# UNIX Distributed
# Programming

# UNIX Distributed Programming

*Chris Brown*

PRENTICE HALL

New York London Toronto Sydney Tokyo Singapore

First published 1994 by
Prentice Hall International (UK) Limited
Campus 400, Maylands Avenue
Hemel Hempstead
Hertfordshire, HP2 7EZ
A division of
Simon & Schuster International Group

© Prentice Hall International (UK) Limited 1994

Typeset in 10/12 pt Times
by Columns Design and Production Services Ltd,
Reading, Berkshire

Printed and bound in Great Britain by
Redwood Books , Trowbridge, Wiltshire

---

Library of Congress Cataloging-in-Publication Data

Brown, Chris.
 UNIX distributed programming / Chris Brown.
   p.   cm.
 Includes bibliographical references and index.
 ISBN 0-13-075896-5
   1. UNIX (Computer file)  2. Electronic data processing–
 Distributed processing.   I. Title.
 QA76.76.063B745   1994
 005.4'3–dc20                          93–49622
                                         CIP

---

British Library Cataloguing in Publication Data

A catalogue record for this book is available from
the British Library

ISBN 0-13-075896-5

1 2 3 4 5    98 97 96 95 94

To Lynne, who won't understand a word of it

# Contents

# Figures

# Preface

The idea for this book grew out of a course I wrote, originally in collaboration with Derek Jones, for the training company Learning Tree International. Beginning as a fairly broadly based course on UNIX networks, covering both system administration and programming, it has evolved to become more focused on distributed (client–server) programming within a UNIX-based network. The structure of this book largely reflects the structure of that course.

Despite the technicality of the subject matter, I have attempted to give the presentation a friendly feel, through both the style of the diagrams and the text, and by occasionally wandering off on tangents, where the tangent held more promise of entertainment than the proper business of the book. I have, however, tried very hard to avoid patronizing the reader.

The book assumes that you have a basic knowledge of C programming. I have tried to avoid unduly complex expressions, data structures or logical flow. However, you need to understand, for example, the notion of a function which returns a pointer to a structure. Otherwise you are going to have a tough time with the examples.

Although many system calls and library routines are mentioned in the text, there is no attempt to introduce every single one systematically, or to explain every possible argument option, or every possible error return. If the descriptions make clear the concept and purpose of the calls, I am content. Serious readers, especially those intending to write their own code, will undoubtedly wish to consult the *Programmer's Reference Manual* pages to learn the additional details, and appropriate references are given to assist in this.

The book includes many examples of C code, most of them in the form of complete, working programs. In all cases, the principle guiding the choice of these examples has been to keep them short, by focusing on the distributed programming mechanisms they are designed to illustrate, and avoiding lengthy sections of application-specific code. Inevitably, this gives many of the examples a rather 'toy' feel. Hopefully, though, they are short enough to inspire the reader to type in and try at least a few of them, and will be useful as templates, or starting points, for his or her own applications. Another ploy used to keep the examples short has been to omit all but the most rudimentary of error checking. The reader is cautioned that such a cavalier approach would be quite unacceptable in production code.

I have chosen to use ANSI C function declaration syntax rather than the older K+R style, on the grounds that most users nowadays either have an ANSI compiler as standard, or use a third party ANSI compiler such as gcc, available from the Free Software Foundation.

Like the course from which it derives, this book presents a rather traditionalist view of UNIX, by which I mean that it concentrates on the underlying structure and mechanisms, rather than dwelling on 'surface' issues such as system administration or graphical user interfaces. I make no apology for this. And also like the course from which it derives, the book is not an attempt to 'sell' UNIX, in any commercial sense. Rather, it is an attempt to pass on to others the 'working enthusiasm' I have developed over the years.

Chris Brown
October 1993
Sheffield, England

# Acknowledgements

Although there is a great deal of new material here compared with the training course (it is amazing how many more words will fit into a book than on 400 training foils), some of the examples are taken from the course, as are some of the diagrams.

The following figures are based on illustrations which originated in the course: 1.3, 1.4, 1.5, 1.6, 1.7, 2.7, 2.8, 2.9, 2.20, 3.1, 3.3, 3.4, 3.5, 3.6, 3.7, 3.8, 3.9, 3.11, 3.12, 3.14, 3.16, 4.1, 4.2, 4.3, 4.5, 4.7, 4.8, 4.10, 4.12, 4.13, 4.15, 4.16, 4.17, 4.18, 4.19, 4.20, 4.21, 5.2, 5.3, 5.4, 5.5, 6.1, 6.2, 6.3, 6.4, 6.6, 6.7, 6.8, 6.10, 7.2, 7.3.

The following demonstration programs are derived from programs which originated in the course:

- Chapter 2: `forkdemo`, `tinymenu`, `menushell`, `whosort`, `pline`, `cline`, `sigcatcher`.

- Chapter 3: `getwordbyuk`, `getwordbyus` and test harness.

- Chapter 4: `hangman` and `rcat` (`tftp` client).

- Chapter 6: Programs 'A' and 'B', `xdr_to_file`, `xdr_writer`, `xdr_reader`, `list`.

I am grateful to Learning Tree International, in particular to their Product Development Manager Rick Adamson, for giving permission to use this material.

# Chapter 1

# Distributed programming concepts

## 1.1  A definition of distributed programming

Since this is a book about distributed programming, it may be appropriate to begin with an attempt at a definition:

> Distributed programming is the spreading of a computational task
> across several programs, processes or processors.

This definition may be broader than you were expecting, and perhaps raises more questions than it answers. What exactly do we mean by a program, a process and a processor? These things will become clear as we proceed; or at least, clearer than they are now. Partly, our definition is vague because the subject itself is very broad. There are many flavours of distributed programming, many different reasons for doing it and a wide range of research activity in the area. In this chapter we will explore the spectrum of distributed programming, and see where UNIX fits in.

## 1.2  The benefits of distributed programming

One way of describing distributed programming and classifying its various forms is to look at the benefits it brings. We summarize here four rather different (but not mutually exclusive) types of benefit; we will examine each of these in more detail as we proceed through the chapter.

1. By splitting the solution to a specific problem into a number of steps, we can use existing general-purpose programs to handle some of these steps, and so reduce the amount of new code we have to write. Often, we may be able to avoid writing any new code altogether. We will refer to this benefit as *tool building*.
2. By using several processors concurrently, we can solve the problem more quickly than if we used a single processor. We will refer to this benefit as *concurrency*.
3. The problem itself is sometimes of the form 'Do A, B and C in parallel'. In this case, the most 'natural' solution may be to use separate parallel processes to perform A, B

and C. Forcing the solution into a strictly sequential form for execution by a single process is unnatural and makes it harder to understand. We will refer to this benefit as *parallelism*.

4.  Sometimes, the resources needed to solve the problem are themselves spread around amongst several computers on a network. *Resources*, in this context, might mean files, tape drives, modems, specialized peripherals, an especially fast CPU, or just the screen and keyboard where we are sitting. We view the network as a whole as a collection of shared resources. We will refer to this benefit as *resource sharing*.

Let us consider each of these benefits in more detail.

## 1.2.1 Tool building

Every experienced UNIX user exploits this form of distributed programming, via shell commands such as

```
ls -l | more

find / -name core -print | mail root

dd if=/dev/dsk/f0q18dt | uncompress | tar xvf -
```

Here, we are splitting a task across two or more different programs, and combining them using a pipeline. The advantage of such pipelines is that they allow us to use a number of general-purpose programs in combination to perform a rather specific task. They allow us to reuse a program in many different contexts. They avoid the need to build commonly used functionality (such as sorting and searching) into each program that needs them. Instead, they allow that functionality to be provided once-and-for-all, in some 'centrally available' way. The advantage is certainly not one of efficiency – it would undoubtedly be more 'efficient' (in terms of run-time CPU, central processing unit, cycles) to incorporate (for example) output browsing capabilites into the `ls` command than to use a totally separate program (`more`) for the job. Of course, for an inherently interactive activity such as browsing a directory listing, run-time efficiency is of little concern. A 'personally efficient' way of devising a suitable command is much more important.

Whether the act of piecing together simple command lines such as these should be graced with the name 'programming' is doubtful. It might better be described as *composing* a solution. This approach figures prominently in the UNIX philosophy and is promoted very convincingly in Kernighan and Pike (1984).

## 1.2.2 Concurrency

Over the past decade, raw processor performance has increased spectacularly. Improved silicon technology has increased internal clock speeds, from around 1 MHz in 1984 to 100 or even 200 MHz in current state-of-the-art devices such as DEC's Alpha processor.

Improvements in architecture, such as instruction pipelining, on-chip co-processors and cache memory, have further improved performance. Together, these developments have resulted in a rate of increase in processor performance which can be approximated by the following equation, sometimes known as *Joy's law*:

$$\text{processor power} = 2^{(\text{year} - 1984)} \text{ MIPS}$$

where MIPS means either 'million instructions per second' or 'meaningless indication of processor speed', depending on your degree of cynicism. In other words, Joy's law says that we had one-MIP processors in 1984, and have doubled this every year since.

---

**An aside:** 'laws' such as Joy's law should be clearly distinguished from physical laws such as Boyle's law (for gas pressure) and Newton's laws (of motion), which are statements of physical principles that have widespread and permanent validity. Joy's law is simply an appealing way of approximating the situation at the time. Another example is Grosch's law which dates from the 1950s and says that the performance of a computer is proportional to the square of its cost.

---

Joy's law held for a number of years, but is beginning to break down. (It predicted a 512-MIP processor by the year 1993 – we are about a factor of 5 below this.) It is generally accepted that the processor designers will find it impossible to maintain this rate of improvement over the next decade. Certainly, if the price/performance ratio is taken as the important measure, it is currently cheaper (in terms of hardware) to build a box containing ten 10-MIP processors than a box containing a single 100-MIP device. If you need a 1000-MIP machine, multiple-processor systems are currently the only solution.

The average end-users who put their computers to work on word processing, spreadsheets and the occasional game of golf may wonder who needs such powerful machines. Some of the power is squandered in providing graphical user interfaces. Dragging a file icon to the trash basket may be more 'intuitive' than typing `rm filename` but you pay an enormous penalty in terms of processor cycles. 'WYSIWYG' (what you see is what you get) text processors and voice mail are similarly expensive. There are other applications which need high performance for more fundamental reasons. These include graphics rendering, virtual reality, real-time image processing and machine vision, finite element analysis, medical imaging and a host of simulation and modelling applications, such as quantum chromodynamics, weather simulation and molecular biology.

All this leads us to the following observation: multiprocessor systems and concurrent programming are the inevitable way forward for very high performance computing. Arthur Trew and Greg Wilson (1991) underline this point:

> All of the major actors in supercomputing today acknowledge that parallelism of one kind or another is the only way that they will be able to meet the market's increasing demand for high-speed, low-cost computing. Even in conservative

areas such as on-line transaction processing, established firms such as DEC and IBM are facing increasing competition from younger companies whose use of parallelism gives them a significant price/performance edge.

Although there are many different variations on the theme of multiprocessor architectures, there is a useful top level classification of machines into *shared memory* architectures (Figure 1.1) and *distributed memory* architectures (Figure 1.2).

Shared memory systems suffer from one fairly obvious design problem: if all the CPUs are fetching instructions and data from the same memory, then that memory (and the bus leading to it) may not have sufficient bandwidth. The problem is alleviated to some extent by using wide data paths (64 or 128 bits) to the global memory, and by using fast cache memories local to each processor; still, shared memory systems generally show a fairly low degree of parallelism, typically having just two or four processors, although multiprocessor shared memory machines with up to ten processors have been announced.

Distributed memory message passing systems, on the other hand, do not have this bottleneck, and are much more suitable for 'massively parallel' systems and for solving problems which can be partitioned to minimize interprocessor message traffic.

Thus, adequate hardware technologies already exist to build machines with tens or hundreds of processors. The software environments and tools needed to program them are another matter. Such environments do exist, but they are relatively immature. Some of them seek to present the end-programmer with the illusion of a fast single-processor machine. This is relatively easy to do on a shared memory architecture, and extremely difficult (one might almost say perverse) on a distributed memory architecture. Other environments require the programmer to think hard about how to divide the work amongst the processors, and to consider issues of message passing and synchronization. In other words, the programmer must explicitly design concurrency into his algorithms. Although some spectacular successes have been achieved in this area, they require skilled, specialist programming and are mostly confined to research laboratories.

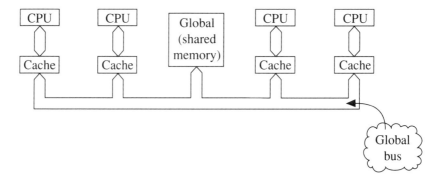

**Figure 1.1** Shared memory multiprocessor architecture.

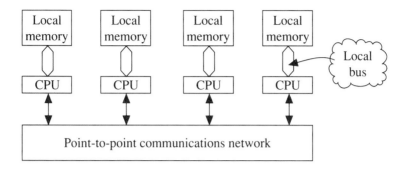

**Figure 1.2** Distributed memory multiprocessor architecture.

As the software technologies to support concurrent programming mature, we can expect this situation to change. At present, however, no mainstream version of UNIX supports 'massively' concurrent programming to any real extent. As such, the topic receives little attention in the remainder of this book, although a simple concurrent application is presented in Chapter 4.

## 1.2.3 Parallelism

There are some programming tasks for which the most natural expression of the solution is a parallel one. Consider the standard UNIX utilities `cu` and `tip`. Although they have a number of fancy features, `cu` and `tip` are basically communications programs which ferry characters back and forth between your terminal and a serial port. Often the serial port has a modem attached, and is used to connect to a remote machine. The illusion created by such a communications program is that your terminal is connected directly to a dial-in line on the remote computer, as shown in Figure 1.3.

A top level specification of the program might read: 'If any characters arrive from the keyboard, copy them to the output port. *At the same time*, copy characters which arrive from the input port to the screen'. Since, in general, the characters will not conveniently take turns to arrive from the keyboard and from the input port, a serial solution ends up looking something like this:

```
while (TRUE) {
    Wait until either the port
        or the keyboard has a character ready
    if (keyboard has a character ready) {
        read character from the keyboard
        write it to the port
    }
    else if (port has a character ready) {
        read character from the port
```

```
        write it to the screen
     }
}
```

It is possible to implement this serial solution as a single UNIX process, by using the select() or poll system calls, which allow us to wait until one of several input streams has data ready for reading. select() is described in Chapter 4. Nonetheless, this is a messy, unnatural solution. A parallel solution might look as follows:

```
Do the following two things in parallel:
    { while (TRUE) {
            read character from the keyboard
            write it to the port
      }
    }
    { while (TRUE) {
            read character from the port
            write it to the screen
      }
    }
```

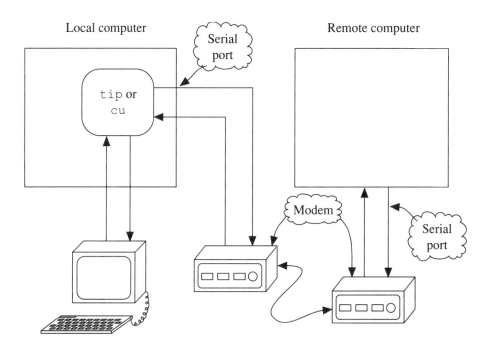

**Figure 1.3** Illustrating cu and tip.

A few programming languages (notably Occam) actually have a construct to say 'Do the following things in parallel' (Jones and Goldsmith, 1989). C has no such feature. However, under UNIX, we can explicitly create two parallel processes, and arrange for one of them to execute one of the loops, and the other to execute the other. Conceptually, the solution looks more like this:

```
start a new process
if (this is the new process) {
    while (TRUE) {
            read character from the keyboard
            write it to the port
    }
}
else {            /* This is the original process */
    while (TRUE) {
            read character from the port
            write it to the screen
    }
}
```

There is 'natural parallelism' in many computing tasks. Unfortunately, many years of writing programs in purely sequential languages, to execute on purely sequential machines, has made many programmers (particularly ageing ones, like me) almost blind to the possibilities for parallel solutions.

## 1.2.4 Resource sharing

A decade ago, a group of people in an organization who wanted access to computing facilities may well have been provided with a time-sharing minicomputer. Each user (if they were lucky) had a terminal in his or her office, attached to it (see Figure 1.4).

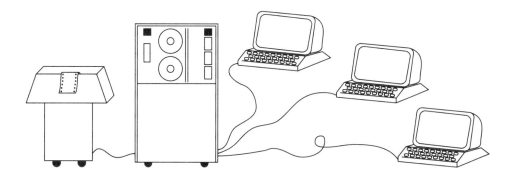

**Figure 1.4** Resource sharing – the multi-user minicomputer.

Such machines provided cost-effective, interactive, communal computing for many years. Sharing files was easy, because everyone's files were part of the same file system. Peripherals such as printers and tape drives were also inherently shared. The problem with such machines was that other, more critical, resources such as the CPU and the memory, were also shared. As more users logged on, performance dropped, sometimes to the point where users preferred to give up and come back at night, when there was less competition.

When the PC came along, things were (in some ways) much better, because it was possible to replicate the critical resources at each 'seat'. (*Critical resources* means CPU, memory, screen and keyboard, i.e. those resources that adversely affect a user's productivity if they are in short supply.) In other ways, things were much worse, because these totally separate PCs made sharing rather difficult. File transfer often meant carrying a floppy disk between machines. Sharing a printer usually involved pushing it down the corridor on a trolley (see Figure 1.5).

So, no sooner had the PC enabled us to separate our computing resources from one another than we began to look for ways to combine them again. The solution (which is of course obvious in the context of the present discussion) was to connect all these single-user machines together in some sort of network, and to provide clever software which allowed remote resources, such as files or printers or other more specialized peripherals, to be conveniently accessed (see Figure 1.6).

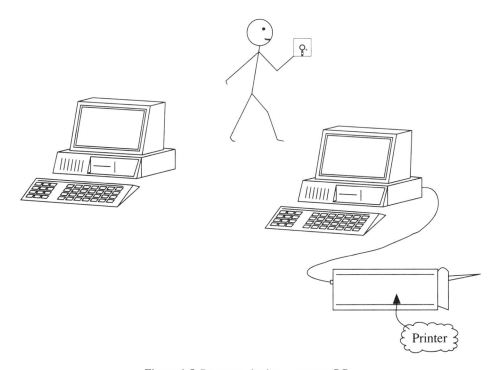

**Figure 1.5** Resource sharing – separate PCs.

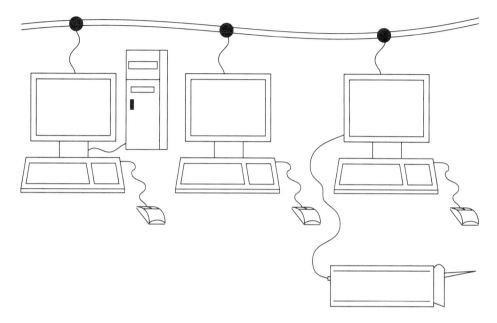

**Figure 1.6** Resource sharing – the network solution.

Networks are frequently described as *transparent*. The term has become overused of late, particularly by sales staff who often confuse it with the word 'opaque'. Let us consider what transparency means. The window of my office is transparent. From in here, I can see things on the outside just as easily as if I *were* on the outside. Having the window in between does not affect the view I get. In network terms, transparency means that you can access the remote resources in just the same way as you access the local resources (i.e. the ones that are attached to the machine you are sitting at). In a well-designed network, users may literally not know where the resource is located.

---

**An aside:** the transparency of a properly configured UNIX network can be high. Recently, whilst deputizing for our system manager, I needed to shut one of our file servers down briefly for maintenance. I walked down the corridor, calling into each office 'If your files are on deepthought (the server in question), go and have a coffee'. This was met by shrugged shoulders and the response 'I don't know where my files are!'

---

Thus, we can view the machines, files and peripherals on a network collectively as a set of shared resources, as shown in Figure 1.7. Programs that run in such an environment often have to 'reach across' to access remote resources, and so are inherently distributed. This form of distributed programming is perhaps the most important in the UNIX market-place, and receives a great deal of attention in this book.

## 1.3 Methods of problem decomposition

In the last section, we examined the various benefits that distributed programming brings. In this section, we look at some ways of decomposing a problem into pieces so that the solution may be distributed.

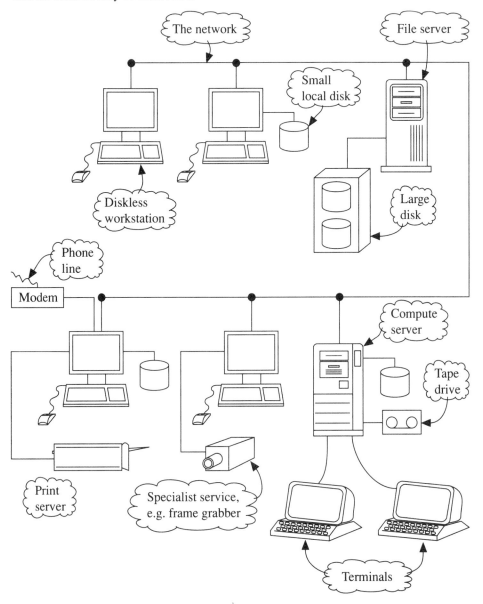

**Figure 1.7** Networks as a shared resource.

## 1.3.1 Data distribution

One very common way of distributing an application is to divide the input data set into pieces, and hand each piece to a separate process. This is known as *data distribution* or *domain decomposition*. Real life abounds with analogies of this technique. For example, at a scout camp a contingent of three scouts is told to peel potatoes for lunch. The input data set (a large pile of unpeeled potatoes) is divided into three roughly equal piles. Each scout tackles his own input pile, producing an output pile of peeled potatoes. Finally, the three output piles are collected together into one large pile. At the risk of insulting your intelligence, the operation is shown in Figure 1.8. Another analogy is that of a team of bricklayers contracted to build the walls of a large house. Each bricklayer is given a pile of bricks and some mortar, and a staked-out section of the perimeter to work within.

These analogies share a couple of key features. First, each worker is doing the same operation (peeling potatoes or laying bricks), but to a different piece of the input data set (a different lot of potatoes or bricks). Second, the workers operate concurrently. Indeed, the whole point of having several workers is to get the job done quicker than it would with one worker.

In both analogies, there is a limit to how many workers can be usefully employed, but this limit could be quite large. In the first example, we could in theory use as many scouts as we have potatoes. It is harder to imagine how a 'bricklayer per brick' arrangement would work; nonetheless the more bricks and the bigger the house, the more bricklayers we could employ.

The problem of having *too many* bricklayers has to do with ordering and synchronization. There is a constraint on the order in which the bricks are laid (you can only put a brick on top of one which is already there) which prevents you laying all the bricks simultaneously. Even in a more realistic situation, say a bricklayer for every five metres of wall, there is still a synchronization issue: each bricklayer has to make sure that each layer of bricks ties in correctly with his neighbours' layers. Over a five metre stretch of wall, that probably is not too bad, but if we increase the number of bricklayers such that each has only one metre of wall, the need to synchronize with his or her neighbours will start to affect productivity. We will not be getting our money's worth out of those bricklayers. (The bricklayer analogy is developed further in Fox *et al.*, 1988.)

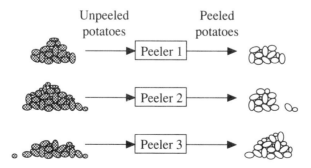

**Figure 1.8** Real-life parallelism through data distribution.

The problem is less acute for the potato peelers because they do not need to synchronize their activities, except initially when the pile of unpeeled potatoes is divided up, and at the end when the peeled potatoes are collected together. In distributed programming jargon, we say that the potato peelers are *loosely coupled* and the bricklayers are more *tightly coupled*. These terms relate to the frequency with which the different workers need to synchronize their activity, and/or to exchange data. These kinds of issues are of great importance to people trying to exploit 'massively parallel' systems (ones with hundreds of processors), because they determine the extent to which one can achieve a speed-up which is linearly related to the number of processors.

Let us consider some computer-related examples of data distribution. The first stage of many image processing applications is to find edges (or other low level features) in the image. To do this quickly, we might divide the image up into slices and send each slice to a different processor. Each would in due course send a list of the features it had found to some 'master' process. The arrangement is shown in Figure 1.9.

---

**An aside:** images are normally represented as two-dimensional arrays of *pixels*; each pixel has an integer value representing the brightness of that part of the image. A typical size for this pixel array is 512 × 512, giving 262 144 pixels. To make matters worse, an ordinary TV camera will drop that amount of data in your lap twenty-five or thirty times a second. An edge might be loosely defined as 'a place where the brightness is changing quickly as you move across the image'. You will note from this definition that to see if a pixel is an edge, you have to look around at its neighbours.

---

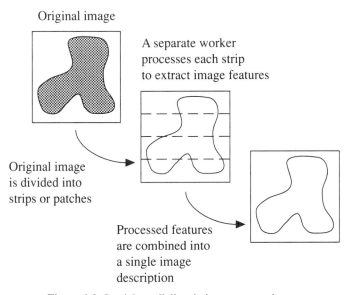

Original image

A separate worker
processes each strip
to extract image features

Original image
is divided into
strips or patches

Processed features
are combined into
a single image
description

**Figure 1.9** Spatial parallelism in image processing.

As another example, suppose we had a large database of theatrical performances which was sorted chronologically, and we wanted to count how many times *Hamlet* had been performed in French. We might divide the database up into fifty year slices, and send each slice to a different processor. Each would in due course send a count of the performances it had found to some 'master' process, which would simply add them up.

As a third example: it is time to do a complete rebuild of our latest program, which is split across sixty source files. The task can be distributed by compiling each file on a different processor.

To summarize: data distribution divides the input data set amongst several processors. The code is replicated on each processor, and each does the same operations, but on a different piece of the data. There will be an upper limit on the number of processors which can be usefully employed, depending on the amount of input data, and the smallest amount of data that can sensibly be processed on its own. This limit may be quite large, often larger than the number of processors actually available. The purpose of data distribution is usually to allow concurrent execution on a multiprocessor system and thus reduce the time taken to solve the problem.

## 1.3.2 Algorithmic distribution

A second important technique for distributing a problem solution is *algorithmic distribution*. For an example we will return to our scout camp. Lunch is over, the potatoes have been eaten, and it is time to wash the pots. To do this quickly four scouts are appointed, one to collect the dirty plates from the tables, one to wash them, one to dry them, and a stacker to put them away in the cupboards. The four operate in a pipeline as shown in Figure 1.10.

A factory production line provides another excellent example of a pipeline. The key characteristic of algorithmic distribution is that each worker sees the same data items, but performs a different operation on them. In the case of a multiprocessor implementation,

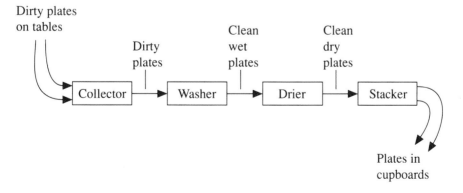

**Figure 1.10** Real-life parallelism through algorithmic distribution.

each processor is running different code. The pipeline imposes some sort of loose synchronization on its individual components. In the washing up example, if the stacker finds his 'input pile' empty, he must wait for the drier to dry more plates. If the collector has amassed a precariously high pile of plates by the sink, he must wait until the washer has processed a few.

The number of workers who can be employed in this way is limited by the number of steps in the pipeline, and is usually quite small. It does not grow as the size of the input data set increases. Of course, the number of workers can be increased by using data distribution *as well*; for example, if washing up turned out to be the bottleneck, two or more washers could be employed. Alternatively, if it was simply necessary to increase the throughput, the entire pipeline could be replicated.

Another fine real-world example of algorithmic distribution may be found if we stand back from our bricklayers and survey the entire building site. There we will find other specialist workers: joiners, plumbers, electricians, plasterers, decorators. There is a very loose sequential flow to the work of these people as the house is built, and a rather complex pattern of synchronization – the plasterer cannot plaster a wall that the bricklayer has not yet built, for example. Yet there is also much scope for parallel operation. Anyone who has had the task of coordinating such an activity will know how difficult it can be.

The classic example of algorithmic distribution in UNIX is, of course, the pipeline. Pipelines are easily built from the command level via commands such as:

```
du  /  |  sort  -nr  |  head  -20
```

First, du generates a list of all directories in the file system, preceded by a count of the number of blocks of disk space they occupy. Next, sort performs a reverse numeric sort (largest first) on this list. Finally, head picks off the first twenty lines of the sorted output.

The cc command provides another example. Although we think of cc loosely as 'the C compiler', it actually distributes the task of compiling a C program amongst five or six programs: the pre-processor, the parser, the code generator, the optimizer, the assembler and the linker, operating in a pipeline.

## 1.3.3 Granularity

Another way of characterizing distributed applications is by their *granularity*. This is not a precise term, but it has to do mainly with the size of the data set operated on by each process. Are we dealing with boulders (*coarse grain*) or grains of sand (*fine grain*)? Table 1.1 summarizes the characteristics of the two.

As we will see later, in UNIX a process is a rather large object, and expensive to create. Also, communication between processes can be expensive, particularly if they are running on different machines across a network. Consequently, UNIX is better suited to coarse grain than fine grain parallelism.

**Table 1.1**

|  | Type of distribution | |
|  | Coarse grain | Fine grain |
| --- | --- | --- |
| Number of processes | Small | Large |
| Amount of data per process | Large | Small |
| Frequency of communication | Low | High |
| Frequency of synchronization | Low | High |

## 1.3.4 Load balancing

When a computing task is to be spread across multiple processors for concurrent execution, it is generally desirable to balance the load; that is, to ensure that each processor has an equal amount of work to do. Despite what our potato-peeling scouts might think, the issue is not one of fairness, but of efficiency. If some workers are given less work than others, they will finish sooner, and stand idle until the others are done. Poor load balancing is one reason why multiprocessor systems often fail to yield linear speed-up. In some applications using data distribution, load balancing is easily achieved by simply giving each worker an equal amount of input data. This works if each data item is equally expensive to process, and each processor has the same speed. The former is not true for many applications and the latter may not be true on a heterogeneous network of UNIX workstations. Another approach is to divide the data up into many more pieces than there are workers, and allow workers to help themselves to a new piece of data when they are ready. We can imagine our scouts taking their input from a single communal pile of potatoes. This paradigm is sometimes called a *processor farm*, and we will see an implementation of one in Chapter 4.

With a pipelined, algorithmic decomposition of the problem, accurate load balancing is more difficult. In this case, we cannot usually 'fine tune' the workload of each worker by adjusting the boundaries between the tasks which they perform.

# 1.4 A brief history of UNIX distributed programming

Having looked at some aspects of distributed computing from a fairly theoretical standpoint, we will examine the distributed programming features of UNIX and see how it fits into the picture. To begin at the beginning ...

## 1.4.1 Early days

Although the really early versions of UNIX were not multiprogramming, UNIX rapidly developed (back in the early 1970s) as a multi-user timesharing operating system, to run on single-processor, multi-user machines such as the PDP-11 and (later) the VAX, from Digital Equipment Corporation. Single-user workstations and networks were unheard of in those days, and multiprocessor machines were even further over the horizon. Not surprisingly, therefore, UNIX provided little support for distributed programming. Indeed, one might argue that since the aim of UNIX was to share a single processor amongst many tasks, and the aim of distributed programming is to spread a single task amongst many processes, the two are exact opposites.

Nevertheless, UNIX did at least support multitasking. Users could run background jobs (by putting an '&' at the end of the command line), and they could create jobs consisting of two or more processes connected by pipelines. Underlying both of these facilities was the `fork()` system call, which is used to create new processes. The ease with which a user program could spawn new processes was a very novel feature of an operating system in the early 1970s. Another underlying system call, `pipe()`, created a one-way communication channel, the ends of which could be 'inherited' by child processes, allowing two processes to communicate provided they had a common ancestor. In terms of interprocess communication facilities, that was about it.

## 1.4.2 'System V' interprocess communication

During the following decade UNIX accumulated many new utilities, but the basic model of process creation and interprocess communication (IPC) stayed the same. Then, around 1984, AT&T introduced a number of additional IPC mechanisms into System V Release 2. These mechanisms were shared memory, message queues and semaphores. They made it possible to implement one-to-many and many-to-one communication patterns, compared with the one-to-one communication of the pipe, and they provided much greater flexibility in process synchronization. Still, they were only useful between processes on the same machine. System V had no networking support. Chapter 2 discusses these 'single-machine' IPC mechanisms of UNIX in detail.

## 1.4.3 The start of UNIX networking

One of the more significant events in the history of UNIX was its adoption by ARPA (the US Advanced Research Projects Agency – later DARPA) as a vehicle to provide cooperative computing amongst ARPA's many researchers spread across North America. The networking support whose development was funded by ARPA resulted in an implementation of the TCP/IP (transmission control protocol/internet protocol) suite, which provided interprocess communication facilities between processes running on different machines, separated by anything from a few metres to a thousand kilometres or more. Particularly significant was the release in 1984 of 4.2 BSD UNIX from the University of California at Berkeley, which provided a set of system calls giving programmers access to the networking services of the TCP/IP protocols. This set of system calls became generally known as 'sockets'. A socket is an end-point of communication; it is where the application program and the transport provider meet (*transport provider* means the protocol stack that conveys the data to the entity at the other end). Using the new system calls in 4.2 BSD, sockets could be created and connected, and data could be passed between them. 4.2 BSD gave UNIX an IPC mechanism which could be used to write applications which were truly distributed across machines.

A number of important utilities were developed to take advantage of TCP/IP. Especially well used were `telnet`, which allowed you to log-in on a remote machine (providing you had an account, of course), and `ftp` , which allowed transfer of files to and from (mostly from) remote machines. These two utilities are not UNIX-specific – you might find yourself connected to a machine running VAX/VMS or IBM/MVS, for example. The Berkeley team wrote some additional programs which are sometimes known as the r* (pronounced r-star) commands, because they have names derived from traditional UNIX commands, but with an r (for remote) in front. Thus we have `rlogin` (remote login), `rcp` (remote file copy) and `rsh` (remote shell, i.e. remote command execution). These commands are UNIX-specific; they are especially convenient when used across a collection of machines which are under a single administrative control, because they will (if suitably configured) let you access the remote machine without supplying a password every time. Look up `rlogin(1)`, `rcp(1)` and `rsh(1)` in the programmer's reference manual for details.

As is perhaps evident from the utilities just described, the type of distributed computing supported by sockets is usually more to do simply with gaining access to remote resources across a network than with achieving true concurrent operation of several machines. Indeed, the client–server model of interaction which is usually used with sockets is explicitly designed to prevent concurrency – a client program requests a remote server program to perform some action, waits until the server has finished and replied, then continues. The only reason for contacting the remote machine at all is because it has some resource which you need, but cannot get locally; a particular data file perhaps, or a very fast CPU, or maybe just an accurate knowledge of what time it is.

Returning to the System V history lesson, around 1986 AT&T introduced a new style of interface to the transport provider in the form of a set of library routines called the transport level interface, or TLI. TLI is conceptually equivalent to sockets; indeed there is an almost one-to-one correspondence between the socket calls which clients and servers use, and the equivalent TLI calls. TLI, however, is modelled after the OSI (open systems interconnection) transport layer definition. It is important to realize that TLI is not a transport provider in its own right, but simply an interface to one. TLI has been adopted as the 'officially recommended' interface to the transport layer by several standards groups, including X/Open (X/Open Co. Ltd, 1988). Nonetheless, the socket interface is still in use by many programmers, and is unlikely to go away in the foreseeable future.

## 1.4.4  The coming of the workstation

The computers which were talking to one another in 1984 using these new-fangled sockets and TCP/IP were mostly still multi-user time-sharing machines. The DEC VAX was especially popular at the time. As hardware technology improved, and the 16/32 bit microprocessors such as the Motorola 68000 (and its derivatives) came onto the market, the idea of a personal computer powerful enough to run UNIX became feasible. Because the term *personal computer* had by that time come to mean a specific family of machines from IBM, these new machines were called *workstations*, presumably to suggest that you could actually get some real work done with them. Sun Microsystems was one of the first companies to pull together the key pieces of technology needed for a workstation: a 32-bit processor (the 68000), a memory management system (Sun's initially came from Stanford University; in fact 'Sun' was originally an acronym for Stanford University Node), a bit-mapped screen and mouse, and a local area network technology (ethernet). Last, but not least, BSD UNIX was available, and able to tie all these pieces together. The oft-quoted Bill Joy, who was the principal architect of BSD UNIX, left Berkeley to become a founder of Sun Microsystems. His original vision, now long-since surpassed, was for a 'three-M' machine: one million pixels on the screen, one million instructions per second and one million bytes of memory.

## 1.4.5 The need for transparent networking

This new generation of workstations ran a UNIX which was every bit as multitasking and multi-user as it had ever been. However, the real strength of these new machines was as high performance single-user systems. As a result, the preferred way to provide UNIX resources for small to medium sized work groups began to change from being a multi-user minicomputer to a network of single-user workstations. Once this had happened, the need for a convenient way of sharing resources (especially files) across the network, became acute. The early network utilities such as `ftp` and `rcp` were not enough; it was just too inconvenient to have to explicitly copy a file from a remote machine just because the file happened to be 'over there', and the user happened to be logged in 'over here'. With a multi-user minicomputer, a user could log in on any visual display unit (VDU) terminal and see the same environment. Why should it be different for a network of workstations? Why should I be tied to a specific machine, any more than I was tied to a specific VDU?

To tackle this problem, Sun introduced a new technology which it called the *Network File System* (NFS). What NFS allowed you to do was to attach a piece of a remote machine's file system onto your local directory structure. Thereafter, remote files were accessed in just the same way that local ones were. From the command level, you could use the same commands to create, copy, move, rename, print, archive or delete remote files as you did for local ones. From the programmer's perspective, you could use the same system calls to open, read, write, seek and close remote files as you did for local ones. If sensibly configured, NFS can be used to distribute the total file system amongst several server machines, in such a way that all files are accessed using the same UNIX pathnames from any machine. Users are no longer tied to specific workstations. Indeed, NFS is so 'transparent' that many users of the network may be totally unaware of which machines their files are actually on. Sun publicly published the specification of the NFS protocols, and had enormous success in getting NFS accepted as a *de facto* standard for distributed UNIX file systems.

Although NFS made networking a great deal easier, it was not of itself a mechanism for distributed programming. However, underneath NFS, Sun released their implementation of a new style of client–server interface called a *remote procedure call* (RPC). As its name suggests, RPC provides a way for a program to call a procedure (or a function, or a subroutine, or whatever name you prefer) which will be executed on a remote machine. The results generated by the procedure are returned to the local machine. Of course, RPC does not enable you to do anything new which you could not already do using sockets, but it does allow you to do it in a much more convenient fashion. Using sockets, communication with a remote program requires input–output (I/O) operations to be explicitly coded into the program. Using RPC, this communication is 'hidden' behind a traditional procedure call. In other words, RPC allows a distributed application to communicate with its remote parts using the same mechanism (a procedure call) as it uses to communicate with its local parts.

The benefits of using RPC (which will become more apparent in Chapter 6) are considerable. Indeed, most new network services are now written using RPC, and some of the older socket-based services have been converted. One of the important new services based on RPC is the Network Information Service (NIS, formerly known as Yellow Pages), which allows system configuration (and other) databases to be stored centrally on a server and distributed to clients as needed.

The bundle of new technologies comprising NFS, RPC/XDR (external data representation), and NIS is sometimes collectively known as ONC (open network computing). NFS and NIS are described in detail in Chapter 3, and RPC/XDR in Chapter 6.

There are some interesting recent developments in the UNIX world which may, in time, change the nature of UNIX distributed programming considerably. These include the following:

1. A number of multiprocessor systems are appearing on the market. Manufacturers such as Sequent and Solbourne have offered multiprocessor UNIX machines for a number of years. More recently (1992), Sun Microsystems released multiprocessor server machines, and the desktop Sparcstation-10, often sold in a single-processor configuration, but capable of accepting more. These mainstream UNIX vendors are sticking with shared memory architectures, and fairly small (two or four) numbers of processors, Currently, the strategy is to maintain the illusion of a single-processor system at the UNIX system call level. This is (relatively) easy on a shared memory architecture. Keeping the processors busy relies on having multiple UNIX processes ready to run simultaneously, either because the machine is being used by many people, or because the user has many tasks running. They do not offer an automatic speed-up for any single task, and at present multiprocessor systems are used primarily as high performance servers and not as desktop machines. There are a few distributed memory (message passing) architectures on the market which offer a 'UNIX compatible' programming environment.

2. Vendors are introducing support for lightweight processes (threads). By allowing concurrency within a single-user process these will allow an application to exploit multiple processors simultaneously (though not without some rethinking by the programmer).

3.  More 'object-oriented' forms of interprocess communication are appearing. Amongst these is the `ToolTalk` messaging service from Sun. Built on top of RPC, ToolTalk provides an even higher level of abstraction for interprocess communication in which applications can despatch messages not to a specific program but to any application with specified *capabilities*.

Some of these developments are reviewed in more detail later.

# 1.5  Summary: where does UNIX fit in?

Historically, UNIX has been a single-processor operating system. As such, it has a rich set of mechanisms for manipulating processes and communicating amongst them. Even on modern multiprocessor machines, most implementations strive to give the illusion of being fast single-processor systems. The UNIX concept of a process is a heavyweight one. Whilst it would be entirely reasonable to distribute an application across four or five processes, it would be quite unreasonable to spread it across four or five hundred.

In practice, UNIX distributed programming is rarely about achieving true concurrency of execution on multiple processors. By far the commonest model is one of coarse grain algorithmic distribution, which is found in two main forms: simple sequential pipelines which are merely 'composed' at the shell command level, and client–server applications which distribute an application across a network.

The focus of attention in UNIX distributed programming is on local area networks. The driving force behind such networks is that they provide a cost-effective shared computing resource to a group of users, with critical resources replicated at each seat, and non-critical resources shared. A very comprehensive set of network services has grown up over the years. One of the greatest strengths of UNIX networks is that the underlying protocols are *not* vendor-specific. The extent to which transparent interoperability of mixed vendor networks is a reality, here and now, with UNIX is something which is often not fully appreciated by the non-UNIX community.

# Chapter 2

# UNIX interprocess communication

## 2.1 Introduction

### 2.1.1 In defence of the chapter

In this chapter we examine the mechanisms available in UNIX to support distributed programming *on a single machine*. We will examine the system calls used to create new processes and to synchronize and communicate amongst them. Recall from Chapter 1 that our definition of distributed programming was 'the spreading of a computational task across several programs, processes or processors'. According to this definition, distributed programming does not necessarily involve multiple processors or networks. You may be unconvinced by this definition and feel that this chapter does not really belong in the book, because it does not deal with intermachine communication. Nonetheless the techniques discussed here are necessary 'stock in trade' for serious network programmers.

### 2.1.2 The user and the kernel

In large measure, this book is about the relationship between user programs and 'the system'. This is a rather formal and strictly enforced relationship, with four distinct layers, as illustrated in Figure 2.1.

The lowest layer is the hardware: processor, memory, disks, tapes, terminal ports, network interfaces and the like. This layer offers a very low level functionality, accepting primitive commands such as 'seek the disk arm to track 86, select head 3 and read sector 0'. Software written to interact directly with the hardware is nonportable and full of low level detail: controller register layouts, interrupt priorities, DMA starting addresses and so on. Few people want to program at this level.

The next layer up is implemented by a resident piece of software called the UNIX *kernel*. Some of the key components of the kernel are the following:

1. Device drivers. These are the routines that 'know about' (and, for the most part, hide) all the low level detail of talking to the real hardware.
2. File system management. This is the code that organizes the storage of data into files and directories, hiding the lower level of disk blocks, free lists and so on.

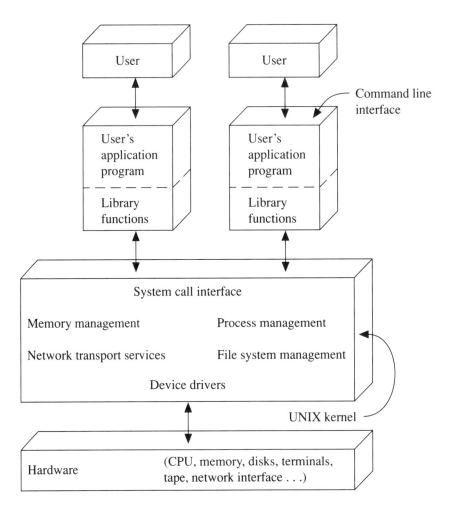

**Figure 2.1**  A layered view of a UNIX system.

3. Process management. This code schedules the running of user processes, time-sharing between them, and ensuring that each has the resources it needs.
4. Memory management. This code manages the sharing of physical memory within the machine to the processes that need it, giving each process the illusion of a separate 'address space'. The programmer is almost entirely unaware of this activity, unless it goes wrong.
5. Network transport services. This code provides machine-to-machine and process-to-process delivery of data across the network.

Between them, these components offer a wide range of services to the user's program. Broadly speaking, the kernel may be viewed as a large collection of routines that user programs may call. (Technically, this is not an accurate view and we will refine it shortly.) These routines offer a much higher level of functionality than the raw hardware: typical instructions we can give to the kernel might be 'change the ownership of this file', 'send the data to the console screen' or 'start a new process'. The repertoire of commands supported by the kernel defines a 'UNIX virtual machine', which is not only higher level, but also platform-independent. The stability and standardization of this 'virtual machine interface' is of great importance to the success of UNIX in the commercial market-place, because it allows the applications that are built on top of it to be portable across a wide range of hardware platforms.

The user program is not actually free to call any function it finds lying around inside the kernel. Access is much more strictly controlled. To enter the kernel, the user program makes a *system call* by executing a *trap* instruction of some sort. This instruction puts the processor into a privileged operating mode (sometimes called supervisor mode, or simply kernel mode) and jumps into the kernel through a well-defined trap address. This is the only way in. Parameters passed with the trap instruction tell the kernel what service is requested. When the operation is done, the processor flips back to its normal operating mode (sometimes called user mode), and returns control to the user program. We talk of executing in 'user space' and in 'kernel space'.

Requesting a service from the kernel is a little like buying something over the counter in a shop. You have to ask the assistant politely. You may be able to see what you want on the shelves behind the counter, but you are not free to leap over and help yourself. The UNIX shop is not self-service. This is in contrast to the MS-DOS world where it is common practice to bypass the operating system and talk directly to the hardware, usually in an effort to improve efficiency.

In addition to the repertoire of services offered by the kernel, user programs have access to a large number of library functions. These represent the third layer in Figure 2.1. Library functions usually offer a 'higher level' of service than system calls; however, the key difference between the two is that a system call is handled by code inside the kernel, whereas a library function is linked in as part of your executable program, in user space. Some library functions operate entirely in user space without making system calls. The function `strcmp()`, which compares two strings, is an example. Other library functions will in turn need to make system calls to get their job done. For example, the formatted output function `printf()`, after doing its fancy format conversions, will call the `write()` system call to actually get the data output.

How can you tell, by looking at a program that

```
write(1, "hello world", 11);
```

is a system call, but

```
printf("hello world");
```

is a call to a library function? More to the point, how can the compiler tell? You might guess perhaps that `write` is a reserved word in the language, in the same way that it is in

Fortran, for example. No, the answer is that, in fact, they are both function calls. You cannot *directly* code a system call into your program at all because no amount of clever C programming will ever persuade the compiler to generate a trap instruction. Instead, you call a tiny 'wrapper' function in the standard C library, which parcels up the parameters correctly, and performs the trap. The wrapper uses a little bit of assembly code to achieve this. There is a separate wrapper function for each system call. You can see them by scanning the standard C library, using the command

```
ar  t  /usr/lib/libc.a  |  more
```

The entries `creat.o`, `fork.o` and `write.o` are examples of system call wrappers. You will also see many other examples of functions in that library which are *not* wrappers.

To a programmer, it does not really matter, at least not in any fundamental sense, whether a particular call is a system call or a library function. There are some minor points to note, however:

1. System calls are documented in section 2 of the reference manual, and library functions are in section 3. It is sometimes easier to find them if you know which section to look in.
2. The business of trapping into the kernel imposes an overhead on system calls which (pure) library functions do not have.
3. When a C program is linked, the standard C library, which includes the system call wrappers, is scanned by default. However, if the program requires routines from other libraries, the linker must be told about them. For example, the flag `-lm` tells the linker to scan the maths library, `libm.a`. In this case the programmer needs to be aware not only that the calls are to library routines, but which library they are in.

The fourth layer in our software structure is the user's command-line interface to the application programs. Here the functionality is at a very high level, with commands of the form 'compile this program', or 'sort this alphabetically'.

## 2.2 The concepts of process and program

### 2.2.1 The difference between a program and a process

Before going any further we must be clear about two key concepts: the *program* and the *process*. A program is a list of instructions (either in binary machine code or in some higher level interpreted language such as a shell script) specifying a sequence of operations to be performed. A program is a relatively passive entity, but has a clear physical existence – one can point to some lines of code or (conceptually at least) to some instructions in memory and say 'There's the program'. A process is an altogether more active, but more abstract, kind of thing. The designers of 4.3 BSD UNIX say that 'Processes constitute a thread of control in an address space', and that 'A process is a program in execution' (Leffler *et al.*, 1988).

A theatrical analogy may help to make clear the distinction between process and program. Consider an actor, reading the script of a play. The script is like a program – it is a list of instructions telling the actor what to say and do. The actor is like a process. He is the agent responsible for reading the script; that is, a process is the agent responsible for executing the program. The actor has an identity quite separate from the script. He has a name, his parents, some children perhaps. These things are quite independent of the script he happens to be reading. If he puts aside *Hamlet* in favour of *King Lear*, he is still the same actor. In the same way, a process may turn from executing one program to executing another, but it is still the same process. The process is an active entity, it 'does things' by executing the code in the program, and by making system calls when necessary. The process will spend some time executing, some time *blocked*, that is, descheduled until some I/O or other operation has completed, and some time simply waiting its turn in the scheduler queue for its allocation of time.

It is harder to visualize the 'physical existence' of a process than of a program. A process carries with it a certain *context*, that is certain *state information*. Some of this information is held in 'user space' and can be manipulated directly by the program; for example, the values of all the variables. Other context is held inside the kernel on behalf of the process and can only be manipulated via system calls; for example, the process's numeric *process ID*, its notion of the current directory and its open file descriptors. Yet other context is maintained which is not visible to the user at all, for example, the position of the process on the scheduler's queue, and (possibly) information about if and where the process's memory image is swapped out onto disk. So the process does have a kind of physical existence after all – one could point to this varied collection of data structures and say 'There's the process'. This brings us to our own definition:

> A process is the context maintained whilst executing a program.

### 2.2.2  The attributes and resources of a process

Table 2.1 lists the main components of a process context in a little more detail. Some of these items are fairly self-explanatory, others will be explained as we proceed. From this list it is clear that UNIX processes carry rather large amounts of 'baggage' around with them in terms of state information. Such processes are sometimes called *heavyweight processes*. This makes the business of creating a new process relatively 'expensive'. It is for this reason that UNIX is best suited to coarse grain distributed applications.

# 2.3  Manipulating processes

## 2.3.1  Creating new processes

One of the central strengths of UNIX is the ease with which new processes can be created. Any process can create a new process using the system call

**Table 2.1**

| Attribute/resource | Description |
| --- | --- |
| Process ID | A unique integer value identifying this process |
| Parent process ID | The process ID of the process which created this one |
| Real user ID | The numeric user ID of the user who started this process |
| Effective user ID | The ID of the user whose access rights are currently being carried; normally, this is the same as the real user ID |
| Current directory | The directory used as the start point for looking up relative pathnames |
| File descriptor table | A table containing data on all input/output streams opened by the process. The table is indexed by a small integer value called a file descriptor |
| The environment | A list of strings, each conventionally of the form VARIABLE=VALUE, used to customize the behaviour of certain programs. The environment is interrogated by calling the library routine getenv() |
| Code space | A piece of memory in which the program code is stored |
| Data space | A piece of memory in which global variables and other static data are stored |
| Stack | A piece of memory used to hold local variables (declared inside functions) |
| Heap | A piece of memory allocated dynamically in response to explicit calls by the process, usually via the library routines malloc() and free() (look up sbrk(2) and malloc(3)) |
| Priority | Parameters that control the scheduling of the process |
| Signal disposition | Masks indicating which signals are awaiting delivery, which are blocked, etc. (signals will be discussed later in the chapter) |
| umask | A mask value used to ensure that specified access permissions are *not* granted when this process creates a file. (Look up umask(1) and umask(2)) |

```
fork();
```

This is, in some ways, the simplest of all system calls. It takes no arguments, and returns a simple integer result. Yet in other ways, it is one of the hardest system calls to understand. The fork() call creates a new process which is an exact copy of the original, as shown in Figure 2.2. One process makes the call to fork(), *two* processes return from it. The two continue execution asynchronously, competing for CPU cycles with all the other processes in the machine. The original process is called the *parent*; the newly created process is called the *child*.

For an analogy, we may return to our actor and script example. The actor sees an instruction saying 'fork'. He calls in from the wings a new actor (the child), and they stand side by side reading from the same script. 'Where are we?' asks the child. 'We're here', says the parent, pointing a finger at the line following the fork() instruction. 'OK', says the child, and they stand side by side, reading from the same script. This analogy is not perfect because it suggests that the new child process already existed in

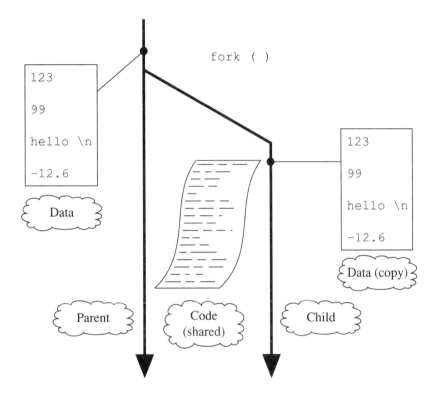

**Figure 2.2** The fork() call illustrated.

some dormant state, waiting to be used. This is not the case. When a fork() is executed, the kernel creates a new child process by making a copy of the parent. (Look up fork(2).)

When we create a child process it is usually because we want it to do something different from the parent. Consequently there must be some way for these two 'identical' processes to know which is which, on return from the fork(). Here is how: in the parent, the return value of the fork() call is the process ID of the newly created child. In the child, the fork() returns zero. Invariably, therefore, the fork() call appears inside an if test, so that the parent and child can branch to different places.

The following program illustrates the operation of fork() and the asynchronous behaviour of the parent and child:

```
/* Demonstration of forking a child process */
/* The program forkdemo.c */

main()
{
    int i;

    if (fork()) {  /* I must be the parent */
```

```
        for (i=0; i<1000; i++)
            printf("\t\t\tPARENT %d\n", i);

    }
    else   {     /* I must be the child */
        for (i=0; i<1000; i++)
            printf("CHILD %d\n", i);
    }
}
```

In this program both the parent and the child execute a loop 1000 times, printing the loop count and the word PARENT or CHILD. To help distinguish the output, the parent's lines are indented three tab stops to the right. When this program is run, the output is of the following form:

```
CHILD 0
CHILD 1
CHILD 2
                        PARENT 0
                        PARENT 1
                        PARENT 2
                        PARENT 3
CHILD 3
CHILD 4
CHILD 5
CHILD 6
CHILD 7
                        PARENT 4
                        PARENT 5
CHILD 8
CHILD 9
CHILD 10
                        PARENT 6
                        PARENT 7
                        PARENT 8
                        PARENT 9
                        PARENT 10
```

. . . and so on.

In practice you may not see such rapid switching between the parent and child output. This will depend on the length of the time-slice allocated by the scheduler to each process, and the number of times your computer is able to execute the loop in that time-slice. The buffering performed in the standard I/O library also complicates the picture, as it will tend to gather up the output from each process into larger chunks. However, the point is this: the output from the parent and child will be interleaved in some random way, as the scheduler switches attention between the two. The output from the program is nondeterministic; that is, it will not be the same each time, and you cannot determine exactly what the output will look like by examining the source code, even though it is a mere twelve lines long.

Also apparent from this example it that the two processes maintain their own count variable, i, quite independently. Changing the value of this variable in one process does not affect its value in the other. This is because the child receives a separate *copy* of the memory space used to hold variables.

## 2.3.2  Concurrent execution of parent and child

In the previous example, both child and parent processes continued to execute from a shared copy of the same code. Usually, when we create a child process, we do so because we want it to execute a totally separate program. We will do that in the next section. First, however, we consider one more example in which parent and child continue to execute the *same* program.

In Chapter 1 we examined pseudo-code for a communications program which ferried characters back and forth between the user's terminal and a serial port. Now that we know about fork(), we can write the program for real. Here it is; it is called talkto:

```
/* Simple communication program - copies characters from
   stdin to a specified port, and from the port to stdout.
*/

#include <stdio.h>
#include <fcntl.h>

main()
{
    int fd, count;
    char buffer[BUFSIZ];

    /* Open the device. /dev/ttya is the UNIX file
       name of the serial port we wish to talk to.
       NB:  The child will inherit the descriptor.
    */
    fd = open("/dev/ttya",  O_RDWR);
    if (fd == -1) {
        fprintf(stderr, "cannot open device ttya\n");
        exit(1);
    }

    if (fork()) {    /* Parent: copy port to stdout */
        while(1) {
            count = read(fd, buffer, BUFSIZ);
            write(1, buffer, count);
        }
    }
    else {           /* Child: copy stdin to port */
```

```
        while(1) {
            count = read(0, buffer, BUFSIZ);
            write(fd, buffer, count);
        }
    }
}
```

Both parent and child enter an infinite loop. The parent reads from the serial port and will block until one or more characters arrive. However many characters are received (up to a maximum of BUFSIZ), the same number is copied to file descriptor 1 (standard output). The child does exactly the same, but reads from file descriptor 0 (standard input) and writes to the serial port. This program relies on two important characteristics of process creation in UNIX. First, the file descriptor fd (created by the parent before the fork()) is inherited by the child. Second, the parent and child have separate copies of the character buffer buffer and the variable count.

---

**An aside:** to make the program at all useful, it would need, at minimum, some way of setting the baud rate of the port after opening it. Many other bells and whistles could be added – terminal emulation, file diversions, auto-dialler support, etc. – but it is easy to imagine that programs such as cu, tip and kermit had beginnings almost as humble as this example.

---

The ps command may be used to examine the process activity in the system, and it is worth running it here to convince ourselves that there really are two processes executing the talkto program. ps has a plethora of flags and options (and what is worse, they are different between the BSD and System V versions); the example here shows a (heavily edited) version of the output from the SVR4 version of ps:

```
eddie% ps -aef

      UID    PID  PPID  C    STIME TTY        TIME COMD

    chris    580   579  0 16:34:20 pts/3      0:01 csh
    chris   1425   580 44 22:33:27 pts/3      0:01 talkto
    chris   1426  1425  0 22:33:27 pts/3      0:00 talkto

eddie%
```

The columns to note are those labelled PID ( = process ID), PPID ( = parent process ID) and COMD ( = command). Notice that there is a shell (PID = 580) which is the parent of one of the talkto processes, and that this process (PID = 1425) is in turn the parent of the other talkto process (PID = 1426). This output also gives us a clue about how the shell works – it forks a child to run the requested command.

### 2.3.3 Program execution and the environment

The previous example is slightly unusual in that both parent and child execute the same program (albeit different parts of it). More often, we make the child execute a separate program. The system call exec() is used to do this. To illustrate the operation of exec(), it may be helpful to return to our analogy of an actor and his script. An 'exec' instruction in the script tells the actor to stop reading his present script and to start reading a new one – 'Go and read *Hamlet*!'. In doing so, he discards the old script entirely, and starts at page 1 of the new one. However, he remains the same actor; he retains his own identity. (He is still John Smith, but he is no longer reading *King Lear*.)

In a similar way, an exec() call in a program causes the process to replace its execution image with that of a new program. In doing so, the process necessarily loses the context that was associated with the old program: the code space, data space, stack and heap. However, it remains the same process – it has the same process ID, the same parent and (if it has any) the same children as it had before. The process keeps other pieces of context as well; for example, all open file descriptors are retained. This is very important, as we will see in later examples.

Before looking at exec() in detail, we will examine the user-level context which is passed to the new program, via the arguments to the main() function. These are shown in Figure 2.3. The argc and argv parameters are well known by C programmers; they provide access to the program's 'command line arguments'. The envp parameter is less well known and less often used. It provides access to the process's *environment*. In this context, the term environment has a specific meaning. It is simply a list of strings, each conventionally of the form VARIABLE=value which is used to customize the behaviour of certain programs. (Look up environ(5).) For example, some programs such as the mailer, which allow you to escape into an editor to help prepare your text, look for an environment variable called EDITOR to see which editor to invoke.

Here is a little program called showenv which will print both its argument list and its environment:

```
/* A program which prints its command line args
   and its environment
*/
main(int argc, char *argv[], char *envp[])
{
    printf("Command line args are:\n");
    while (*argv != 0) {
        printf("%s\n", *argv++);
    }
    printf("Environment strings are:\n");
    while (*envp != 0) {
        printf("%s\n", *envp++);
    }
}
```

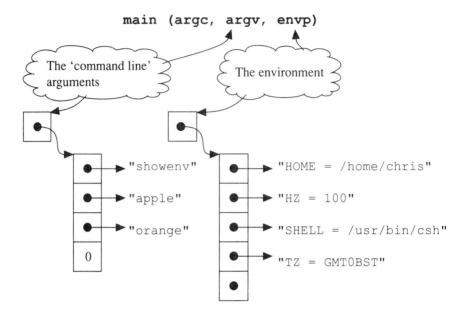

**Figure 2.3** The arguments to `main()`.

When executed, the output appears as follows. (Some of the environment variables have been elided out.) Notice that the initial command line argument retrieved by the program (`showenv` in the example) is in fact the name by which the program is invoked.

```
eddie% showenv apple orange
Command line args are:
showenv
apple
orange
Environment strings are:
HOME=/home/chris
HZ=100
SHELL=/usr/bin/csh
TZ=GMT0BST
...
eddie%
```

In practice, it would be unusual for a program to scan through its entire environment in this way. More often, it would interrogate the value of a specific environment variable by calling `getenv()`. (Look up `getenv(3)`.)

Let us return to our discussion of `exec()`. There are in fact six versions of it. They differ in three areas:

1.  Is the name of the program to be executed specified as an absolute pathname, or as a relative pathname which is looked up in each directory specified in the PATH environment variable?
2.  Is the environment to be passed to the new program simply to be the one we already have (i.e. inherited), or do we want explicitly to pass a new one?
3.  Do we want to pass the 'command line' arguments as an explicit list appearing in the exec() call, or as a vector?

Figure 2.4 shows a decision tree leading to the correct choice of exec() call in each case. For details of these, look up exec(2). Notice that not all of the possible eight combinations are catered for.

Arguably, the easiest version of exec() to use is execlp(). Suppose we wish to execute the sort program, passing arguments '-n' and 'foo'. The call to execlp() would appear as follows:

```
execlp("sort", "sort", "-n", "foo", 0);
```

Note that the call takes a variable number of parameters. The zero argument is essential to mark the end of the list. Why does the 'sort' argument appear twice? Is this redundant information? Well, yes, in a way, but the point is that the first argument specifies the name of the executable file that we want to execute, while the second argument specifies what the program is to receive as its argv[0] argument. It is only by convention that the two are the same. (That is, the shell does things this way.)

The following program illustrates the use of execlp() to implement a rather trivial menu-driven command interpreter:

```
/* The program tinymenu.c */
#include <stdio.h>

main()
{
    /* Hard-wired list of commands */
    static char *cmd[] = { "who", "ls", "date" };
    int i;
    /* Prompt for, and read a command number */
    printf("0=who, 1=ls, 2=date : ");
    scanf("%d", &i);

    /* Execute the selected command */
    execlp(cmd[i], cmd[i], 0);
    printf("command not found\n"); /* exec failed */
}
```

Apart from the abysmal lack of error checking, the most fundamental limitation of this program is that it is a 'one-shot' affair. Having selected a menu item, the requested program is executed, then the process terminates. Unfortunately, we cannot simply put the whole thing into a loop, because the execlp() call never returns (unless it fails for

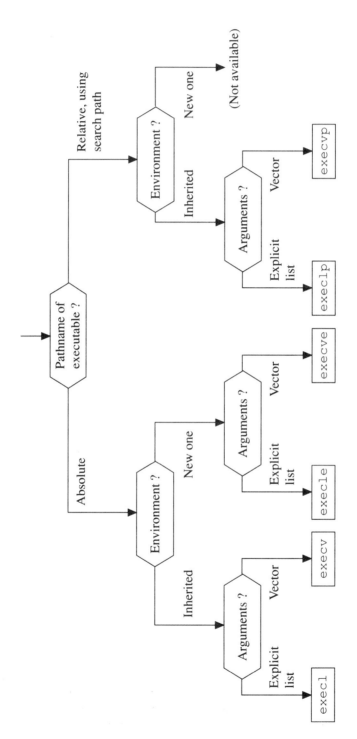

**Figure 2.4** Decision tree for the `exec()` family of calls.

some reason; for example, if it cannot find the file we asked it to execute). If the `execlp()` succeeds, control is transferred to the new program. All context within the old program is lost; there is no way back.

How might we change the program to keep hold of its context whilst the selected command is executing, so that we can get control back afterwards? The answer is, we can `fork()` to create a new process to execute the command, and have the original process (the parent) wait until the child has finished. Remember, processes are good at maintaining context. That is what they are for.

## 2.3.4  Basic process control using `exit()` and `wait()`

To do the menu program properly, we need two additional system calls. The `exit()` call is used by a process that wishes to terminate voluntarily. It takes a single-integer parameter, known as the *exit status* of the process. By convention, an exit status of zero indicates 'success'; a nonzero exit status indicates a 'failure' of some kind. Secondly, the `wait()` system call is used by a parent to wait for one of its children to terminate. The `wait()` call can return two pieces of information:

1.  The process ID of the child whose termination caused the `wait()` call to wake up.
2.  The exit status of the child.

We will ignore these details for now, and simply note that the call `wait(0)` may be used to wait for a child to die.

---

**An aside:** the terminology has become rather morbid here. It is normal (though not compulsory) for a parent to outlive its children in the UNIX world.

---

Using `exit()` and `wait()`, here is a reworked version of the program:

```
/* File menushell.c */

#include <stdio.h>

main()
{
    /* Hard-wired list of commands */
    static char *cmd[] = { "who", "ls", "date" };
    int i;

    while (1) {
        /* Prompt for, and read a command number */
        printf("0=who, 1=ls, 2=date : ");
        scanf("%d", &i);
        /* If selection is invalid, parent terminates */
        if (i<0 || i>2)
```

```
                exit(1);
        if (fork() == 0) {  /* Child */
                /* The child executes the selected command */
                execlp(cmd[i], cmd[i], 0);
                printf("command not found\n");
                exit(1);
        }
        else {
                /* The parent waits for the child to finish */
                wait(0);
        }
    }
}
```

The use of `fork()`, followed by an `exec()` in the child and a `wait()` in the parent, is a very common idiom in UNIX programming. It is, essentially, the sequence of operations performed by the shell to execute a command. Figure 2.5 illustrates this.

## 2.3.5 Inheritance of process attributes and resources

Table 2.2 summarizes the inheritance of some of the important process attributes and resources across a `fork()` and an `exec()`.

**Table 2.2**

| Attribute | Inherited by child? | Retained on `exec`? |
|---|---|---|
| Process ID | No | Yes |
| Real user ID | Yes | Yes |
| Effective user ID | Yes | Depends on whether the 'setuid' bit of the executable file is set |
| Static data | Copied | No |
| Stack | Copied | No |
| Heap | Copied | No |
| Code | Shared | No |
| Open file descriptors | Copied; file pointers are shared | Usually, but can be explicitly prevented using an `fcntl()` call on the descriptor |
| Environment | Yes | Depends on which version of `exec()` is used |
| Current directory | Yes | Yes |
| Signal-handling behaviour | Copied | Partially |

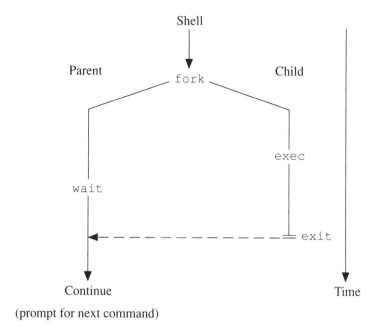

**Figure 2.5** Process activity when the shell executes a program.

## 2.4 Pipes

We have seen how to create new processes, and how to synchronize with them in a primitive way using `wait()`. In this section we examine how we may communicate with those processes, and how to synchronize with them a little more closely, using that most traditional of UNIX interprocess communication mechanisms, the *pipe*.

The easiest channels of communication for a process to use are its standard input (file descriptor 0) and standard output (file descriptor 1). These are inherited from the process's parent (the shell, for example), and by default are connected to the keyboard and screen. Most UNIX users know how to redirect these streams, using notations such as

```
who  >  temp_file
sort <  temp_file
```

Most UNIX users are also familiar with the concept of a pipe, and know how to ask the shell to create one, with commands of the form

```
who  |  sort
```

which runs who and sort as two concurrent processes, with the standard output of who connected to the standard input of sort. Simple pipelines like this are at the heart of the UNIX philosophy of coarse grain algorithmic distribution, with solutions to specific problems being 'composed' by combining two or more general-purpose tools. We will examine the steps performed by a program, such as the shell, to create such a pipeline.

## 2.4.1  Creating pipes

A pipe is a unidirectional mechanism. It has an upstream end, which can be written to, and a downstream end, which can be read from. Pipes are created using the pipe() system call which is illustrated in Figure 2.6. The argument to pipe() is a pointer to an array of two integers. On return from the call, element 0 of the array contains a file descriptor referencing the downstream end of the pipe, and element 1 contains a file descriptor referencing the upstream end. (Look up pipe(2).)

---

**An aside:** traditionally, pipes have always been unidirectional. They are documented as such in the original System V Interface Definition, in the SunOS 4.1 manual and in the OSF/1 manual. However, the SVR4 manual explicitly states that pipes are *bidirectional* – a read() from either end will return data written to the other end. Such a pipe is, in effect, two independent communication channels, one in each direction. We will not rely on this capability in our examples.

---

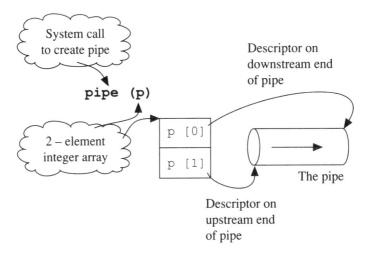

**Figure 2.6** Creating a pipe.

Pipes are most commonly used to establish one-way communication between two child processes that have a common parent. Figure 2.7 shows a process A which arranges for two children, B and C, to communicate through a pipe. The stages are as follows:

- Stage 1: Process A creates a pipe, receiving descriptors on each end.
- Stage 2: Process A forks twice, creating children B and C. The children both inherit both descriptors, so at this point all three processes have descriptors open on both ends of the pipe.
- Stage 3: Each process closes the ends of the pipe it does not need. B closes the downstream end, C closes the upstream end and A closes both ends. (We will see why it is important to close the unused ends, particularly the upstream end, shortly.)

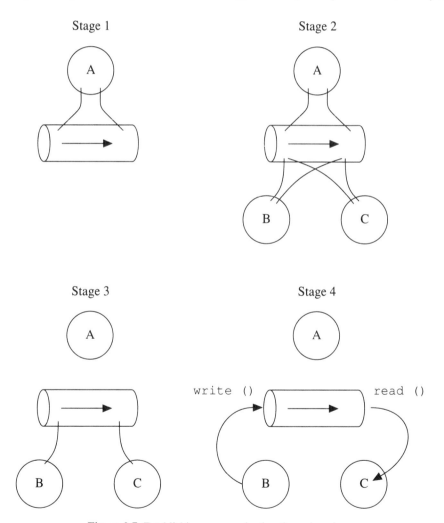

**Figure 2.7** Establishing communication through a pipe.

- Stage 4: Processes B and C usually then execute some other program. The file descriptors on the ends of the pipe remain intact across the `exec()` calls. B writes to the pipe using normal `write()` system calls, C reads from it using `read()`.

We will see the code to do these things in Section 2.4.3.

## 2.4.2 Synchronization using pipes

Pipes have a finite capacity (typically a few thousand bytes) and impose a loose synchronization between the upstream and downstream processes. If the upstream process tries to write to the pipe when it is full, the process will block until the downstream process consumes some of the data. It is particularly important to understand the behaviour of the downstream process. Consider a program that processes a stream of data read from a pipe, reading up to 100 bytes at a time, and continuing until there are no more data available – that is, until the `read()` call returns zero. Its processing loop will have the following form:

```
while((count = read(fd, buffer, 100)) > 0) {
    /* process data in buffer */
}
```

Let us suppose that the descriptor `fd` references the downstream end of a pipe, and that the upstream process has written 230 bytes of data into it. Within the downstream process, the first two passes through the loop will request, and receive, 100 bytes of data. The third pass will request 100 bytes but receive only 30, because that is all there is left in the pipe. On the fourth pass, the `read()` will block, because the pipe is empty. If the upstream process writes more data, the downstream process will immediately receive it. However, if the upstream process has finished, and closes the descriptor on its end of the pipe (or simply exits), the downstream process's `read()` call will return an end of file (EOF) indication (that it, it will return zero). Let us summarize this behaviour:

> A `read()` on an empty pipe will block. However, if *no* process has the upstream end open, the read will return zero, to indicate 'end of file'.

## 2.4.3 A pipeline example

In Section 2.4.1 we examined a four-stage process used to establish a pipe between two child processes. The classic example of this scenario is seen when the shell executes a command such as

```
who  |  sort
```

In this case (referring to Figure 2.7), process A is the shell, process B executes `who` and process C executes `sort`. In fact, the shell's task in establishing this pipeline is a little more complicated than these four steps. The shell cannot simply create a pipe, hand the two file descriptors down to its children, and expect who and sort somehow to know that they are supposed to read and write these descriptors. All who does is write to standard output (file descriptor 1), and sort will simply read its standard input (file descriptor 0), sort it and write the results to its standard output. Somehow, the shell has to get the output from who connected to the upstream end of the pipe, and the input to sort connected to the downstream end.

The dup2() call may be used to rearrange the 'plumbing' in the required fashion. The call

```
dup2(old, new);
```

takes an existing file descriptor, old, and duplicates it onto new. If new is already an open descriptor, it will be closed first. In other words, after the call, new will refer to the same stream as old does. (Look up dup2(3) and dup(2).) For example, after executing the following code fragment:

```
int p[2];

pipe(p);
dup2(p[1], 1);
```

the standard output of the process will be connected to the upstream end of the pipe.

Using dup2(), we are now able to set up the 'who piped into sort' scenario, using the following program:

```
/* File whosort.c */

main()
{
    int fds[2];

    pipe(fds);                    /* Create the pipe */
    /* First child reconnects stdin to downstream
       end of pipe and closes the upstream end
    */
    if (fork() == 0) {
      dup2(fds[0], 0);
      close(fds[1]);
      execlp("sort", "sort", 0);
    }
    /* Second child reconnects stdout to upstream
       end of pipe and closes the downstream end
    */
    else if (fork() == 0) {
      dup2(fds[1], 1);
      close(fds[0]);
```

```
        execlp("who", "who", 0);
}
/* Parent closes both ends of pipe
    and waits for both children to finish
*/
else {
close(fds[0]);
close(fds[1]);
wait(0);
wait(0);
}
}
```

There are some important comments to be made about this example. The close() performed by the first child, to close the upstream end of the pipe, is essential. Without it, this child will never see an EOF when it reads from the pipe. Even though the process has no intention of writing to the pipe, the fact that it holds a descriptor open on the upstream end will prevent the EOF from being seen. Why the pairs of calls to close() and wait() in the parent? The calls to wait() are to ensure that the parent does not return until both children have finished. If we do not do this, the shell (which in turn is waiting for its child – i.e. the process that is executing the whosort program – to complete) may resume and prompt us again before the who and sort programs have completed. The close() on the upstream end of the pipe is there for the reason already stated. Without it, sort will never see an EOF from the pipe.

---

**An aside:** if there is one single program that captures the essence of UNIX, this may be it. All UNIX system programmers should be required, by law, to rewrite this program annually.

---

## 2.4.4  Limitations of pipes

Although pipes are very elegant, they do have some limitations:

1.  Pipes are unidirectional (at least, as noted above, in most implementations). This is not a fundamental limitation; it is easy to create two for two-way communication.
2.  Pipes offer no mechanism to 'authenticate' the process at the other end. For example, the process reading from the pipe has no idea who the writer is. This is closely related to the next point.
3.  Pipes must be pre-arranged. Two *unrelated* processes cannot make a pipe and connect to each end. They must have a common ancestor who created the pipe, and handed the file descriptors down to its descendants.
4.  Pipes do not work across the network. Both processes must be running on the same machine.

## 2.4.5 Named pipes

Named pipes (also known as FIFOs, because they provide first-in, first-out operations) overcome one of the limitations listed above: they allow unrelated processes to establish communication. A named pipe has an entry in the file system, and as such, it has an ownership and an access mode in the same way as does a file. Named pipes can be created with the command mknod ( look up mknod(1) ), and show up on a directory listing as type 'p'. For example:

```
eddie% mknod my_fifo p
eddie% ls -l my_fifo
prw-r--r--    1 chris     other       0 Dec  1 09:22 my_fifo
eddie%
```

---

**An aside:** named pipes can also be created with the mknod() system call. Look up mknod(2). The use of mknod() for this purpose is not especially intuitive, even by UNIX standards. It is just one of those things you have to *know*.

---

Named pipes are very easy to use: one process opens the pipe for writing, another process opens it for reading. Thereafter, they behave much like ordinary pipes.

## 2.5  Shared memory

### 2.5.1  Shared memory concepts

At any one time during the operation of a UNIX system, there will be a number of active processes sharing the physical memory of the machine. Memory management software within the kernel, working in close conjunction with memory management hardware which is interposed between the processor and the actual memory, gives each process the illusion of having the address space to itself. (Indeed, in a virtual memory implementation of UNIX, which most versions are nowadays, each process can have the illusion of having more memory than is physically present – in theory, up to the architectural limit of the processor.) Part of the job of this memory management system is to ensure that no process is able to access memory that belongs to another process. This is an essential feature of any multi-user operating system; the system must prevent a malicious (or merely errant) process from interfering with the operation of other processes, or, worse still, from bringing the system down completely by overwriting parts of the kernel. The point is this:

> Normally, UNIX explicitly prevents a user process from accessing any
> data in memory belonging to another process.

There are times, however, when shared memory can be a very effective form of communication amongst a group of processes which are specifically written to cooperate as part of a distributed application. Consequently, most versions of UNIX support a mechanism whereby a group of processes can explicitly elect to share a piece of memory.

The basic idea is illustrated in Figure 2.8. Some process (say, process A in the figure) initially creates a shared memory segment. This process specifies a size for the segment, and it also allocates to the segment a numeric *key* value. Since the process presumably wishes to access the segment it has just created, it will normally then proceed to 'attach' the segment into its own address space. This operation returns to the process a pointer through which it can reference to access data in the segment, in much the same way as `malloc()` returns a pointer to a piece of memory allocated from the heap. At some later time another process (B in the figure) can choose to attach the segment also. All B needs to know is the numeric key of the segment. Any change made to the data in the segment by one process is immediately visible to any other process which has the segment attached.

---

**An aside:** shared memory has been likened to the 'mind melding' practised by Star Trek's Mr Spock. You may or may not find this analogy helpful!

---

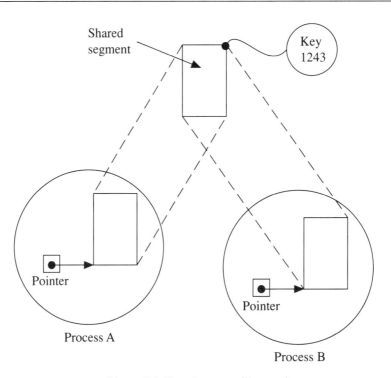

**Figure 2.8** Shared memory illustrated.

You should not think of a shared memory segment as a piece of memory which belongs to the address space of one particular 'master' process. Much like a file, a shared memory segment has an existence quite independent of any one process. The segment remains present in the system even if no process has it attached. Shared memory segments have other attributes in common with files, too. They have access permissions and modification timestamps, for example. The `ipcs` command may be used to obtain a listing of shared memory segments, much like `ls` is used to list files in a directory. We will see an example of this shortly.

## 2.5.2  Shared memory operations

Figure 2.9 illustrates the two key shared memory operations. `shmget()` is used to create a new segment or to obtain a 'handle' on an existing segment. In this call, the segment is identified by its key. The `shmat()` call is used to attach an existing segment into the address space of the calling process. (Look up `shmget(2)` and `shmop(2)`.)

## 2.5.3  A shared memory example

The two programs `cline` and `pline` presented here provide a simple example of the use of shared memory. The program `pline` ('print line') simply prints a line of characters every four seconds. The length of the line, and the character to be printed, are taken from a small data structure of type `struct info` held in a shared memory segment. The idea is that some other program can attach the segment and change the numbers. The program `cline` ('change line') takes two arguments: a single character and a count. These are written into the shared memory segment, where they will be seen by `pline` (if it is running) the next time it prints a line.

The two programs need to agree on the key of the segment, and the structure of the data within it. Because this information is shared, we will place it in a header file:

```
/* The header file line.h */
struct info {
    char c;
    int  length;
};

#define KEY            ((key_t)(1243))
#define SEGSIZE        sizeof(struct info)
```

The choice of a key number here is arbitrary. The only requirement is that it does not clash with keys used by other applications on the same machine. As there is no official register of key values, it is up to local system administrators to maintain a list of keys if necessary.

Here is the `pline` program. It gets a segment, creating it if necessary, then attaches it, and writes default values into the `info` structure. Then it loops, printing a line of data

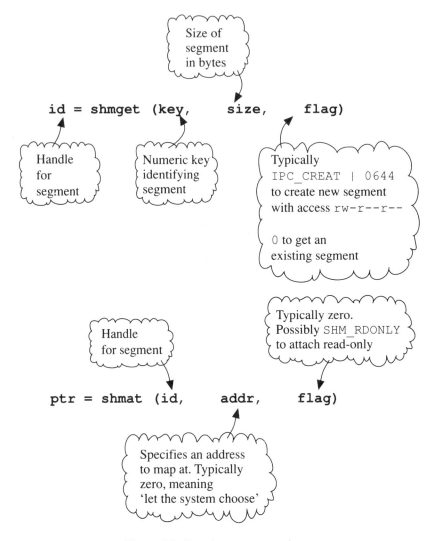

**Figure 2.9** Shared memory operations.

every four seconds under control of the two numbers in the shared segment. The loop terminates when the character count is set to zero.

```
/* This is an example of using shared memory. The program
   prints a line of text every four seconds. The length of the
   line, and the character printed, are controlled by two
   numbers held in a small data structure in a shared memory
   segment. Some other program can attach the segment and
   change the numbers.
```

```
*/

#include <stdio.h>
#include <sys/types.h>
#include <sys/ipc.h>
#include <sys/shm.h>
#include "line.h"

main()
{
    int    i, id;
    struct info *ctrl;
    struct shmid_ds shmbuf;

    id = shmget(KEY, SEGSIZE, IPC_CREAT | 0666);
    if (id < 0) {
        perror("pline: shmget failed:");
        exit(1);
    }

    ctrl = (struct info *)shmat(id, 0, 0);
    if (ctrl <= (struct info *)(0)) {
        perror("pline: shmat failed:");
        exit(2);
    }

    /* Set default parameters */
    ctrl->c      = 'a';
    ctrl->length = 10;

    /* Main loop - print a line every 4 seconds */
    while (ctrl->length > 0) {
        for (i=0; i<ctrl->length; i++)
            putchar(ctrl->c);
        putchar('\n');
        sleep(4);
    }
    exit(0);
}
```

Here is the `cline` program. In this case, it assumes that the shared segment already exists, and will fail if it does not. Having obtained a handle on the segment and attached it, the program simply takes a character and a count from the command line, and writes them into the shared segment.

```
/* This is an example of using shared memory. The program
   operates in conjuntion with the pline program. It allows
   the line length and character parameters of that program
   to be manually adjusted, by writing them into a shared
   memory segment.
*/
```

```c
#include <stdio.h>
#include <sys/types.h>
#include <sys/ipc.h>
#include <sys/shm.h>
#include "line.h"

main(int argc, char *argv[])
{
    int    id;
    struct info *ctrl;
    struct shmid_ds shmbuf;

    if (argc != 3) {
        fprintf(stderr, "usage: cline <char> <length>\n");
        exit(3);
    }

    id = shmget(KEY, SEGSIZE, 0);
    if (id < 0) {
        perror("cline: shmget failed:");
        exit(1);
    }

    ctrl = (struct info *)shmat(id, 0, 0);
    if (ctrl <= (struct info *)(0)) {
        perror("cline: shmat failed:");
        exit(2);
    }

    /* Copy command line data to shared memory region */
    ctrl->c      = argv[1][0];
    ctrl->length = atoi(argv[2]);

    exit(0);
}
```

Here is an annotated sample of the dialogue when this program is run:

```
eddie% pline &          # Start pline in background
aaaaaaaaaa
[1] 727                 # Shell reports process ID
eddie% aaaaaaaaaa
aaaaaaaaaa              # pline is busy printing 10 a's
aaaaaaaaaa
cline x 20              # write new values to the segment
eddie% xxxxxxxxxxxxxxxxxxxx
xxxxxxxxxxxxxxxxxxxx
xxxxxxxxxxxxxxxxxxxx    # now pline is printing 20 x's
xxxxxxxxxxxxxxxxxxxx
xxxxxxxxxxxxxxxxxxxx
cline f 0               # set count to zero
```

```
eddie%                  # pline will now terminate
[1]     Done     pline  # Shell reports termination
```

Even after `cline` and `pline` have both finished, the shared memory segment still exists, and may be seen using the `ipcs` command. The `key` value of 0x000004db shown below is in hexadecimal and corresponds to the decimal value 1243 defined in our header file `line.h`.

```
eddie% ipcs -bm
IPC status from /dev/kmem as of Tue Dec  1 12:34:42 1992
T    ID    KEY          MODE         OWNER    GROUP  SEGSZ
Shared Memory:
m    200 0x000004db -Crw-rw-rw-      chris    other   1024
```

Finally, we can delete the segment using `ipcrm`, then execute `ipcs` again to check that the segment has gone:

```
eddie% ipcrm -m 200
eddie% ipcs -bm
IPC status from /dev/kmem as of Tue Dec  1 12:34:55 1992
T    ID    KEY          MODE         OWNER    GROUP  SEGSZ
Shared Memory:
eddie%
```

For details of these commands, look up `ipcs(1)` and `ipcrm(1)`.


## 2.5.4  The characteristics of shared memory

The shared memory mechanism is sometimes criticized as being unnecessarily complicated to use. It is true that the business of dealing with ownership and access modes of the segment make for a rather messy set of system calls in order to perform something which is conceptually rather straightforward. It must be remembered, however, that a shared memory segment can be attached by any process, providing the key is known, just as any process can open a file if they know its name. Consequently, some form of access controls is essential, and it makes sense to use the familiar ownership and 'rw-r-r–' style of controls that UNIX uses for files and devices.

Let us digress for a moment and compare shared memory with pipes as a communication mechanism. The two most important advantages of shared memory are *efficiency* and *random access*. Shared memory is more efficient than pipes because the data do not need to be copied. A pipe is a buffer inside the kernel, so data must be copied from the address space of the upstream process into the kernel, then again from the kernel into the address space of the downstream process. Also, shared memory provides random access: a process may choose to update just a small piece in the middle of a data structure, whereas pipes provide a purely sequential byte stream. Shared memory provides a many-to-many communication mechanism (i.e. many processes can attach the segment), and there is no clear 'producer–consumer' relationship defined amongst these processes. Pipes, on the other hand, provide a one-to-one communication mechanism, with a well-defined producer–consumer relationship.

One of the strengths of pipes is that they automatically impose a loose synchronization between the upstream and downstream processes, as we saw in Section 2.4.2. The sharing of memory, on the other hand, imposes no synchronization whatever. For example, if we wish to implement a 'consumer' process which blocks until new data are written to a shared segment, we would have to use some additional mechanism to provide this synchronization. Depending on the form of synchronization required, we may choose to use semaphores (Section 2.6), or signals (Section 2.8), or we may even choose to write a short message down a pipe.

Because shared memory provides random access, it is tempting to use it to share graph structures such as linked lists or trees. You must be very careful here; the usual C technique of linking the structure together with pointers may not be usable. The point is this:

> Pointers created by one process are valid in the address space of that process. They will not be valid in the address space of some other process unless such a process can guarantee to attach the shared memory segment at the same address.

The neat solution here would be to use *based* pointers, that is, pointers that hold values relative to some fixed base address (in this case, the address at which the segment is attached). Unfortunately, C does not provide based pointers, although they can be simulated with explicit address arithmetic.

## 2.5.5 Shared memory using `mmap()`

An alternative approach to shared memory is to use the `mmap()` system call. The manual page for `mmap()` explains that it 'establishes a mapping between a process's address space and a virtual memory object' which is no doubt very helpful if you happen to know what a virtual memory object actually is. `mmap()` comes from BSD UNIX. The early implementations were far from complete and the only kind of object which you could `mmap()` was a pseudo-device driver corresponding to the physical system address space. This allowed programmers to map a specified piece of the physical address space into their program. It was used, for example, to allow user access to devices such as TV frame buffers without writing a full-blown kernel device driver. More recent implementations of `mmap()` are more complete – in particular, they support the use of *files* as memory-mapped objects.

The `mmap()` call is illustrated in Figure 2.10. For details, look up `mmap(2)`. The basic operation is as follows:

1. The process obtains a file descriptor by opening a regular disk file.

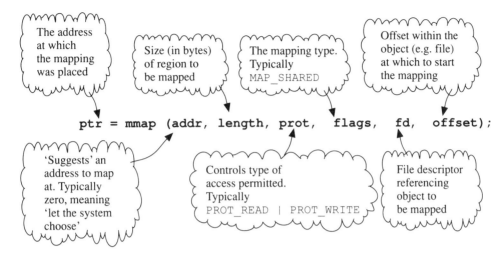

**Figure 2.10** The mmap() call.

2.  The process calls mmap() specifying the file descriptor as one of the parameters. Other parameters control which section of the file is to be mapped in, and may provide some degree of control over the address at which it is attached. (However, the safest thing to do is to allow the system to choose this address for you.) mmap() returns a pointer to the address at which the object has been attached, in much the same way as malloc() returns a pointer to the memory it has allocated.

3.  The process examines or modifies the content of the file via normal memory references off the pointer.

As an example, here are reworked versions of our pline.c and cline.c programs which share memory through the mmap() call. First, the header file. Instead of agreeing on a shared memory key, the two programs must now agree on the name of the file to be mapped in, here shown as pline.conf:

```
#define CONFIG_FILE     "pline.conf"

struct info {
    char        c;
    int         length;
};
```

Here is the mmap() version of pline. Note that the 'config file' must already exist, and must be big enough to hold the info structure. mmap() will not 'grow' the file.

```
/* This is an example of shared memory using the mmap() system
   call. The program prints a line of text every four seconds.
   The length of the line, and the character printed, are
```

```
        controlled by two numbers held in a configuration file
        which the program maps in. Some other program can map in
        the same file (or simply write() to it) and change the
        numbers.                        File "mmpline.c"
*/

#include <stdio.h>
#include <sys/types.h>
#include <fcntl.h>
#include <sys/mman.h>
#include "mmline.h"

main()
{
    int   i, fd;
    struct info *ctrl;

    /* NB The file must already exist */
    fd = open(CONFIG_FILE, O_RDWR);
    if (fd < 0) {
        perror("mmpline: open failed:");
        exit(1);
    }

    ctrl = (struct info *)mmap(0, sizeof (struct info),
                            PROT_READ|PROT_WRITE, MAP_SHARED,
                            fd, 0);
    if (ctrl <= (struct info *)(0)) {
        perror("mmpline: mmap failed:");
        exit(2);
    }

    /* Set default parameters */
    ctrl->c      = 'a';
    ctrl->length = 10;

    /* Main operating loop - print a line every 4 seconds */
    while (ctrl->length > 0) {
        for (i=0; i<ctrl->length; i++)
            putchar(ctrl->c);
        putchar('\n');
        sleep(4);
    }
    exit(0);
}
```

Here is the `mmap()` version of `cline`:

```
/* This is an example of shared memory using the mmap() system
    call. The program operates in conjunction with the mmpline
    program. It allows the line length and character parameters
```

```
        of that program to be manually adjusted, by writing them
        into a file which is mapped into the program's address
        space.    File "mmcline.c"
*/

#include <stdio.h>
#include <sys/types.h>
#include <fcntl.h>
#include <sys/mman.h>
#include "mmline.h"

main(int argc, char *argv[])
{
    int     fd;
    struct info *ctrl;

    if (argc != 3) {
        fprintf(stderr, "usage: mmcline <char> <length>\n");
        exit(3);
    }

    /* Open the configuration file */
    fd = open(CONFIG_FILE, O_RDWR);
    if (fd < 0) {
        perror("mmcline: open failed:");
        exit(1);
    }

    /* Map the file in */
    ctrl = (struct info *)mmap(0, sizeof(struct info),
                        PROT_WRITE, MAP_SHARED, fd, 0);
    if (ctrl <= (struct info *)(0)) {
        perror("mmcline: mmap failed:");
        exit(2);
    }

    /* Copy command line data to mapped file */
    ctrl->c      = argv[1][0];
    ctrl->length = atoi(argv[2]);

    exit(0);
}
```

As a mechanism for creating shared memory objects, the mmap() call is, arguably, better integrated into UNIX than the shared memory calls. Because the shared objects *are* files, the mechanism uses the same naming schemes as files use (i.e. pathnames), it uses existing system calls for creating and deleting the shared objects (open() and unlink()), and it uses existing system calls for changing ownership and access permissions (chown() and chmod()). The System V shared memory mechanism, on the other hand, uses totally new system calls for these operations. Also, of course, the shared object is *nonvolatile*; that is, it will survive a power cut or a reboot of the machine. This is not the case for System V shared memory segments.

The implementation of mmap() is closely tied up with the virtual memory architecture of the machine. If one process has a file mmaped, and another has it opened for reading and writing in the normal way, a change made to the file by one process will propagate immediately to the other process's view of the file. When the change actually reaches the disk is another matter. SVR4 has a call, msync(), which forces modified pages within a process's address space to be flushed to disk.

The more devious readers may be wondering if, by applying mmap() to a file descriptor open on a remote file (using NFS), it might be possible to achieve some sort of network-wide 'virtual shared memory'. Some implementations of UNIX do indeed support mmap() operations on remote NFS file systems; however, the systems tested by the author were either very slow at propagating changes from one virtual memory object to another, or else failed to do so completely. Consequently, mmap() cannot be seriously considered as a network-wide communication mechanism.

## 2.5.6  How not to share memory

We will end this section with a warning about how *not* to share memory. SVR4 UNIX provides a mechanism to access the address space of an active process through special file entries of the form /proc/xxxxx where xxxxx is the process ID. Although it is possible to examine and modify the data space of a process in this way, it is a highly specialized task, requiring detailed knowledge of the layout of the process's memory image, and should definitely not be considered as an IPC mechanism.

---

**An aside:** this mechanism is really intended for use by programs such as truss, which in SVR4 traces the system calls executed by a process. For an example of truss in action, try:

```
truss  date
```

To see how truss itself operates, try:

```
truss  truss date
```

You will observe that truss forks, and opens the /proc entry corresponding to the child. It then applies a sequence of ioctl(), lseek() and read() operations on this descriptor to trace the process. In deciphering the output, one is reminded of those wonderful recursive stories of the tortoise and the hare told by Douglas Hofstadter in his book *Godel, Escher, Bach – An Eternal Golden Braid* (Hofstadter, 1979).

---

# 2.6  Semaphores

## 2.6.1  Critical code sections

The example programs `pline` and `cline` shown earlier in the chapter have a small but significant bug. Consider the following. Program `pline` is running, looping around printing rows of ten letter 'a's, say. The `cline` program is invoked with the command

```
cline  t  50
```

and has just executed the statement:

```
ctrl->c      = argv[1][0];
```

to place the ASCII 't' into the shared memory segment, when unfortunately it gets descheduled in favour of `pline`. The `pline` program sees the new character code 't' but the old length (10). What gets printed is a line of ten letter t's, which no one asked for. In other words, `pline` sees the data whilst `cline` is in the middle of updating, and therefore finds the date in an inconsistent state. The point is, `cline` has a *critical section* of code during which it should not be interrupted; or at least, not by another process using the shared memory segment. In this example, the critical section consists of the lines:

```
/* Copy command line data to shared memory region */
ctrl->c      = argv[1][0];
ctrl->length = atoi(argv[2]);
```

The `pline` program also has a critical section within which the shared data should not be altered; it is the loop:

```
for (i=0; i<ctrl->length; i++)
   putchar(ctrl->c);
```

It is easy to imagine that the probability of `cline` being descheduled in between the two lines of code which make up its critical section is so small as to not be worth considering. Surely the chances are one in a million? Well, yes, that figure is probably about right. Indeed, since this particular critical section is executed only once each time `cline` is (manually) invoked, the failure rate is probably undetectable. However, if the update operation is occurring within a tight loop, our program may fail every few seconds. Of course, programs that fail every few seconds are not too bad to debug. At least there is something vaguely reproducible to look for. It is the programs that fail once a month that are really hard to fix. Failures that occur rarely, randomly and without any apparent data dependencies are often due to unfortunate timing coincidences, known as *race conditions*, such as the one described above.

**An aside:** stories of hard-to-find bugs abound in the folklore of computing. One especially nice tale was popular in the Radio Astronomy Group at Cambridge University, England. The group had a steerable radio telescope dish at a remote site at Lord's Bridge, in the fenland south of Cambridge. (Remote, that is, until the M11 motorway was build alongside.) The dish was steered by a computer which periodically read a new set of coordinates from a paper tape. The system worked fine, except that occasionally it would send the dish to a grossly incorrect position. There was no apparent pattern to this failure, except that it only happened at night, when the site was unmanned. A student was therefore delegated to spend the night in the control hut, to see if he could figure out what the problem was. Several nights of vigil revealed nothing. As long as the student remained in the room, the fault did not occur. A meeting was called. 'As far as I can see', said the student, 'the only difference is that while I'm there, I leave the light on.' The next night, of course, the student found himself sitting in the control hut in the dark, whereupon the problem was soon revealed. A moth, attracted by the bright light of the paper tape reader, had settled on the tape.

Much harder to believe is a report in the November 1992 edition of *Scientific American*, of a study by Edward N. Adams of the Thomas J. Watson Research Centre, who 'empirically analysed "bug sizes" over a worldwide database that involved the equivalent of thousands of years of a particular software system.'

About a third of all bugs found 'produced a failure only about once in 5,000 *years* of execution.' One knows not whether to laugh or cry.

## 2.6.2 Boolean semaphores

Computer science has a standard mechanism called a *semaphore*, designed to prevent simultaneous access by more than one process to a shared resource such as a shared memory segment. At its simplest a semaphore is a boolean variable which is associated with a resource. If the semaphore is set, then the resource is 'in use' and other processes should leave it alone. If the semaphore is clear, the resource is free for use. There are two key operations on a boolean semaphore:

1. Wait (if necessary) until the semaphore is clear, then set it. This is referred to as raising the semaphore, or locking the resource.
2. Clear the semaphore. This is also known as lowering the semaphore, or unlocking the resource.

It is tempting to try to implement such a semaphore in our `cline` and `pline` programs by adding an extra member to the `info` structure, like this:

```
struct info {
    char c;
    int    length;
    int    locked;
};
```

and then to code the critical section of `cline` like this:

```
/* Wait until ctrl structure is free, then lock it */
while (ctrl->locked)
    /* Empty loop body */ ;
ctrl->locked = 1;

/* Copy command line data to shared memory region */
ctrl->c      = argv[1][0];
ctrl->length = atoi(argv[2]);

/* Unlock the ctrl structure */
ctrl->locked = 0;
```

There are two problems with this. First, the busy–wait loop that polls the semaphore is a waste of processor cycles, and best avoided in a multitasking operating system. We would prefer to have the process descheduled if the resource is locked, and automatically re-awakened when it becomes free. The second problem with this solution is that it does not solve the problem. It simply moves the race condition from one place to another. Consider the following: `cline` has just tested the `ctrl->locked` semaphore and found it to be clear. It is just about to set the semaphore when unfortunately it gets descheduled in favour of `pline`, which also tests the semaphore and finds it cleared. Both processes now believe they have exclusive access to the shared memory segment, and will enter their critical section.

For both of these reasons, semaphores cannot be implemented entirely within user code. We need help from the kernel.

## 2.6.3 UNIX semaphores

The necessary help is provided by system calls that manipulate semaphores held *inside the kernel*. UNIX semaphores are more complex than the simple binary semaphores described above in a number of ways:

1. You can create a whole array of semaphores with a single call.
2. The semaphores are multivalued, not binary. The idea is to restrict the maximum simultaneous number of users of a resource to some upper limit, but not necessarily to one. The semaphore's value indicates the number of 'units' of the associated resource that are currently available. When used as binary semaphores, they work the other way round from our earlier description: a value of 1 or more indicates the resource is free, a value of 0 indicates it is locked.
3. You can specify not just a single operation on a single semaphore, but a whole array of operations on a whole array of semaphores.
4. There are facilities to allow UNIX automatically to release all the locks that a process holds on its semaphores when it exits.
5. Semaphores have ownerships, access modes and timestamps, similar to those for shared memory.

All this flexibility is far more than most people really need, and makes for a complicated and confusing set of system calls to manipulate the semaphores.

We will present here a minimum of detail and a simplified interface that will enable us to create, lock and unlock arrays of binary semaphores. For the full details, look up semget(2), semop(2) and semctl(2).

Figure 2.11 shows the semget() call, used to create a new array of semaphores or to obtain a handle on an existing set. Like shared memory segments, semaphore sets are identified by a numeric key. They exist quite independently of any particular process, and they remain in existence after the process that created them has terminated. One process must call semget() with the IPC_CREAT bit set in the flag argument in order to create the semaphore set. Later, other processes obtain access to that set by calling semget() with the same numeric key, and a flag argument of zero.

Figure 2.12 shows the semop() call, used to manipulate semaphore values. semop() handles an array of semaphore operations in a single call, and may be used to obtain or release locks on multiple resources. The system guarantees to perform the entire array of operations 'atomically'; that is, it will perform either all the operations, or none of them. This can be important if you need to obtain locks on a number of resources before proceeding, but wish to avoid deadlock – a situation in which two processes are each waiting for a resource which the other process has already locked.

We will hide much of the complexity of this by writing three wrapper functions that will allow us to create sets of binary semaphores and to lock and unlock a specified semaphore within a specified set. The functions are as follows:

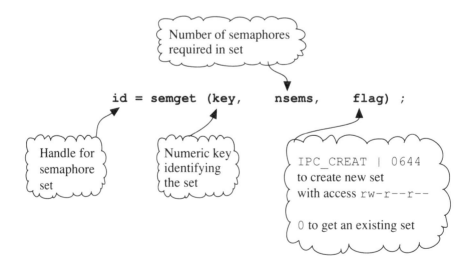

**Figure 2.11** Creating a set of semaphores.

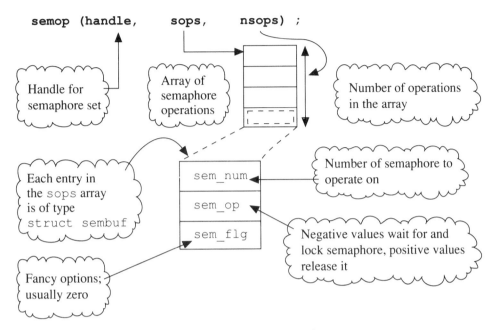

**Figure 2.12** Semaphore operations.

```
/* Make an array of n semaphores with key k */
int make_semas(key_t k, int n)
{
    int semid, i;

    /* Try to get an existing sema set with this key.
       If this succeeds, there must already be such a set,
       which we must first destroy
    */

    if ((semid=semget(k, n, 0)) != -1)
       /* Destroy existing semaphore set */
       semctl(semid, 0, IPC_RMID);
    if ((semid=semget(k, n, IPC_CREAT | 0600)) != -1) {
       /* The semaphore values are initialized to zero,
          which implies that all resources are locked.
          We therefore need to unlock each one. (The
          semctl() function with a SETALL command is
          a more efficient way to do this!)
       */
       for (i=0; i<n; i++)
          unlock(semid, i);
    }
    return semid;
}
```

```
/* Lock semaphore n from set sem */
void lock(int sem, int n)
{
    struct sembuf sop;  /* Build a 1-element array .. */
    sop.sem_num = n;    /* .. of semaphore operations */
    sop.sem_op  = -1;   /* -1 locks one "unit"        */
    sop.sem_flg = 0;
    semop(sem, &sop, 1); /* Block until resource free */
}

/* Unlock semaphore n from set sem */
void unlock(int sem, int n)
{
    struct sembuf sop;  /* Build a 1-element array .. */
    sop.sem_num = n;    /* .. of semaphore operations */
    sop.sem_op  = 1;    /* +1 unlocks one "unit" */
    sop.sem_flg = 0;
    semop(sem, &sop, 1);
}
```

These functions achieve simplicity by sacrificing flexibility. In particular, they are intended to support only binary semaphores, and they allow only a single semaphore operation per call.

## 2.6.4  A semaphore example

Rather than add semaphores to our `cline` and `pline` programs, we will apply them to a different example – one that fails rather more convincingly if semaphores are not used.

Our new example uses a shared memory segment to hold a simple spreadsheet. Our spreadsheet is merely a 2D array of numbers, maintained such that the last number of each row is the sum of all the other numbers in that row, and the last number of each column is the sum of all the other numbers in that column, as shown in Figure 2.13. The spreadsheet is accessed by two processes, an *updater* and a *checker*. The updater periodically changes a randomly selected cell of the spreadsheet to a random value, and updates the row and column totals accordingly. The checker periodically prints the spreadsheet out, and checks that the totals are correct. The example may be contrived, but it provides a convincing demonstration of the use of semaphores.

Pseudo-code for these two operations is as follows:

```
updater:
        choose a random cell and a random value
        /* Start of critical section */
        write the random value into the chosen cell
        compute and update the row total
        compute and update the column total
        /* End of critical section   */
```

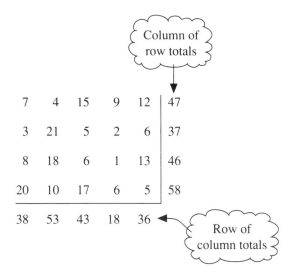

**Figure 2.13** A simple spreadsheet.

```
checker:
        loop over all rows {
            /* Start of critical section */
            compute sum of all cells in row
            if (sum != total in spreadsheet)
                print an error message
            /* End of critical section   */
        }
        loop over all columns {
            /* Start of critical section */
            compute sum of all cells in column
            if (sum != total in spreadsheet)
                print an error message
            /* End of critical section   */
        }
```

Both operations have critical sections, as marked by the comments in the pseudo-code. Our purpose in choosing this example is to show that without semaphores, the checker will in fact find wrongly totalled spreadsheets. This will occur if the checker is scheduled to run inside the critical section of the updater.

We need to consider what 'granularity' of locking to provide. The simplest approach is to use a single semaphore, so that each time we enter a critical section, we lock the entire spreadsheet. However, this is unnecessarily restrictive. If the updater is changing the cell at row 2, column 1, it needs to lock that row and column. However, there is no reason why the checker cannot check some other row or column at this time.

Consequently we will choose to lock the individual rows and columns of the spreadsheet, using two arrays of semaphores, one for the rows, and another for the columns. Figure 2.14 shows the scheme, along with a possible locking scenario. The updater holds locks on row 2 and column 1; the checker holds a lock on row 0. These locks do not overlap, so both processes may proceed.

Although our example runs as two asynchronous processes (the `updater` and the `checker`), we have chosen to have the `updater` created as a child of the `checker`. This is done largely as a matter of convenience, to keep all the source code of the example in a single file, rather than have them separate. It also allows us to demonstrate that children inherit shared memory segments and semaphores from their parents. Thus, the only calls to `shmget()` and `semget()` are in the parent before it forks. The child does not need to execute these calls.

Here is the complete program. Two functions, `make_random_entry()` and `print_and_check()`, implement the `updater` and `checker` operations. The `main()` function creates the shared memory segment, initializes it to zero, creates the semaphore arrays for the rows and columns, forks, and has the child make repeated calls to the `updater` function whilst the parent makes repeated calls to the `checker` function. The `make_semas()`, `lock()` and `unlock()` functions are the ones we saw earlier, and are not repeated here.

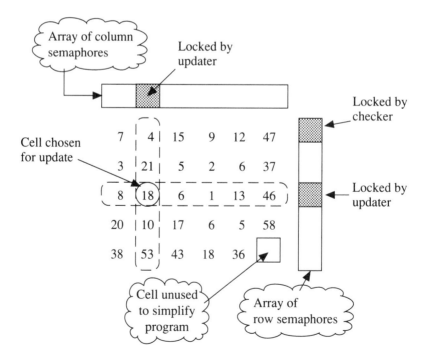

**Figure 2.14** Locking spreadsheet rows and columns.

```
/* Spreadsheet example showing shared memory and semaphores.
   The spreadsheet consists simply of a 2-D array of integers.
   The array is maintained such that the last element of each
   row is the sum of the other elements in the row, and the
   last element of each column is the sum of the other elements
   in the column.
*/

#include <stdio.h>
#include <sys/types.h>
#include <sys/ipc.h>
#include <sys/shm.h>
#include <sys/sem.h>

/* Row and column where the totals are */
int totalrow, totalcol;

/* Handles for the row and column semaphore arrays */
int row_semas, col_semas;

/* Macro for accessing cell at row r, col c of spreadsheet s */
#define CELL(s,r,c) (*((s)+((r)*NCOLS)+(c)))

/* Size of sheet -- fixed for simplicity */
#define NROWS       8
#define NCOLS       8

/* Key used both for shared memory segment and row semas.
   Column semas use SHEET_KEY+1
*/

#define SHEET_KEY   1841

/* ---------------- make_random_entry() ----------------- */

/* Selects a random spreadsheet cell, inserts a random
   value into it, and updates the row and column totals
*/
void make_random_entry(int *s)
{
    int row, col, old, new;

    /* Pick a random cell to update and a random value */
    row = rand() % (NROWS-1);
    col = rand() % (NCOLS-1);
    new = rand() % 1000;
    /* Start of critical section */
    lock(row_semas, row);
    lock(col_semas, col);

    /* Install new entry into sheet */
    old = CELL(s, row, col);
    CELL(s, row, col) = new;
```

```
    /* Update the row and column totals */
    CELL(s, row, totalcol) += (new-old);
    CELL(s, totalrow, col) += (new-old);
    /* End of critical section */
    unlock(col_semas, col);
    unlock(row_semas, row);

    /* The following call deschedules the process for
       5000 microsec. This allows the other process to
       get a look in!
    */
    usleep(5000);
}

/* ------------------- print_and_check() ------------------ */
void print_and_check(int *s)
{
    int row, col, sum, totalbad;
    static int scount = 0;  /* Count of spreadsheets */

    totalbad = 0;
    scount++;        /* Count another spreadsheet */
    for (row=0; row<NROWS; row++) {
        sum = 0;
        /* Start of critical section */
        lock(row_semas, row);
        for (col=0; col<NCOLS; col++) {
            if (col != totalcol)
                sum += CELL(s, row, col);
            printf("%5d", CELL(s, row, col));
        }
        if (row != totalrow)
            totalbad += (sum != CELL(s, row, totalcol));
        /* End of critical section */
        unlock(row_semas, row);
        printf("\n");
    }

    /* Check the column totals */
    for (col=0; col<totalcol; col++) {
        sum = 0;
        /* Start of critical section */
        lock(col_semas, col);
        for (row=0; row<totalrow; row++)
            sum += CELL(s, row, col);
        totalbad += (sum != CELL(s, totalrow, col));
        /* End of critical section */
        unlock(col_semas, col);
    }
    if (totalbad)
```

```
        printf("\nSpreadsheet no %d failed\n", scount);
    if ((scount % 100) == 0)
        printf("\nSpreadsheet no %d processed\n", scount);
    printf("\n-------------------------------------\n");
    sleep(1);
}
/* ---------------------- main() ----------------------- */
main()
{
    int id, row, col, *sheet;

    setbuf(stdout, NULL);

    /* For simplicity, the size of the spreadsheet is fixed */
    totalrow = NROWS-1;
    totalcol = NCOLS-1;

    /* Create and attach the shared segment */
    id = shmget(SHEET_KEY, NROWS*NCOLS*sizeof(int),
                IPC_CREAT | 0600);
    if (id < 0) {
        perror("ssheet: shmget failed:");
        exit(1);
    }

    sheet = (int *)shmat(id, 0, 0);
    if (sheet <= (int *)(0)) {
        perror("ssheet: shmat failed:");
        exit(2);
    }

    /* Clear the sheet entries to zero */
    for (row = 0; row < NROWS; row++)
        for (col = 0; col < NCOLS; col++)
            CELL(sheet, row, col) = 0;

    /* Create sets of semaphores to protect rows and columns */
    row_semas = make_semas(SHEET_KEY,   NROWS);
    col_semas = make_semas(SHEET_KEY+1, NCOLS);
    if ((row_semas < 0) || (col_semas < 0)) {
        perror("ssheet: semget failed");
        exit(2);
    }

    /* Now fork. The parent loops round, printing the
       spreadsheet repeatedly, and checking it for self-
       consistency. The child loops round, making random
       entries into the sheet.
    */

    if (fork()) {
```

```
            while(1)
                print_and_check(sheet);
        } else {
            while(1)
                make_random_entry(sheet);
        }
    }
}
```

In addition to printing out the spreadsheet values, the `print_and_check()` function also prints out 'progress reports' and 'failure reports'. Progress reports are messages of the form

```
Spreadsheet no 200 processed
```

which occur every 100 passes. Failure reports are messages of the form

```
Spreadsheet no 182 failed
```

which occur if the totals are not correct. This would happen if the `checker` ran in the middle of an update operation.

Here are some samples of output from this program. First, a look at the complete output:

```
eddie% semsheet
      0      0      0      0      0      0      0      0
      0      0      0      0      0      0      0      0
      0      0    886      0      0      0      0    886
      0      0      0      0      0      0    964    964
      0      0    899      0      0    288      0   1187
      0      0      0    685    104      0    519   1308
      0      0      0      0    827      0      0    827
    404    262   2588   1418   1692   1047   2512      0
------------------------------------
    821      0    821    212    761      0    834   3449
    159      0     65    521      0      0      0    745
    655    262    886    912      0    759      0   3474
      0     42    992      0     98      0    781   1913
    375      0     69      0      0    182    116    742
     44      0      0    685    734      0    714   2177
      0    849      0      0    643     37    351   1880
   1625   1153   3110   4117   2648   2559   3751      0
------------------------------------
```

and so on. This is really not very interesting, so we will filter the output using `grep` to show just those lines containing 'progress reports' and 'failure reports':

```
eddie% semsheet | grep sheet
Spreadsheet no 100 processed
```

```
Spreadsheet no 200 processed
Spreadsheet no 300 processed
Spreadsheet no 400 processed
Spreadsheet no 500 processed
Spreadsheet no 600 processed
```

and so on. This is not very interesting either, except it does show that there are *no* failure reports. (In fact the program ran for 100 000 passes without producing a failure report.)

To prove that the semaphores are actually doing some good, here is some output from the program after commenting out the calls to `lock()` and `unlock()`:

```
eddie% semsheet | grep sheet
Spreadsheet no 33 failed
Spreadsheet no 59 failed
Spreadsheet no 61 failed
Spreadsheet no 78 failed
Spreadsheet no 100 processed
Spreadsheet no 114 failed
Spreadsheet no 134 failed
Spreadsheet no 152 failed
Spreadsheet no 182 failed
Spreadsheet no 200 processed
Spreadsheet no 234 failed
Spreadsheet no 259 failed
Spreadsheet no 261 failed
Spreadsheet no 271 failed
Spreadsheet no 273 failed
Spreadsheet no 277 failed
Spreadsheet no 289 failed
Spreadsheet no 300 processed
```

and so on. We see that in this situation, about 5 per cent of the spreadsheets fail to check out correctly, according to the `checker` process. The exact behaviour of this program (without the semaphores) is rather unstable – it depends strongly on the value of the parameter to `usleep()` in the `updater` process. Smaller sleep times lead to higher failure rates, as one would expect. If you try running the example, the failure rates you see will also depend on the speed of your processor, the length of a scheduler time-slice, and how busy the machine is with other work. The point is this: without the semaphores, this program exhibits a race condition leading to a demonstrable and unacceptably high failure rate. With the semaphores, the problem is apparently solved.

---

**An aside:** we have not 'proved', in a mathematical sense, that the semaphores fixed the problem, we have merely accumulated some statistics that give us confidence that the program operates correctly. Formal proof of correctness is an issue we do not pretend to address here.

---

## 2.6.5  Some closing comments on semaphores

We deliberately refrained from computing or checking a 'grand total' for the spreadsheet, that is, the cell in the bottom right-hand corner. It is left as an exercise to consider what locking strategy would be needed if the grand total *were* used.

UNIX semaphores have one further feature which we did not use in the previous example. The details are a little messy but the intent is quite simple – it allows UNIX automatically to reclaim any locks that a process is holding when it terminates. When a process has a set of semaphores 'attached', the kernel keeps an 'adjustment value' (semadj) for each semaphore. It starts at zero when the process initially attaches the semaphore set, and is adjusted up or down when semop() operations are performed. Thus, the semaphore value itself indicates how many units of the resource are free, whereas the semadj value indicates the number of those resource units currently held by that process. In the case of binary semaphores, the semadj value is simply a flag indicating whether the process holds a lock on the semaphore. Note that the semaphore values are system-wide, but the semadj values are per process. When a process exits, the semadj values are added on to the semaphore values, i.e. the resources held by that process are given back. For this to work, the sem_flg field of the sembuf structure used in the semop() call must be set to SEM_UNDO (see Figure 2.12).

Our examples of shared resources have used data items held in a shared memory segment, but there are many other possibilities. For example, we may wish to lock a file, or a section of a file, or we may wish to gain exclusive access to a hardware device, such as a frame grabber.

Shared resources can be even more abstract. Consider a computer used to control a number of assembly robots in a factory workspace. The robots operate relatively independently, but share physical space – that is, they can hit one another if they are not careful. To prevent this, the physical space is divided into a three-dimensional array of cubes (known as volume elements, or 'voxels') and a semaphore is allocated to each voxel. When a robot arm wishes to execute a move, it computes all the voxels through which it will pass, and obtains a lock on each of them. When the move is complete, the voxels are released.

Multivalued semaphores are rather rare in practice. A car park provides a real-world example of a resource that has a fixed maximum number of 'resource units', i.e. parking spaces. A multivalued semaphore, whose value represents the number of remaining spaces in the car park, might be used to control entry via any of several entrances. As another example, some third party software products are sold with a licence that imposes a maximum number of simultaneous users of that product. A semaphore might be used to track the remaining number of unused licence tokens.

You will notice from the previous example that the use of a semaphore to protect a resource requires the voluntary cooperation of the programs involved. The semaphore does not physically restrain a process from accessing a resource; the programs must be written to honour the semaphore. In other words, it is the programmer's responsibility to remember to place lock and unlock operations around the critical sections of his or her code. In a similar way, traffic lights do not physically prevent cars from colliding at road junctions. The car drivers must all agree to stop if their light is red. This form of locking is in contrast to the mandatory file locking provided by UNIX, which will cause an attempt to write to a file to block if some other process holds a lock on the file. Mandatory locking is described in Section 3.5.

## 2.6.6 Using files as a locking mechanism

Before proper semaphores were introduced into UNIX, it was common practice to use files as locks. The technique is rather heavy-handed; it would be unthinkable to use it in our spreadsheet example, where the locks come and go very rapidly. Indeed the method is usually used to lock a resource for the entire duration of a program.

The idea is really simple: we associate a file name with the resource we want to lock. To obtain the lock, we attempt to create a file of that name, and open it for exclusive use. If we succeed, we have the resource. If we fail, we must give up, or wait and try again later. In the following example we associate the file name /tmp/grabberlock with the 'TV Frame Grabber' resource (whatever that is – it does not matter for the purposes of this example) which we wish to lock for the duration of the program. The two functions lock() and unlock() illustrate this locking mechanism. The reason for choosing /tmp as the directory for the lock file is twofold. Firstly, this directory has 'world write' permission, so that anyone can create and delete files here. Secondly, /tmp is usually cleared out when the system is booted. This helps ensure that unwanted locks are not left lying around after a system crashes and reboots.

```
/* Program to illustrate the use of files as semaphores */

#define  GRABBERLOCK  "/tmp/grabberlock"
#include <stdio.h>
#include <fcntl.h>
#include <sys/types.h>
#include <sys/stat.h>
#include <pwd.h>

lock(char *f)
{
    int fd;
    struct stat statbuf;

    if ((fd = open(f, O_WRONLY | O_CREAT | O_EXCL, 0644))
                == -1) {
        printf("Sorry, %s is already locked by ", f);
        stat(f, &statbuf);
        printf("%s\n", getpwuid(statbuf.st_uid)->pw_name);
        return -1;
    }
    else {
        close(fd);
```

```
        return 0;
    }
}

unlock(char *f)
{
    unlink(f);
}

main()
{
    if (lock(GRABBERLOCK) == -1) {
        exit(1);
    }
    else {
        printf("Using grabber for 5 seconds ...\n");
        sleep(5);
        printf("Done using grabber\n");
        unlock(GRABBERLOCK);
        exit(0);
    }
}
```

In this example, the presence of the lock file does slightly more than signal the presence of a lock. We are also able to deduce the identity of the user who created the lock file, by using `stat()` to determine the numeric user ID of the file's owner, and `getpwuid()` to map the numeric user ID onto the login name. (Look up `stat(2)` and `getpwent(3)`.)

---

**An aside:** this means that instead of merely muttering 'It's already locked', you can shout 'Hey, Ken, how long y'gonna be ?'

---

In the same way, it is also possible to deduce when the lock was created, by looking at the `st_ctime` field of the structure returned by `stat()`. This information is also retrieved from the file's inode. It is *not* useful to store the user name or other information in the file itself as, by definition, only the process holding the lock can actually access the file's data. Note that this locking technique works even if the programs run with super-user identity.

Here is an example run showing three successive invocations of the program; the first and last are successful, the second fails:

```
eddie% getfilelock &
[1] 723
eddie% Using grabber for 5 seconds ...
getfilelock
Sorry, /tmp/grabberlock is already locked by chris
```

```
eddie% Done using grabber
getfilelock
Using grabber for 5 seconds ...
Done using grabber
[1]   + Done                    getfilelock
eddie%
```

The first invocation is run in the background, where it proceeds to hold the grabber locked for five seconds. The second invocation, launched within this five-second time window, finds the lock file present and fails. The third invocation, launched after the first has finished, is able to lock the grabber again.

# 2.7  Message queues

## 2.7.1  Message queue concepts

The message queue is the third type of IPC mechanism generally known as 'System V IPC', shared memory and semaphores being the other two. (Look up `ipcs(1)`.) They are relatively infrequently used, and we will be content here briefly to describe their functionality and present a simple example. For the details, look up `msgget(2)`, `msgop(2)` and `msgctl(2)`.

A message queue is an ordered list of messages, held in the kernel. It has some features in common with a shared memory segment: it is identified by a numeric key value, it has ownership and access modes, and it exists quite independently of any particular user process. Subject to the usual access permissions, any process that knows the key of a message queue can send messages to it and retrieve messages from it.

Each message on the queue carries user data and has a *type* associated with it. The type is simply a positive integer, and is used to give some control over the order in which the messages are retrieved from the queue. Figure 2.15 shows a single message queue and the `msgsnd()` and `msgrcv()` calls used to send and receive messages.

In terms of functionality, message queues are mid-way between named pipes and shared memory. They offer more flexible access than the strictly first-in first-out scheme of a pipe, but they do not offer the completely random access provided by shared memory.

## 2.7.2  Message queue operations

Figure 2.16 shows the `msgget()` call which is used to obtain a handle on an existing segment (by setting the `flag` argument to zero), or to create a new one (by setting the `IPC_CREAT` bit in the `flag` argument). This operation is conceptually like performing an `open()` on a file.

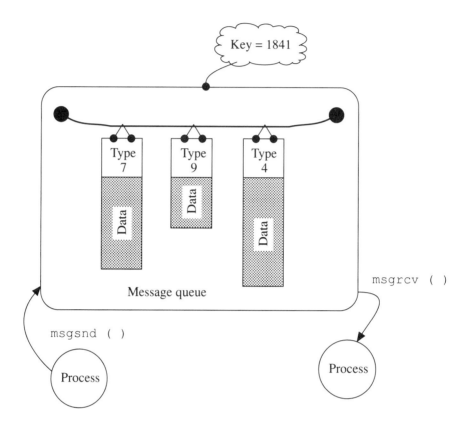

**Figure 2.15**  Message queues illustrated.

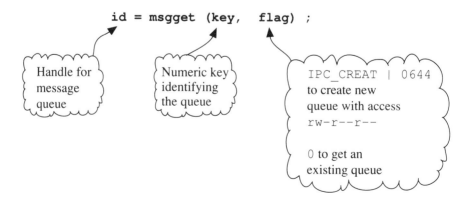

**Figure 2.16**  Creating a message queue.

Figure 2.17 shows the `msgsnd()` call which is used to place a message on the queue. The user is required to assemble a message with a type field at the beginning followed by the data. (An alternative and perhaps more convenient interface might have been to pass the type as an additional parameter.) The queue has a maximum capacity, typically only a few kbytes. If the queue is full, `msgsnd()` will block. Nonblocking operation is achieved by setting the `flag` parameter to `IPC_NOWAIT`. This flag causes `msgsnd()` to return an error, rather than waiting, if the queue is full.

Figure 2.18 shows the `msgrcv()` call which is used to retrieve a message from the queue. The user has some control over the order in which messages are retrieved through the `type` parameter. This is the most complicated part of the whole thing. Requesting a `type` of zero gets the first message on the queue. A positive value of `type` gets the first message of that type. A negative value of `type` gets the first message of the lowest type which is less than or equal to the absolute value of `type`. This rather complex and curious third case allows priority message schemes to be implemented.

## 2.7.3  A message queue example

To illustrate the mechanics of manipulating message queues, here are two programs, `msgsnd` and `msgrcv`, which provide a command line interface to queues of text messages.

The `msgsnd` program is invoked as in the following example:

```
% msgsnd  100  7  "hello world"
```

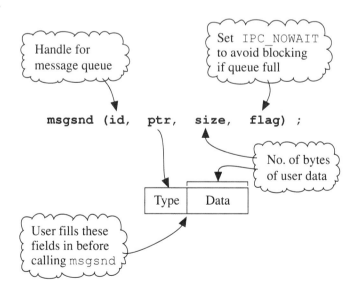

**Figure 2.17** Sending to a message queue.

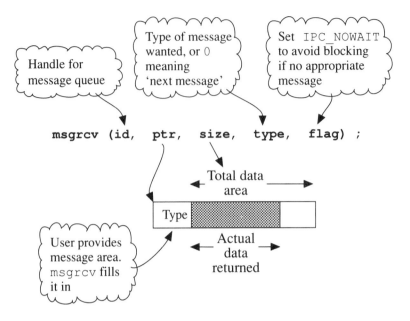

**Figure 2.18** Reading from a message queue.

which will place a message containing the text 'hello world' on the message queue with
key 100, with type 7. The message queue is created if it does not exist.

The `msgrcv` program is invoked as in the following example:

```
% msgrcv  100  7
[7] hello world
```

which retrieves the first message of type 7 from the message queue with key 100. The
message is written to standard output, preceded by the message type in square brackets.

Here is the `msgsnd` program. Note the declaration of a `text_message` structure, and
the requirement to `strcpy()` the message text into this structure.

```
/* A program to send a message to a message queue.

   Usage:  msgsnd <key> <type> "text of message"
*/

#include <stdio.h>
#include <sys/types.h>
#include <sys/ipc.h>
#include <sys/msg.h>

struct text_message {
    long mtype;
    char mtext[100];
```

```
} ;

main(int argc, char *argv[])
{
    int msid, v;
    struct text_message mess;

    if (argc != 4) {
        printf("usage: msgsnd <key> <type> <text>\n");
        exit(1);
    }

    /* Get the message queue, creating it if necessary */
    msid = msgget((key_t)atoi(argv[1]), IPC_CREAT|0666);
    if (msid == -1) {
        printf("cannot get message queue\n");
        exit(1);
    }

    /* Assemble the message */
    mess.mtype = atoi(argv[2]);     /* The type */
    strcpy(mess.mtext, argv[3]);    /* The text */

    /* Write message onto the queue */
    v = msgsnd(msid, &mess, strlen(argv[3])+1, 0);
    if (v<0)
        printf("error writing to queue\n");
}
```

Here is the `msgrcv` program. It is quite similar to `msgsnd`; note, however, that the `IPC_CREAT` flag is not set in the `msgget()` call. This program expects that the queue already exists. There would be little point in creating a new queue, then attempting to read a message from it! Note also the use of the `IPC_NOWAIT` flag in the `msgrcv()` call. If there is no suitable message we do not wait, we just report the fact.

```
/* A program to read a message from a message queue.

   Usage:  msgrcv <key> <type>
*/

#include <stdio.h>
#include <sys/types.h>
#include <sys/ipc.h>
#include <sys/msg.h>
#include <errno.h>

struct text_message {
    long mtype;
    char mtext[100];
} ;

main(int argc, char *argv[])
{
```

```
    int msid, v;
    struct text_message mess;

    if (argc != 3) {
        printf("usage: msgrcv <key> <type>\n");
        exit(1);
    }

    /* Get the message queue, do not create it */
    msid = msgget((key_t)atoi(argv[1]), 0);
    if (msid == -1) {
        printf("cannot get message queue\n");
        exit(1);
    }

    /* Read a message of the specified type, do not block */
    v = msgrcv(msid, &mess, 100, atoi(argv[2]), IPC_NOWAIT);
    if ((v<0)) {
        if (errno==ENOMSG)
            printf("no appropriate message on queue\n");
        else
            printf("error reading from queue\n");
    } else
        printf("[%d] %s\n", mess.mtype, mess.mtext);
}
```

The ipcs command may be used to examine the message queues in the system. A useful combination of flags is '-qo' which says to report 'outstanding' usage of message queues only. The following dialogue illustrates the use of ipcs and our programs msgsnd and msgrcv. First, four messages with types 4, 8, 9 and 7 are placed on the queue with key 100. The subsequent ipcs -qo command confirms that there are now four messages, totalling 70 bytes, on the queue with key 64 hex (100 decimal). The command msgrcv 100 0 retrieves the first message from the queue, regardless of type. The command msgrcv 100 9 retrieves the first message of type 9, and so on.

```
eddie% msgsnd 100 4 "hello world"
eddie% msgsnd 100 8 "flee all is discovered"
eddie% msgsnd 100 9 "stop dave I'm afraid"
eddie% msgsnd 100 7 "what's up doc"
eddie% ipcs -qo
IPC status from /dev/kmem as of Fri Dec  4 11:23:56 1992
T    ID    KEY          MODE         OWNER    GROUP CBYTES  QNUM
Message Queues:
q    150 0x00000064 --rw-rw-rw-    chris    other     70     4
eddie% msgrcv 100 0
[4] hello world
eddie% msgrcv 100 9
[9] stop dave I'm afraid
eddie% msgrcv 100 -5
no appropriate message on queue
```

```
eddie% msgrcv 100 -10
[7] what's up doc
eddie% ipcs -qo
IPC status from /dev/kmem as of Fri Dec  4 11:25:53 1992
T     ID    KEY          MODE         OWNER    GROUP CBYTES  QNUM
Message Queues:
q    150 0x00000064 --rw-rw-rw-    chris    other     23    1
eddie%
```

### 2.7.4 Uses for message queues

Message queues may be used to multiplex data streams from multiple producers to a single consumer. The producer of the message could be identified within the message type (for example, the type might be set to the process ID of the producer). It is also possible to demultiplex data from a single producer to multiple consumers. The consumers might be 'generalists', each processing the next message on the queue, whatever type it happened to be, or they could be 'specialists', each one taking messages of a specific type from the queue.

Message types may be used to implement a priority scheme. Using message types between (say) 1 and 1000 would provide a simple ordered priority, with type=1 being the highest priority and type=1000 being the lowest. A call to msgrcv() requesting a type of −1000 would then retrieve the highest priority message from the queue. A slightly more complex scheme could be used to separate 'normal' from 'urgent' messages, with types in the range (say) 1 to 10 being considered urgent and larger types considered normal. A consumer could check for the presence of urgent messages in the queue by calling msgrcv() with a type of −10 and the IPC_NOWAIT flag set. If no urgent messages were present, this call would return −1, whereupon the consumer could go ahead and read the first (non-urgent) message from the queue.

As IPC mechanisms, message queues and shared memory have the rather unusual property that the communicating parties do not need to be active at the same time. They provide an indirect form of communication. Indeed, producers of data do not direct their output at specific consumers, they simply know that they must deposit their data in a particular shared memory segment, or on a particular queue. There is, of course, an IPC mechanism with this property that has been around for a very long time, that has the added advantage of being nonvolatile. It is called a file.

## 2.8  Signals

### 2.8.1  Signals as asynchronous events

A signal is an asynchronous event which is delivered to a process. 'Asynchronous' means that the event can occur at any time; it is not related to or synchronized with any particular operation in the program. Broadly speaking, a signal is usually a notification to a process that something 'unexpected' or 'unusual' has happened, which may require the process to leave what it is doing for a moment, and take special action.

Signals impact the lives of all UNIX users, whether they know it or not. Most users know that they can usually kill a program by typing ^C (or maybe DELETE; it depends which character they have set as their interrupt character). Most users (and certainly all programmers) have seen the message Segmentation fault (core dumped) appear on their terminal. Both of these actions are the result of the delivery of a signal.

---

**An aside:** some versions of UNIX used to report Memory fault rather than Segmentation fault. The first UNIX system I used was a PDP-11/60. Shortly after commissioning the machine, I ran a program (I think it was nroff) which resulted in the system printing out 'Memory fault' on the console. Taking this to mean that there was, well, a fault in the memory, I shut the system down and spent the rest of the day running hardware diagnostics. Nowadays, of course I am wise to the fact that most UNIX error messages are the result of historical accident rather than an actual description of the problem. The message 'not a typewriter', for example, is about as relevant in the modern world as being asked not to covet my neighbour's ox.

---

## 2.8.2 Signal types

Signals have a *type* (a small integer), and thirty or so different types are defined, although only about half a dozen of these are of interest to most programmers. The types have symbolic names such as SIGINT defined in the file /usr/include/sys/signal.h. Some of the important signal types, and their meanings, are listed in Table 2.3. The column headed 'Default action' indicates the effect that the signal will have if the process has not made alternative arrangements to deal with it. We will look at this in detail shortly.

**Table 2.3**

| Name | Default action | Description/cause |
| --- | --- | --- |
| SIGHUP | Terminate process | Hangup of dial-in line |
| SIGINT | Terminate process | Interrupt character typed |
| SIGQUIT | Create core image | Quit character typed |
| SIGKILL | Terminate process | Usually the result of kill -9 |
| SIGSEGV | Create core image | Invalid memory reference |
| SIGPIPE | Terminate process | Write on pipe with no one to read it |
| SIGALRM | Terminate process | Alarm clock timer expired |
| SIGTERM | Terminate process | A general 'please stop now' signal |
| SIGURG | Discard signal | Urgent condition on socket, etc. |
| SIGWINCH | Discard signal | Window size changed |
| SIGUSR1 | Terminate process | User-defined signal type |

## 2.8.3  Where signals come from

Signals originate from a variety of places, as shown in Figure 2.19. One such place is the terminal driver (a part of the kernel which reads characters from the keyboard and hands them to the user process). This driver monitors the incoming data for a number of special characters, among them an *interrupt* character (often ^C) and a *quit* character (often ^\). These characters may be changed using the stty command. When one of these special characters is received by the terminal driver, it does not hand the character to the process, but instead delivers a signal (either SIGINT or SIGQUIT) to the process. Other signals originate in the hardware. For example, an attempt to access an invalid memory address will result in the delivery of a SIGSEGV signal. Some signals are generated directly by the kernel. For example, an attempt to write to a pipe when no process has the downstream end open for reading will result in the delivery of a SIGPIPE signal. Yet other signals originate in user processes. For example, if a window manager has resized a window, it may send a SIGWINCH signal to the process responsible for maintaining that window.

Finally, the kill command is a general-purpose signal-sending program, allowing signals to be delivered under manual control, from the shell command level. As an example, the command

```
kill  -KILL  4481
```

can be used to send a SIGKILL signal to process ID 4481. The symbolic names used by this command to specify the signal type are the same as those that appear in signal.h, with the SIG prefix removed.

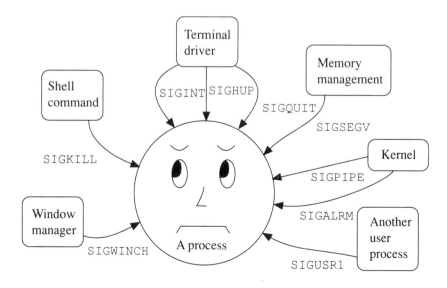

**Figure 2.19** Signal sources.

Notice that whilst signals may originate from a variety of places, it is always the kernel that delivers the signal to the process. Remember, the kernel controls all processes.

## 2.8.4 How a process responds to a signal

A process may choose how it will respond when a signal of a particular type is delivered. This choice is known as the *disposition* of the signal. There are three possibilities:

1. The process can choose to ignore the signal.
2. The process can choose to execute a specified *signal-handler* function when the signal is delivered, and then continue where it left off.
3. The process can accept the default behaviour of the signal. The default actions were listed in Table 2.3. In most cases, this default is to terminate the process.

The disposition of a signal is set using the `signal()` system call. The general form is:

```
signal(sig, handler);
```

where `sig` is the signal type and `handler` is the address of the handler function. For example, the call

```
signal(SIGTERM, cleanup);
```

specifies that the function `cleanup()` is to be called when a signal of type `SIGTERM` is delivered. Figure 2.20 shows a typical flow of control through a signal handler when a signal is delivered. There are two special values that can be used instead of a handler function. `SIG_IGN` specifies that the signal is to be ignored, and `SIG_DFL` specifies that the default handling of the signal should be used. As mentioned above, the default in most cases is to terminate the process. In some cases, the system will also create a 'core file' containing a snapshot of the memory image of the process at the instant the signal was delivered. In principle, core files can be used for *post-mortem debugging,* the rather unsavoury business of dismembering the corpse of a process to find out why – or at least where – it died. The signals whose default is to create a core file are those that indicate deviant behaviour by the process itself, such as 'bus error' and 'segmentation violation'.

---

**An aside:** for the benefit of readers who are too young to remember core memory, computers used to store their bits magnetically in tiny toroidal pieces of ferrite called 'cores', arranged in a 2D array on an amazingly fine mesh of wires which carried the current pulses needed to magnetize and sense the core's state. Core memory was expensive, bulky and slow, but it did have one saving grace – it was inherently nonvolatile; that is, it retained its data with the power off. I once watched an engineer install a core memory upgrade (from 16 to 32 kbytes, I believe) in a Data General NOVA computer. I was most impressed that he had had the foresight to load the memory diagnostic program into the board before bringing it. 'Dumping

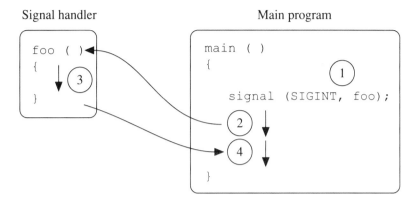

① Program specifies handler for SIGINT signal

② SIGINT occurs; handler is called.

③ Handler executes

④ Handler returns, main program continues

**Figure 2.20** Flow control on receipt of a signal.

core' meant writing the core's contents to a file. Core memories are now history, but for some reason the term 'core dump', referring to the memory image of a process, has stuck.

Here is a simple example of a process that installs a signal handler. In this example, the signal is of type SIGINT, and may be generated simply by typing ^C on the keyboard. When the signal is delivered, the handler merely prints a message, then the main program continues.

```
/* The Program sigcatcher.c */

#include <sys/signal.h>

void catcher(int sigtype)
{
    printf("I got the signal\n");
    signal(SIGINT, catcher);
}

main()
```

```
{
    int i;

    signal(SIGINT, catcher);

    for (i=0; i<1000; i++) {
        printf("working ... %d\n", i);
        sleep(1);
    }
}
```

Why the call to `signal()` inside the signal handler? When a signal is delivered, the disposition of the signal is reset to `SIG_DFL`. We need to re-establish the handler explicitly each time. If we do not, then only the first `SIGINT` would be trapped. A second would terminate the process.

## 2.8.5  Sending a signal

Most often, a programmer's concern with signals is in determining his or her program's response to 'unsolicited' signals sent to it from other parts of the system. Occasionally, however, he or she may choose to use signals explicitly as a form of synchronization mechanism between processes acting together as part of a distributed application. As an example, if a producer process and a consumer process are communicating via shared memory, the producer may signal the consumer to indicate that it has changed the data in the shared memory segment.

A process may send a signal to another process by a call of the form:

```
kill(pid, sig);
```

where `pid` is the ID of the process to receive the signal and `sig` is the signal type. A particularly distasteful example is:

```
kill(getppid(), SIGKILL);
```

which will ensure the death of your parent. (Signals of type `SIGKILL` can be neither caught nor ignored.) There are restrictions on who can send signals to whom. Essentially, a process can only signal a process with the same user ID.

---

**An aside:** the name `kill`, both for the signal-sending function and the signal-sending utility program, is not a good one. It is chosen because the default behaviour on receipt of the signal, in most cases, is to kill the process. The name `send_signal` might be better. This is all part of the traditional UNIX obsession with short names, on the assumption that the average user would prefer to remember what commands such as `mv`, `rm`, `ls` and `ar` do than to type complete words like move, remove, list and archive. The classic example is the system call for creating files. It is called `creat()`, on the basis (presumably) that 'create' is over-threshold on length. The fashion seems to have passed, at least in some quarters. I note from my OSF/1 manual the existence of a function called `pthread_condattr_delete()`.

---

## 2.8.6 Six things to do with a signal

In this section we will examine six possible uses for signals, and present a basic program schema for each.

### Use number 1: Ignoring a signal

One of the most common reasons for needing to know about signals is so that a program can choose to ignore them. Remember, signals may get sent to a process whether it wants them or not. The default response for most signal types is to terminate the process. The basic schema for ignoring signals is as follows. Remember, however, that SIGKILL signals cannot be ignored or caught.

```
main()
{
    signal(SIGINT,  SIG_IGN);
    signal(SIGQUIT, SIG_IGN);
    /* ... and so on          */

    /* Now get on with some work */
}
```

### Use number 2: Clean up and terminate

Sometimes we are happy to have signals such as SIGINT result in the termination of our program, but wish to perform some clean-up operation first. Clean-up may include the removal of temporary work files, message queues or shared memory segments, and perhaps the termination of a child. A typical schema is as follows:

```
/* Global variables */
int my_childs_pid;

void clean_up(int sigtype)
{
    unlink("/tmp/my_work_file");
    kill(my_childs_pid, SIGTERM);
    wait(0);
    fprintf(stderr, "program terminated\n");
    exit(1);
}

main()
{
    signal(SIGINT, clean_up);
```

```
/* ... maybe create a temporary file */
open("/tmp/my_work_file", O_RDWR | O_CREAT, 0644);

/* ... and maybe spawn a child */
my_childs_pid = fork();

/* Get on with some work ... */
}
```

The library function `atexit()` is also useful in ensuring that clean-up actions are taken. It allows a stack of clean-up functions to be established, which will be executed automatically on a 'normal' termination of the process – that is, if it calls `exit()`, or if the `main()` function returns. However, the clean-up functions are *not* executed if the process terminates abnormally, in response to an un-caught signal.

## Use number 3: Handle dynamic reconfiguration

Many programs read configuration data of some sort from a file. Often, they read the file only on start-up, and need to be stopped and restarted if the configuration is changed. By installing a signal handler that rereads the configuration data, the program can be re-configured dynamically, without restarting it. Here is a typical schema:

```
void read_config_file(int sigtype)
{
    int fd;

    fd = open("my_config_file", O_RDONLY);
    /* Do the hard part
        ... i.e. read configuration parameters
    */
    close(fd);
    signal(SIGHUP, read_config_file);
}

main()
{
    /* Set up initial configuration */
    read_config_file();

    /* Enter service loop */
    while (1) {
        ...
    }

}
```

## Use number 4: Report status/dump internal tables

Long-running programs often accumulate a large amount of internal state information such as routing tables or statistical summaries. Installing a signal handler to give an on-demand printout of this information can be a valuable aid to debugging. Note that the state information has to be globally visible for this method to work because it must be accessible from within the signal handler. A simple example illustrated in the schema below shows how a long-running tape copy program might be queried to find how many blocks it has copied.

```
/* Global state info */
int count;

void print_debug_info(int sigtype)
{
    /* Print out state information */
    printf("%d blocks copied\n", count);
    signal (SIGUSR1, print_debug_info);
}

main()
{
    signal (SIGUSR1, print_debug_info);

    for (count=0; count<A_BIG_NUMBER; count++) {
        /* Read block from input tape */
            ...
        /* Write block to output tape */
            ...
    }
}
```

## *Use number 5: Turn debugging on/off*

The idea here is to sprinkle `printf()` calls around the code to provide some kind of debug trace printout, but to have these calls enabled and disabled dynamically, i.e. whilst the program is running. In this example, the boolean variable `debug_flag` keeps track of whether debugging is on or off. The flag is flipped each time a `SIGHUP` is delivered.

```
int debug_flag;

void toggle_debug_flag(int sigtype)
{
    debug_flag ^= 1;  /* Flip the flag */
    signal(SIGHUP, toggle_debug_flag);
}

main()
{
    /* Disable debugging initially */
    debug_flag = 0;

    /* Install the signal handler */
    signal(SIGHUP, toggle_debug_flag);

    /* Get on with some work ... */
```

```
/* Within the code, statements to implement a
   debug trace might be written as follows:
*/
if (debug_flag) printf("something useful");
}
```

## Use number 6: Implement a timeout

This is a more complex example and worthy of a complete program rather than just an outline schema. The idea is to take an operation which may block indefinitely (that is, which waits for an event that might never happen), and add to it a timeout mechanism that will force control back into the program if the event does not occur within some specified number of seconds. In our example, the operation is simply to read a line of text from standard input and place it in a buffer. There is of course a routine `gets()` in the standard I/O library to do this, but it will not time out. Our plan is to implement a new function, `t_gets()`, which includes a timeout. So that we know where we are heading, here is a brief manual page specifying the function:

```
NAME
    t_gets - get a string from stdin, with timeout

SYNOPSIS
    int t_gets(char *s, int t)

DESCRIPTION
    t_gets reads characters from the standard input
    stream into the array pointed to by s, until a
    newline character is read, waiting for input for a
    maximum of t seconds.

DIAGNOSTICS
    If an end-of-file, or a read error, is encountered,
    -1 is returned.  If no input is received before the
    timeout, -2 is returned. Otherwise the length of the
    string is returned.
```

The key mechanism in implementing the timeout is the `alarm()` system call, which tells the kernel to send the process a SIGALRM signal after a specified number of seconds. (Look up `alarm(2)`.) Specifying an argument of zero turns the alarm off. By nominating a signal handler for SIGALRM, and calling `alarm()` just prior to calling `gets()`, we can arrange to get control back into the signal handler if the operation times out. But how does this help us? We need to force control back into the `t_gets()` function, so that it can return −2 to its caller. Of course, C provides the `goto` statement to force a transfer of control, but it does not allow us to jump *between* functions (thank goodness!).

The problem can be solved by using a pair of library routines, `setjmp()` and `longjmp()`. Though simple enough to use, their operation is confusing. A call to `setjmp(env)` takes a 'snaphot' of the machine's state (in particular, the stack context) and saves it in the buffer `env`. This call will return zero. A subsequent call to `longjmp()`, specifying the same environment buffer, will restore the stack frame from the buffer and thus transfer control back to the point at which the setjmp() was executed. As the manual page puts it: 'longjmp(env,val) restores the environment saved by the last call of setjmp, and then returns in such a way that execution continues as if the call of setjmp had just returned the value val to the function that invoked setjmp.' Thus, longjmp() provides a sort of 'global goto' operation, but only to somewhere you have already been, and left a place marker behind by calling setjmp().

The business about the return value from setjmp() is to allow us to distinguish the case where we are returning from setjmp() because we just called it, from the case where a longjmp() has just jumped there.

We now know enough to implement the t_gets() function. Here it is, along with a simple main() function to provide a test harness:

```
/* A program to illustrate the use of SIGALRM, setjmp, and
   longjmp to implement a timeout
*/

#include <stdio.h>
#include <setjmp.h>
#include <sys/signal.h>

jmp_buf timeout_point;

/* This is the handler for the SIGALRM signal */

void timeout_handler(int sigtype)
{
    longjmp(timeout_point, 1);
}

/* This is the important bit */

int t_gets(char *s, int t)
/* char *s;            Buffer to read into      */
/* int t;             Timeout value in seconds */
{
    char *ret;

    signal(SIGALRM, timeout_handler);
    if (setjmp(timeout_point) != 0)
        return -2;                  /* Timed out */
    alarm(t);
    ret = gets(s);
    alarm(0);               /* Cancel the alarm */
    if (ret == NULL) return -1;     /* EOF */
    else return strlen(s);
}

/* This is just a test harness. We keep calling t_gets,
   and reporting the outcome, until we see EOF
*/
```

```
main() {
    char buffer[100];
    int v;

    while(1) {
        printf("enter a string: ");
        v = t_gets(buffer, 5);
        switch (v) {
            case -1: exit(1);    /* Probably EOF */
            case -2: printf("timed out!\n");
                    break;
            default: printf("you typed %d characters\n", v);
        }
    }
}
```

The call to `alarm()` to cancel the alarm signal after `gets()` has returned is very important. Without it, the `t_gets()` function would return, and the SIGALRM would be delivered some time later. At that point, the signal handler would attempt a `longjmp()` to a context which was no longer valid; that is, the (non-existent) stack frame of `t_gets()`, resulting in chaos.

Here is an annotated dialogue resulting from running this program:

```
eddie% timeout
enter a string: timed out!      # For a while we type nothing
enter a string: timed out!
enter a string: hello           # This time we respond
you typed 5 characters
enter a string: goodbye         # This time we respond
you typed 7 characters
enter a string: timed out!
enter a string: eddie%          # Here we typed ^D
```

## 2.8.7  Advanced signal handling

Both BSD and SVR4 UNIX provide fancier signal-handling features than we have examined here, but unfortunately, the details are different between the two versions of UNIX. Indeed, the `signal()` and `kill()` calls are about all one can use to remain completely compatible between the two. This is unfortunate, because *functionally* the SVR4 and BSD enhancements are much the same.

---

**An aside:** SVR4 UNIX claims to include most of the BSD features. This is largely true, but it does not always do so in a compatible way. Signals was one area in which System V and BSD had already significantly diverged before the adoption of BSD technology into System V took place.

---

A key enhancement is the addition of a *signal mask* which specifies a set of signals that are *blocked* from delivery. Blocking a signal postpones its delivery; this is not the same as setting the signal disposition to SIG_IGN, which causes the signal to be discarded. Blocking and unblocking may be used to protect a critical section of code which needs to execute without interruption by a specified set of signals. We will not describe these enhancements in detail, but here are a couple of code fragments to show the idea. In SVR4, a critical section might be implemented as follows:

```
sighold(SIGINT);
sighold(SIGQUIT);

/* critical section ... */

sigrelse(SIGQUIT);
sigrelse(SIGINT);
```

In BSD the calls sigblock() and sigsetmask() may be used for the same purpose, as follows:

```
int old_mask;

old_mask = sigblock(sigmask(SIGINT) | sigmask(SIGQUIT));

/* critical section ... */

sigsetmask(old_mask);
```

Another enhancement relates to signals arriving while a previous signal of the same type is still being handled. As we saw in our first signal-handling example, when a handler is installed with signal(), the disposition of the signal is reset to its default when the signal is delivered. This is why we had to reinstall the handler by calling signal() again within the handler. This is not an entirely satisfactory solution, as a second signal arriving before the handler is reinstalled will trigger the default action – probably terminating the process. The modern BSD and SVR4 implementations provide for permanent installation of the handler which can avoid this problem.

In the modern implementations, when a signal is caught it is automatically masked from delivery whilst the handler is invoked. This avoids recursive behaviour in the handler if signals of the same type arrive in quick succession.

BSD and SVR4 provide system calls sigvec() and sigaction() respectively which allow these aspects of signal behaviour to be controlled in great detail. Both implementations also provide simpler wrapper functions to handle the common cases. In particular, SVR4 provides a function sigset() which is like signal() except that it causes the handler to be installed 'permanently', and provides for automatic masking of the signal during execution of the handler, as discussed above. sigset() is recommended in preference to signal(). Finally, both implementations provide the original signal() call, for backwards compatibility.

## 2.9  UNIX and multiprocessor machines

### 2.9.1 Message passing vs. shared memory architecture

In Chapter 1 we noted that multiprocessor machines are increasingly seen as the most cost-effective way to provide continued growth in the power of UNIX systems. We noted that the most fundamental distinction in the architectures of these machines was between distributed memory (message passing) architectures and shared memory architectures. The mainstream UNIX vendors are currently opting for shared memory architectures, because on these machines it is (relatively) easy to maintain the illusion of a fast single-processor machine from the programmer's standpoint, and thus provide an evolutionary path forward for their customers. Manufacturers offering shared memory multiprocessors include Convex, Solbourne, Sequent and Sun.

In the distributed memory market-place, one of the most successful processors is the Inmos Transputer, largely because of its four on-chip 10 Mbit/s communication links and excellent microcoded support for interprocess communication, making the construction of large-scale message passing architectures fairly easy. These devices are not capable of supporting a fully fledged UNIX – they have no memory management or paging support, for instance – and indeed are sometimes programmed almost 'naked'; that is, without any operating system code loaded onto the processor at all. This is not so bad as it might seem, for the transputer provides on-chip support for interprocess communication and process scheduling, perhaps the two most fundamental operating system services. Some of the operating environments developed for these systems are very UNIX-like, such as Helios (Perihelion, 1989) or Chorus. (For a comparative review of parallel operating systems, see Schuilenburg *et al.*, 1992.)

There is another market sector – the so-called SIMD (single instruction, multiple data stream) machines, which can deliver extremely high performance through the use of a large number (typically 4K–64K) of relatively simple processors which operate in lock-step. Vendors active in this field include Active Memory Technology, Maspar and Thinking Machines Corporation. Such processor arrays do not themselves run UNIX, and are typically viewed as peripherals attached to a host workstation. The programming of such systems is usually supported by special-purpose Fortran or C compilers with libraries of functions to handle standard operations such as Fast Fourier Transforms or matrix operations. We will not consider them further here.

A survey of available parallel computing systems is given in Trew and Wilson (1991).

### 2.9.2  Asymmetric vs. symmetric multiprocessing

Let us return to the mainstream shared memory multiprocessor systems. Because of the bottleneck imposed by the shared memory bus, such systems usually have a rather small number of processors; four is typical. The benefit of these machines is that they are able to run several processes concurrently – one per processor. The scheduler assigns ready-to-run processes to the processors, until all processors are busy. When one of these processes subsequently blocks, or reaches the end of its time-slice, or terminates, it relinquishes the processor on which it is running. The scheduler then assigns the next ready process from the queue to that processor. At different times in the life of a process, it will be executed by different processors. Because all processors share a common memory, it is straightforward for any processor to resume execution of a process where the previous one left off.

To exploit such a system properly, there must be at least as many ready-to-run processes as there are processors. On a busy time-sharing machine, or on a file server handling multiple concurrent requests, this is likely to be the case. However, on a machine whose workload is dominated by one application running as a single UNIX process, no benefit will be seen by moving to a multiprocessor architecture, because all but one of the processors will be left mostly idle. It is important to bear this in mind when evaluating the potential of multiprocessor machines. (In Section 2.10 we will look at the use of *multi-threading* as a way of enabling an application running as a single UNIX process to exploit multiple processors.)

The concurrency offered by multiprocessor UNIX systems generally falls into one of two categories: *asymmetric* and *symmetric* multiprocessing.

Asymmetric multiprocessing allows genuine concurrency for processes executing in 'user space' but allows only one process at a time to be executing inside the kernel, that is, whilst processing a system call or a page fault. Symmetric multiprocessing allows genuine concurrency both in user space and inside the kernel. That is, several processors may simultaneously execute kernel code. Of the two, symmetric multiprocessing is much harder to implement. The problem is that the kernel manipulates many system-wide data structures, such as the scheduler table. To allow updates to these data structures to proceed reliably in the face of concurrency, all these structures need to be individually protected by some form of locking mechanism. The problems are akin to those we encountered in our 'spreadsheet' example in Section 2.6. Thus, converting a single-threaded kernel to a multi-threaded one requires the identification of all places where shared objects are manipulated, and the placing of locks around the appropriate critical sections of code. (For a more detailed discussion of these issues, see Powell *et al.*, 1991, and Eykholt *et al.*, 1992.)

## 2.9.3  Microkernel architectures

Another fairly recent trend in the design of operating systems has been towards *microkernel* architectures. As the name implies, the key idea behind these systems is to place just a bare minimum of functionality inside the kernel, and move many of those functions which are traditionally kernel-based out into user space. Typically, the microkernel provides the following:

1.  A basic process creation and scheduling mechanism.
2.  A low level message passing mechanism.
3.  A memory management mechanism.

Functions typically provided in user space include the following:

1. The file system.
2. Concepts of user identity and access controls.
3. Network transport providers.

How does a microkernel work in practice? Suppose a process wishes to open a file. Using the message passing mechanism provided by the microkernel, it sends a message to the file system module (in user space). This module may, in turn, send a message to the access control module (also in user space), and collect a reply. Finally, the file system module may call the microkernel to perform the required low level disk I/O. Of course, this complexity is readily hidden from the programmer by library functions, which may be designed to preserve a completely traditional interface. To open a file, the programmer merely calls a function such as open(), and receives a file descriptor.

Even from this brief example it is perhaps clear that microkernels provide *mechanisms* but do not impose *policy*. That is, the microkernel does not determine the 'look and feel' of the operating system as seen by the programmer. It is not appropriate to speak of a 'UNIX microkernel' any more than it would be appropriate to speak of a 'UNIX instruction set'. The microkernel can be thought of as a kind of 'hardware abstraction layer' (to coin the Windows NT terminology) on top of which the operating system services are built. It would be possible, in theory, to run a set of servers providing UNIX functionality alongside a set of servers providing Windows functionality. In practice, the user services are usually modelled closely on UNIX.

The advantages of microkernels include the following:

1. A microkernel isolates the hardware dependencies, making it easier to port to new hardware.
2. Pushing operating system services out into user space improves modularity and makes the code much easier to debug. (Debugging code in kernel space is an order of magnitude harder than debugging code in user space.)
3. On large-scale message passing multiprocessor systems, many of the processors may have almost no hardware resources other than memory. For example, they may have no disk and no connection to a local area network (LAN). It is pointless, and very wasteful of memory, to load onto these processors a full-blown UNIX kernel including file system code and TCP/IP support. Using a microkernel architecture, these user services may be present on just a few selected processors within the machine. We achieve a truly distributed operating system, in the sense that the total functionality is spread around many processors, with no single processor offering all services.
4. As noted above, it is possible to emulate several operating systems simultaneously on the same machine. Windows NT does this (Custer, 1993). Even if there is only one operating system interface, it is convenient to be able to develop and test new versions of the operating system without stopping the old one.

The two microkernel systems which currently stand out in terms of having a high degree of UNIX compatibility and good support for multiprocessor machines are *Mach* and *Chorus/MiX*. Mach was developed at Carnegie-Mellon University, and is significant in having been chosen by the Open Software Foundation as the basis for OSF/1. Early versions of Mach contained most of the BSD 4.2 code in the kernel and so cannot really be considered as microkernels. The microkernel version did not appear until version 3.0 in 1989. There is a good overview of Mach in Tanenbaum (1992).

Chorus is a microkernel from the French company *Chorus Systèmes*. Provided with it is a UNIX server called *MiX*, which provides a high degree of SVR4 compatibility. Currently, Chorus/MiX is one of the few operating systems capable of delivering UNIX compatibility with support for large-scale (100-processor) distributed memory machines.

# 2.10  Threads

A traditional UNIX process, as discussed in Section 2.2, provides a single 'thread' of execution through a program. Within that process, everything happens sequentially; there is no concurrency. As noted in the previous section, such a process can effectively make use of just a single processor. *Multi-threading*, the subject of this section, allows concurrency within a single process.

## 2.10.1  Thread concepts

Rather similar to a process, a thread is an abstract concept, and impossible to capture in a one-line definition. However, the name is fairly descriptive, if you think about it the right way.

Figure 2.21 shows a flow diagram of a hypothetical program. Though out-moded as a design aid, flow diagrams provide a good graphical representation of the possible 'execution paths' through the loops and branches of the program. As the code is executed, an actual execution path, or *thread of control* is traced out. Imagine handing the process a ball of string, and keeping hold of one end at the start of the flow diagram. As the process proceeds and meanders around the diagram, it unwinds this string to leave a record of its travels. This *thread* shows the path of execution through the code, as shown in Figure 2.22.

## 2.10.2  Shared and private threads' resources

Multi-threaded environments allow several such threads of execution to be active within the overall context of a single process. Most of this context is shared by all the threads within a process. This includes the following:

1. The code. All the threads within a process are executing the same program.
2. All static and global data. For C programs, this means all variables declared outside functions.

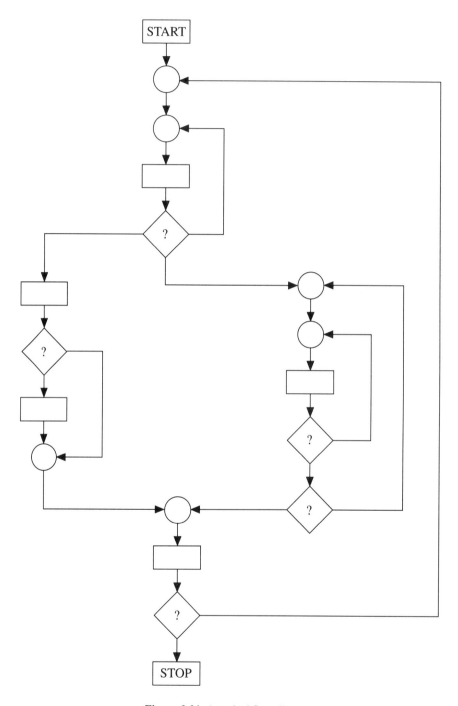

**Figure 2.21** A typical flow diagram.

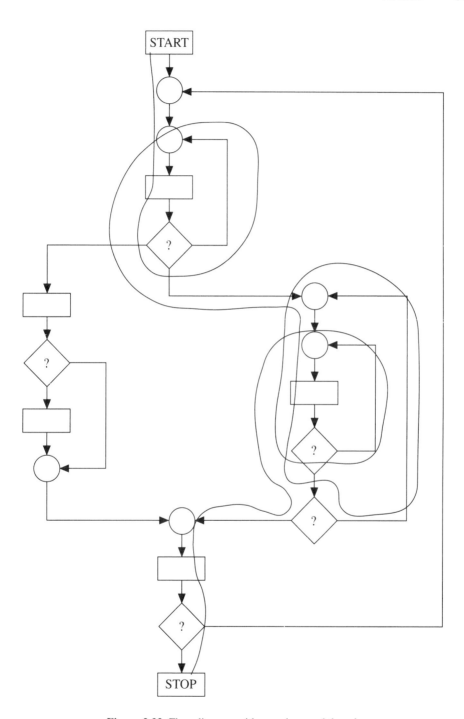

**Figure 2.22** Flow diagram with superimposed thread.

3. The heap (i.e. memory obtained by calling `malloc()`).
4. All process attributes and resources held by the kernel. This includes the real and effective user IDs, the current directory and any open file descriptors.

The amount of context private to each thread is usually very small, but typically includes the following:

1. Its own register state, and stack. (Local variables declared inside functions.)
2. Its own priority level.
3. Its own identifier.

This is the minimum context necessary to maintain an independent flow of control through the program. Depending on the implementation, the thread may have other private context, such as its UNIX signal-handling behaviour.

Because threads carry so much less context with them than UNIX processes, they are sometimes called *lightweight processes*. Whilst it would be unusual for an application to be distributed across more than half a dozen UNIX processes, it would be quite reasonable to think of an application which created a thousand threads.

## 2.10.3 Thread scheduling and synchronization

In additional to their minimal context (and hence small memory requirements), another aspect of the lightweight-ness of threads is their fast context switch times. Typically the context switching and scheduling of threads within the process is handled by the thread library, without calling the kernel. The kernel is responsible for scheduling the process as a whole, and knows little or nothing of the internal thread structure. Within the process, a degree of cooperation is required between the threads if one thread is not to hog all the CPU time. Functions such as `thread_yield()` are provided to allow a thread to relinquish control voluntarily. (If the kernel *does* schedule the threads, the amount of per thread context required increases, as does the context switch time. Such threads are sometimes called *heavyweight threads*.)

When a process begins execution in a multi-threaded environment, a single thread is launched, which begins executing the `main()` function of the program. Unless the program explicitly creates new threads, it will continue as a traditional single-threaded UNIX process. New threads are created by a call which is typically of the form:

```
thread_create(char *stack, int stack_size,
              void (*func)(), void *arg);
```

The first two arguments specify the location and size of a stack available to the new thread. This is usually allocated by the parent thread from the heap. Setting the size of the stack can be difficult, and comes as a shock to UNIX programmers who are accustomed to the luxury of having the operating system grow the stack for them as necessary. The third argument, `func`, names the function where the thread should begin execution. From the thread's viewpoint, this function is equivalent to the `main()` function of a traditional process. If the thread ever returns from the function `func`, the thread terminates. The fourth argument, `arg`, is passed to the function. Commonly, it is used to allow multiple threads, running the same function, to have some form of individual identity, or to locate the data on which they are to operate.

Because so much context is shared between threads, a lot of responsibility rests upon the programmer to ensure that threads do not interfere with one another in unwanted ways; for example:

1.  If a thread changes to a different directory, all threads within the process see the new current directory.
2.  If a thread closes a file descriptor, the descriptor becomes closed in all threads.
3.  If a thread calls `exit()`, the whole process, with all its threads, terminates.
4.  If a thread modifies data in memory shared by the other threads (static data, or the heap), it must arrange for sufficient locking so that no other thread can corrupt or obtain an inconsistent view of the data. This problem is basically the one we addressed (at the process level) in Section 2.6. Thread libraries invariably provide a variety of mechanisms for synchronization, including semaphores, *mutex* locks and *condition variables*.
5.  If a thread sits in a compute-bound loop, all other threads in that process will be starved of CPU time. The kernel will not pre-empt the thread and switch to a new one. Thus, threads offer a form of 'cooperative concurrency'.

## 2.10.4  Advantages of threads

Why bother with threads? There are two key reasons for writing multi-threaded applications:

1.  On a multiprocessor shared memory machine, each thread can run on a different processor. Thus, threads provide a way for the programmer to exploit multiple processors and achieve genuine concurrency *within a single application.*
2.  Some applications have inherent concurrency. Threads provide a natural way to express this. For example, a database system may have many user interactions in progress at any one time. A network server may wish to manage multiple simultaneous clients. A windowed application may wish to respond to user input, such as operating a scroll bar, whilst computationally intensive image rendering is in progress.

These advantages may be summarized thus: threads allow a degree of parallelism, either 'logical' parallelism or true parallelism on multiprocessor platforms, within a single application process.

## 2.10.5  Disadvantages of threads

1.  The idea of combining concurrency with such a high level of resource sharing is new to many UNIX programmers. A certain amount of retraining and a great deal of care is needed to write robust multi-threaded applications.

2.  It is not obvious how to extend the semantics of some UNIX operations into multi-threaded environments. For example, if a thread calls `fork()`, should the new process be born with copies of all the running threads that the parent had, or should it just have a copy of the thread which performed the `fork()`? If a signal is delivered to a process, which thread should it be delivered to? The one executing at the time? All of them? Should each thread be allowed to nominate its own signal handler?

## 2.10.6  Implementations of threads

Although there have been a number of implementations of threads on UNIX, none of them could really claim to be definitive; however, a POSIX draft standard P1003.4a for multi-threading (known as *pthreads*) is in preparation (POSIX, 1990). SunOS Release 4 included a lightweight process library which operated entirely within user space. *Mach*, from Carnegie-Mellon University, provides a threads interface which is much more closely integrated with the kernel. OSF/1 supports multi-threading, again based on the Mach kernel, although the programmer's normal interface to this is POSIX pthreads (Open Software Foundation, 1991).

Recent versions of Solaris offer a two-level threading mechanism: the first level is called threads, and is the level at which programmers mostly work, to express the 'logical' concurrency in their programs; the second level is the lightweight process (LWP). (Confusingly, an LWP in this context is *not* the same as a thread, and is *not* the same as the lightweight processes offered in SunOS 4.) The LWP level gives the programmer control over the extent of the true (multiprocessor) concurrency within an application (Powell *et al.*, 1991).

# Chapter 3

# Distributed UNIX services

## 3.1 An introduction to network services

In this chapter we discuss some of the standard facilities which UNIX provides to support distributed operation across a network. These include remote command execution, the Network Information Service, and the Network File System. We will briefly examine these utilities from the end-user's perspective, then go on to look 'behind the scenes' at their implementation. All these facilities are based on the so-called *client–server* model for distributed applications. We begin the chapter, therefore, with a look at the basic concepts and terminology of client–server.

### 3.1.1 Clients, servers, daemons and protocols

A *server* is a program that provides a service, that is, it makes some resource available to other programs running somewhere on the network. The resource could be almost anything, a database perhaps, or a complete file system. The resource may be a piece of hardware, such as a printer, or a fax modem, or a screen and keyboard, or some more specialized device such as a television frame grabber or document scanner. The server program runs on the machine which the resource is attached to, and waits *passively* until its services are required. Servers are often started up at boot-time, via commands in a start-up script. We will see examples of this in Chapter 7. Servers usually spend most of their time asleep, waiting for work.

A *client* is a program that *uses* a resource. It may be running on the machine to which the resource is attached, or on a different machine; indeed, the main point of clients and servers is to provide access to resources irrespective of their physical location. A client *actively* makes a connection across the network to the server it requires.

The terms client and server are sometimes used to refer to a *machine*. For example, we may point out a computer on our network which has a large disk attached and say 'That is our file server, and these diskless workstations here are its clients'. Or we may refer to a machine with a printer attached as a 'print server'. In the present context, however, the terms client and server refer to the relationship between individual *programs*, not to machines. In general, machines cannot simply be labelled as clients and servers. One machine, for example, might be a server for a piece of the file system, but a client of a remote print server. In fact, the same duality can sometimes apply within a single program. For example, a program which is a server for a database might itself contact a time server, to obtain an accurate timestamp to attach to a new record in the database. At that moment, the database server is a client of the time server.

In the UNIX world, the term *daemon* is sometimes used to refer to a server. Usually,. it means that the server is 'permanently available', which implies (as discussed above) that it is started at boot-time. Also, daemons usually provide a 'system-related' service, such as remote login. However, the distinction between system services and application services is blurred. Is there any good reason to consider mail delivery as a 'system service' and document scanning as an 'application service'? It depends on what your users use the network for.

Whatever the definition of a daemon might be, many servers have names ending in 'd' in honour of the name. For example, one of the servers that supports remote login is called rlogind, and the server that supports the network file system is called nfsd. On some systems, daemons have names such as in.rogind. The in. at the beginning of the name indicates that the server is started via a special server called inetd. This topic is discussed in Section 7.1. Of course, these names are just conventions – there is no necessity to follow this pattern.

A *protocol* is a set of rules describing how a client and server interact. It defines the commands accepted by the server, and the precise format of the messages which pass between them.

As an example of a real-life protocol, here is an example of a dialogue with sendmail (a mail delivery server; one of the few daemons whose name *does not* end in 'd'). The example shows the dialogue during the delivery of a mail message from Richard on machine eddie to Chris on machine trillian. Lines marked with a '<' prefix came from the server, lines marked '>' were sent to it. The upper case words such as HELO and DATA are keywords of the sendmail protocol:

```
< 220 trillian Sendmail 4.1/SMI-4.1 Fri, 18 Dec 92 22:19:32 GMT
> HELO eddie
< 250 trillian Hello eddie (localhost), pleased to meet you
> MAIL From: Richard Greenlaw <richard>
< 250 Richard Greenlaw <richard>... Sender ok
> RCPT To: Chris Brown <chris>
< 250 Chris Brown <chris>... Recipient ok
> DATA
< 354 Enter mail, end with "." on a line by itself
> Flee - all is discovered!
> .
< 250 Mail accepted
> QUIT
< 221 trillian delivering mail
```

As the example shows, sendmail uses a text-based protocol. This protocol is widely used, and is called SMTP (simple mail transfer protocol). It is documented in RFC 821.

Other servers use binary protocols; often, C structures are used to define the message formats. We will examine a simple binary protocol when we write a client for the `tftp` server in Chapter 4. The protocol may also specify the error conditions that can arise in the server, and how they are notified back to the client.

Many servers provide general-purpose services and will be used by a variety of clients engaged on a variety of specific tasks. The time server and the X Windows server are examples of general-purpose servers. The user is concerned only with writing the clients, and the protocol used to communicate with the server is pre-ordained.

Other servers are written specifically for use with particular clients, as part of a distributed application. The users write both the server and the client code, and are responsible for defining their own protocols.

## 3.1.2 Locating a service

In Chapter 4 we examine in detail the operations performed by a client to obtain a connection to a server. It is appropriate here, however, to describe in general terms the way in which a service is located, or 'addressed' on the network.

To find a service, a client must first know which machine to contact. At the highest level the machine is identified by a text name such as 'eddie' or 'trillian'. At lower levels, this name is translated to a numeric network address, typically an IP (internet protocol) address, which is a 32-bit number. Within the machine identified by this address, there will usually be several 'communication endpoints' at which servers are listening for connections. These endpoints are identified by a *port number*, usually 16 bits. As an analogy, to telephone an individual in a company, you first dial the company's switchboard number. This is analogous to the IP address, identifying a specific machine. You then ask to be connected to a particular telephone extension. This is analogous to the port number, identifying one particular service within the machine.

Each service has a particular port at which it listens for connections. The `sendmail` server mentioned above, for example, always listens on port 25. The `rexecd` daemon, which offers a remote command execution service and is discussed in Section 3.2, always listens on port 512, and so on.

This correspondence between services and port numbers is held in the file `/etc/services`. Here is an extract:

```
daytime        13/tcp
daytime        13/udp
netstat        15/tcp
chargen        19/tcp          ttytst source
chargen        19/udp          ttytst source
ftp-data       20/tcp
ftp            21/tcp
telnet         23/tcp
smtp           25/tcp          mail
time           37/tcp          timserver
```

```
time            37/udp          timserver
   ...
exec            512/tcp
login           513/tcp
shell           514/tcp         cmd
printer         515/tcp         spooler
```

The last line, for example, says that a service called `printer` listens for connections on port 515 and uses TCP. (We will meet both TCP and UDP (user datagram protocol) in Chapter 4.) The entry also says that `spooler` can be used as an alternative name for the service. On many networks this information is not in fact stored on a local file which is replicated at each machine, but is obtained from a central database via a network information server. The same is true for a number of other system configuration files. We will discuss the Network Information Service later in this chapter. Programmers usually access this information using *resolver* routines such as `getservbyname()` which isolates them from needing to know whether the information comes from a local file or a remote server. Resolvers are described in Section 3.3.

Figure 3.1 illustrates the use of machine addresses and port numbers in identifying a service. In light of the generally very well-developed network services in UNIX, this method of locating a service is surprisingly primitive. You cannot simply attach a text name, such as 'fax_modem' to a service and ask the system to locate a machine offering that service. You have to specify the machine. It is true that the RPC (remote procedure call) based services (discussed in Chapter 6) offer a dynamic mapping from the service identifier to the port number, but the client still needs explicitly to specify the host on which the service is located. In contrast, AT&T's distributed file system, RFS, introduces the concept of named *resources* and automatically locates the machine providing that resource, even switching to a backup 'provider' if the original fails. However, this is only in the context of sharing files (and possibly devices). The key point is this: there is no central registry of services available network-wide.

---

**An aside:** the Open Software Foundation's Distributed Computing Environment (DCE) wins here. It provides a 'cell directory service' which allows services to register and be found, network-wide. A two stage look-up is used. First, the cell directory service maps the service name on to the name of a machine providing that service. Second, a daemon on the specified machine maps the service name on to a port number.

---

## 3.1.3 Reserved ports

The port number at which `sendmail` (for example) listens for connections is called a *well-known* port number. `sendmail` always listens at this port. If a `sendmail` decided to listen at port 26 instead of 25, it would have a very quiet life, because no one would know where to find it. When a client connects to a server, it must create a transport endpoint of

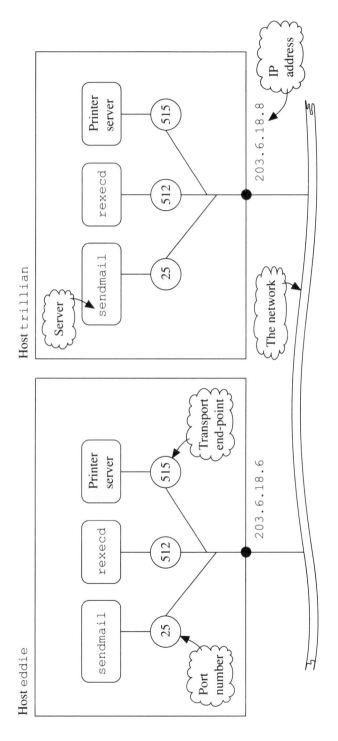

**Figure 3.1** Identifying a server.

its own, and it, too, will have a port number. This choice is largely arbitrary; the client does not really care what port it uses. However, there is one important exception: port numbers less than 1024 are *reserved*, which means that only a process running with the effective user identity of `root` can use these port numbers. These reserved ports form the basis of a sort of low level security amongst the network services. Most servers use reserved ports. This is supposed to give the client assurance that it is talking to the genuine server, and not some program that a third-year student has just written to capture passwords. Of course, all it really proves is that the server is running with root privileges. Less commonly, some servers demand that clients use a reserved port (they do not care which one) so that they can be sure it is the genuine client to whom they are offering their service. We will meet an example of this in Section 3.2.2.

With this background out of the way we will move on to examine a network service in more detail.

# 3.2  Remote command execution

The ability to execute a command on a remote machine is one of the most fundamental network services. It conforms closely to the general model of a network service discussed in the previous section, consisting of a server, a client and an agreed protocol.

Before describing the implementation, we will examine the remote command execution services from an end-user's perspective.

## 3.2.1  Command line utilities: `rsh` and `on`

The most widely used remote execution command is `rsh`. (On some systems it may have a different name because the name `rsh` is used for a *restricted* shell, which is not the same thing at all.) `rsh`, of course, is the *client* program, which runs on the local machine. It connects to a server called `rshd`, although most end-users are probably unaware of this detail. The form of the command is:

```
rsh   remote_host   command
```

For example, the command

```
rsh   desiato   who
```

would run the `who` command on the machine `desiato`, reporting the results to the local screen. That is, `rsh` collects the standard output from the remote `who` and delivers it to its own standard output. `rsh` will also ferry its own standard input across the network to the remote command's `stdin`; for example:

```
cat   greeting   |   rsh   desiato   mail   jane   brian
```

will mail `jane` and `brian` on the remote machine `desiato`, sending them the contents of the local file `greeting`. One needs to keep a clear picture of the 'plumbing' in these situations; in the above example, the pipe is between the two local programs `cat` and `rsh` as shown in Figure 3.2(a). And in this example:

```
rsh   desiato   who   >   who_list
```

it is the local shell which redirects the standard output of the `rsh` command to the local file `who_list`, and the command seen by the remote shell is simply `"who"`, as shown in Figure 3.2(b). However, in this example:

```
rsh   desiato   who   '>'   who_list
```

the local end treats the '>' literally, passing the command `"who > who_list"` to the remote shell. Thus, it is the output from `who` which is redirected now, to a file on the remote machine, as shown in Figure 3.2(c).

An alternative remote execution utility, named `on`, is available on some systems as part of the ONC facilities. `on` is an RPC-based service supported by the daemon `rexd`. It is used much like `rsh`, with the same general form of command:

```
on   remote_host   command
```

From an end-user's viewpoint, the chief feature of `on` is that it creates an environment on the remote system which is very similar to that on the local machine. All the local environment variables, for example, are explicitly passed to the remote end as part of the protocol. We will return to this point in Section 3.2.3. An additional feature of `on` is that it supports interactive remote commands, i.e. commands which like to think they are talking directly to a terminal. For example, the command

```
on   desiato   vi   my_file
```

should (in theory) work, whereas the same command using `rsh` will certainly *not* work.

## 3.2.2  Authentication of remote execution requests

On my local machine, I have a user identity. I established that identity, and authenticated it with a password, when I logged in. However, my identity (and resultant access privileges) on the local machine will not necessarily be good on a remote machine. Just because I can send a message to a machine across a network does not mean I am allowed to use it. So the question is, on what basis does the remote machine decide whether I am allowed to execute the requested command, and in particular, how does it know who I am? Different remote execution servers use different methods to authenticate their users,

Local host                                    Remote host  `desiato`

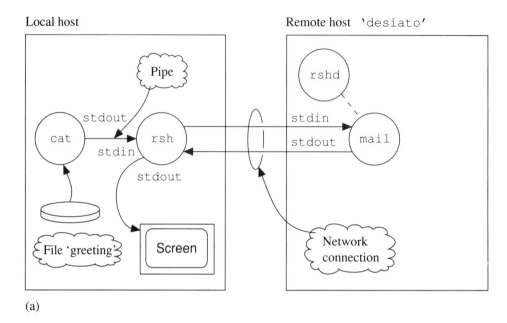

(a)

Local host                                    Remote host  `desiato`

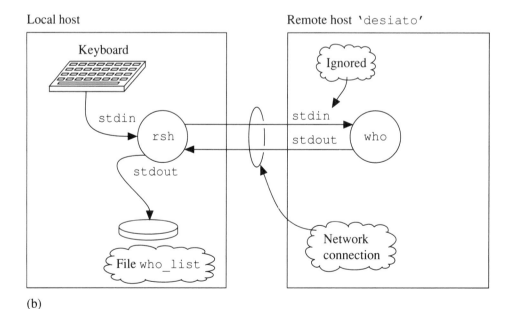

(b)

**Figure 3.2** Plumbing for `rsh` commands: (a) `cat greeting | rsh desiato mail jane brian`; (b) `rsh desiato who > who_list`.

**Figure 3.2** *continued* (c) rsh desiato who '>' who_list.

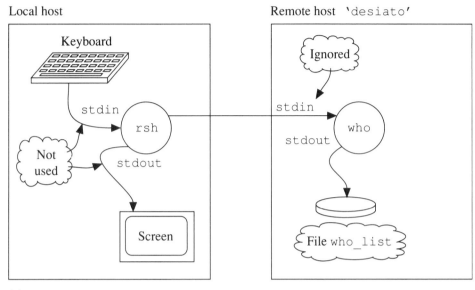

(c)

but one method is that performed by rshd. It uses a scheme of *trusted hosts* to provide 'transparent' remote command execution; that is, to avoid the need to specify a user name and a password each time a remote command is executed. It works as follows. Suppose I am logged in on host eddie, and wish to execute a command on trillian. For this to succeed, two conditions must be satisfied:

1. I must have an account on trillian. Normally, I will have the same user name on both machines.
2. The /etc/hosts.equiv file on trillian must contain an entry for eddie, or failing that my home directory on trillian must contain a file called .rhosts which contains an entry for eddie.

The authentication tests made by rshd are summarized in Figure 3.3. Putting an entry for a machine in my /etc/hosts.equiv file means that I consider it a *trusted* host. If that host tells me it is sam who is trying to log in, I believe it, and I assume it has taken whatever steps are necessary to verify sam's identity.

At minimum, an entry in /etc/hosts.equiv consists simply of a machine name, allowing any user on the named machine to have transparent access (assuming they have a local account). Some implementations support fancier formats; for example, in SunOS, the following entry:

```
eddie  -sam
```

means that any user *except* sam can execute commands from eddie.

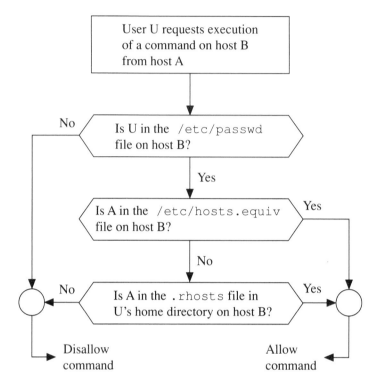

**Figure 3.3** Validation of remote command execution request by rshd.

So far, so good. But how does the remote machine get to know my user name? Of course, the client tells it. How can the remote machine be sure that the client is telling the truth? Surely any competent C programmer could read the manual page for rshd, and write a client program that sent across any user name it chose? The answer is that the rshd server also demands that the client connects to it using a *reserved* port. As we saw in Section 3.1.3, a process can only use a reserved port if it is running with an effective identity of root . To construct a client with root privileges requires the user to attain super-user status on the local machine. This, then, is the basis of the authentication performed by the rshd server.

---

**An aside:** in these days of single-user workstations, the assumption that root is a totally trustworthy user is a poor one. In many cases, the 'owners' of individual workstations know their root password so that they can perform routine tasks such as rebooting the machine. Any DOS-based PCs connected to the network present a similar problem. A knowledgeable user on such a machine could readily impersonate a UNIX user attempting a rsh command.

---

Programmers who are not entrusted with the super-user password will have a hard time developing clients which connect to `rshd()` because they will need to ask their system administrator to execute the commands required to make their executable run 'setuid to root' each time they recompile it. There is an alternative remote execution server `rexecd` which does not rely on the client having root privilege for its authentication. This server does not have a widely available client program (analogous to `rsh`), but has a client wrapper function `rexec()` to help users write their own clients. We will present a detailed example of `rexec()` in Section 3.2.3; meanwhile we merely note that the `rexecd` daemon performs authentication by demanding a user name and a password each time it is called.

## 3.2.3 The remote execution environment

A little earlier we discussed the example

```
rsh  desiato  who  '>'  who_list
```

saying that it redirected the output of `who` to a file on the remote machine. An interesting question is 'In which directory will the `who_list` file be created?', which leads on to the broader question 'What environment is seen by the remote command?'. The answer is that the environment will be much as if you had actually just logged in to that machine; for example, the current directory will be your home directory. The shell that is started up will be the shell specified by your account on the remote machine, and normal start-up processing for a nonlogin shell occurs; for example, a `csh` will read your remote `.cshrc` file but *not* your `.login` file. Neither `sh` nor `ksh` read your `.profile` in this situation. Because of this, your search path on the remote machine might not be set up as you expect it, so commands that are in non-standard places may not be found unless they are given as absolute pathnames.

The `on` command goes to much greater lengths to make the remote environment look like the local one. The current directory on the remote machine is set to the current directory on the local machine. This really only makes sense in a context where the two machines see the same (distributed) file system, so that the user can reference (say) his or her home directory using the same pathname on both machines.

The difference between `rsh` and `on` in this respect is easily demonstrated by comparing two remote `pwd` commands:

```
eddie% cd /home/chris/reports
eddie% rsh trillian pwd
/home/chris              # In home directory on remote
eddie% on trillian pwd
/home/chris/reports      # Current dir preserved on remote
eddie%
```

On some systems, the `rexd` daemon goes further, actually remotely mounting the current directory, if possible, from the appropriate machine. The difference between `rsh` and `on` may be summed up as follows:

Using rsh is like performing a short-term login for a single command.
The environment is much as if you had logged in 'over there'. Using on
is like stealing some other machine's CPU cycles to execute in the
environment 'over here'.

## 3.2.4 Remote execution client functions

For the most part, the remote execution daemons are used only by the standard client utilities such as rsh. However, it is possible to write programs that invoke these services directly. The protocols used by these daemons are documented in the manual pages (look up rshd(1) and rexecd(1)); however, for most purposes programmers will use the client wrapper functions rcmd() and rexec() which hide the details of the protocol and provide a convenient interface to the programmer. Table 3.1 summarizes the three remote execution daemons, and their associated client programs and wrapper functions.

The rex() client function uses an RPC-based service which we will not discuss in detail here. The rshd and rexecd servers, along with their client functions rcmd() and rexec(), are quite similar to one another. They both allow a command to be executed on a remote machine, and they both make connections to the stdin and stdout of the command. In both cases, an 'intermediate' shell is started (on the remote machine) to interpret the command line. In both cases, there is an option to obtain a separate network connection to the command's stderr stream, or it may be merged with the stdout. The chief difference lies in the form of authentication used; that is, how is it determined if the user is allowed to execute this command on the remote machine?

Both servers require that the user has an account on the remote machine. As mentioned in Section 3.2.2, rshd uses the /etc/hosts.equiv mechanism, along with a requirement that the client is using a reserved port, for its authentication. In contrast, rexecd requires that a user name and a password (verified on the remote machine) are provided each time.

**Table 3.1**    Remote execution servers and clients

| Server | Client function | Typical client application | Comments |
| --- | --- | --- | --- |
| rshd | rcmd() | rsh, rcp | Part of the BSD r* utilities. Authentication is based on the use of a reserved port, and the /etc/hosts.equiv file. |
| rexecd | rexec() | No standard applications | Similar to rshd, but authentication is via explicit user name and cleartext password. |
| rexd | rex() | on | An RPC-based service; passes more environment data than the others, and supports interactive use. |

## 3.2.5 A remote execution example

Let us examine a simple client which connects to the remote execution server `rexecd` using the client function `rexec()`. The `rexec()` call is illustrated in Figure 3.4.

As mentioned above, `rexec()` requires a user name and a password for the authentication process. This information may be supplied in three ways:

1. The user name and password may be passed as arguments to the `rexec` call. Of course, hard-wiring these into the code is an appalling choice from a security standpoint; even if the source code is kept from the prying eyes of others, it is an easy matter to extract these strings from the executable, using the `strings` utility. (Look up `strings(1)`.) In any case, this method would require that the program be recompiled for use by a different user.
2. The information may be placed in a file called `.netrc` in the user's home directory. In this case, you supply null pointers in place of these strings in the call to `rexec()`.
3. The information may be entered from the keyboard at run-time. If the user name and password are not present in the call to `rexec()`, and there is no `.netrc` file, the user will automatically be prompted to enter them when the function is called.

We will begin by using method (3). Our example program simply runs the `apropos` command on a specified remote machine. (The `apropos` command lists those manual pages relating to a specified keyword. On some systems the command `man -k` is used instead.) Our program is called `rap` (remote apropos) and is invoked like this:

```
rap   remote_host   keyword
```

Here is the program:

```c
/* A simple example of remote command execution.
   This program runs 'apropos' on a remote machine
*/

#include <sys/types.h>
#include <stdio.h>

main(int argc, char *argv[])
{
    int fd, count;
    char buffer[BUFSIZ], command[80], *host;

    if (argc != 3) {
        printf("usage: rap host keyword\n");
        exit(1);
    }

    host = argv[1];

    /* Assemble a command string for the remote machine */
    sprintf(command, "/usr/ucb/apropos %s", argv[2]);
```

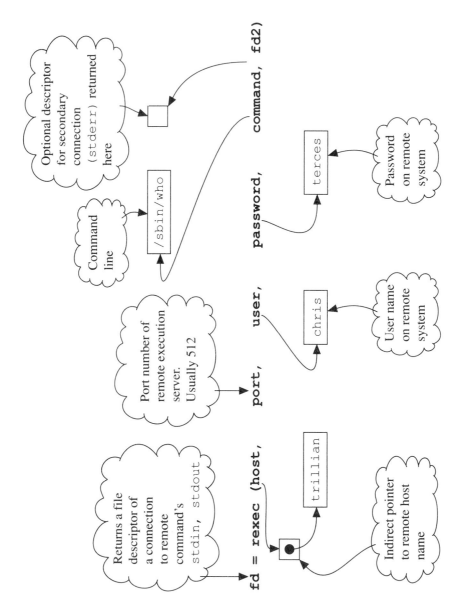

**Figure 3.4** The rexec() call.

```
    /* Start up the remote program. 512 is the port number
       of the rexecd daemon, NOT a buffer size!
    */
    fd = rexec(&host, htons(512), 0, 0, command, 0);
    if (fd == -1) {
       printf("rexec failed\n");
       exit(1);
    }
    /* Now we just relay the standard output from the
       remote command to our own stdout, until we see
       an EOF on the network connection,  indicating
       that the remote end has closed down
    */
    while ((count = read(fd, buffer, BUFSIZ)) > 0)
        fwrite(buffer, count, 1, stdout);
}
```

There are some subtleties to note about the `rexec()` call:

1. Why do we pass `&host` instead of just `host` as the first argument? The answer is subtle (and barely relevant to the present discussion). A machine can be known under several names, and may be referenced by any of these names in the `rexec()` call. If the name you supply is not the 'official' name of the machine (the one listed first in the `/etc/hosts` file), then `rexec()` alters the `host` pointer to point to the official name. It is not clear why, if you already know one valid name for the machine, you might want to know another one. Nonetheless, it is designed that way.

2. What is the purpose of the `htons()` call in the second argument? We will answer the question properly in Chapter 4; meanwhile we merely note, rather mysteriously, that the port number must be in 'network byte order', and the `htons()` function (actually it is usually a macro) sorts this out.

3. Note that the remote command is specified as a single text string, with the arguments separated by white-space, and not as a set of separate strings, as is used in the `exec()` family of calls. You should be aware that this 'command line' is interpreted by a shell at the remote end. Shell metacharacters such as the filename wildcards * and ? *will* be interpreted at the remote end.

4. Notice that we have been careful to specify an absolute pathname for the `apropos` command on the remote machine. This is because it is difficult to be sure that the command will lie on our search path in the remote environment.

Since we have not specified a user name and a password to `rexec()`, it will prompt us for them. Here is a sample run in which we ask remote host `trillian` to find manual entries containing the keyword `kill`.

```
eddie% rap trillian kill
Name (trillian:): chris      # Prompt for user name
Password (trillian:chris):   # Password does not echo
kill(1): kill - terminate a process by default
```

```
killall(1m): killall - kill all active processes
kill(2): kill - send a signal to a process
killpg(3b): killpg - send signal to a process group
eddie%
```

To improve the 'transparency' of this operation (that is, to avoid having to specify a user name and a password each time), we can place appropriate entries in our `.netrc` file. (Look up `.netrc(4)`.) For example:

```
machine trillian login chris password terces
machine desiato  login crb   password milliway
```

These entries say that if I execute a remote command on `trillian`, I should do so as user `chris`, supplying the password `terces`, and if I execute a remote command on `desiato` I should do so as `crb` with password `milliway`. You may be (justifiably) reluctant to place cleartext passwords into a file, but your security is not really compromised providing you make sure that no one but you has read permission on the file. It is up to you to remember to do this. However, `rexec()` will explicitly remind you (with an error message) if it finds a `.netrc` which is readable by 'group' or 'other'. Let us suppose we have created a `.netrc` file as shown above, and set the correct access permissions with the command:

```
chmod  go-rw  .netrc
```

We can now run the `rap` program again, noting that this time we are not prompted for a name or password:

```
eddie %rap trillian kill
kill(1): kill - terminate a process by default
killall(1m): killall - kill all active processes
kill(2): kill - send a signal to a process
killpg(3b): killpg - send signal to a process group
eddie %
```

There are other programs, notably `ftp`, which will also use the entries in `.netrc` to give a more transparent login.

In practice, user-written clients of `rshd` and `rexecd` are not very common. The reason is simply that for most purposes, the general-purpose client `rsh` is all that is needed. Indeed, we could provide an alternative implementation of `rap` using a shell script or a shell function, without writing any C code at all. For example, defining the Korn shell function:

```
function rap
{
    rsh $1 /usr/ucb/apropos $2
}
```

will produce a `rap` command with the same functionality as the one we wrote.

However, these client functions are occasionally useful for starting up remote non-interactive processes, ones that perhaps reconnect their standard input and output to files (or other network connections) and continue to operate in the background. For example, they provide a way for clients to start up servers that are not started via the normal boot-time procedures discussed in Section 7.4.

## 3.3 The Network Information Service

The remote command execution mechanisms described in the previous section are not at all transparent, in so far as the programmer has to make a function call that explicitly 'reaches across' to the remote machine. In this section we turn our attention to a rather different type of network service which, whilst being very frequently used, is normally so transparent that we are not even aware of it.

---

**An aside:** before we proceed further, a note about the name. NIS, the Network Information Service, was formerly called Yellow Pages, and is still colloquially known as such – or simply as 'YP'. The name was changed to avoid a clash with a registered trademark of British Telecom. Nevertheless, most of the programs and library functions which make up NIS are called 'yp..something' in remembrance of the old name (not to mention backwards compatibility).

---

### 3.3.1 The need for a Network Information Service

NIS was developed by Sun primarily to make it easier to administer large groups of workstations, by centralizing a number of system configuration databases which previously had to be replicated in text files on each workstation. For example, if a new workstation is added to an existing network of fifty machines, a new entry must be made in the /etc/hosts file on all fifty machines, and a complete /etc/hosts file must be provided on the new machine. Of course, it is possible to devise a shell script that partially automates this, by copying an updated hosts file from some 'master' machine to each of the others. If a new user account is added, the new entry must similarly appear in each machine's /etc/passwd file. A script could be used for this also, but life is not so easy here, as often there will be 'private' accounts specific to individual machines. There are other configuration files, such as /etc/services and /etc/aliases (containing system-wide mailing lists) to which similar comments apply. NIS simplifies the administration of these databases by centralizing this information on a 'master NIS server' machine. A server program, ypserv, running on this machine answers requests from clients running on workstations for information in these databases as required.

The main use of NIS, then, is to replace (or in some cases, supplement) local system configuration files with centrally maintained databases that can be queried by clients as required. As such, NIS is primarily the province of the system administrator, and is largely transparent, both to end-users and to programmers, if it is set up correctly. However, NIS may be viewed in a more general way than this, as a network-wide look-up mechanism for any database the user cares to devise. By constructing a hashed index for the database, it performs this job very efficiently, even for huge files. In this section we first provide an overview of the NIS system, and discuss the server and client components. We briefly discuss its use by the system administrator, and we will then show how users can create, and provide look-up functions for, NIS databases of the user's devising.

## 3.3.2 An overview of NIS

Machines that use NIS are grouped into NIS *domains*. A domain, in this context, is simply a group of machines that share common system configuration information (and by implication, are under common administrative control). A domain has a text name. NIS domains do not (necessarily) correspond to particular physical networks, or to particular ranges of IP addresses, or to particular parts of the internet namespace.

---

**An aside:** for example, there is no reason why all machines whose names end in .cs.oxbridge.ac.uk must be in the same NIS domain – the two concepts of domain are completely unrelated. In practice, because system administrators like to keep life simple, it is likely that the machines in the cs.oxbridge.ac.uk part of the internet name space *would* form an NIS domain, and moreover, the NIS domain name may well be cs.oxbridge.ac.uk.

---

Within each domain, a *master server* machine is chosen. On this machine, a single copy of each of the configuration files such as /etc/services and /etc/hosts is maintained by the system administrator. These files are converted into an indexed database format called a *map*, for efficient access. Each entry in the map consists of a *key* and an associated *value* both of which are text strings. A map is designed to be efficiently searched by a *key* value only. Herein lies a small problem. Some of the system configuration files are often used 'two ways round'. For example, the /etc/hosts file is used both to map hosts' names on to IP addresses, and vice versa. For this reason, *two* maps are built from /etc/hosts, one that can be looked up by name and one that can be looked up by address. These maps are called hosts.byname and hosts.byaddr. Similar comments apply to several other maps. All the maps are placed in a directory that is 'well known' to the NIS server ypserv. The database access routines on top of which ypserv is built are documented in dbm(3).

Optionally, slave servers can be allocated for the domain. Slave servers help reduce the workload on the master, and provide continuity of service in the event that the master goes down. At least one slave server is pretty much mandatory even on a small network – domains with only one server are difficult to manage because the server cannot be taken out of service without disabling the entire domain. The master sends copies of the maps to the slave servers on a regular basis.

The NIS client machines dynamically select a server for their NIS domain. This process of selection is called *binding*, and is performed by the daemon ypbind. This daemon, confusingly, runs on the *client*. A client may well change its mind, over time, about which server to use. This will happen if the server it is currently bound to goes

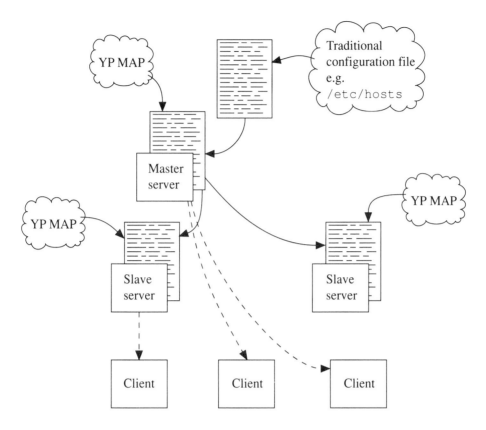

**Figure 3.5** NIS masters, slaves, clients and maps.

down, or simply becomes slow in responding. At any one time, however, the client uses the same server for *all* the maps. (It is possible, however, for a client to request map information from some domain other than the default.)

Figure 3.5 shows the relationship between masters, slaves, clients and maps.

### 3.3.3 The server side of NIS

On the NIS master server, the text files from which the maps will be derived are collected together in the directory /etc/yp. NIS maps are built from these files using the program makedbm. For details, look up makedbm(1). The general form of the command is simply:

```
makedbm   infile   outfile
```

Each line in the text file infile generates one record in the map. The first field of the line (up to the first white-space character) is taken to be the *key* of the record, and the remainder of the line is taken to be the value associated with that key. The output from makedbm is a pair of files called outfile.dir and outfile.pag. The .pag file holds the actual data and the .dir file contains the hashed index. Together, these two files make up the map. All the maps for each domain are placed in a single directory. For example, NIS maps for the domain bradway would be placed in the directory /var/yp/bradway. Note that a single server can hold maps for more than one domain. Knowing the domain name for which an enquiry has been received, the server simply selects the appropriate subdirectory of /var/yp.

A certain amount of massaging is usually required to get the original files into the right form for makedbm. For example, consider how the hosts.byaddr map is built from the hosts file. As mentioned above, hosts.byaddr is the map that is designed to be indexed 'by address'; i.e. it uses the IP address as the key.

For example, the following entry from the hosts file:

```
201.96.44.7      trillian  trilly
```

generates an entry in the hosts.byaddr map with '201.96.44.7' as the key, and '201.96.44.7 trillian trilly' as the associated data. As this example shows, it is conventional to repeat the key as part of the value. To do this, we need to get makedbm to see the input line

```
201.96.44.7      201.96.44.7      trillian  trilly
```

The awk utility (Aho *et al.*, 1988) excels at reformatting files in this way, and this particular task may be accomplished by the command

```
awk '{ print $1, $0 }' /etc/yp/hosts | \
makedbm  -  /var/yp/bradway/hosts.byaddr
```

Note the '-' as the first argument to makedbm which tells it to read standard input, in this case the output from awk. Some of the maps are rather harder to handle. For example, to build the hosts.byname map, the single hosts entry shown above must expand into the following *two* input lines seen by makedbm:

```
trillian    201.96.44.7      trillian  trilly
trilly      201.96.44.7      trillian  trilly
```

This may also be handled by awk. Other complications arise when the key field includes embedded white-space characters. These must be replaced by nonwhite-space characters (usually an underscore) before they are seen by makedbm. Another issue is the removal of comment lines which typically begin with '#'.

Figure 3.6 illustrates the building of an NIS map, and the resolver functions (described in Section 3.3.4) used to query it. For the standard maps handled by NIS, the commands needed to build the maps are provided with the system. For some really awesome examples of sed, awk and shell commands to prepare files for makedbm, take a look at the file /var/yp/Makefile, which controls the rebuilding of all the NIS maps.

Apart from creating the maps, the only other important issue on the NIS server machine is to ensure that the server ypserv is running. Usually this is started via an entry

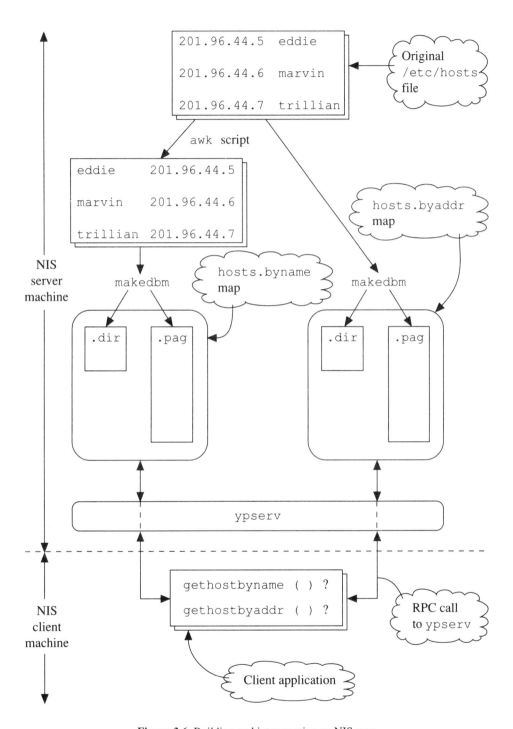

**Figure 3.6** Building and interrogating an NIS map.

in a boot-time script. `ypserv` is an RPC-based server. (We examine RPC-based servers in detail in Chapter 6.)

## 3.3.4 The client side of NIS

Client support for NIS is provided at three levels:

1.  Command line utilities for interrogating the maps.
2.  Library functions called *resolvers*, each designed for interrogation of a specific map.
3.  Low level general-purpose functions for map interrogation.

We will consider these three levels in turn.

At the command level the programs `ypcat` and `ypmatch` are available for interrogation of the maps. `ypmatch` performs a look-up for one or more keys in a specified map. For example, the command

```
ypmatch trillian eddie hosts.byname
```

will search for hosts `trillian` and `eddie` in the `hosts.byname` map, returning the associated values.

The command `ypcat` is used to 'read out' the entire map. For example, the command

```
ypcat passwd.byname
```

will display the complete `passwd.byname` map, and is equivalent to typing

```
cat /etc/passwd
```

on machines that are not running NIS. As another example, the command

```
ypcat hosts.byname | fgrep '200.14.97.'
```

may be used to find all hosts on the net `200.14.97`. Note that this is a much less efficient way to search the host's database than the `ypmatch` example because the entire map is shipped from the server to the local machine and searched locally, rather than performing a look-up of the map on the server. In this example, this is the best we can do, because we are searching for something (the network address) that is not a key of the map.

By default, `ypcat` and `ypmatch` both consult the maps from the NIS domain to which the local machine belongs. Both commands accept a `-d` flag to specify an alternative domain.

The middle level of client support within NIS consists of a library of so-called *resolver* functions that are available to the application programmer. We will examine the resolvers which interrogate the maps derived from the file `/etc/passwd` as an example. As for the `hosts` file, there are two maps: `passwd.byname` which uses the user name as the key, and `passwd.byuid` which uses the numeric user ID as the key. To interrogate these maps, three resolver functions are provided:

1. getpwuid() takes a numeric user ID as argument and returns the corresponding value from the passwd.byuid map.
2. getpwnam() takes a user name as argument and returns the corresponding value from the passwd.byname map.
3. getpwent() takes no argument. By calling it repeatedly, successive entries from the map are returned.

Each of these functions returns a pointer to a passwd structure which contains the map entry broken out into its various fields, each stored in a member of the structure. This behaviour is typical of the resolvers for each of the maps, as summarized in Table 3.2, which shows the most commonly used maps, their resolvers and the type of structure returned.

Let us return to the resolvers for the passwd maps to provide a more detailed example. These resolvers return a pointer to a passwd structure which is declared as follows:

```
struct passwd {
        char    *pw_name;    /* User name */
        char    *pw_passwd;  /* Encrypted password */
        /* Next two are ints in some versions */
        uid_t   pw_uid;      /* Numeric user ID */
        gid_t   pw_gid;      /* Numeric group ID */
        char    *pw_age;
        char    *pw_comment;
        char    *pw_gecos;   /* Personal info about user */
        char    *pw_dir;     /* User's home directory */
        char    *pw_shell;   /* User's shell */
};
```

The members of this structure (with the exception of pw_age and pw_comment) correspond to the fields within the /etc/passwd file. Here is a sample entry:

```
chris:ESwxx94NP32V.:21:90:Chris Brown:/eddie/chris:/bin/csh
```

Let us see how the getpwuid() resolver may be used to map numeric user IDs back on to user names. Here is a short program called getusername which takes a numeric user ID as an argument, and shows the corresponding user name:

```
#include <pwd.h>

main(int argc, char *argv[])
{
    struct passwd *pwp;
    int id = atoi(argv[1]);

    pwp = getpwuid(id);
    if(pwp != 0)
        printf("User ID %d is %s\n", id, pwp->pw_name);
    else
        printf("User ID %d unknown\n", id);
}
```

**Table 3.2**

| Map | Resolvers | Structure |
|-----|-----------|-----------|
| group | getgrent(), getgrid(), getgrname() | group |
| passwd | getpwent(), getpwuid(), getpwnam() | passwd |
| hosts | gethostent(), gethostbyaddr(), gethostbyname() | hostent |
| services | getservent(), getservbyport(), getservbyname() | servent |
| networks | getnetent(), getnetbyaddr(), getnetbyname() | netent |
| rpc | getrpcent(), getrpcbynumber(), getrpcbyname() | rpcent |

Here is an example run:

```
eddie% getusername 21
User ID 21 is chris
eddie%
```

As a real example of use, when you execute the command `ls -l`, the `ls` program uses `getpwuid()` to show file ownerships as user names rather than numeric IDs.

Historically, many of these resolver functions existed before NIS. Originally, of course, they obtained their information simply by searching the local configuration files. The NIS versions of the resolvers are smart enough to revert to scanning the local file if the NIS system is not running, i.e. if they cannot bind to a server for their domain. This is important because it makes NIS transparent to the application programmer. The programmer uses the resolvers in the same way whether the look-up is in a local file or via a remote server. Indeed, programs do not even need relinking with different resolvers to move between NIS and non-NIS environments. An important design consideration for NIS was backwards-compatibility with the old way of looking up the local files.

In some cases, the NIS map completely replaces the traditional local configuration file. The `hosts` and `services` maps are in this category. In other cases, the NIS map *supplements* the entries held in the local file. The `passwd` and `group` maps are handled this way. This allows each machine to have a private, machine-specific set of accounts (defined in the local `/etc/passwd` file), and a communal shared set of accounts (defined in the NIS maps). Special notations are used in the `/etc/passwd` and `/etc/group` files to tell the resolvers to go to the NIS maps for further entries. The simplest notation is just a line starting with a '+' sign. For example, here is an (abridged) example of the `/etc/passwd` file on an NIS client:

```
root:1zEKufan5EbjQ:0:1:Operator:/:/bin/csh
uucp::4:8::/var/spool/uucppublic:/usr/lib/uucp/uucico
sync::1:1::/:/bin/sync
ftp::499:499:Anonymous Ftp:/douglas/anon_ftp/:/usr/ucb/ftp
+::0:0:::
```

The four accounts listed in this file are private to this machine. The last line, beginning with the '+', cues the resolver to look in the NIS map for further entries.

Fancier notations are available; for example, it is possible to include *specific* users or groups of users from the NIS map. It is important to realize that these facilities are simply bells and whistles implemented by the resolvers. They are not handled by the NIS server.

The resolvers are built on top of a number of low level NIS client functions which provide a generic interface to the NIS look-up service. There are quite a number of these functions. They are described in detail in `ypclnt(3)`. We will content ourselves with a look at just two of them:

1.  `yp_get_default_domain()` returns the name of the local machine's default NIS domain. This is needed by the `yp_match()` call, described below, and by several other client functions.
2.  `yp_match()` specifies a domain, a map name and a key, and returns the value associated with that key. Note that `ypmatch()` simply returns the value as an uninterpreted text string. It knows nothing of the internal structure of this string, and does not attempt to pick it apart into fields. That is left to the resolvers.

These two functions are illustrated in Figure 3.7. The following section provides examples of using these functions.

## 3.3.5 Home-made maps and resolvers

In this section we will bring together many of the issues already discussed by showing how to develop NIS maps and resolvers for a database of the user's devising. We will use a rather frivolous database giving a list of North American versus British vocabulary differences.

---

**An aside:** it has been said that America and Britain are two nations divided by a common language. Of course, the differences go deeper than mere discrepancies in vocabulary. I remember trying to explain to American friends about 'bonfire night', a curious English festival held on November 5th. 'There was this Guy Fawkes . . .' I began. 'Fawkes who?' they asked.

---

Here is an abridged version of the database, which we assume begins life as a simple text file called `words`. Each line consists of the British word followed by the American word. For simplicity, we have avoided entries that contain embedded white-space.

```
autumn        fall
bonnet        hood
boot          trunk
car           automobile
chemist       pharmacy
chips         fries
cradle        bassinet
```

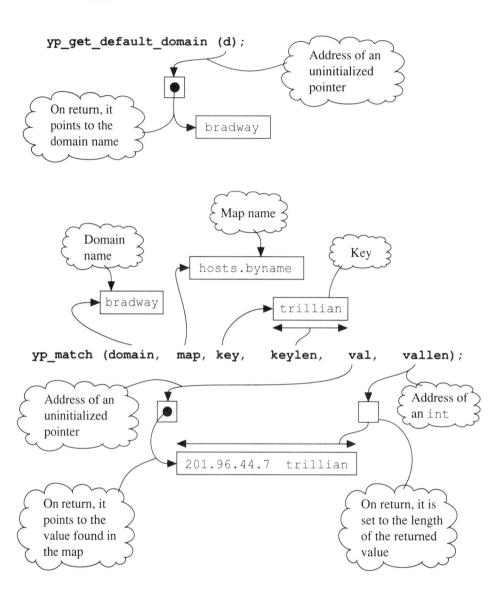

**Figure 3.7** Low level NIS client functions.

```
exhaust      muffler
film         movie
fringe       bangs
garden       yard
handbag      purse
hire         rent
```

```
holiday      vacation
lift         elevator
lorry        truck
motorway     freeway
nappy        diaper
notes        bills
pavement     sidewalk
petrol       gas
pram         baby-carriage
push-chair   stroller
railway      railroad
roundabout   rotary
rubber       eraser
rubbish      trash
sacked       fired
saloon       sedan
sweets       candies
tick         check
trousers     pants
windscreen   windshield
wing         fender
```

We will begin by creating the maps on the NIS server. There will be two maps, words.byuk, which uses British words as the key, and words.byus, which uses American words as the key. The text file as it stands is fine as input to makedbm to build the words.byuk map. The words.byus map is a little harder; it needs the key and value reversing. We use awk for this. Thus, the following commands will build the maps:

```
makedbm  words  words.byuk
awk '{ print $2, $1 }' words | makedbm - words.byus
```

Notice that neither map replicates the key string as part of the value. For example the value associated with the key petrol in the words.byuk map is simply gas. We will need to bear this in mind when we write the resolvers.

We now have four new files:

```
words.byuk.dir
words.byuk.pag
words.byus.dir
words.byus.pag
```

To make them accessible to ypserv we must copy them into the directory for the NIS domain of which they are a part. This operation needs root privilege. If this is a new domain, we must also create the subdirectory. In this example, bradway is the domain name:

```
mkdir  /var/yp/bradway
cp words.by* /var/yp/bradway
```

Assuming `ypserv` is already running, no other steps are needed to add the new maps to the system. However, to make the map easier to maintain we should add an entry to the NIS `Makefile` so that the map may be readily rebuilt if it needs to be changed. We will do this in Section 3.3.6.

We can immediately access the new map from a client using either `ypmatch` or `ypcat`. For example:

```
eddie% ypmatch  fall  words.byus
autumn
eddie%
```

To provide proper support on the client side we need to write resolver functions. Following the naming convention for such functions, we will call them `getwordbyuk()` and `getwordbyus()`. Despite the frivolity of the example we will try to make our resolvers have a similar 'look and feel' to the standard NIS resolvers. Here is a manual page for them:

```
NAME
        getwordbyuk, getwordbyus - get word list entry

SYNOPSIS
        #include "words.h"

        struct wordent *getwordbyuk(char *ukword);

        struct wordent *getwordbyus(char *usword);

DESCRIPTION
        getwordbyuk() and getwordbyus() each return a pointer to an
        object with the following structure containing the broken-out
        fields of a line in the words database.

          struct  wordent {
              char *w_uk;      /* String containing British  word */
              char *w_us;      /* String containing American word */
          }

DIAGNOSTICS
        A NULL pointer is returned if the word is not found in the
        database, or if the database cannot be located.

RESTRICTIONS
        The information returned is contained in a static area which
        is overwritten on each call.
```

Here is the implementation. First, the header file which simply defines the `wordent` structure:

```
/* word.h */

struct wordent {
```

```
    char *w_uk;    /* String containing British  word */
    char *w_us;    /* String containing American word */
};
```

Now, the resolver functions themselves. Two details to note here are that the key string is *not* replicated as part of the value returned by `yp_match()`; the return value is simply the 'translated' word. Secondly, the value is returned with a newline appended. We replace this with a null terminator.

```
struct wordent *getwordbyuk(char *ukword)
{
    static struct wordent item;
    int val_len, i;
    char *domain;

    item.w_uk = ukword;
    if(yp_get_default_domain(&domain) != 0)
        return (struct wordent *) NULL;
    if (yp_match(domain, "words.byuk", ukword, strlen(ukword),
            &item.w_us, &val_len) != 0)
        return (struct wordent *) NULL;
    /* Remove the trailing '\n' */
    item.w_us[val_len] = '\0';
    return &item;
}

struct wordent *getwordbyus(char *usword)
{
    static struct wordent item;
    int val_len;
    char *domain;

    item.w_us = usword;
    if (yp_get_default_domain(&domain) != 0)
        return (struct wordent *) NULL;
    if (yp_match(domain, "words.byus", usword, strlen(usword),
            &item.w_uk, &val_len) != 0)
        return (struct wordent *) NULL;
    /* Remove the trailing '\n' */
    item.w_uk[val_len] = '\0';
    return &item;
}
```

Lastly, a small test harness to show that everything works:

```
main()
{
    struct wordent *w;
```

```
    w = getwordbyuk("bonnet");
    if (w != (struct wordent *)NULL)
        printf("getwordbyuk gave %s: %s\n", w->w_uk, w->w_us);
    else
        printf("getwordbyuk failed\n");

    w = getwordbyus("sidewalk");
    if (w != (struct wordent *)NULL)
        printf("getwordbyus gave %s: %s\n", w->w_uk, w->w_us);
    else
        printf("getwordbyus failed\n");
}
```

The output when this program is run appears as follows:

```
getword.byuk gave bonnet: hood
getword.byus gave pavement: sidewalk
```

## 3.3.6  Administrative components of NIS

In this section we will examine those parts of NIS that are the province of the system administrator. Our treatment will be brief, since administration is not the prime focus of this book. For a much more detailed discussion, see Stern (1991).

The shell script `ypinit` is used to initialize the NIS system, both on the master server (-m flag), and on the slave servers (-s flag) and in some versions, on the clients too (-c flag). On the master server, `ypinit` queries the user interactively for a list of slave servers and builds a special map called `ypservers` from this list. It creates a subdirectory in /var/yp for the domain, then uses the `Makefile` in /var/yp to generate initial copies of all the maps.

The file /var/yp/Makefile handles all the nitty-gritty details of building the maps. Files with names of the form `mapname.time` are used as timestamps to record when each map was last built. The `Makefile` is heavily parametrized, with variables used for the names of the various NIS management commands, and the system directories. Here is the additional `Makefile` entry to rebuild the two maps from our 'words' database:

```
words.time:     $(DIR)/words
        $(MAKEDBM) $(DIR)/words $(YPDBDIR)/$(DOM)/words.byuk
        awk '{ print $$2, $$1 }' $(DIR)/words | \
        $(MAKEDBM) - $(YPDBDIR)/$(DOM)/words.byus; \
        touch words.time; \
        echo "updated words"; \
        if [ ! $(NOPUSH) ]; then \
            $(YPPUSH) words.byuk; \
            $(YPPUSH) words.byus; \
            echo "pushed words"; \
        fi

words: words.time
```

If a map is to be rebuilt, all the system administrator normally needs to do is edit the text file from which the map is derived, `cd` into the `/var/yp` directory, and type `make`.

Things get a little more complicated if there are slave servers in the domain. Additional commands are used to ensure that the slaves receive copies of any maps that have been updated on the master. The `ypxfr` utility is run on the slave to obtain an up-to-date copy of a map. It contacts the master server, walks through the entries in the master server's map, and rebuilds a map of its own from the data thus received. `ypxfr` is normally invoked under two circumstances:

1. When a map has been rebuilt on the master server, and an explicit `yppush` command has been issued from the master to the slave server. There are two lines in the sample `Makefile` entry shown above concerned with the execution of `yppush`.

2. In response to entries in the system `crontab` file, which is used to schedule activities which need to occur on a regular basis. Typically, scripts with names such as `ypxfr_1perday` are started up by the `crontab` entry. These scripts simply contain a sequence of `ypxfr` commands. For example:

```
ypxfr group.byname
ypxfr group.bygid
ypxfr protocols.byname
ypxfr protocols.bynumber
```

Having these `crontab` entries ensures that a slave server does not miss out on an update entirely if it happened to be down when the master did a `yppush`.

Under SVR4 UNIX, the file `/var/yp/aliases` may be used to give 'nicknames' to the maps. For example, an entry of the form:

```
words   words.byus
```

allows the map name `words` to be used in place of `words.byus` in commands such as `ypcat` and `ypmatch`, as well as in the low level NIS client functions. In other implementations, a fixed set of nicknames is built into the `ypcat` and `ypmatch` commands themselves.

## 3.3.7 Limitations of NIS

As we have discussed, NIS was developed as a system administration aid, to avoid the replication of configuration data across a group of workstations under common administrative control. It was designed to be backwards compatible with the 'old way' of doing things – applications which thought they were querying local files such as `/etc/hosts` needed to be relinked but still worked after NIS was installed. In the context of this motivation, NIS is a great success. Viewed more generally as a 'network information service', however, NIS does have some strange design features and limitations:

1. NIS is highly asymmetric with respect to reading and writing the maps. Reading is very efficient, even for huge maps. It is available to any client, and is supported at a variety of levels on the client side. Writing is not supported within the NIS protocol, and is a cumbersome process, involving the regeneration of the entire map on the master server, and the propagation of the complete new map to any slave servers. In general, these operations require `root` privilege and are carried out manually by the system administrator. The `passwd` map is an exception. To allow users to change their passwords, a `yppasswd` command, operating in conjunction with a `yppasswdd` daemon on the master NIS server, is provided. Even so, a full map rebuild is needed to incorporate a single change of password.

2. There are no access controls. Any NIS map is accessible to any client. There is no way to say things such as 'this map is owned by Jenny and is only accessible to Jenny and members of her group'.

3. There is no local caching of 'frequently asked questions' in the clients. Of course, this helps ensure that all clients see consistent copies of the data, but it is inefficient in that every time a resolver is called, network traffic is generated to contact the NIS server.

4. The NIS maps are centralized. NIS is sometimes called a 'distributed database system', but this description is misleading. The data are *not* distributed across many machines, they are held on a single system. That is the whole point. For groups of machines where updates to the database are all made via a central authority (the system manager) this is fine. Consider, however, the problem of providing a database of name-to-IP address mappings for every host on the Internet. There are simply too many hosts, they are changed too frequently, and by too many people, for a centralized database to be even remotely practical. What is needed in this case is a truly distributed database, in which specific servers are responsible for keeping authoritative data on only a portion of the entire system. The Domain Name Service (DNS) is an example of such a system. The *Global Directory Services* of OSF/1, based on the ISO X.500 standard, is another example.

## 3.3.8 NIS+

A new network information service, NIS+, introduced by Sun into Solaris 2.1, is designed to overcome the previously mentioned limitations of NIS. The complexity of NIS+ warrants a complete chapter in its own right but, briefly, its key advantages are as follows:

1. Within NIS, a domain represents a set of machines under a central administrative control. There is no way to delegate authority to administer *parts* of the domain. NIS+ uses hierarchical domain names, similar to the hierarchical machine names used on the Internet. For example, the Widget Corporation might have NIS+ domains `widget.com` (the top level domain, containing company-wide information) and subdomains `sales.widget.com`, `eng.widget.com`, and so forth.

2. Maps are replaced by *tables*. The tables have multiple columns, and any number of columns may be designated as 'searchable'. For example, a single `hosts` table can be used to support both `gethostbyname()` and `gethostbyaddr()` look-ups. Separate 'byname' and 'byaddr' maps are not needed. The tables have names within the hierarchical name-space, for example, `personnel.sales.widget.com`. Each table has a 'schema' specifying the table layout – the number of columns, which of the columns are searchable, and which of the columns is to be considered case-sensitive in searches. Figure 3.8 illustrates the structure of the NIS+ domains and tables.

3. Look-up operations on NIS tables can specify search criteria for multiple columns of the table. An *indexed name*, such as `[name=helen,site=hemel],personnel .sales.widget.com` specifies search criteria for table columns `name` and `site` in the `personnel` table in the `sales.widget.com` domain.

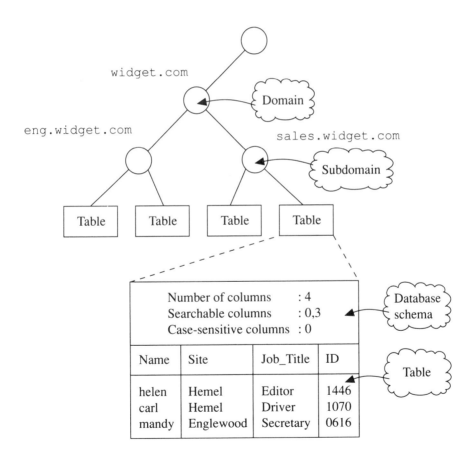

**Figure 3.8** NIS+ domains and tables.

4.  The NIS+ server uses authentication data passed as part of the RPC call to identify the user making the request. Using that identity, the server establishes access rights for the requester. Access rights in tables can be granted at three levels: for the table as a whole, for a specific entry (row) in the table and for a specific column. There are four access rights – read, modify, create and destroy – and four classes of user – (1) the object's owner, (2) the object's group owner, (3) all other users who are known to NIS+ and can be authenticated and (4) users who are not authenticated to NIS+. Clearly, this provides a great deal of flexibility. As a specific example, it can make available `passwd` file entries to all authenticated users, except for the encrypted password field, which might be made readable only by requesters with `root` identity.

5.  It is possible, in principle, to replace the underlying database engine used by the NIS+ server with a user-supplied system. The functions forming the server-to-database interface are described in the `nis_db(3N)` manual page in the Solaris documentation. A default *structured storage manager* is provided as the database engine.

The benefits of NIS+ will probably be felt largely by system administrators, with most programmers continuing to use the usual resolver functions such as `getpwuid()` as their main interface to it, and most end-users remaining unaware of its existence. For building user-defined network databases, NIS+ provides a lot of functionality, but has a correspondingly complex user interface, with in excess of forty client functions. Whether it will achieve popularity as a general-purpose network information service remains to be seen.

A more detailed overview of NIS+ may be found in McManis (1991).

# 3.4 Distributed file systems

Many network services can be thought of as making *code* available across the network. That is, they provide access to the functionality of a specific remote program. A distributed file system, on the other hand, is concerned with making *data* available across the network. As such, it is one of the most general-purpose, and certainly the most heavily used, of all network services.

In this section we will look primarily at one particular distributed file system technology: NFS. We will see how the traditional file system concepts in UNIX have been extended across the network. We will examine the server, client and administrative aspects of NFS, we will look at how NFS affects the programmer, and we will consider some of its limitations.

NFS was developed by Sun Microsystems and introduced in 1984. Sun placed the protocol specifications in the public domain (see RFC 1094), and promoted NFS heavily (and very successfully) as a vendor-independent distributed file system. Since then, NFS has been widely embraced by the UNIX industry and there can be few, if any, UNIX vendors who do not support it.

**An aside:** at a recent meeting of the UK UNIX Users' Group a show of hands was taken of the number of people using distributed file systems. Almost all of the 250 delegates were using NFS. The number of people using RFS (Remote File Sharing – the main competitor to NFS in the UNIX world) was zero. Of course such samplings may be biased. A poll of the number of people sporting beards and wearing sandals would probably also have returned a surprisingly high figure!

## 3.4.1  Local and remote mounts

Even back in the early days, long before networks, UNIX had a way of piecing a file system together from separate physical parts in a largely transparent way. This was important, because the disk drives on the minicomputers where UNIX grew up had capacities of typically 2.5 or 5.0 Mbytes, and it was commonplace to have the file system spread across two, three or four drives. (You may laugh, but believe me, they were a great step forward after paper tape.) Nowadays, a small UNIX system might use, say, a single 330 Mbyte SCSI (Small Computer Systems Interface) drive. Nonetheless, even if there is only a single drive, it is common practice to divide that drive into two or more different *partitions*. Although these partitions are rotating around the same spindle, they are effectively treated as separate devices. Each partition has a separate device file entry in the `/dev` directory, and each has its own file system complete with its own inode table. For example, the names `/dev/dsk/c0t1s0`, `/dev/dsk/c0t1s1` and `/dev/dsk/c0t1s2` might refer to partitions 0, 1 and 2 of drive 1 on controller 0.

These pieces of the file system are assembled by *mounting* devices onto directories. Figure 3.9 shows an example in which the file system is built from three parts: partitions 1 and 2 on disk drive 0, and partition 0 (the whole disk) of drive 1. The partition that contains the top level of the directory hierarchy, including the root directory, is called the *root partition*. Within that partition, empty directories are created to act as *mount points* for the other partitions.

The mount operations are performed via the `mount` command. For example:

```
mount   /dev/dsk/1s0   /users
```

would mount the partition `/dev/dsk/1s0` onto the directory `/users`. Thereafter, a file may simply be referenced as (for example) `/users/sue/something`, and the UNIX kernel, in trying to locate this file, will note that `/users` is a mount point, and will continue the look-up of the filename on the mounted partition.

None of this has anything to do with networking, or with distributed file systems. However, the concept of piecing a file system together by mounting disk partitions generalizes rather nicely to the network situation. Using NFS, it is possible to mount part of a remote machine's file system tree onto a local directory. Figure 3.10 shows a small file system distributed between two machines, `venus` and `pluto`. The home directories for users bob and tom are on `venus`, whilst those for users sue and jim are on `pluto`. Two

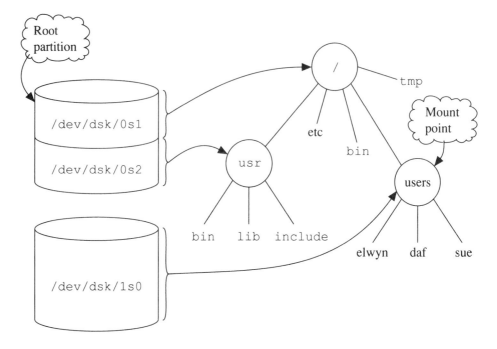

**Figure 3.9** Disk partitions and mount points.

remote mounts are used to make each set of home directories accessible on the other machine. Remote mounts are performed by a variation of the mount command. The general form is:

```
mount   -F nfs  machine:/remote_dir   /local_dir
```

In the situation shown in Figure 3.10, each machine performs one local and one remote mount. For example, on venus:

```
mount  /dev/dsk/0s1  /venus
mount -F nfs pluto:/pluto  /pluto
```

Notice that the mount points /venus and /pluto are named after the machine whose file system is mounted at that point. It is not essential to do things this way, but it is a convention that minimizes confusion, is easily extended to more machines and (perhaps most importantly) maintains the same view of the file system tree on all machines. For example, tom sees his home directory as /venus/tom whichever machine he has logged on to. Be aware, however, that NFS does not enforce or guarantee a globally consistent view of the file system; it is up to the system administrator to set things up this way.

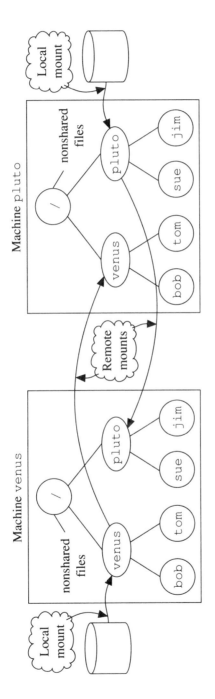

**Figure 3.10** A distributed file system.

The example of Figure 3.10 shows clearly that machines are not necessarily *purely* NFS servers or NFS clients. In the situation shown, each machine is a server for some parts of the file system, and a client for other parts.

## 3.4.2 Server and client components of NFS

Two daemons must be present on an NFS server machine:

1.  `nfsd` – this daemon retrieves NFS requests for file operations from the network and passes them to the local disk system. It is normal to run multiple instances of `nfsd` to allow a degree of concurrency in processing NFS requests. Each daemon processes one packet from the network at a time, passing it to the disk subsystem. Small systems typically run four or eight daemons; high performance dedicated NFS servers may run as many as fifty. To achieve genuine concurrency it is also necessary for the server to have multiple disk drives (on multiple controllers), and perhaps multiple network interfaces too.
2.  `mountd` – this daemon is responsible for servicing remote mount requests, as well as implementing some form of access control. Because mounting is a (relatively) infrequent operation, there is only one instance of this daemon.

On the client side, the NFS software is hardly visible to the user. Other than `mount`, there is no command-level utility that the user invokes to contact the NFS service, in the way that, for example, `rsh` is used to contact the `rshd` server. Instead, most of the client side of NFS is inside the kernel, which intercepts system calls from user processes to operate on remote files, and converts these into requests which are sent to the `nfsd` on the server from which that file is mounted.

To improve performance, clients normally run several instances of a daemon called `biod` – typically four or eight. These daemons perform read-ahead and write-behind on behalf of processes using NFS files.

Although the `nfsd` and `biod` servers are visible to the user (they will show up on a `ps` listing, for example), they barely have any existence as user processes, and spend all their time executing inside the kernel. Indeed, the only reason for having them exist as user processes at all is to provide the kernel some way of maintaining the context for multiple concurrent threads of execution through these services. In most versions of UNIX, the kernel does not support multi-threading internally. In Solaris 2.1, which does support kernel multi-threading, the `biod` daemons are not used.

To provide a uniform way of applying operations such as `open()`, `read()` and `write()` to both local and remote file systems, UNIX uses a data structure called a `vnode`. The vnode is a per file data structure which is allocated within the kernel for each open file, current directory, etc. It provides an interface to a 'virtual file system' (VFS) object, and contains an array of pointers to functions that support a standard set of operations on files in that file system. Lying 'behind' the vnode can lie multiple file system types. In the context of the present discussion, the important distinction is between local and remote (NFS mounted) file system types, but the idea can be generalized to provide multiple types for both local and remote file systems. For example:

1.  The s5 file system which is derived from the original System V system.
2.  The UFS file system which derives from the so-called 'fat fast file system' developed at Berkeley. This is the most efficient and commonly used UNIX file system, but SVR4 for example supports both s5 and UFS file systems.
3.  The PCFS file system which provides access to DOS files, either on floppy disks imported from PCs or (when UNIX is run directly on the PC) on other partitions of the hard disk.
4.  The TMPFS file system which is essentially a 'RAM disk' providing fast access to temporary files which are not required to survive a reboot. Sometimes mounted on /tmp.
5.  The HSFS (High Sierra File System) which supports file systems on CD-ROM.
6.  The block and character devices. Of course, devices were integrated into the file system long before vnodes were invented, through the use of 'device special files'.
7.  The NFS file system, as discussed in this section.
8.  The RFS file system, an alternative file-sharing technology.

Within each file system type, a per file data structure appropriate to that file system is maintained. For an MS-DOS file system, for example, we have pcnodes. For a normal UNIX file system, we have inodes. For a remote file system, we have rnodes. Figure 3.11 illustrates the vnode and the various file system types which may lie behind it, and Figure 3.12 shows the relationships between the client and server components of NFS.

## 3.4.3  The NFS protocol

The NFS protocol defines the set of file system operations supported by the server, along with the format of the requests sent by the client and the format of the replies. Before looking at details we note three key points about the protocol:

1.  NFS is built using the RPC protocol, which in turn relies on the XDR, external data representation. As a result of this, the protocol is independent of specific machine architecture and data representation differences. All of these issues are discussed in Chapter 6.
2.  The set of file system operations defined by NFS is not UNIX-specific (although it must be said that it *is* somewhat UNIX-oriented, and it *does* assume a tree-structured file system). NFS server and client implementations exist for several other operating systems; one commonly used product is PC-NFS, which provides a client (only) implementation for DOS machines.
3.  The NFS protocol is *stateless*. In other words, an NFS server does not need to retain any state information from one NFS transaction to the next. This implies that each NFS request must be complete in itself, containing all the information required to perform it. The RPC calls themselves are made using a connectionless delivery protocol (UDP). This fits in nicely with the statelessness of the protocol.

The statelessness of NFS has the important practical advantage that a server (or the network) can go down temporarily without the clients having to take special recovery

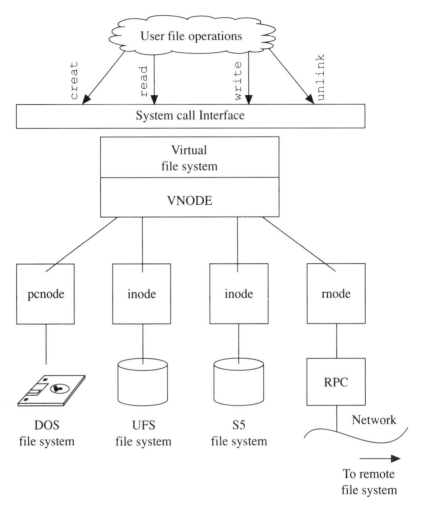

**Figure 3.11** The virtual file system.

action – they simply retry their requests until the server or network recovers. (Most UNIX users will have seen message sequences like

```
NFS server mickey not responding ... still trying
NFS server mickey OK
```

which can sometimes occur even if a server is simply overloaded and slow in responding.)

An important concept in the NFS protocol is the *file handle*. This is a data structure which is meaningful only on the server; its internal format is not specified by the protocol, and it is *opaque* to the client. That is, the client cannot make any sense of it. The

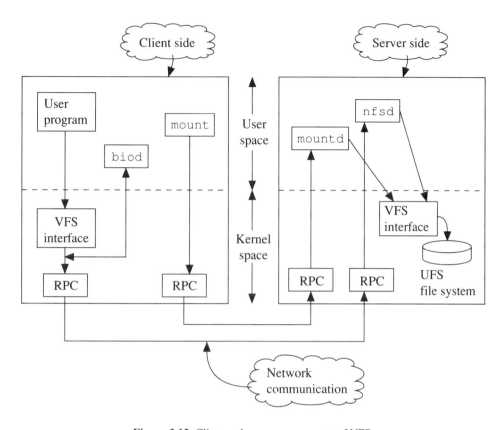

**Figure 3.12** Client and server components of NFS.

file handle contains all the information needed by the server to identify a file, and is passed in each NFS call that needs to reference a file or directory. As an example, on a UNIX-based server the file handle might contain the inode number of the file along with the major and minor device numbers of the disk partition on which it resides.

Table 3.3 gives a list of the RPC procedures defined by the NFS protocol, and a brief description of each. This list corresponds to version 2 of the protocol, as defined in RFC 1094. We will illustrate the use of these NFS procedures with a simple example. Returning to the scenario of Figure 3.10, suppose that a process running on `venus` wishes to read the file `/pluto/jim/jobs`.

When it opens the file, the local UNIX system begins a search along the components of the pathname, constructing a vnode for each (if there is not one already) as it goes. The following sequence of events occurs (see Figure 3.13):

1. The root directory '/' is searched for the file `pluto`.
2. Noting that this is a mount point, the local machine contacts the `mountd` daemon on the server from which the file system is mounted, requesting a file handle for the directory `/pluto` on the server.

**Table 3.3**

| Server operation | Description |
| --- | --- |
| NFSPROC_NULL | Does nothing except 'succeed'. A mandatory procedure in all RPC servers, so clients can test if the server is active. |
| NFSPROC_GETATTR | Returns the attributes (ownerships, access modes, timestamps and type) of a file. |
| NFSPROC_SETATTR | Sets (some of the) attributes of a file. |
| NFSPROC_LOOKUP | Looks up a file (specified by name) in a directory (specified by file handle) and returns a handle for that file. |
| NFSPROC_READLINK | Returns the contents of a symbolic link. |
| NFSPROC_READ | Reads a specified number of bytes from a file (specified by file handle). Note that the file offset at which the read starts must be passed with *every* read request, unlike the UNIX read() system call which implicitly continues reading 'where the last one left off'. Since NFS servers are stateless, they cannot maintain knowledge of their clients' file offsets. |
| NFSPROC_WRITE | Writes a specified number of bytes to a file (specified by file handle). As for NFSPROC_READ, a file offset is passed on every request. |
| NFSPROC_CREATE | Creates a file with a specified name in a directory (specified by file handle), and gives it a set of initial attributes (specified in the call). |
| NFSPROC_REMOVE | Removes a file (specified by name) from a directory (specified by file handle). |
| NFSPROC_RENAME | Renames a file (and like the UNIX mv command, it may move the file to a different directory). |
| NFSPROC_LINK | Creates a new link (specified by name) in a directory (specified by file handle) to an existing file (specified by file handle). |
| NFSPROC_SYMLINK | Creates a symbolic link. A symbolic link is a file containing the *pathname* of another file. This pathname is interpreted by the *client*, not by the server. |
| NFSPROC_MKDIR | Creates a directory with a specified name in a directory (specified by file handle). |
| NFSPROC_RMDIR | Removes an (empty) directory with a specified name from a directory (specified by file handle). |
| NFSPROC_READDIR | Returns directory entries (essentially a list of file names) from a directory (specified by file handle). |
| NFSPROC_STATFS | Returns information about the file system containing a given file (specified by file handle). The information includes the size of the file system, the number of free blocks and the 'optimum transfer size' for READ and WRITE requests to the server. |

3.  mountd returns a handle (h1, say).
4.  The local machine sends an NFSPROC_LOOKUP request to the nfsd server to find the file named jim in the directory specified by handle h1.
5.  The nfsd server returns another handle (h2, say).
6.  The local machine sends an NFSPROC_LOOKUP request to the nfsd server to find the file named jobs in the directory specified by handle h2.

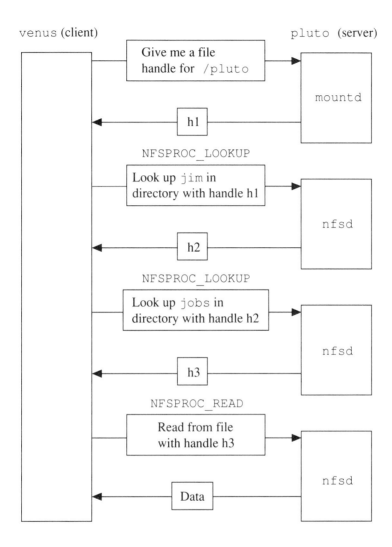

**Figure 3.13** NFS transactions required to read /pluto/jim/jobs.

7.  The nfsd server returns another handle (h3, say).
8.  Finally, the local machine sends an NFSPROC_READ request to the nfsd server requesting data from the file specified by handle h3. The request includes an explicit starting offset in the file, and a byte count.
9.  The server sends the data.

By looking up the pathname components in turn, the NFS protocol itself never has to deal with pathnames such as /pluto/jim/jobs, so it has no inbuilt assumptions about whether the server's operating system uses pathname syntax like `/pluto/jim/jobs` or `\pluto\jim\jobs` or even `jobs@jim@pluto`.

You may have observed that there are no procedures called `NFSPROC_OPEN` or `NFSPROC_CLOSE` to correspond to the UNIX system calls `open()` and `close()`. The server, being stateless, has no concept of holding a file open for a client. When a file is opened (on the client side), the client will perform a `LOOKUP` operation and obtain a handle for the file. When data are written to an open file, any buffering takes place at the client end. At the server end, `write` operations are synchronous. That is, when the `write` returns, the client can assume that the data are safely on disk, even if the server were to crash immediately afterwards. This requirement makes writing somewhat less efficient than reading for NFS files.

## 3.4.4  The administrative components of NFS

Conceptually, NFS is straightforward to administer. There is a configuration file on the servers which controls file system availability and another on the clients which determines which file systems will be mounted at boot-time. We will briefly examine these two files. On large networks (several tens of servers and several hundred clients) system managers must find ways of configuring NFS such that the effort involved in maintaining the configuration is not proportional to the number of hosts on the network. That is, administrative methods that involve going round manually and 'doing something' at each host are not practical. A good reference for NFS administrators is given at the end of this section.

All network services provide some form of access control, and NFS is no exception. Access control within NFS exists at two levels:

1.  The file `/etc/exports`, or on some systems `/etc/dfs/sharetab`, is used on NFS servers to restrict which of their file systems may be remotely mounted, and by which clients.
2.  Once a file system is remotely mounted, normal UNIX 'rwx' access controls are applied for individual files. (The RPC protocol used by NFS uses `AUTH_UNIX` credentials, which allow the server to know the user and group ID of the process making the request. For more details of this mechanism, see Chapter 6.)

The exact syntax of the `/etc/exports` file and the range of options supported vary a little from one implementation to another. At minimum, the syntax contains a list of directories on the local machine that we are willing to 'export', i.e. that are available for mounting by remote clients. This example is taken from SunOS 4.1:

```
/home1
/bucket                 -root=jeltz:trillian
/var/spool/pcnfs        -access=peecee:faraday
/cdrom                  -ro
```

Taken in order, these entries say the following:

1. The directory `/home1` can be mounted by any client.
2. The `/bucket` directory may be mounted by any client, and `root` retains super-user privilege if accessing this file system from `jeltz` or `trillian`. This point is discussed further in Section 3.4.6.
3. The directory `/var/spool/pcnfs` can be mounted by clients `peecee` and `faraday`.
4. The directory `/cdrom` can be mounted read-only by any client.

Information about the status of NFS may be obtained using the `showmount` command.

```
showmount  -e
```

may be used on a server to obtain a list of exported file systems, and

```
showmount  -a
```

gives a list of all currently mounted file systems. In SVR4, the `dfshares` command is also available; it shows RFS mounted file systems as well as NFS. Note that these administrative commands may be in obscure directories such as `/usr/etc` which are not on your search path.

So much for the servers. On NFS clients, remote file systems may be mounted in one of three ways:

1. By explicit use of the `mount` command, as in the example in Section 3.4.1. This method might be used to mount a removable medium such as a floppy disk manually, or to mount remote file systems on a 'trial' basis. It is not used as the normal way of assembling a distributed file system.
2. Via entries in the 'file system table', either `/etc/fstab` or `/etc/vfstab`, depending on the version of UNIX. These entries are read in response to a `mount  -a` or `mountall` command, again depending on version. This is the normal method used to establish permanent mounts at boot-time.
3. Via the *automounter*, a program that mounts file systems on demand, and unmounts them again if they are not accessed within a few minutes. Automounter operation is controlled through a set of automounter *maps* which can be either local files or NIS maps. This is the preferred method of setting up a distributed file system if there are many servers, as it avoids establishing large numbers of cross-mounts at boot-time. It also scales well to large networks, because the maps that determine what gets mounted where can be administered centrally and distributed via NIS.

As an example, here is a simple `/etc/fstab`, again taken from SunOS 4.1:

```
/dev/sd0a              /                4.2 rw          1 1
/dev/sd0g              /usr             4.2 rw          1 2
douglas:/usr/man       /usr/man         nfs ro,bg,soft  0 0
marvin:/usr            /marvin          nfs rw,bg        0 0
magrathea:/usr         /magrathea       nfs rw,bg        0 0
```

```
desiato:/disk1      /disk1      nfs rw,bg      0 0
desiato:/disk2      /disk2      nfs rw,bg      0 0
```

The fields in this file are as follows:

1. The name of the local disk partition, or the name of the remote file system, to be mounted.
2. The mount point (within the local file system).
3. The file system type. '4.2' means a Berkeley file system; more modern versions would call this type 'UFS'.
4. Special options used when mounting. Here, `rw` means read/write, `ro` means read-only. The `bg` option requests that mounts be retried in the background if they fail the first time. This can be useful to prevent a bunch of servers from deadlocking if they all try to boot and cross-mount each others' file systems at the same time. The `soft` option controls the behaviour of an NFS client if a request times out. Normally (on a `hard` mount, which is the default) the client will retry the request indefinitely. On a `soft` mount, the client-side NFS returns an error to the program if the request times out. This point is discussed further in Section 3.4.5.
5. Two numbers which control dumping and checking of the file system. These are not of interest to us here, except to note that they should both be zero for NFS-mounted files.

The automounter maps provide much the same information. Here are two sample entries:

```
/disk1          -rw  desiato:/disk1
/usr/man        -ro  desiato:/usr/man trillian:/local/man
```

The first field specifies the directory (on the client machine) at which the mount is to occur. The `-rw` and `-ro` entries are options passed to the `mount` command. The next field specifies the name of the remote machine and the file system on that machine which is to be mounted. The second line illustrates a useful feature of the automounter: it is possible to specify alternative servers. In this example, a user on the local machine would have access to the `/usr/man` directory if *either* of the hosts `desiato` or `trillian` were available.

An excellent reference for the NFS system administrator is Stern (1991).

## 3.4.5 The programmer's view of NFS

NFS provides a very high degree of transparency both to the programmer and to the end user of the file system. Those system calls that manipulate files, such as `open()`, `close()`, `read()`, `write()`, `lseek()` and `unlink()`, work the same with local and remote files. As a result, command level utilities for performing file system housekeeping, such as `cp`, `mv`, `rm` and `ln`, work identically with local and remote files. Consequently, there is very little that the programmer needs to know about NFS.

Performance is one issue. NFS provides good performance for reading, not quite so good for writing. This is because the NFS specification says that the data must actually have reached the disk before a `write()` call is acknowledged back to the client. Record locking is particularly inefficient. Some programs which do a lot of record locking can work fine on local files but become unusably slow when applied to NFS mounted file systems.

There are a few curiosities in the behaviour of the UNIX file system which are difficult or impossible to emulate using NFS, and which might possibly break 'old' UNIX programs that rely on them. For example, UNIX lets you delete open files. The file remains accessible to the process that has it open, even though it has no entry in the file system, and does not completely disappear until it is closed. The NFS server, being stateless, cannot do this. Also, UNIX checks file access permissions only when a file is opened. If a process has write permission on a file, and has opened it, it will still be able to write to that file even if some other process removes write permission in the meantime. The NFS server, however, checks access permissions on every read or write.

Soft-mounted file systems (mounted using the `soft` option in the `/etc/fstab` file) can present problems to the programmer. Operations such as `read()` and `write()` on soft-mounted file systems may time out and return errors if the NFS server is down, or just very busy. The programmer should be prepared to catch such errors, and retry the operation if necessary. Many 'network naïve' programs treat any error return on a `read()` operation as meaning 'end of file' and simply stop processing. Writing to soft-mounted file systems is especially problematic; some versions of the `mount` manual page advocate that only read-only file systems should be soft mounted.

## 3.4.6  User identity mapping with NFS

When access is made to an NFS mounted file, access permission checks are applied on that file's server to determine if you have read, write or execute permission on the file. (We assume that the NFS server is a UNIX system.) Your numeric user identity, as defined on the local (NFS client) machine, is used in determining these access permissions. Usually, system administrators are careful to keep user IDs consistent (so that a given user always has the same user ID) across a group of machines that share files via NFS. If the machines all use the same NIS map to obtain their account information, this consistency is of course assured. Occasionally, however, inconsistently configured machines can cause surprises. Consider the two machines A and B configured as shown in Figure 3.14, which we assume have cross-mounted each other's user file system using NFS.

The figure shows a cut-down version of the password file on the two machines – we are only interested in the mapping from user name to numeric user ID. Also shown are a few sample files on each machine; here, we are interested only in the file names and ownerships (as would be shown by an `ls -l` on that machine).

Suppose stuart is logged in on machine A. He appears as the owner of the local file `rum` and the remote file `coffee` on machine B. Why? Because his numeric user ID is 36,

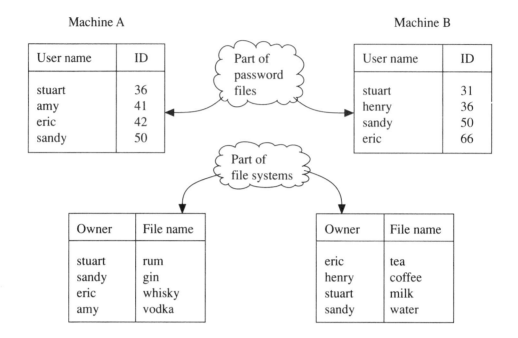

**Figure 3.14** Inconsistent user ID allocation.

and those two files have user ID 36 as their owner. On the other hand if stuart logs in on machine B he has user ID 31 and owns the file `milk` (only). The point is: when you reach across into a remote file system, it is your numeric user ID that remains constant, not your login name. When an `ls -l` command displays the owner of a file, it maps the numeric user ID of the owner back to the user name by looking it up using the `getpwuid()` resolver on the *local* machine. So an `ls -l` executed on machine B to list the files on machine A would show that `rum` was owned by henry, and `gin` was owned by sandy. It would be unable to find user names for the files `whisky` and `vodka` because the user IDs 41 and 42 do not appear in its password file, and would simply report the numeric user ID in the 'owner' column of the listing.

The only user for whom life is sane on these two machines is sandy, because she has the same user ID on both. The situation depicted in this example is clearly intolerable, and stresses the importance of maintaining consistent user IDs across machines which share files using NFS.

This rule about keeping the same user ID when you reach across for a remote file does not apply to the super-user. His numeric ID, by definition, is 0, but on the remote machine it is mapped to the value −2. On many systems there is actually an entry in the password file for this user ID, under the name `nobody`. In some systems, the user ID is defined as an `unsigned short` and the user ID for `nobody` is consequently defined to be

65534. In any event, the ID is intended to represent a miserable wretch who owns no files at all. This can lead to a curious situation where remote files accessible to you under your normal account become inaccessible to you if you are logged in as `root`.

Some implementations support an option in the `/etc/exports` file to allow a remote super-user to retain his identity when he accesses your local file system from specified hosts. For example, the entry

```
/usr/gnu  -root=neptune:pluto
```

allows `root` to access the local `/usr/gnu` file system with `root` privilege from machines `neptune` and `pluto`.

## 3.4.7 Limitations of NFS

NFS does not maintain any kind of central agent to keep track of which file systems are available from which servers. Servers do not 'advertise' or 'register' the file systems they are willing to export. A client cannot simply make requests like 'I want to mount the manual pages' or 'I want to mount the C libraries for MIPS architecture'; the client must know *which server* these resources may be found on. Following on from this, there is no way to specify a backup server in the way that slave servers can be designated for NIS. If a client has its manual pages mounted from the host `titan`, and `titan` is down, then the client cannot access the manual pages, even if other servers on the same network have them available. Similarly, it is not easy to move file systems from one server to another (to help balance the disk space load, for example). Every client needs to know about the change. (Using the automounter helps here, because it can centralize NFS mounting information in an NIS map.) All of these issues are primarily for the system manager.

There are some functional issues, too. When a server is working its way down the components of a pathname to locate a file for a client, if it should come across a directory which is itself a mount point for a remote NFS file system, it does not 'follow the link' to the other server. In other words, an NFS server can only export file systems which reside on its own disks, *not* those of other servers.

NFS does not support *caching* of file data on the client, even for read-only file systems. Every client access to a remote file results in network traffic to the server. However, the read-ahead performed by the `biod` daemons helps here. When NFS was invented, small client-side disks were usually quite slow – slower than the network bandwidth – so that client-side caching would have made little difference to performance. Disk drives have got much faster since then, and small high performance disks on NFS clients have become the norm. In this context, client-side caching of file system requests makes a lot of sense.

Finally, NFS does *not* provide access to remote devices.

# 3.5  File and record locking

## 3.5.1  The need for record locking

Within a distributed application it is common to have several processes writing and reading a shared file. To ensure the consistency of the data in the file, it is sometimes necessary to guarantee that a sequence of file updates are performed 'atomically'; that is, once a process begins an update, it must be sure that it can complete it without interference from other processes. Similarly, it is sometimes necessary to prevent processes from obtaining an inconsistent view of data by reading parts of a file whilst some other process is in the middle of an update. Purely *read-only* sharing of files is generally not a problem.

We will illustrate the problem with a simple example, a toy airline seat reservation program. Suppose that an airline keeps a record of seat availability for its flights in a file seatfile. The file contains a sequence of binary records, indexed by flight number. Each record is simply an integer giving the number of seats currently available for that flight.

To sell a seat on a flight we must perform the following operations:

1. Open the seat file.
2. Seek to the record for the required flight.
3. Read the current number of seats.
4. Decrement it.
5. Write it back to the file.

Here is a program called sellseat to perform these operations:

```
/* Sell seat program -- no record locking */

#include <stdio.h>
#include <sys/types.h>
#include <sys/stat.h>
#include <fcntl.h>

main(int argc, char *argv[])
{
    int flight, seats, fd;

    fd = open("seatfile", O_RDWR);
    if (fd<0) {
        perror("cannot open seat file");
        exit(2);
    }

    if (argc != 2) {
        printf("usage: %s flight_number\n", argv[0]);
        exit(1);
    }
```

```
    flight = atoi(argv[1]);

    lseek(fd, flight*sizeof(int), SEEK_SET);
    read (fd, &seats, sizeof(int));
    seats--;
    sleep(1);  /* To increase likelihood of a problem */
    printf("%d seats remaining on flight %d\n",
            seats, flight);
    lseek(fd, (off_t)(flight*sizeof(int)), SEEK_SET);
    write(fd, &seats, sizeof(int));
    close(fd);
}
```

The program is designed to be invoked with a single numeric argument, specifying the
flight number for which the seat is to be sold. The code contains a `sleep(1)` call,
intended to simulate the processing that a real-world application would perform during
the transaction.

To get things started we need a couple of administrative programs. The first,
`seatcreate`, is used to create the seat file in the first place, and to enter an initial
allocation of seats for each flight. Here it is:

```
/* Utility to initialize seatfile */

#include <stdio.h>
#include <sys/types.h>
#include <sys/stat.h>
#include <fcntl.h>

main(int argc, char *argv[])
{
    int numflights, numseats, i, fd;

    if (argc != 3) {
        printf("usage: %s flights seats\n", argv[0]);
        exit(1);
    }

    /* Create the seat file, read/write by owner only */

    fd = open("seatfile", O_RDWR | O_CREAT, 0600);
    if (fd<0) {
        perror("cannot open seat file");
        exit(2);
    }

    numflights = atoi(argv[1]);
    numseats  = atoi(argv[2]);

    for (i=0; i<numflights; i++)
        write(fd, &numseats, sizeof (int));

    close(fd);
}
```

The program expects two arguments; for example:

```
seatcreate 6 230
```

will create a seat file containing six records, each of which is initialized to the value 230.

The second program, `seatlist`, simply lists the seat availability for all flights. Here it is:

```
/* Utility to list seat file contents */

#include <stdio.h>
#include <sys/types.h>
#include <sys/stat.h>
#include <fcntl.h>

main(int argc, char *argv[])
{
    int numseats, fd, i=0 ;

    /* Open existing seat file */

    fd = open("seatfile", O_RDWR);
    if (fd<0) {
        perror("cannot open seat file");
        exit(1);
    }

    while(read(fd, &numseats, sizeof(int)) > 0)
        printf("flight%4d: %4d seats available\n",
                i++, numseats);
    exit(0);
}
```

The following dialogue illustrates the operation of these programs:

```
eddie% seatcreate 6 230              # Create initial seat file
eddie% ls -l seatfile
-rw-------   1 chris     other    24 Mar 11 17:57 seatfile
eddie% seatlist                      # Examine the initial file
flight   0:  230 seats available
flight   1:  230 seats available
flight   2:  230 seats available
flight   3:  230 seats available
flight   4:  230 seats available
flight   5:  230 seats available
eddie% sellseat 3                    # Sell two seats on flight 3
229 seats remaining on flight 3
eddie% sellseat 3
228 seats remaining on flight 3
eddie% seatlist                      # Examine new seat availability
```

```
flight    0:   230 seats available
flight    1:   230 seats available
flight    2:   230 seats available
flight    3:   228 seats available
flight    4:   230 seats available
flight    5:   230 seats available
eddie%
```

So far, so good. The problems arise when we run two instances of `sellseat` concurrently:

```
eddie% sellseat 3 & sellseat 3
227 seats remaining on flight 3
227 seats remaining on flight 3
eddie%
```

What has happened here? The first instance of `sellseat` has read the seat count for flight 3 (the number 228) and blocked on its `sleep()` call. The second instance of `sellseat` has read the same number (228) from the file. Each instance has then decremented the number, and written it back to the file. In effect, the same seat has been sold twice.

---

**An aside:** this whole example is dedicated to those readers who have spent hours pacing airport departure lounges because their flight was overbooked. This is not because airlines have never heard of record locking. It is because they deliberately sell more tickets than the plane has seats.

---

## 3.5.2 The `flock()` and `lockf()` locking functions

The ability to lock a file to prevent this kind of problem was, for many years, absent from UNIX, and a long-running intellectual debate raged about if and how it should be implemented. The argument was not so much over whether record locking was needed – there was little question over that – but about whether it should be provided *inside the kernel* or as a user-level service. To quote one commentator: 'The kernel needs to provide record locking about as much as it needs to provide trigonometric functions' (Rochkind, 1985). Despite these arguments, UNIX *did* acquire kernel-based locking mechanisms. BSD added the `flock()` system call, and System V introduced the `lockf()` function. Of these two, `flock()` is the more primitive. It supports only the locking of entire files, rather than specific sections of them. The locking it provides is only *advisory*, not *mandatory*. (We will explain the difference shortly.) And thirdly, it has never been extended to work across the network. For these reasons, we will confine our discussion to the System V `lockf()`-style call.

The `lockf()` call is illustrated in Figure 3.15. For details, look up `lockf(3)`. Strictly speaking, `lockf()` does not provide *record* locking, because UNIX has no notion of file records. Instead, it provides a totally general mechanism which allows locks to be placed on any specified byte range within the file. To lock (or unlock) a range within a file, we must first lseek() to the beginning of the range and then call lockf(), specifying the size (in bytes) of the range to be locked. A negative size implies that the locked range is to extend backward (i.e. towards the beginning of the file) from the current file offset position. There is no requirement to unlock exactly the same size range as was originally locked. For example, I might lock bytes 1000–2000 of a file, then unlock bytes 1400–1500. That will leave me with *two* locked ranges, one from 1000–1399, and another from 1501–2000.

Here is our sellseat program with record locking added. All that is new are the two calls to lockf():

```
/* Sell seat program --  with record locking */

#include <stdio.h>
#include <sys/types.h>
#include <sys/stat.h>
#include <fcntl.h>
#include <unistd.h>

main(int argc, char *argv[])
{
    int flight, seats, fd;

    fd = open("seatfile", O_RDWR);
    if (fd<0) {
        perror("cannot open seat file");
        exit(2);
    }

    if (argc != 2) {
        printf("usage: %s flight_number\n", argv[0]);
        exit(1);
    }

    flight = atoi(argv[1]);

    lseek(fd, flight*sizeof(int), SEEK_SET);
    lockf(fd, F_LOCK, sizeof(int));     /* NEW */
    read (fd, &seats, sizeof(int));
    seats--;
    sleep(1);
    printf("%d seats remaining on flight %d\n",
            seats, flight);
    lseek(fd, (off_t)(flight*sizeof(int)), SEEK_SET);
    write(fd, &seats, sizeof(int));
    lockf(fd, F_ULOCK, -sizeof(int));   /* NEW */
    close(fd);
}
```

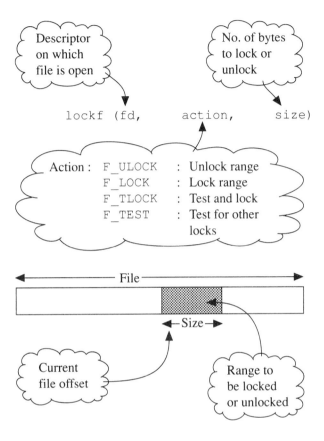

**Figure 3.15** The lockf() function.

Note that we lock a 'positive' range (following the current file offset) and unlock a 'negative' range (preceding the current file offset). This is because the intervening write() has moved the file offset to the end of the locked range. With this modification, concurrent instances of the program behave correctly:

```
eddie% sellseat 3 & sellseat 3
227 seats remaining on flight 3
226 seats remaining on flight 3
eddie%
```

Now, both instances of sellseat correctly decrement the seat count.

### 3.5.3 Advisory vs. mandatory locking

The locking used in the above example is termed *advisory*. It works only if the programs wishing to share the file agree to abide by the rules – that is, to call lockf() at the beginning and end of the critical region of code. Some other program which simply rushes ahead and writes to the file will not be prevented from doing so by the lock.

In later versions of System V UNIX, the mechanism was extended to support *mandatory* locking. Rather than extend the lockf() call itself, a cunning (if somewhat bizarre) method was devised to determine if the locks on a file should be considered mandatory. The trick concerns the file's 'access mode'. If a file has the 'set group id' bit *on*, and the group execute permission bit *off*, then locking on that file is mandatory. This combination is one that was deemed to be inappropriate in normal use. For details, look up chmod(2). Newer versions of the chmod command provide a special permission flag, +l, to set this mode combination. Similarly, newer versions of ls -l display an 'l' in the 'group execute' permission position if mandatory locking is enabled. For example:

```
eddie% chmod 644 seatfile
eddie% ls -l seatfile
-rw-r--r--   1 chris     other      24 Mar 13 18:05 seatfile
eddie% chmod +l seatfile
eddie% ls -l seatfile
-rw-r-lr--   1 chris     other      24 Mar 13 18:05 seatfile
eddie%
```

When mandatory locking is enabled, any attempt to read or write a locked range will block until the lock is released. This implies that every read and write operation must be checked by the kernel on a file for which mandatory locking is enabled.

### 3.5.4 Network-wide lock management

How are file locking operations extended to operate across the network? Here, multiple clients on different hosts may be competing for file locks. The design goal is clear – the network should remain transparent. That is, locking of records in remote files should be done in the same way as the locking of records in local files. One approach would be to include additional commands in the NFS protocol to support the acquisition and release of file locks. However, this would violate the important NFS design goal of statelessness. Locks are, by definition, state information held by the server.

To avoid compromising the statelessness of NFS, network-wide record locking is handled by a separate protocol and a separate lock manager daemon, lockd. The lockf() function passes lock requests to the local lockd daemon. If the request relates to a remote file, the local lockd makes an RPC call to the lockd on the NFS server where the file is held. This process is illustrated in Figure 3.16.

Locking information for a file is therefore held by the lockd daemon on the NFS server where the file resides. Since this is inherently stateful, a problem arises if the server crashes. When the server reboots, how does it recreate the state information about the locks it holds on behalf of its clients? To tackle this, one further daemon, statd, is used. statd monitors machine status. When client machine A establishes a lock on a file served from machine B, it informs machine B's statd that it has an interest in machine B's state. This information is held on machine B in the file /etc/sm.bak (or /var/statmon/sm.bak under Solaris). If B crashes, then subsequently reboots, its statd notifies the statd on all machines which have registered an interest in machine B's state. In turn, each statd notifies the clients that any locks they may have held are lost. Each client then has a 'grace period' (45 seconds by default) during which it may resubmit each lock request it previously held. During this period, the lock manager will only accept requests to reclaim previously held locks. It will not accept requests for new locks until after the end of the grace period. The reclamation of locks is handled automatically by the lockd daemon and is transparent to the user program. However, if the lockd daemon fails to re-establish a lock within the grace period on the client's behalf, the client will receive a SIGLOST signal.

If a client crashes and reboots, its statd informs the statd daemons on the NFS servers, which will cancel all the locks held by that client. Presumably, if the client application that obtained the lock in the first place is restarted, it will attempt to establish its locks from scratch.

This design is complicated and not entirely satisfactory, and most implementations are not bug-free. In particular, if a client crashes and does not recover (perhaps it is waiting for an engineer to come to replace the CPU card), any locks it held at the time of the crash will remain on the server (unless the server is rebooted), and may well prevent other clients from going about their business. To prevent this, some form of 'keep-alive' would need to

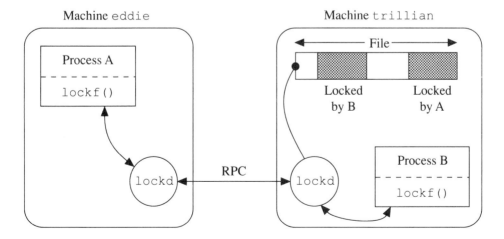

**Figure 3.16** Locking local and remote records.

be added to the `statd` protocol, whereby each `statd` would periodically poll each `statd` on every client which held locks on that machine. Lack of a response would indicate that the client was down, and that the server should cancel all locks held by that client. The problem with a periodic keep-alive is that it consumes network bandwidth.

# 3.6 Internet access utilities

The facilities described so far in this chapter are used primarily within local area networks, in which the hosts are typically all at the same site, and are connected by a high speed LAN such as ethernet. It is important to note, however, that there is no technical reason why the machines making up an NIS domain should not be spread throughout Europe, or why a machine in Boston should not lock a record in an NFS-mounted file on a server in San Francisco. That is part of the magic of layered network protocols – once you can get IP packets to flow between two machines, everything that is built on top automatically follows.

Having made the point, however, such usage is not the norm. In practice, communication between machines which are widely dispersed across the Internet is generally in one of three ways:

1.  Using `telnet`, which supports remote login.
2.  Using `ftp`, which supports file transfer.
3.  Using e-mail, which supports personal communication.

These utilities are designed to be more frugal in their use of bandwidth, and to operate between machines which are under totally independent administrative control.

## 3.6.1 `telnet`

The `telnet` client program, together with the `telnetd` server, provide remote login facilities across TCP/IP networks. The access controls are up to the server; if the server is a UNIX machine (which it often is, although it should be noted that the `telnet` protocol is *not* UNIX-specific), you must have an account on the remote machine, and are required to enter your user name and password just as for a local login. Some machines offer 'guest' login facilities which require no password; usually they provide a non-standard and very restricted shell. The `archie` server is an example. (A `telnet` session to `archie` is shown in Section 3.6.3.)

`telnet` is usually given the name (or the IP address) of the remote host as a command line argument. For example:

```
telnet  prep.ai.mit.edu

telnet  18.71.0.38
```

As mentioned above, `telnet` is not UNIX-specific. It also makes minimal assumptions about the type of terminal in use at the local end, and the type of terminal the programs at the remote end expect to deal with. It does this by defining a *network virtual terminal*, which is a kind of lowest common denominator for real-world terminals. The terminal capabilities may then be extended by negotiation between client and server. For details, look up `telnetd(1)` and RFCs 854 and 855.

Normally `telnet` connects to the `telnetd` server at the standard TCP port number 23. Optionally, it may be given an alternative port to use. For example:

```
telnet  localhost  1220
```

will connect to port 1220 on the local machine. Used in this way, `telnet` is a sort of general-purpose client which can be used to ferry lines of text back and forth to the server. This can be useful for testing text-oriented servers; we will see an example of this in Chapter 4.

## 3.6.2 FTP

FTP (the file transfer protocol) is both the name of a protocol, and of the client that implements it. The server, as you might guess, is usually called `ftpd`. The access control is similar to `telnet`, that is, you must have an account on the remote machine and you must supply your user name and password. However, there is an important exception to this, called *anonymous* FTP, discussed below. The `ftp` server is best thought of as a kind of mini-shell, offering a restricted repertoire of commands to browse the file systems and to send and receive (mostly receive) files. Some of these commands are listed below:

```
bye                Terminate the connection to the server, and exit
cd <dir>           Change directory to the directory <dir>
                   on the remote machine
lcd <dir>          Change directory on the local machine
dir                List the current directory on the remote machine
get <file>         Get the specified file from the remote machine
mget <files>       Get multiple files, using whatever kind of
                   file name wildcard expansion the remote system
                   offers
put <file>         Put the specified local file onto the remote system
mput <files>       Put multiple files, using file name wildcard
                   expansion, on the local system
```

Bear in mind that the remote machine is not necessarily running UNIX. For example, the result of a `dir` command may look like the familiar UNIX `ls -l` output, or it may not.

Anonymous FTP may be used to provide read-only access to files on machines on which you do not have an account. This mechanism is extensively used to retrieve files from the vast repository of public domain software, RFCs, news articles and other resources held on archive servers around the Internet. A small amount of special set-up is required on a server to 'activate' anonymous FTP; instructions are given, for example, in Nemeth *et al.* (1989) and in the manual page for `ftpd(1)`.

To use anonymous FTP on the client-side, the user simply connects to the server and logs in as user `anonymous`. He does not have to supply a valid password; sometimes he is asked to supply 'guest' as the password, sometimes he is asked to provide his e-mail address. The latter is typically only used for logging, rather than for authentication. (This is just as well, as the author finds it difficult to type his e-mail address accurately when echoing is turned off!) There is an example anonymous FTP session in Section 3.6.4.

## 3.6.3 Locating internet resources

The amount of source material held in Internet repositories is truly enormous. There is a huge amount of public domain software, much of it of high quality, such as the GNU software, including ANSI C and C++ compilers and debuggers, latex, perl, the X11R5 software, plus lots of contributed X software. There is a strong UNIX bias to this software, but not a complete monopoly. For example, there is software for MS-DOS, Windows, Macintosh and Atari. Much of the material is duplicated and held on many servers.

To help in locating this software, a number of sites operate a special service called *archie*, which was developed at the School of Computer Science at McGill University. Archie is well able to describe itself and we will allow it to do so by reproducing one of its help texts:

> Archie is a pair of software tools: the first maintains a list of about 600 Internet ftp archive sites. Each night software executes an anonymous ftp to a subset of these sites and fetches a recursive directory listing of each, which it stores in a database. We hit about 1/30th of the list each time, so each site gets updated about once a month, hopefully balancing timely updates against unnecessary network load. The 'raw' listings are stored in compressed form on `quiche.cs.mcgill.ca` (132.206.2.3), where they are made available via anonymous ftp in the directory `~ftp/archie/listings`.
>
> The second tool is the interesting one as far as the users are concerned. It consists of a program running on a dummy user code that allows outsiders to log onto the archive server host to query the database. This is in fact the program we call Archie.
>
> Users can ask Archie to search for specific name strings. For example, `prog kcl` would find all occurrences of the string 'kcl' and tell you which hosts have entries with this string, the size of the program, its last modification date and where it can be found on the host along with some other useful information. In this example, you could thus find those archive sites that are storing Kyoto Common Lisp. With one central database for all the archive sites we know about, archie greatly speeds the task of finding a specific program on the net.

Complete anonymous ftp listings of the various sites that we keep in the database may be obtained via the 'site' command and for a list of the sites which we keep track of, see the 'list' command.

Archie also maintains a 'Software Description Database' which consists of the names and descriptions of various software packages, documents and datasets that are kept on anonymous ftp archive sites all around the Internet. The 'whatis' command allows you to search this database.

A more recent service known as *gopher* makes the task of searching for Internet services somewhat easier, or at least, better integrated. Gopher is a distributed document location and delivery service. The user interface is in the form of a set of hierarchical menus, through which the user navigates. In essence, one is browsing a 'virtual hierarchical file system' of documents. A gopher server can be used to provide access to local (i.e. campus-wide or company-wide) documents such as the staff telephone directory, the campus bookshop's price list, and the location and opening hours of the libraries. When gopher servers 'know about' other gopher servers, the result is a 'gopherspace' of documents that can span the entire Internet. When used in this way, one of gopher's strengths is that it removes from the user any concern about where (i.e. on which host) the documents are located. The user simply navigates down the menus to find the required document.

For example, a user may select a top level menu item *books*, then *Shakespeare* from the next menu, *Midsummer Night's Dream* from the next, and *Act 1* from the final menu. Alternatively the user might have selected *books*, then *The Bible*, then *Romans*, then *Chapter 2*. The fact that the Bible and the complete works of Shakespeare are stored on machines in different continents is not noticeable to the user. Although gopher calls itself a distributed document delivery service, the term *document* needs liberal interpretation; *data source* might be a better description. In addition to plain text files, a data source might be a binary file or an image. It may also be a connection to a *search server* which can be interrogated to provide 'virtual directories' of documents matching user-specified criteria. A data source might even be a `telnet` connection to a specialized information service, typically offering yet another hierarchy of information to browse. For example, a local gopher server in the UK provides access to British Telecom's 'Electronic Yellow Pages' (EYP) service (a nation-wide trades and business services directory) via a `telnet` login under the account name `eyp`. Gopher integrates these varied and geographically dispersed data sources in a relatively seamless way. For more information, see Krol (1993).

Unlike `telnet` and FTP, gopher is generally not shipped as part of a standard UNIX distribution. However, source code for client and server implementations for a variety of platforms, including UNIX, Windows, Macintosh and VMS, is available from various archive servers (via anonymous FTP, of course!).

## 3.6.4 An example internet session

The following transcript of a simple internet 'session' is perhaps the best way of illustrating the use of these tools. First we will use anonymous FTP to retrieve an RFC document. Because computer programmers enjoy self-referential examples, we will obtain a copy of RFC 959, which describes the `ftp` protocol itself. Many sites archive the RFC; here we have chosen to go direct to the Network Information Center, `nic.ddn.mil`.

```
eddie% ftp nic.ddn.mil
Connected to nic.ddn.mil.
220-*****Welcome to the Network Information Center*****
    *****Login with username "anonymous" and password "guest"
Name (nic.ddn.mil:pc1crb): anonymous
331 Guest login ok, send "guest" as password.
Password:
230 Guest login ok, access restrictions apply.
ftp> cd rfc
250 CWD command successful.
ftp> ls
200 PORT command successful.
150 Opening ASCII mode data connection for file list.
rfc-by-author.txt
rfc-by-title.txt
rfc-index.txt
rfc10.txt
rfc1000.txt
rfc1001.txt
rfc1002.txt
```

... a very long list continued here ...

```
226 Transfer complete.
10069 bytes received in 25 seconds (0.4 Kbytes/s)
ftp> get rfc959.txt
200 PORT command successful.
150 Opening ASCII mode data connection for rfc959.txt (147316 bytes).
226 Transfer complete.
local: rfc959.txt remote: rfc959.txt
151249 bytes received in 14 seconds (11 Kbytes/s)
ftp> bye
221 Goodbye.
```

Next, let us retrieve some source code. Suppose we have read somewhere that a program we require, called `tcpd`, is available for anonymous FTP. (In fact, `tcpd` is just a small TCP test program, but it will suffice as an example.) Since we do not know *where* to find this program, we first conduct a `telnet` session to our nearest archie server, which in this example is at Imperial College, London.

```
eddie% telnet archie.doc.ic.ac.uk
Trying 146.169.11.3 ...
Connected to archie.doc.ic.ac.uk.
```

```
Escape character is '^]'.
        Welcome to the UK archie server

Login as archie for the archie service, enter control-d to abandon the login.
For general archive services connect to src.doc.ic.ac.uk (146.169.2.1)
which supports both anonymous-ftp and telnet with a login name of sources

erase character is DEL    erase line is control-U

archie.doc.ic.ac.uk (ttyp7) 11:04AM on Sunday, 17 January 1993
login: archie
This server is really meant for use by UK/European sites.  If you are not
in this area please try and find a nearer archie server.

archie.doc.ic.ac.uk [146.169.11.3]     UK/European  Imperial, London, UK
archie.funet.fi      [128.214.6.100]    European     FUnet, Helsinki, Finland
archie.au            [139.130.4.6]      Australian   Deakin, Geelong, Australia
archiecs.huji.ac.il [132.65.6.15]       Israel       Israel
archie.sura.net      [128.167.254.179]  World        SURAnet, Maryland, USA
archie.rutgers.edu   [128.6.18.15]      World        Rutgers, New Jersey, USA
archie.unl.edu       [129.93.1.14]      World        Lincoln, Nebraska, USA
archie.ans.net       [147.225.1.2]      World        ANS, New York, US
archie.mcgill.ca     [132.206.2.3]      World        McGill, Montreal, Canada

There are a lot of commands, use 'help' for details. Here is a barebones intro:
  set term TYPE    set terminal type. Eg 'set term vt100'.
  set pager        turns on output paging.
  set maxhits N    reset the number of hits returned (default 999)
  prog PATTERN     searches for matches.  Eg 'prog bios'.

If you have any problems/queries please email ukuug-soft@doc.ic.ac.uk
archie>
```

So far, that was all background information. Now we asked archie to locate `tcpd` for us. The list of sites it found ran to several hundred entries. Having found a fairly local site, we aborted the remainder of the listing.

```
archie> prog tcpd

Host ftp.uu.net    (192.48.96.9)
Last updated 03:02 16 Jan 1993

    Location: /systems/unix/bsd-sources/sys/tests/nfs/unix-tests/tools
      FILE      r--r--r--      985  Jan 10  1990   tcpd.c.Z

Host ftp.denet.dk   (129.142.6.74)
Last updated 04:30 15 Jan 1993

    Location: /mirror1/bsd-sources/sys/tests/nfs/unix-tests/tools
      FILE      r--r--r--      985  Jan 10  1990   tcpd.c.Z

Host wuarchive.wustl.edu   (128.252.135.4)
Last updated 04:03 10 Jan 1993
```

```
        Location: /mirrors4/4.3bsd-reno/sys/tests/nfs/unix-tests/tools
            FILE      r--r--r--      985  Jan  9  1990  tcpd.c.Z

    Host unix.hensa.ac.uk    (129.12.21.7)

    Last updated 03:37  9 Jan 1993

        Location: /pub/uunet/systems/unix/bsd-sources/sys/tests/nfs/unix-tests/tools
            FILE      r--r--r--      985  Jan 11  1990  tcpd.c.Z
```

. . . Many more entries were listed. However, having found one on a fairly local (UK) machine, we have what we need.

```
archie> bye
Connection closed by foreign host.
eddie%
```

The next step is to `ftp` to the site which archie found for us, and retrieve the file(s) we need:

```
eddie% ftp unix.hensa.ac.uk
Connected to unix.hensa.ac.uk.
220 nutmeg.ukc.ac.uk FTP server (Version 6.20 01 Oct 92 15:13:00) ready.
Name (unix.hensa.ac.uk:pc1crb): anonymous
331 Guest login ok, send e-mail address as password.
Password:
230-Please read the file README
230-  it was last modified on Wed Nov  4 15:43:50 1992 - 73 days ago
230 Guest login ok, access restrictions apply.
ftp> cd /pub/uunet/systems/unix/bsd-sources/sys/tests/nfs/unix-tests/tools
250-Please read the file README.Z
250-  it was last modified on Thu Jan 11 01:42:31 1990 - 1101 days ago
250 CWD command successful.
ftp> ls -l
200 PORT command successful.
150 Opening ASCII mode data connection for /bin/ls.
total 18
-r--r--r--  1 netlib         585 Jan 11  1990 Makefile.Z
-r--r--r--  1 netlib         376 Jan 11  1990 README.Z
-r--r--r--  1 netlib        1494 Jan 11  1990 dirdmp.c.Z
-r--r--r--  1 netlib        1066 Jan 11  1990 dirprt.c.Z
-r--r--r--  1 netlib        5320 Jan 11  1990 pmapbrd.c.Z
-r--r--r--  1 netlib         850 Jan 11  1990 pmaptst.c.Z
-r--r--r--  1 netlib        1025 Jan 11  1990 tcp.c.Z
-r--r--r--  1 netlib         985 Jan 11  1990 tcpd.c.Z
-r--r--r--  1 netlib        1018 Jan 11  1990 udp.c.Z
-r--r--r--  1 netlib         944 Jan 11  1990 udpd.c.Z
226 Transfer complete.
remote: -l
```

```
570 bytes received in 0.2 seconds (2.7 Kbytes/s)
ftp> binary
200 Type set to I.
ftp> get README.Z
200 PORT command successful.
150 Opening BINARY mode data connection for README.Z (376 bytes).
226 Transfer complete.
local: README.Z remote: README.Z
376 bytes received in 0.0046 seconds (80 Kbytes/s)
ftp> get tcpd.c.Z
200 PORT command successful.
150 Opening BINARY mode data connection for tcpd.c.Z (985 bytes).
226 Transfer complete.
local: tcpd.c.Z remote: tcpd.c.Z
985 bytes received in 0.2 seconds (4.8 Kbytes/s)
ftp> bye
221 Goodbye.
eddie%
```

At this point, back on our local machine `eddie`, we have the RFC we pulled from the Network Information Center, and the source code for `tcpd` . The latter is in a compressed format (the `.Z` at the end of the file name gives a pretty good hint of this) and must be uncompressed. This is true for many files in the Internet archives. The UNIX command `uncompress` replaces a '`.Z`' file with its uncompressed version, as the following dialogue shows:

```
eddie% ls
README.Z                rfc959.txt       tcpd.c.Z
eddie% uncompress tcpd.c.Z
eddie% uncompress README.Z
eddie% ls
README                  rfc959.txt       tcpd.c
eddie%
```

These examples hopefully show that accessing the Internet is relatively easy. What they cannot hope to show is the vast amount of archived material which is available. To the UNIX community, the Internet is a latter-day Aladdin's cave.

# Chapter 4

# Client–server programming using sockets

## 4.1 Underlying protocols

### 4.1.1 Introduction

The network services such as remote command execution and NIS discussed in the previous chapter are all provided for us as part of a normal UNIX distribution. In many cases, we access them using standard client programs such as `rsh` and `ypmatch`, and do not need to write any client code at all. In other cases, we write programs that access these services via special functions such as `rexec()` or `gethostbyname()` which provide a convenient interface to the service and hide most of the details of the low level protocol.

In this chapter, we will start to examine the business of providing new network services by writing our own servers and clients. In other words, we will begin to explore the mechanisms available to build distributed applications which operate across the network. This requires us to work at a slightly lower level than client wrappers such as `rexec()` and `gethostbyname()` – we will need to devise our own application protocol, and we will need to deal directly with our 'transport provider', i.e. those underlying parts of the networking software that perform the humble but important task of simply transporting data between machines. These low level data-transporting services are themselves organized in layers, forming what is known as a *protocol stack* beneath the user's application program.

We do not need to know much about the physics of internal combustion engines to drive a car. However, knowing a little about what goes on under the bonnet (or hood!) can make it easier to understand the finer points of motoring, helping us to see, for example, why it is a bad idea to press the brake and the accelerator at the same time. In a similar way, we do not need to know much about these lower 'transport provider' layers in order to write distributed applications – we merely need to be grateful for them. However, there are a few details of the transport provider of which we ought to be aware. In particular, we need to understand the difference between a connectionless transport and a stream transport, and we need to know about the addressing schemes that are used. Consequently, we begin this chapter with a brief discussion of the underlying network protocols.

164

## 4.1.2 Protocol stacks

Figure 4.1 shows a simple example of a protocol stack. The top boxes, marked FTP Client and FTP Server, are examples of application programs that usually execute in 'user space'. That is, they are not part of the kernel, they are programs that we write, compile and execute in the normal way. The middle two layers of the stack, marked TCP and IP, usually reside primarily in the kernel, although a small part of them may be implemented as library functions which are linked into the application program. The bottom layer of the stack, marked ethernet, is almost always implemented in hardware on a network interface card.

The client and server in this example communicate using the file transfer protocol. We saw examples of this protocol in Section 3.6.4. The protocol, of course, defines the format of the messages that pass between the server and the client, and conceptually we do indeed imagine that client and server 'talk to one another' directly. This direct

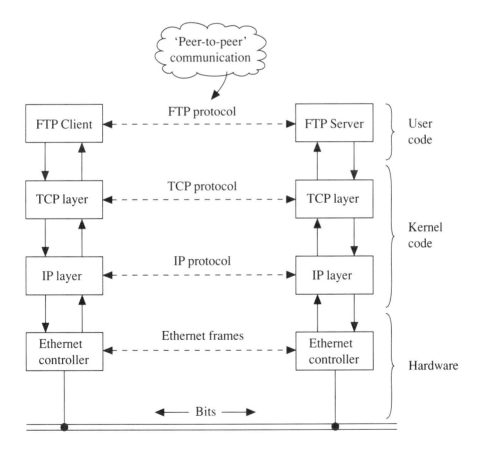

**Figure 4.1** A typical protocol stack.

communication is an illusion. In reality, the data pass down the protocol stack at the sending end, and back up the stack at the receiving end. Entities at the same level in the protocol stack are called *peers*, and the (conceptual) communication between them is called *peer to peer* communication.

We see that a programmer writing an application such as the FTP server therefore needs to understand two separate interfaces:

1.  The peer-to-peer application protocol, i.e. the format and meaning of the messages that pass between server and client.
2.  The interface to the transport provider layer (TCP in this example) in the kernel. This interface consists of a small number of system calls and/or library routines through which the application obtains the services of the transport provider.

Real-world application protocols are usually rather complicated, and the code to implement them is correspondingly lengthy. The examples in this chapter are deliberately chosen to de-emphasize the application-specific part of the code by making the application protocols really simple. We are learning how to place a telephone call, not how to sell double glazing to the guy at the other end.

## 4.1.3 The ethernet layer

What do these lower layers of the protocol stack actually do? We will begin by examining the lowest layer shown in Figure 4.1 – the ethernet layer. This corresponds approximately to the bottom two layers (the physical layer and the data link layer) of the ISO OSI reference model (Tanenbaum, 1988). The ethernet layer is concerned with the transmission of units of data (called frames) between machines that are on the same physical network. Figure 4.2 shows the format of these frames. Briefly, the fields are as follows:

1.  A preamble which is simply a bit sequence intended to help the receiving interface get into synchronization.
2.  A 48-bit destination address (sometimes called the physical address) which is used to specify which network interface the frame is intended for. Each interface has its physical address 'hard-wired' in, so that it knows which frames to receive and which to ignore.
3.  A 48-bit source address indicating which machine the frame came from.
4.  A type field that contains a 'magic number' indicating which higher level protocol this frame is being carried on behalf of. For example, a value of 800 (hex) indicates an IP packet, 6003 (hex) indicates a Decnet Phase-4 packet, and 809B (hex) indicates an Appletalk packet. This type field is important in enabling multiple vendors' protocols to coexist on the same physical network.
5.  The data. In the case of TCP/IP this will be an IP datagram – or a fragment of one.
6.  A 32-bit cyclic redundancy check (CRC) field which allows the receiving network interface to verify that the frame has not been corrupted.

| Preamble | Destination address | Source address | Packet type | Data (e.g. IP datagram) | CRC |
|----------|---------------------|----------------|-------------|-------------------------|-----|
| 64 bits | 48 bits | 48 bits | 16 bits | 368–12 000 bits | 32 bits |

**Figure 4.2** Ethernet frame format.

## 4.1.4 Data encapsulation

Included within the frame, of course, is a field for the actual data being carried on behalf of the layer above. This field has a variable length. Here we see an example of an important concept in protocol stacks – *encapsulation*. Encapsulation is the addition of header (and sometimes trailer) information to a packet of data by a layer. The header contains just the information needed for that layer to do its job, i.e. to deliver the packet to the 'peer entity' at the other end. The process of encapsulation can be seen occurring at each layer of the protocol stack, as shown in Figure 4.3. The packet grows longer as the headers are progressively added to it on its way down the protocol stack at the sending end. Each layer's header becomes part of the lower layers' data. At the receiving end, the headers are progressively stripped off at each layer, once they have done their job.

The following analogy may help. Chris wishes to send a letter to Helen, who lives in Oxford. He writes the letter and passes it to his secretary with the instructions 'Please send this to Helen'. The secretary, knowing that she cannot simply send a loose sheet of paper through the post, puts the letter into an envelope, writes Helen's address on the front, and sticks a stamp on. The letter is now ready to be committed to the mercy of the postal service. Next day (with any luck), Helen's secretary receives the letter. She takes the letter out of the envelope, throws the envelope away, and hands the letter to Helen. This analogy has two important characteristics:

1. Neither Chris nor Helen ever see the envelope.
2. Neither secretary needs to read the letter.

In a similar way, each layer of a protocol stack is not aware of the header added by the lower layer, and each layer does not attempt to interpret the data that have been handed down from the layer above – it merely sets about delivering them to the peer entity at the other end. The data are sometimes described as *opaque*.

---

**An aside:** applications such as `rlogin` which ferry single characters across the net as they are typed make very inefficient use of network bandwidth. Each one-byte message has acquired a total of 74 bytes of 'packaging' by the time it reaches the network cable. One is reminded of the deplorable surfeit of packaging we see nowadays in the distribution of food and many other items, and is led to wonder if a more ecologically minded implementation of TCP/IP might be written which saves the old headers for reuse.

Before leaving the ethernet layer, we should note that ethernet is by no means the only physical medium used to transport data around UNIX networks, although it is dominant. Other standards such as IEEE 802.5 (Token Ring) and ANSI X3T9.5 (FDDI) are also in use. The IEEE 802.3 standard is very similar to ethernet, but has not been widely embraced by the UNIX community. Although the frame formats used by these standards are not identical to ethernet, the basic ideas are much the same – header and trailer information which includes both the source and the destination physical address, surrounding a variable length data field.

## 4.1.5 The IP layer

Proceeding a level further up the protocol stack, we find the Internet protocol (IP) layer. This layer (which corresponds approximately to the network layer in the OSI seven layer reference model) is also concerned with transporting packets from one machine to another, but adds a very important capability over the ethernet layer – it facilitates the routing of the packet through intermediate gateway machines, if necessary. Thus it allows data to be sent to machines that are not directly connected on the same physical network.

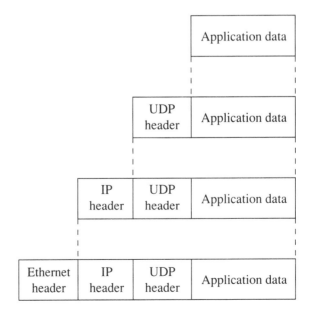

**Figure 4.3** Packet encapsulation.

The unit of data transported by the IP layer is called an IP datagram. The business of routing IP datagrams across an internet is based not on a physical address such as ethernet, but on a 'higher level' address called the internet address, or IP address. The IP address is a 32-bit number which is logically divided into two parts. The first part identifies a network (and is therefore used to route the datagram), and the second part identifies a specific host connection on that network.

The delivery service offered by IP is 'connectionless'. Each IP datagram is routed around the internet quite independently of any other. This has a number of important consequences:

1.  Because a gateway has to make a routing decision for every single datagram, such decisions must be made very efficiently. (This does not impinge greatly on the life of an application programmer, but it is certainly a challenge for the designers and implementors of the internet protocol suite itself.)
2.  There is no guarantee that two successive datagrams will follow the same route, even if travelling from the same source to the same destination. This has the important consequence that IP datagrams are not necessarily delivered in the same order as they were sent.
3.  Because no resources are permanently committed within the gateways to any particular connection, the gateways may occasionally have to discard a datagram because of lack of buffer space or other resources. Thus, the delivery service offered by IP is a 'best effort' service rather than a guaranteed service.

Figure 4.4 shows the format of an IP datagram, slightly simplified.

## 4.1.6  The transport layer

Proceeding further up the protocol stack we come to the transport layer. As application programmers, this is the layer of greatest interest to us, because it is the one we have to deal with directly. In fact there are two transport protocols commonly used in UNIX: the user datagram protocol (UDP) and the transmission control protocol (TCP). These two protocols offer connectionless and connection-oriented transport services respectively.

UDP and TCP can be likened to the postal service and the telephone service, as illustrated in Figure 4.5. Consider first the characteristics of the postal service:

1.  Every letter has to have an address on it. The letter is routed through the postal system purely on the basis of that address. There is no way I can come to some sort of private understanding with a post box that all letters I deposit there are to be delivered to a particular person. Similarly, whenever I pass a datagram to UDP for delivery, I must pass the address of the transport endpoint to which it is to be delivered.
2.  The postal service does not confirm that it has delivered a letter, or even that it has failed to deliver a letter (except for a few specialized and expensive postal services which we will ignore). Consequently, when I post a letter I do not know for certain

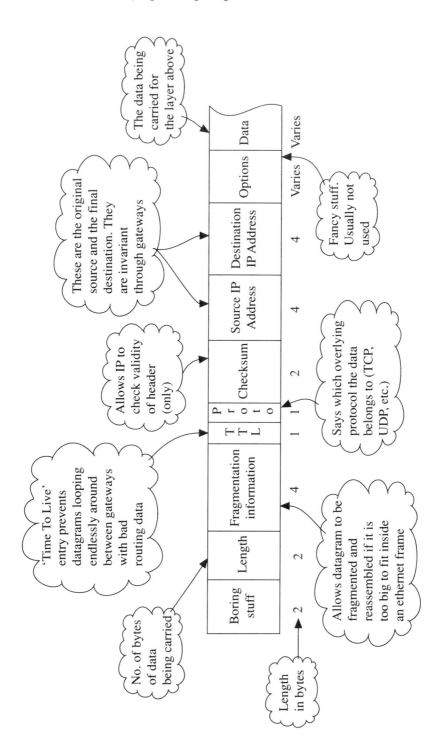

**Figure 4.4** IP datagram format.

when or if it will arrive at its destination. Similarly, UDP has no built-in mechanism to acknowledge the receipt of datagrams, and consequently, there are no automatic arrangements to resend a lost datagram, or to notify the sender of failure to deliver.

3.  The postal service does not guarantee to deliver letters in the same order as they were posted. Similarly, UDP may not necessarily deliver datagrams in the order they were transmitted.

4.  If I send three separate letters to the same person, that person receives three separate letters. Even if they represent three consecutive instalments of my memoirs, they do not all merge into one *en route*. The recipient knows where each letter ends and the next begins. Similarly, UDP datagrams are sent and received as separate entities. We say that UDP 'preserves message boundaries'.

Now consider the characteristics of the telephone service. The analogy with TCP is not so close, but there are a few important points:

1.  When I place a telephone call I have to supply 'addressing information' (in this case a telephone number) just once, when I dial the call. During the call, my telephone somehow 'knows' that the words I speak into it are to be conveyed to that particular recipient. I do not have to preface each sentence with 'please deliver this sentence to so-and-so'. Similarly with TCP, I supply an address just once, when I establish the connection. Thereafter I simply send data to the connection.

2.  The person at the other end hears the words I speak in the same order as they were spoken. Similarly, TCP guarantees to deliver the bytes of the data stream in the same order as they were transmitted.

3.  Once the call is connected, a telephone works both ways. I can both speak into it and listen to it. Similarly a TCP connection is bidirectional.

4.  The telephone delivers a continuous stream of audio signal. It does not divide it up into pieces. Similarly, TCP provides a purely stream-oriented connection; it does not preserve message boundaries. The analogy is weak here so let us be more explicit. If I write 100 bytes to a TCP connection, then another 100, then another 50, the receiving end simply finds 250 bytes waiting to be read. It has no idea that they were written in packets of 100, 100 and 50. The receiving end may choose to read all 250 bytes in one operation, or to read just 10 bytes at a time, or whatever it pleases. In contrast, with UDP I have to read exactly one whole datagram at a time. Application protocols running over TCP should therefore provide some way for the recipient to know when it has received a complete message. For example, the application may use fixed length messages, corresponding to some C structure perhaps. If variable length messages are unavoidable, messages might include an initial value which explicitly tells the recipient how much more data to expect. Alternatively, a server may send a sequence of strings to a client, each string terminated by a null character.

The above analogies broadly illustrate the differences between a connectionless transport service (UDP) and a connection-oriented transport service (TCP). We will examine these two protocols in a little more detail.

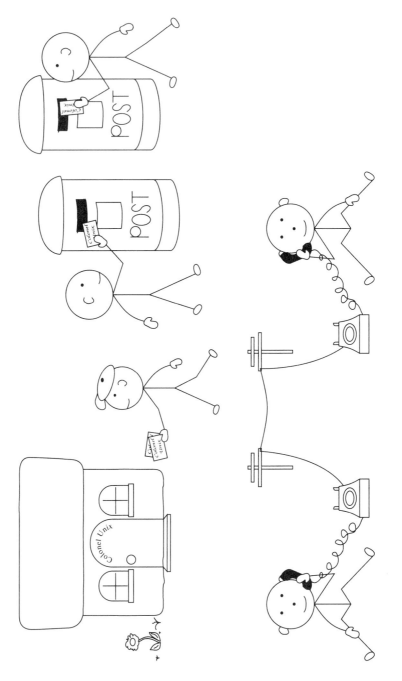

**Figure 4.5** Datagram and stream delivery.

## 4.1.7 User datagram protocol

The format of a UDP datagram is shown in Figure 4.6. It is extremely simple, reflecting the fact that UDP offers very little over and above the service offered by IP. Its most important function is to deliver datagrams to and from specific transport endpoints (in effect, specific processes) within the machine. The transport endpoint is identified by a 16-bit *port number*. To return to our postal analogy, the IP layer corresponds to the postman who delivers letters to the front door of your company's premises. UDP plays the role of an internal delivery service which distributes those letters to specific individuals within the company.

The UDP header also provides a checksum which allows the UDP layer at the receiving end to check the validity of the data. Beyond that, UDP inherits all the 'shortcomings' of IP – it does not check that the datagrams have been received, or retransmit them if they have gone astray. Also, it does not guarantee that the datagrams are received in the same order as they were transmitted.

## 4.1.8 Transmission control protocol

Like UDP, TCP uses the notion of a port number to direct messages to specific transport endpoints within the machine. Also like UDP, TCP provides a checksum to allow the recipient to verify that the data have been received correctly. Beyond that, the resemblance ends.

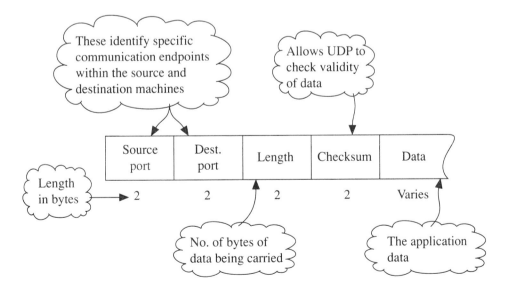

**Figure 4.6** UDP datagram format.

In order to achieve a data delivery service that is reliable and correctly sequenced over a network layer (IP) that offers neither of these, TCP uses a technique called *positive acknowledgement with retransmission*. The basic idea is illustrated in Figure 4.7. Each time TCP sends a segment of data, it starts a timer. When the receiving end gets the segment, it immediately sends an acknowledgement back to the sender. When the sender receives the acknowledgement, it knows all is well, and cancels the timer. However, if the outgoing segment (or the return acknowledgement) gets lost by the IP layer, the timer at the sending end will expire. At this point, the sender will retransmit the segment.

Figure 4.7 illustrates a simple lock-step scheme in which the sending end waits to receive an acknowledgement of each segment before sending the next. The maximum communication bandwidth achievable with this scheme is

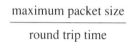

$$\frac{\text{maximum packet size}}{\text{round trip time}}$$

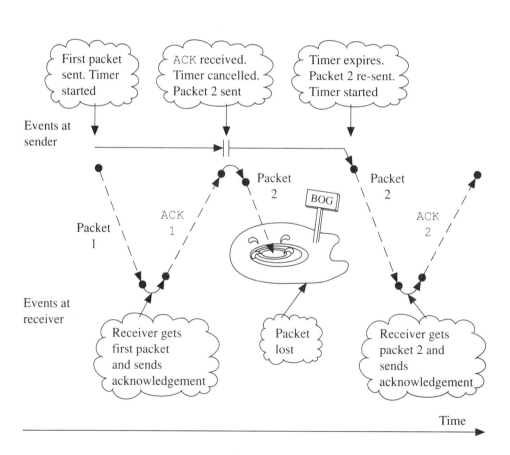

**Figure 4.7** Positive acknowledgement and retransmission.

which is almost certainly much lower than the network is actually able to sustain. (Imagine you are trying to conduct a dialogue with a friend via postcards. If you wait for each card to be acknowledged before sending the next one, and if a card takes two days on average to be delivered, you can only send a postcard every four days. The postman can handle more than that.)

To overcome this problem, TCP uses a *sliding window* protocol which allows several unacknowledged segments to be present in the network. As shown in Figure 4.8 the window gradually slides down the data stream as the transmission proceeds. Bytes behind the trailing edge of the window have been both transmitted and acknowledged. Bytes in front of the leading edge of the window have not been sent yet. To control this sliding window, there are three fields within the TCP header. The *sequence number* is placed in the header by the sender and indicates the byte offset within the data stream at which this segment begins. The data is used by the recipient to ensure that misordered segments are

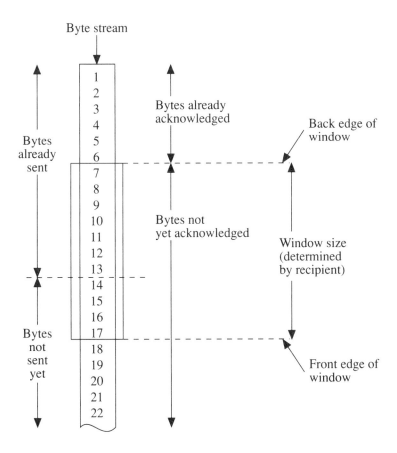

**Figure 4.8** A sliding window.

re-assembled correctly, and to reject duplicate segments. The *acknowledgement number* is used in the acknowledgements returned by the recipient; it indicates which segment is being acknowledged. (Acknowledgement packets use the same header format as outgoing packets, but they do not usually contain data.) A third field is used to control the size of the window. This field is used in acknowledgement packets and is filled in by the recipient to indicate how many more bytes of data (beyond the one that is currently being acknowledged) the recipient is willing to accept before further acknowledgements are sent. Consider the scenario in Figure 4.8. The recipient has acknowledged receipts of bytes 1 to 6, and specified a window size of 11. This gives the sender licence to send as far as, but not beyond, byte 17. At the instant shown on the diagram, the sender has sent up to byte 13. Bytes 14–17 may be sent without waiting for further acknowledgements. Beyond that, however, the sender must stall until the recipient has sent further acknowledgements and the back end of the window can advance. In effect, the window size indicates the amount of buffer space available at the recipient for storage of incoming data. (The byte numbers used in this example are of course unrealistically small.)

The sliding window protocol allows TCP to flow-control the data stream accurately. Over the years, as TCP has matured, algorithms for adapting the window size have improved, ensuring that good use is made of the network bandwidth whilst at the same time guaranteeing that the recipient is never forced into discarding data by being sent more than it can handle. Figure 4.9 shows the format of the TCP header.

It should be noted that the particular sets of features found in the UDP and TCP transport services are simply the combinations that were chosen by the designers. There is nothing really fundamental about them – other combinations are possible. For example, one could imagine a 'reliably sequenced packet' service which preserved message boundaries (like a UDP) but guaranteed that the packets were in the correct order, were never duplicated, and so on. Indeed, it is easy to find applications for which such a transport service would be ideal. Alternatively, one could imagine a connection-oriented transport service that guaranteed delivery of all the data but did not guarantee the sequence. It is extremely difficult to find applications for which such a service would be any use whatsoever.

---

**An aside:** the late and much loved comedian Eric Morecambe once did a sketch in which he attempted to play Grieg's Piano Concerto in A minor under the baton of show guest André Previn. Challenged by an outraged Previn at the end of the performance, Eric defended himself with the reply 'I played all the right notes – just not necessarily in the right order.'

---

## 4.1.9 Summary

Let us summarize the characteristics of the layers of the TCP/IP protocol stack in Table 4.1.

**Table 4.1**

| Layer | Correspondence with OSI layers | Characteristics |
|---|---|---|
| Ethernet | Physical and data link | Delivers frames between directly connected machines. Other technologies (e.g. token ring, Fibre Distributed Data Interface) offer much the same. |
| IP | Network | Delivers IP datagrams between any two machines on a connected internet. The machines may be separated by intervening gateways. Handles routing and fragmentation issues but does not guarantee delivery or correct sequencing of the datagrams. |
| UDP | Transport | Delivers datagrams between transport end-points (i.e. specific programs) for any two machines on a connected internet. Preserves message boundaries but does not guarantee delivery or correct sequencing of the datagrams. |
| TCP | Transport | Provides a reliable, correctly sequenced, flow-controlled stream delivery service between transport endpoints (i.e. specific programs) for any two machines on a connected internet. Does not preserve message boundaries. |

## 4.1.10 Dissecting a real packet

There are a number of packet monitor programs available on the market which will capture and display network traffic. The product Lanwatch, from FTP Software, is a typical example. It runs on a PC, under DOS, and is capable of displaying a wide variety of network protocols (not just TCP/IP), interpreting packet headers up to and including the transport layer.

The `snoop` utility, a part of Solaris 2.1, has the advantage of running over a live UNIX system. It is more focused on TCP/IP, but it can extend its interpretation of the protocol stack up into the higher layers, for example to show the 'op-codes' of a `tftp` packet, or the parameters to an NFS request.

Packet monitors usually operate the network interface in what is quaintly known as 'promiscuous' mode, which means that the interface will accept all packets, whatever their destination address. Such programs can be very useful both as diagnostic aids and as teaching tools. To illustrate, here is an example of the 'verbose' output from `snoop` for a single packet which is a read request `tftp` packet from the host `magrathea` to `desiato`. The packet encapsulation is clearly apparent, with each layer's header displayed in turn:

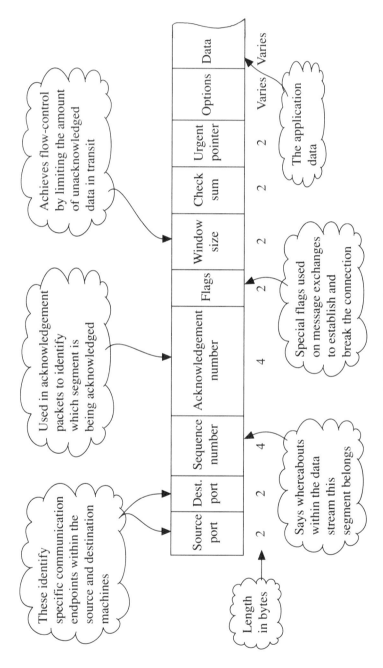

**Figure 4.9** TCP datagram format.

```
ETHER:   ----- Ether Header -----
ETHER:
ETHER:   Packet 1 arrived at 15:39:35.08
ETHER:   Packet size = 62 bytes
ETHER:   Destination = 8:0:20:e:7e:24, Sun
ETHER:   Source      = 8:0:20:e:7c:9a, Sun
ETHER:   Ethertype = 0800 (IP)
ETHER:
IP:      ----- IP Header -----
IP:
IP:      Version = 4
IP:      Header length = 20 bytes
IP:      Type of service = 0x00
IP:            xxx. .... = 0 (precedence)
IP:            ...0 .... = normal delay
IP:            .... 0... = normal throughput
IP:            .... .0.. = normal reliability
IP:      Total length = 48 bytes
IP:      Identification = 62014
IP:      Flags = 0x0
IP:            .0.. .... = may fragment
IP:            ..0. .... = last fragment
IP:      Fragment offset = 0 bytes
IP:      Time to live = 60 seconds/hops
IP:      Protocol = 17 (UDP)
IP:      Header checksum = 7c47
IP:      Source address = 192.9.200.18, magrathea
IP:      Destination address = 192.9.200.17, desiato
IP:      No options
IP:
UDP:     ----- UDP Header -----
UDP:
UDP:     Source port = 3969
UDP:     Destination port = 69 (TFTP)
UDP:     Length = 28
UDP:     Checksum = 0000 (no checksum)
UDP:
TFTP:    ----- Trivial File Transfer Protocol -----
TFTP:
TFTP:    Opcode = 1 (read request)
TFTP:    File name = "/etc/passwd"
TFTP:    Transfer mode = octet
```

# 4.2  Socket concepts

Having looked at how the TCP and UDP transport services operate, we will now turn our attention to how these services may be accessed from our application program. The original interface to TCP and UDP came from the 4.2 BSD release of Berkeley UNIX. It consisted of about eight new system calls, and went under the general name of *sockets*. We will examine these system calls, and see how to use them to write clients and servers, in the remainder of this chapter. In the next chapter we will look at an alternative (and in some ways more modern) interface to the transport layer, called TLI.

## 4.2.1 What is a socket?

A socket is an 'endpoint for communication'. It is where the application program and the transport provider meet. As an analogy, perhaps at work you have a box in which you place outgoing mail. Twice a day, the mail man (the transport provider) picks up the mail from this box, and sets about delivering it. At the recipient's end, there is probably also some kind of mailbox where the mail man leaves the letters, and from where the recipient picks them up. The mail boxes are like datagram sockets. They are the point of contact between the user's program and the connectionless transport provider (see Figure 4.10).

Similarly, a telephone is an endpoint for communication analogous to a stream socket; it is the point of contact between the user and a connection-oriented transport provider (the telephone company). We see from these analogies that sockets have a *type*, which indicates the kind of transport provider they are associated with. Although several types of socket are defined, we will primarily be interested in the two mentioned above, namely datagram sockets and stream sockets. Sockets can only interact with sockets of the same type. This makes sense: you cannot post someone a letter and have it emerge as a monologue from the recipient's telephone.

## 4.2.2 Socket address families

Before looking at any code, we must examine the issue of how sockets are addressed. Whenever two unrelated processes want to get together, there has to be *something* they both know – some 'agreed place' at which they can rendezvous. For example, in the case of shared memory or message queues which we saw in Chapter 2, there is a simple numeric key which the parties concerned must agree on. In the case of a named pipe, there is a filename which must be opened by both programs. In the case of sockets, there are several different ways of giving the socket a name. These naming methods are called *address families*.

The simplest address scheme is the so-called UNIX address family, in which sockets have UNIX pathnames, such as /tmp/mysock, associated with them. Under BSD UNIX, these sockets show up as entries of type 's' on a long directory listing; for example:

```
douglas% ls -l /tmp/mysock
srwxrwxrwx  1 chris      0 Jul  1 21:38 /tmp/mysock
douglas%
```

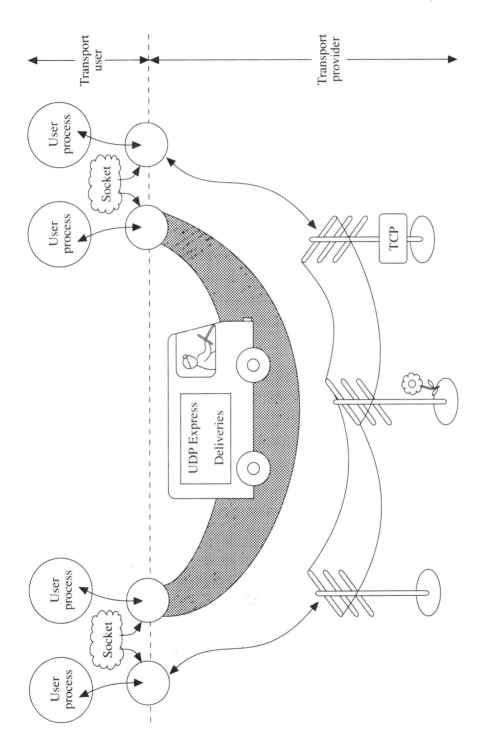

**Figure 4.10** Illustrating sockets – a transport endpoint.

Under SVR4 UNIX, this socket type is implemented as a named pipe, and shows on a directory listing as type 'p'. Named pipes can also be created from the command line using

```
mknod  filename  p
```

Although simple, UNIX address family sockets are of no use as a network-wide IPC mechanism, because the client and the server must both be on the same machine. Consequently we will not use them in any of the examples here.

The other commonly used scheme for naming sockets is called *internet domain addressing*. In this scheme, the socket's 'name' actually consists of two numbers: the 32-bit IP address of the host where the socket resides, and a 16-bit port number. This is the address family which we will use in the examples in this chapter.

The socket system calls which take socket addresses as arguments (such as bind() – the call that actually associates the name with the socket) are flexible enough to cope with these different families of addresses. Indeed, the function interface itself is flexible enough to handle any arbitrary style of socket address. The price paid for this flexibility is a little extra complexity in the code.

Structures are defined for the two types of socket address. A UNIX domain address looks like this:

```
struct sockaddr_un {
    short   sun_family;              /* Tag: AF_UNIX */
    char    sun_path[108];          /* path name    */
};
```

and an internet domain address looks like this:

```
struct sockaddr_in {
    short   sin_family;             /* Tag: AF_INET */
    u_short sin_port;               /* Port number  */
    struct  in_addr sin_addr;       /* IP address   */
    char    sin_zero[8];            /* Padding      */
};
```

Notice that both structures have an initial *tag* member whose value must be set to indicate the type of address which is actually in use. This is because functions like bind() receive only a pointer to the structure – they rely on this tag to discover what kind of structure it really is. The sockaddr_in structure has an included struct in_addr which contains an internet address. This is defined as follows (although some implementations try hard to make it look more complicated):

```
struct in_addr {
    u_long s_addr;
};
```

These data structures are illustrated in Figure 4.11.

There is also a 'generic' socket address structure, `struct sockaddr`, defined as follows:

```
struct sockaddr {
    u_short  sa_family;
    char     sa_data[14];
};
```

This structure type exists so that socket addresses may be passed into functions in an address family-independent manner.

The other complication raised by this 'address family independence' of the socket system calls is that whenever you pass a socket address, you must also pass an additional parameter specifying the length of that address. For example, a call to `bind()` might appear as follows:

```
struct sockaddr_in server;

bind (sock, (struct sockaddr *)&server, sizeof server);
```

Note also the cast on the second argument to convince the compiler that you are passing a 'generic' socket address pointer.

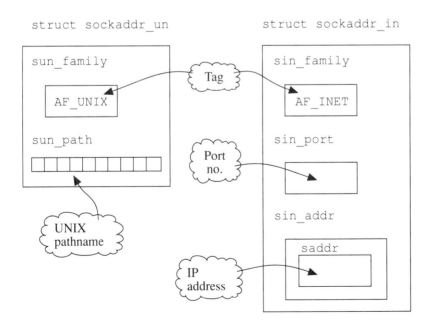

**Figure 4.11** Socket address data structures.

### 4.2.3 Socket types

Another property of sockets, quite separate from their address family, is their *type*. The type of a socket refers to the type of the underlying transport. Likely values are:

```
SOCK_STREAM        /* A connection-oriented transport, eg TCP */
SOCK_DGRAM         /* A connectionless transport, eg UDP */
SOCK_RAW
```

SOCK_RAW is used – on occasion – to talk directly to the IP layer. Our examples will use only SOCK_STREAM and SOCK_DGRAM.

## 4.3 Connection-oriented server operations

### 4.3.1 Establishing the connection

With these initial concepts out of the way, we now look in detail at the operations performed by a connection-oriented server and client. We saw in Chapter 3 that the client–server relationship is asymmetric. A server sits passively waiting for work; it does not know where that work will come from. A client actively goes out and connects to the server it requires. This asymmetry is reflected in the different sequence of socket system calls required in the server and client, as illustrated in Figure 4.12.

We will examine the steps performed by the server in order:

1.  A socket of the required address family and type is created:

    ```
    int sock;
    sock = socket ( AF_INET,  SOCK_STREAM,  0 );
    ```

    The first argument specifies the address family, and the second says what type of socket we want. The third argument may be used to specify which underlying protocol is to be used, but is usually set to zero, meaning 'let the system choose'.

    The return value is a 'socket descriptor', used when we later want to refer to this socket.

2.  An address is *bound* to the socket. The address, as we have seen, consists of an IP address and a port number, and it has to be placed in a sockaddr_in structure, along with the tag value AF_INET to say what kind of address this is. This structure is then passed to the bind() system call. The code typically looks something like this:

    ```
    #define SERVER_PORT      4321
    struct sockaddr_in       server;

    server.sin_family      = AF_INET;      /* Tag value */
    server.sin_addr.s_addr = INADDR_ANY;
    ```

```
server.sin_port        = htons(SERVER_PORT);

bind (sock, (struct sockaddr *)&server, sizeof server );
```

If this is a new or experimental service, the port number is to some extent arbitrary, although of course it must be agreed with the client. As it is impossible to reuse a

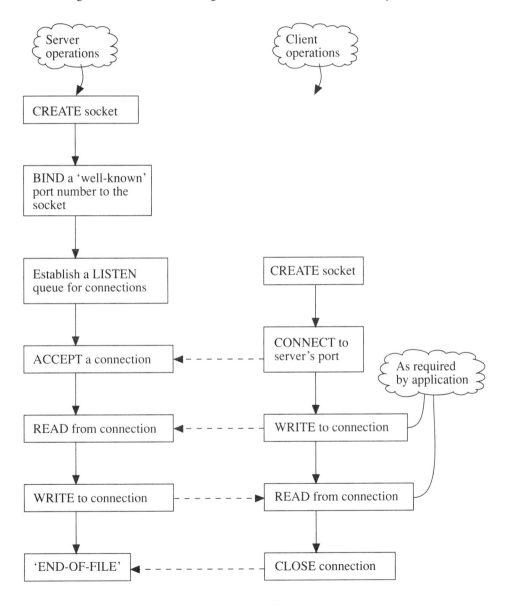

**Figure 4.12** Connection-oriented client and server operations.

port that is already assigned, we should at least avoid the ports listed in
`/etc/services`, which correspond to standard internet servers. You may wish to
choose a port less than 1024. These so-called *reserved* ports can only be used by
programs running with super-user privileges. They were the basis of what passed for
security in the original BSD networking support, being considered a sort of 'verifier'
which convinces the client that it really was connecting to the 'official' server and
not some imposter. Of course, all it really proves is that the client is connecting to a
server which is running with root privileges.

The function `htons()` (usually implemented as a macro) converts the port
number from host to network byte order. We will discuss byte ordering later; for now
it is sufficient to know that `htons()` converts the port number to a common form
which all machines can understand. For details, look up `byteorder(3)`.

The value `INADDR_ANY` assigned to the IP address of the socket address is a kind
of 'wildcard'; it means 'this socket will accept connections from any of the network
interfaces on this machine'. Usually, of course, the machine has only one network
interface and one IP address. A gateway, however, has more than one, and we can
elect that a socket should only accept connection requests via one of them, by using
the appropriate IP address here. Note that `INADDR_ANY` has nothing to do with which
*client* IP addresses we will accept connections from.

3.  Next, we need to inform the kernel that we wish to accept connections on this socket,
    as follows:

    ```
    listen ( sock, 5 );
    ```

    The second argument specifies how many pending connection requests the system
    should queue. Requests become pending if new clients try to connect whilst the
    server is busy talking to an existing client. When the limit on pending connections
    has been reached, any further attempts to connect will be refused rather than queued.
    Five is a typical value here (some implementations also say it is the maximum).

4.  The final stage in establishing communication is to wait for, and accept, a connection
    request from a client. The code is typically as follows:

    ```
    struct sockaddr_in  client;
    int fd, client_len;

    client_len = sizeof client;
    fd = accept ( sock, &client, &client_len);
    ```

    This call will block (i.e. will not return) until a client connects. The second argument
    to `accept()` points to a structure in which will be returned the socket address of the
    client that connected. We can ignore this if we do not care who the client is. In some
    situations, the server may wish to check that the client has bound a reserved port as a
    verifier. In others, we may wish to check the client's IP address by mapping it back
    to a symbolic name, and looking that name up in some list of clients that we are
    willing to serve. (Recall, for example, from Chapter 3 that the `mountd` daemon looks

at the `/etc/exports` file to decide what requests to honour, and from whom.) The third argument is a so-called 'value-return' argument used both to pass a value into a function and return a value from it. We use it to tell `accept()` how big our data structure is, and on return `accept()` modifies the value to tell us how much data it actually put in there.

The return value from `accept()` is a new descriptor relating to the connection now established to the client. This new descriptor behaves like a regular file descriptor and we can use it to `read()` and `write()` on. Some people are confused by the presence of two descriptors (`sock` and `fd` in our example). To distinguish them clearly, the terms *rendezvous descriptor* (`sock`) and *connection descriptor* (`fd`) are sometimes used. The rendezvous descriptor cannot be used for doing I/O on – it is not connected to anything – but it can be used to accept further connections. The connection descriptor, on the other hand, is exactly what we need to communicate with the client.

Once the connection is established, the situation appears as in Figure 4.13. Note that there are five items defining the connection between the client and server:

(a) the protocol in use;
(b) the client's IP address;
(c) the client's port number;
(d) the server's IP address;
(e) the server's port number.

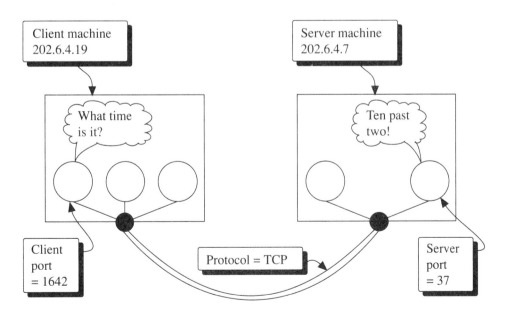

**Figure 4.13** Associations between processes.

The significance of this comment is that if any of the five items is different, it is a different connection. For example, if a second client on the same client machine were to connect to the same server, we would have two quite distinct connections. In this case, only one of the five items defining the connection is different – namely, the client's port number.

The utility `netstat` can be used to display a variety of network activity and status information. With the `-a` flag, it lists all transport endpoints present on the local machine. Here is a cut-down example of the output from machine `eddie`:

```
eddie% netstat -a
Active connections (including servers)
Proto Recv-Q Send-Q  Local Address     Foreign Address   (state)
tcp      0      0    eddie.ftp         ford.3099         ESTABLISHED
tcp      0      0    eddie.1022        trillian.login    ESTABLISHED
tcp      0      0    eddie.1023        trillian.login    ESTABLISHED
tcp      0      0    *.ftp             *.*               LISTEN
tcp      0      0    *.telnet          *.*               LISTEN
tcp      0      0    *.shell           *.*               LISTEN
tcp      0      0    *.login           *.*               LISTEN
tcp      0      0    *.exec            *.*               LISTEN
tcp      0      0    *.time            *.*               LISTEN
tcp      0      0    *.finger          *.*               LISTEN
tcp      0      0    *.printer         *.*               LISTEN
tcp      0      0    *.smtp            *.*               LISTEN
tcp      0      0    *.1038            *.*               LISTEN
tcp      0      0    *.1036            *.*               LISTEN
tcp      0      0    *.1035            *.*               LISTEN
tcp      0      0    *.1034            *.*               LISTEN
tcp      0      0    *.sunrpc          *.*               LISTEN

udp      0      0    *.1112            *.*
udp      0      0    *.1111            *.*
udp      0      0    *.1109            *.*
udp      0      0    *.1108            *.*
udp      0      0    *.1104            *.*
udp      0      0    *.tftp            *.*
udp      0      0    *.syslog          *.*
udp      0      0    *.biff            *.*
udp      0      0    *.talk            *.*
udp      0      0    *.time            *.*
udp      0      0    *.name            *.*
```

The local address and foreign address columns show endpoint addresses in the form `machine_address.port_number`. If the machine address appears in the `/etc/hosts` file, it will be shown as a symbolic name and not as a numeric IP address. Similarly, if the port number appears in the `/etc/services` file it will be shown as a service name. The first three lines of output show established TCP connections. The five items defining the connection are clearly shown. The first line shows a connection from an `ftp` client on host `ford` to the `ftp` server on the local machine. The second and third lines show `rlogin` connections, both from `eddie` to `trillian`. The only item differentiating these two connections is the local port number. Several other TCP-based services are shown in the output; these are idle, listening for connections. The services in the list which are not at 'well-known' port numbers are RPC servers, which we will discuss in Chapter 6.

## 4.3.2  Data transfer using sockets

Once our connection is established, the descriptor `fd` behaves like any other file descriptor. We can `read()` and `write()` it, `dup()` it, `close()` it and so on. We can even call `fdopen()` on it to obtain a 'standard I/O' stream, and write to it using `fprintf()`, although care is needed here to consider the effects of the buffering done within the `stdio` library.

The dialogue between client and server depends, of course, on the application protocol. Usually it consists of requests from the client followed by responses from the server. Some servers, such as the time server, send their data as soon as the connection is established; it is not necessary for the client to send anything.

Often, the protocol includes a way of indicating explicitly that the dialogue is complete (for example, a response from the server to say 'I have no more data for you', or a message from the client saying 'I have no more questions'). In that case, both ends know to close the connection. Sometimes, the client (or server) will simply close the connection without warning. In this case, the server (or client) will receive an EOF indication when it next tries to read from the connection.

Once the server has finished with one client, it will usually close that connection and loop round to accept the next one. Thus, the schema of the server's main loop is typically like this:

```
struct sockaddr_in  client;
int fd, client_len;
char inbuf[1000];         /* Data from client */
char outbuf[1000];        /* Data to   client */

client_len = sizeof client;

while (1) {
    fd = accept (sock, &client, &client_len);
    while ( read (fd, inbuf, 1000) > 0) {

        /* Process the data in inbuf, placing the result
           in outbuf */
        ...

        write ( fd, outbuf, 1000);
    }
    /* When client closes its end of the connection, we close
```

```
        our end.  Otherwise we would eventually run out of file
        descriptors.   Then   we  loop   round  to   pick up another
        connection.
    */
    close (fd);
}
```

This type of server is generally called an *iterative* server because it loops around
serving one client at a time. Any further clients who try to connect whilst the server is
busy simply have to wait. This is fine for servers (such as the time server) which maintain
only a very brief connection with the client, but clearly unacceptable for (say) the `telnet`
server which may remain connected to a client for hours on end. We will look at two
ways of simultaneously serving multiple clients later in the chapter.

## 4.3.3  Example: a network game server

We will now bring all these fragments of code together into a complete program. The
program plays the word guessing game 'hangman'. The protocol is as follows: the client
sends a message consisting of a single letter guess. The server responds by showing the
word it has chosen, with as-yet-unguessed letters shown as '-'. If the client's guess does
not appear in the word, the client's 'number of lives', initially set to 12, is decremented.
The process continues until either all the letters have been guessed (the client has won),
or the 'lives' count has reached zero (the server has won).
    Here is the code:

```
/* Network server for hangman game  (iterative schema) */
/* File hangserver.c */

#include <sys/types.h>
#include <sys/socket.h>
#include <netinet/in.h>
#include <stdio.h>
#include <syslog.h>
#include <signal.h>
#include <errno.h>
extern time_t time();

int maxlives = 12;
char *word[] = {
#include "words"
                };

#define NUM_OF_WORDS    (sizeof(word)/sizeof(word[0]))
#define MAXLEN  80      /* Maximum size of any string in the world */
#define HANGMAN_TCP_PORT        1066

main()
{
```

```
    int sock, fd, client_len;
    struct sockaddr_in server, client;

    srand((int)time((long *)0));          /* Randomize the seed */

    sock = socket(AF_INET, SOCK_STREAM, 0);
    if (sock < 0) {
        perror("creating stream socket");
        exit(1);
    }

    server.sin_family      = AF_INET;
    server.sin_addr.s_addr = htonl(INADDR_ANY);
    server.sin_port        = htons(HANGMAN_TCP_PORT);

    if (bind(sock, (struct sockaddr *) &server, sizeof (server)) < 0) {
        perror("binding socket");
        exit(2);
    }

    listen(sock, 5);

    while (1) {
        client_len = sizeof(client);
        if ((fd = accept(sock, (struct sockaddr *) &client,
                         &client_len)) < 0) {
            perror("accepting connection");
            exit(3);
        }
        play_hangman(fd, fd);
        close(fd);
    }
}

/* ----------------- play_hangman() ---------------------- */

/* Plays one game of hangman,  returning when the  word has been
   guessed or all the player's 'lives' have been used.  For each
   'turn' of the game, a line is read  from  stream 'in'.  The
   first character of this line is  taken as the player's guess.
   After each guess and prior to the first guess, a line is sent
   to stream 'out'. This consists of the word as guessed so far,
   with - to show unguessed  letters,  followed by the number of
   lives remaining.
   Note that this function neither knows nor cares  whether its
   input and output streams refer to sockets, devices or files.
*/

play_hangman(int in, int out)
{
    char *whole_word, part_word[MAXLEN],
         guess[MAXLEN], outbuf[MAXLEN];
```

```
int lives   = maxlives;    /* Number of lives left */
int game_state = 'I';       /* I ==> Incomplete    */
int i, good_guess, word_length;
char hostname[MAXLEN];

gethostname(hostname, MAXLEN);
sprintf(outbuf, "Playing hangman on host %s:\n\n", hostname);
write(out, outbuf, strlen(outbuf));

/* Pick a word at random from the list */
whole_word = word[rand() % NUM_OF_WORDS];
word_length = strlen(whole_word);
syslog(LOG_USER|LOG_INFO,
        "hangman server chose word %s", whole_word);
/* No letters are guessed initially */
for (i=0; i < word_length; i++)
   part_word[i] = '-';
part_word[i] = '\0';

sprintf(outbuf, " %s   %d\n", part_word, lives);
write(out, outbuf, strlen(outbuf));

while ( game_state == 'I')
    /* Get guess letter from player */
  { while (read(in, guess, MAXLEN)<0)
     { if (errno != EINTR)
            exit(4);
        printf("re-starting the read\n");
     } /* Re-start read() if interrupted by signal */
   good_guess = 0;
   for (i=0; i<word_length; i++)
     { if (guess[0] == whole_word[i])
         { good_guess = 1;
           part_word[i] = whole_word[i];
         }
     }
   if (! good_guess) lives--;
   if (strcmp(whole_word, part_word) == 0)
       game_state = 'W';    /* W ==> User Won */
   else if (lives == 0)
     { game_state = 'L';    /* L ==> User Lost */
       strcpy(part_word, whole_word); /* Show User the word */
     }
   sprintf(outbuf, " %s   %d\n", part_word, lives);
   write(out, outbuf, strlen(outbuf));
  }
}
```

Note that we have added error handling into the code – a vital part of real-world network applications. A large fraction of the above code is devoted to the `play_hangman()` function. The internal details of this function are not important to us. We merely need to know that it conducts a dialogue via two file descriptors, which are passed as arguments. Think of `play_hangman()` as symbolizing the work which a real-world server must do. When this function is called, the network connection `fd` is passed as both descriptors.

The list of words from which the program chooses is taken from a file called 'words' which gets compiled into the code. This file should appear as follows:

```
"aardvark",
"abacus",
"albatross",
  ...
"zoology"
```

If this program is compiled, it can be started up in the background, and tested. We can use `telnet` as a client to try things out. Normally, of course, `telnet` contacts the `telnetd` server on port 23, and embarks on its usual protocol negotiation. However, by supplying an extra argument, `telnet` can be made to connect to a different port. In that case, it does not attempt the protocol negotiation, but merely ferries text back and forth to the server. (This is *observed*, rather than *documented* behaviour.) Here is a typical dialogue. We first compile the server, then launch it in the background. Then we use `netstat` to verify that we do indeed have a socket on port 1066, in the LISTEN state. Finally we use `telnet` to connect to this port.

```
douglas% cc hangserver.c -o hangserver
douglas% hangserver &
[1] 3646
douglas% netstat -a | grep 1066
tcp        0      0  *.1066           *.*      LISTEN
douglas% telnet localhost 1066
Trying 127.0.0.1 ...
Connected to localhost.
Escape character is '^]'.
 -----------   12
e
 ------e----   12
s
 ------e--s-   12
t
 ------e--s-   11
n
 ------e--s-   10
i
 ------e-is-   10
m
 ------e-ism   10
```

```
a
 -a-a--e-ism    10
d
 -a-a--e-ism    9
r
 -ara--e-ism    9
p
 para--e-ism    9
l
 parallelism    9
Connection closed by foreign host.
douglas%
```

## 4.4  Serving multiple clients at the same time

As noted above, iterative servers which maintain long-lived connections to their clients
are unsatisfactory in that new clients have their connection requests put 'on hold' for an
arbitrarily long time. To solve this we clearly need a server that can maintain connections
with multiple clients at the same time. In this section we examine two approaches to this.

### 4.4.1  Concurrent servers

The first approach involves having the server spawn a child process to deal with each
client. All the parent does is to `accept()` the connections; each one is handed over to a
new child. Servers which operate in this way are known as *concurrent* servers. Given that
a child process in UNIX always inherits open file descriptors from its parent, concurrent
servers are surprisingly easy to implement. A simple schema might look like this:

```
sock =  socket ( ... );
bind ( sock, ... );
listen (sock, 2);

while (1) {
    fd = accept ( sock, ...);
    if (fork() == 0) {
        /* Child - process the request */
            play_hangman(fd, fd);

        exit(0);         /* Child is done */
    } else
        close (fd);      /* Parent does not use the connection */
}
```

Notice that after accepting a connection and forking, all the parent does is immediately
close it again, and loop round to accept another. Having the parent close its descriptor on

the connection socket does not, of course, break the connection in the client. The parent *must* do a close on `fd`, otherwise it will eventually run out of descriptors.

## 4.4.2 Preventing zombies: System V style

It is easy to turn the `hangserver` program into a concurrent server. If this is done, it will be capable of playing multiple simultaneous games with `telnet` clients coming in from multiple hosts. As it stands, however, the code has one rather serious flaw. This becomes apparent if we do a `ps` on the server machine after a few connections have come and gone. We will see something like this:

```
douglas% ps -l
        F UID   PID  PPID CP PRI NI  SZ  RSS WCHAN    STAT TT  TIME COMMAND
20008000  21  5525  3660  0   1  0  24    0 socket    IW   b   0:00 hangserver
    8401  21  5527  5525  0  25  0   0    0           Z    b   0:00 <defunct>
    8401  21  5529  5525  0  25  0   0    0           Z    b   0:00 <defunct>
    8401  21  5531  5525  0  25  0   0    0           Z    b   0:00 <defunct>
20000001  21  5537  3660 26  31  0 200  504           R    b   0:00 ps -l
douglas%
```

The three processes marked <defunct> are the corpses of three children spawned by the hangserver parent. (Note that they all have 5525 as their parent process ID.) Although these processes have exited, they have one tiny piece of information – their exit status – that they are waiting to pass back to their parent. Usually, a parent explicitly executes a `wait()` system call to synchronize with the termination of the child. This call retrieves the child's exit status and allows the child process to disappear totally. In some programs, the parent itself exits, leaving the children still running. In this case, each child is inherited by `init` (process no. 1), which always has a `wait()` call outstanding, again allowing the child to be 'mopped up'.

In the concurrent server example given above, neither of these conditions prevails. Indeed, the whole point is to have the server loop back to the `accept()` without waiting. The children, therefore, find themselves with exit status to return, but no one who wants it. Processes in this <defunct> state are impossible to get rid of in the usual way. Killing them does not help – they are already dead. (The 'Z' in the STAT column of the `ps` output stands for 'Zombie'.) Over time, these zombies will gradually fill up all the process table entries in the kernel. They would, of course, all disappear if their parent (process 5525) were killed, because they would be inherited by `init`.

In SVR4 UNIX there is an easy solution to this problem. We simply need to add the call:

```
#include <signal.h>
signal(SIGCHLD, SIG_IGN);
```

into the parent. Since the default disposition of the SIGCHLD signal is SIG_IGN, this call appears to have no purpose. However, it has the useful (and documented) side-effect of preventing zombies from being formed under the circumstances we have just described.

### 4.4.3 Preventing zombies: BSD style

Under BSD UNIX derivatives, the solution just shown does not work, and a more complex fix is needed. The basic idea is this: we can use the SIGCHLD signal to tell us when a child has died. At that point (i.e. in the SIGCHLD signal handler) we can execute a wait() call to mop up the child, and be sure that the wait() will not block. Enabling delivery of the SIGCHLD signal, however, has another unfortunate side-effect which we must cope with. There are certain system calls such as read(), accept() and select() which can be interrupted if a signal is delivered. If this happens, the system call returns with an *apparent* error, and with errno set to EINTR. In our example, the parent will almost certainly be blocked on the accept() call when the signal arrives. We must modify this call to trap the EINTR error return, and restart the accept().

Bringing these various changes together, here are the necessary modified fragments of code for a concurrent BSD-style hangman server:

```
#include <signal.h>              /* Additional header file */

...

/* This is the signal-handling function */
void waiter()
{
   wait(0);                      /* Mop up the child */
   signal(SIGCHLD, waiter);   /* Reinstall signal handler */
}

...

/* Somewhere in the initialization code in main(), we add : */
signal (SIGCHLD, waiter);

...

/* Here is how the main server loop now looks: */

while (1) {
    client_len = sizeof(client);
    RE_ACCEPT:
    msgsock = accept(sock, (struct sockaddr *) &client, &client_len);
    if (msgsock < 0) {
        if (errno == EINTR) {
            /* accept() interrupted by signal. Go try again */
            goto RE_ACCEPT;
        }
        else {
            perror("accepting connection");
            exit(3);
        }
    }
```

```
    rand();                    /* Advance the random generator */
    if (fork() == 0) {
        close(sock);           /* Child - Process Request */
        play_hangman(msgsock, msgsock);
        exit(0);
    }
    else
        close(msgsock);
}
```

Notice the `goto` statement which has quietly crept into the logic that handles the error return from the `accept()` call. It can, of course, be avoided, as follows:

```
while ((msgsock = accept( ...)) < 0) {
    if (errno != EINTR) {
        perror("accepting connection");
        exit(3);
    }
}
```

It is for you to decide which expresses the logic most clearly.

## 4.5  Concurrent servers using the select() call

### 4.5.1  Concurrency and state

There is an alternative approach to writing concurrent, connection-oriented servers which requires only a single process. It relies on the `select()` system call to multiplex between the messages being received on each client connection. We will meet `select()` in detail shortly, but for now, it suffices to know that it provides a way for a process to wait until any of a specified set of network connections has data available to be read. The advantage of this technique, compared with the child per client solution, is that it uses less system resources (memory and process table slots) as there is only a single process. The disadvantage, which can be considerable, is that it may require the server to keep state information to record the progress of the interaction with each client. (In the hangman server, this state information would consist of the complete word, the word as guessed so far and the number of 'lives' remaining.) In the child per client solution, of course, this state information is held in the local variables of each child. Maintaining context is something that processes are very good at. In a single process server, the per client state information is typically bundled up into a structure, and an array of such structures is declared. The array is indexed by the file descriptor referencing the client connection.

Using `select()` also radically affects the control flow in the server. It is necessary to return to the main processing loop (the one with the `select()` call at the top) after every interaction with every client. In the hangman server, an interaction consists of a single guess/response. Thus it is not possible for control to stay inside the `play_hangman()` function for the duration of a game.

For these reasons, the use of `select()` is not a particularly appropriate approach to writing a concurrent hangman server. (It is possible, of course, and you are welcome to try, but you will find it quite messy.)

## 4.5.2  A new example: a stock server

Let us consider a totally new example. The Fritterbuck Supermarket chain has a single distribution warehouse which contains a stock of the various products sold in its retail stores. The warehouse requires a stock-control server to keep track of the stock level of each product. The stock database is simply a series of records of the form

```
{ product_name , stock level }
```

For example, the database might include the following:

```
knife     1600
fork       840
spoon     1255
cup           0
saucer     200
```

The server is required to accept three types of request:

```
BUY    product_name   quantity
SELL   product_name   quantity
SHOW   product_name
```

For example:

```
BUY    knife    250
SELL   cup       85
SHOW   saucer
```

where BUY is an operation requested by one of Fritterbuck's suppliers, and results in an increase in the stock level maintained by the server for the specified product. The server responds to a BUY request with a reply of the form:

```
BOUGHT knife 250
```

SELL is an operation requested by one of the retail stores and results in a decrease in the stock level for the specified product. The server responds to a SELL request with a reply of the form:

```
DELIVER  cup  85
```

The number of items 'delivered' should be the smaller of the number that was requested in the SELL request, and the number actually in stock. The terms BUY and SELL here are from the server's standpoint. Selling means transferring stock from the server to the client.

SHOW requests a report on the stock level of a specific item and results in a response of the form:

```
STOCK saucer 200
```

The server, clients and stock list are illustrated in Figure 4.14.

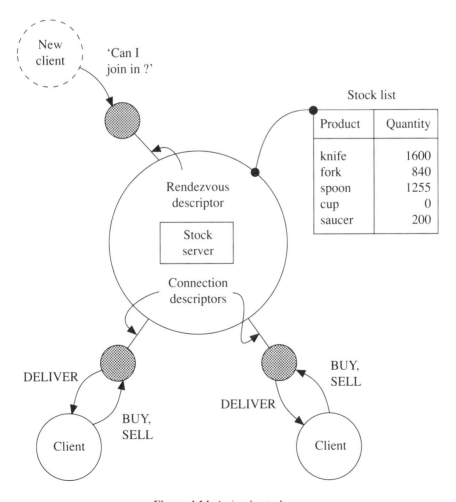

**Figure 4.14** A simple stock server.

We will assume that the client requests come in sufficiently frequently that we do not want the overhead of establishing and closing a connection for each one. That implies that our server will need to maintain multiple concurrent connections with its clients. The server needs to maintain state information too (namely, the stock list), but this information is 'global' (i.e. common to all clients), and not on a per client basis. If this server were written using the child per client technique we used for the hangman server, we would need to arrange some way for the child processes to share the stock list. We might use a shared memory segment perhaps, or a file. In addition, the SELL command requires the server to perform a test and decrement operation on the stock level, and we would need some mechanism to ensure that this operation was 'atomic' – that is, indivisible. For this we might use a semaphore, or a file lock. On the other hand, if the server is written as a single process that reads from all the client connections, the data are inherently global. Also, since there is only one process manipulating the stock levels, there is no possibility of it being pre-empted, so the 'atomic test and decrement' issue simply does not arise.

The conceptual differences in the design issues between the hangman server and the stock server are important. To summarize:

> The concurrent hangman server needs to maintain separate state information for each client, but the dialogues with the clients do not interact. A child per client server works well here. The concurrent stock server does not need to maintain separate state information for each client, but the dialogues with the clients do interact, via 'global' state information. A single-threaded server using select() is a better choice here.

Before looking at the stock server itself we must examine the select() call in more detail.

### 4.5.3 Using select()

Formally, the synopsis of select() appears as follows:

```
select(int nfds,
       fd_set *readfds,
       fd_set *writefds,
       fd_set *exceptfds,
       struct timeval *timeout)
```

The parameters readfds, writefds and exceptfds point to three 'descriptor sets'. The select() call will return if any of the descriptors in the readfds set is ready for reading, or if any of the descriptors in the writefds set is ready for writing, or if any of the descriptors in the exceptfds set has an 'exceptional condition' pending. The term *ready for reading* simply means that there are data waiting to be read on that descriptor, i.e. a `read()` on the descriptor would not block.

In the old days when we were quite happy to tolerate a limit of thirty-two file descriptors per process, the descriptor sets were simply represented by integers. Each bit of the integer represented one descriptor. Of course in these enlightened days it is poor style to have a hard limit of thirty-two implicit in the code, so the exact type of a descriptor set is hidden behind the typedef `fd_set`.

---

**An aside:** also, of course, to avoid being branded as assembly language programmers we must not openly demonstrate in our code that we know how to represent anything as sophisticated as a 'set of' in anything as humble as an integer.

---

In addition, the business of clearing, setting and testing individual descriptors within a set is hidden behind four macros:

```
FD_ZERO(&fdset)        /* Remove all descriptors from set fdset */
FD_CLR(fd, &fdset)     /* Remove descriptor fd from set fdset */
FD_SET(fd, &fdset)     /* Add descriptor fd to set fdset */
FD_ISSET(fd, &fdset)   /* True if fd is present in the set fdset */
```

The timeout parameter may point to a `timeval` structure which should be filled in to indicate the maximum length of time the call should block before it gets 'tired of waiting', and returns anyway. We do not require a timeout facility in this example, so we may set this parameter to `NULL`.

The use of descriptor sets in the `select()` call is illustrated in Figure 4.15. As a simple example, suppose we wanted to wait indefinitely until either of file descriptors 3 or 4 were ready for reading. The code fragment might appear as follows:

```
#include <sys/types.h>

fd_set  myset;

/* Put file descriptors 3 and 4 into myset */

FD_ZERO(&myset);
FD_SET(3, &myset);
FD_SET(4, &myset);

/* In the call below, 5 is the number of descriptors to examine
   i.e. from 0 to 4.  The three NULL parameters mean that we do
   not want to check if any  descriptors are ready for writing,
   we do not want to check if any descriptors have 'exceptional
   conditions' pending, and we do not want to timeout.
*/
```

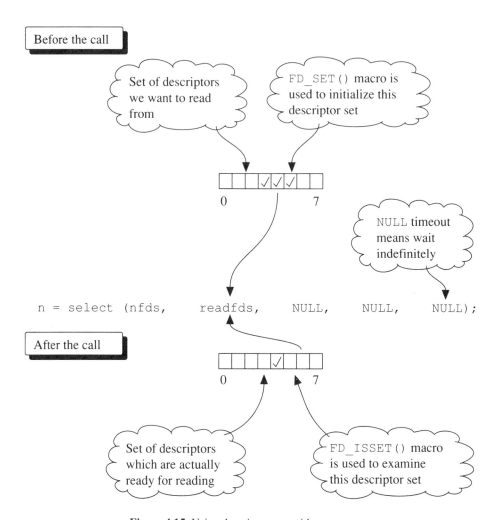

**Figure 4.15** Using descriptor sets with `select()`.

```
select(5, myset, NULL, NULL, NULL);
if (FD_ISSET(3, &myset)) {
    /* Go read from descriptor 3 ... */
}
else if (FD_ISSET(4, &myset)) {
    /* Go read from descriptor 4 ... */
}
else {
    printf("This should never happen");
}
```

There are two slightly messy aspects of using `select()`. First, because your descriptor sets get overwritten by the call, you usually have to keep a separate copy of them around. Secondly, when the call returns, there is no immediate indication of which file descriptor has woken you up. There will probably only be one, but to find it you have to poll each in turn.

## 4.5.4 The design of the stock server

With the details of `select()` out of the way, we will now begin to consider the design of our stock server. To keep the application-specific part of the code as short as possible, we will make a number of simplifying assumptions that would not be acceptable in a real-world implementation. In particular, we will keep the stock list in a pre-declared, fixed length array. It will be kept only in memory, and will not be written to a file. We will use a simple linear search strategy to find products in the list, and we will use a sentinel entry, with a stock level of $-1$, to mark the end of the list.

From a networking viewpoint, the most interesting aspects of the design of the server are in the manipulation of the file descriptors, and the formation of a 'test set' for use in the `select()` call. We must use `select()` to wait until either a transaction is received from an existing client, or a connection request is received from a new client. Initially, there are no client connections, so the only descriptor in the test set is the rendezvous descriptor we are using to accept new connection requests. (Perhaps surprisingly, `select()` considers a rendezvous descriptor on which a connection request has been received as being 'ready for reading'.) Thus, at any one time, our test set consists of a number of descriptors relating to connections already established to existing clients, plus the rendezvous descriptor.

The program listing `stock.c` shows the code for the stock server.

```
/* Stock server. This is an example of a single-process,
   concurrent server using TCP transport and select()
   File stock.c
*/

#include <sys/types.h>
#include <sys/socket.h>
#include <netinet/in.h>
#include <sys/time.h>
#include <sys/resource.h>
#include <stdio.h>

#define STOCK_PORT   7777    /* Our 'well-known' port number  */
#define LIST_SIZE    1000    /* Maximum number of stock items */

/* This structure holds all the data about a single stock item */
struct stock_item {
    char    product[32];    /* The product name */
    long    quantity;       /* The current stock level */
```

```
};

/* This array constitutes the stock list database */
struct stock_item stock_list[LIST_SIZE];

/* --------------------------- main() --------------------------- */
main()
{
    int sock, fd, client_len;
    struct sockaddr_in server, client;
    int max_fd;
    FILE **stream;
    struct rlimit limit_info;

    /* These are the file descriptor sets used by select() */
    fd_set test_set,   ready_set;

    /* We need an array of stream descriptors (of type FILE *). There is
       no portable way to know a priori how many open descriptors we can
       have.  Thus, we find this out at run time, using getrlimit(), and
       dynamically allocate an array of the required size.
    */
    if (getrlimit(RLIMIT_NOFILE, &limit_info) < 0) {
        perror("getting file descriptor limit");
        exit(1);
    }

    stream = (FILE **) malloc(limit_info.rlim_cur * sizeof (FILE *));
    if (stream == NULL) {
        fprintf(stderr, "failed to allocate stream descriptor table\n");
        exit(1);
    }

    sock = socket(AF_INET, SOCK_STREAM, 0);
    if (sock < 0) {
        perror("creating stream socket");
        exit(1);
    }

    server.sin_family      = AF_INET;
    server.sin_addr.s_addr = htonl(INADDR_ANY);
    server.sin_port        = htons(STOCK_PORT);

    if (bind(sock, (struct sockaddr *) &server, sizeof (server)) < 0) {
        perror("binding socket");
        exit(2);
    }

    listen(sock, 5);
    max_fd = sock;

    /* Initially, the 'test set' has just the rendezvous descriptor */
    FD_ZERO(&test_set);
```

```
    FD_SET(sock, &test_set);

    /* The end of the list is marked by an entry with a negative
       stock level. Mark the list as being initially empty */
    stock_list[0].quantity = -1;

    /* Here is the head of the main service loop */
    while (1) {
        /* Because select overwrites the descriptor set, we must
           not use our 'permanent' set here, we must use a copy
        */
        memcpy(&ready_set,   &test_set,   sizeof test_set);
        select(max_fd+1, &ready_set, NULL, NULL, NULL);

        /* Did we get a new connection request? If so, simply
           accept it and add the new descriptor into the read set
        */
        if (FD_ISSET(sock, &ready_set)) {
            client_len = sizeof client;
            fd = accept(sock, &client, &client_len);
            FD_SET(fd, &test_set);
            if (fd > max_fd) max_fd = fd;
            stream[fd] = fdopen(fd, "r+");
            setbuf(stream[fd], NULL);        /* IMPORTANT? */
        }

        /* Now we must check each descriptor in the read set in
           turn.  For each one which is ready, we process the
           client request.  Remember NOT to check the rendezvous
           descriptor.
        */
        for (fd=0; fd<=max_fd; fd++) {
            if ((fd != sock) && FD_ISSET(fd, &ready_set)) {
                if (process_request(stream[fd]) < 0) {
                    /* If the client has closed its end of the
                       connection, we close our end, and remove
                       the descriptor from the read set
                    */
                    close(fd);
                    FD_CLR(fd, &test_set);
                }
                else {
                    fflush(stream[fd]);
                }
            }
        }
    }
}

/* This is the application-specific part of the code */
```

```
/* ----------------------- find_product() ----------------------- */
/* Return a pointer to the stock_item for the specified product name in
   the stock list, or NULL if none found
*/
struct stock_item *find_product(char *name)
{
    struct stock_item *p;
    for (p = stock_list; p->quantity >= 0; p++) {
        if (strcmp(name, p->product) == 0)
            return p;
    }
    return NULL;
}

/* ----------------------- add_product() ----------------------- */
void add_product(char *name, int quantity)
{
    struct stock_item *p;

    /* Scan to find the end of the current list */
    for (p = stock_list; p->quantity >= 0; p++)
        ;      /* Empty loop body */
    if (p - stock_list >= LIST_SIZE-1)
        return;              /* List is already full */
    strcpy(p->product, name);
    p->quantity = quantity;
    /* Mark new end of list */
    (p+1)->quantity = -1;
    return;
}

/* ----------------------- process_request() ----------------------- */
/* Return 0 for normal return, or -1 if encountered EOF from client */
int process_request(stream)
FILE *stream;
{
    char req_buffer[100];
    char request[32], product[32];
    int quantity;
    struct stock_item *p;

    /* Read the request from the client */
    if (fgets(req_buffer, 100, stream) == NULL)
        return -1;                          /* End of file? */

    /* This next call is meaningless for the socket, but is
       needed to allow the stream to change  direction from
       input to output. (Look up fopen() for details.)
    */
    rewind(stream);
```

```
        sscanf(req_buffer, " %s %s %d", request, product, &quantity);
        if (strcmp(request, "BUY") == 0) {
            /* Bump up the stock level for this product by the quantity */
            if ((p = find_product(product)) == NULL) {
                add_product(product, quantity);
            }
            else
                p->quantity += quantity;
            /* Confirm transaction to the client */
            fprintf(stream, "BOUGHT %s %d\n", product, quantity);
        }
        else if (strcmp(request, "SELL") == 0) {
            if ((p = find_product(product)) == NULL) {
                fprintf(stream, "ERROR: product %s is unknown\n", product);
            }
            /* If we have enough, send as many as were asked for */
            else if (p->quantity >= quantity) {
                fprintf(stream, "DELIVER %s %d\n", product, quantity);
                p->quantity -= quantity;
            }
            /* ... otherwise, send as many as we have */
            else {
                fprintf(stream, "DELIVER %s %d\n", product, p->quantity);
                p->quantity = 0;
            }
        }
        else if (strcmp(request, "SHOW") == 0) {
            product[strlen(product)-1] = '\0';
            if ((p = find_product(product)) == NULL) {
                fprintf(stream, "ERROR: product %s is unknown\n", product);
            }
            else {
                fprintf(stream, "STOCK %s %d\n", product, p->quantity);
            }
        }
        else            /* Don't recognize command from client */
            fprintf(stream, "ERROR: request type not recognized\n");
        return 0;              /* Normal return */
    }
```

## 4.5.5 A tour of the stock server code

The application-specific parts of the code, consisting of the functions find_product(), add_product() and process_request() are of relatively little interest to us and we will not comment on them further, except to note that process_request() returns −1 if it encounters an EOF condition when reading from the client connection.

This implementation of the server uses stream descriptors (i.e. descriptors of type `FILE*`) to reference the network connections. This has the advantage that the server can use output functions such as `fprintf()` to formulate replies to the client. The stream descriptors are built from the low level (plain integer) descriptors returned from `accept()` by a call to `fdopen()` – this is done inside the main service loop after a new client connection has been accepted. To store these stream descriptors we need an array (indexed by the corresponding low level descriptor). Because the maximum number of open file descriptors per process is implementation-dependent, we make a call to `getrlimit()` to retrieve the maximum number of descriptors, and use this to `malloc()` an array of the right size. (Older, BSD-based versions of UNIX have a system call `getdtablesize()` to get the size of the file descriptor table, but this is not present in SVR4.)

`getrlimit()` returns a structure declared as follows:

```
struct rlimit {
    rlim_t  rlim_cur;    /* Current limit */
    rlim_t  rlim_max;    /* Hard limit    */
};
```

The hard limit specifies the maximum value that the current limit may be set to.

The most interesting part of the code is the service loop inside `main()`. A call to `memcpy()` is used to make a copy of our descriptor set for `select()` to scribble over. The variable `max_fd` tracks the largest file descriptor, for use in the `select()` call. An alternative would be to use the limit returned by `getrlimit()` here, and dispense with `max_fd`. On returning from the `select()` call we first test the rendezvous descriptor to see if a client is waiting to connect. If it is, we accept the connection, add the new descriptor to the test set and create the corresponding stream descriptor. We call `setbuf()` to disable the standard I/O library's buffering of this stream. In the author's experience, such buffering interacts badly with the network connection. Note also the curious call to `rewind()` immediately after the server has read the client's request. This apparent piece of nonsense is necessary to persuade the standard I/O library to reverse the direction of the stream from input to output.

The service loop also tests for readiness of each existing client connection, passing it to `process_request()` if necessary. If the `process_request()` function indicates that the client has closed the connection, the service loop closes the descriptor and removes it from the test set.

Because this server uses a simple text protocol, it may easily be tested, like the hangman server, by using `telnet` as the client. Here is a sample dialogue:

```
eddie% stock &
[1] 590

eddie% telnet localhost 7777
Trying 127.0.0.1 ...
Connected to localhost.
```

```
Escape character is '^]'.
BUY plate 100
BOUGHT plate 100
SELL plate 35
DELIVER plate 35
SHOW plate
STOCK plate 65
```

Of course, this does not demonstrate the server's ability to sustain simultaneous conversations with multiple clients. You will have to use your imagination!

---

**An aside:** there are many excellent precedents for this (using your imagination, that is). For example, Shakespeare asks us to

> Piece out our imperfections with your thoughts:
> Into a thousand parts divide one man, and make imaginary puissance;
> Think when we talk of horses that you see them,
> printing their proud hoofs i'the receiving earth.

(*Henry V*, Act 1, Scene 1). Had he been writing a play about UNIX he would doubtless have chosen more appropriate imagery.

---

# 4.6  Connection-oriented clients

Because the protocols used by the hangman and stock control servers in the previous sections were so simple, we were able to use an existing client (`telnet`) to test them. In general, this will not be the case. Usually, specific client code will be needed to work with each server. In this section we examine the boiler-plate network code used by a connection-oriented client.

## 4.6.1  Creating a socket

The steps performed by the client are summarized in Figure 4.16. Clients, like servers, begin by creating the socket. The call is just the same:

```
sock = socket(AF_INET, SOCK_STREAM, 0);
```

## 4.6.2  Setting a local address

Unlike the server, the client does not need explicitly to bind an address to this socket. You can simply use it, in which case the system will automatically bind an address for you, choosing an arbitrary port number. Usually the client does not care what port number it is using, but there is an important exception for clients which must bind a reserved port number (< 1024) as a verifier to the server. In this case, the client will need explicitly to bind an address. It will also need to be running with root privileges. In BSD (but not SVR4), the `rresvport()` function may be helpful in obtaining a socket with a reserved port bound; we assume that this is not required here.

### 4.6.3  Connecting to the server

The next step is to connect the client's socket to the server's. This is done using the `connect()` system call. One of the parameters to this call is a `sockaddr_in` structure, which must be filled in with the address of the server. Recall that this structure has three members:

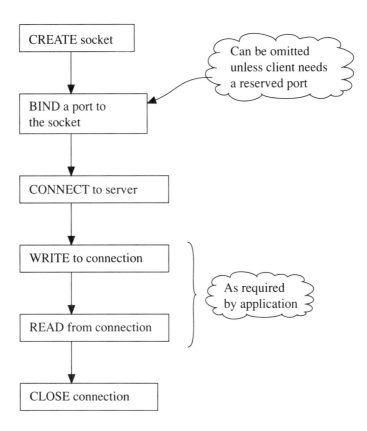

**Figure 4.16** Connection-oriented client operations.

1. A tag value AF_INET indicating the type of address in use.
2. The port number at which the server is listening.
3. The IP address of the server machine.

The simplest way of obtaining the port number and the IP address is to write them explicitly into the program. Hard-wiring the port number into the code is often satisfactory, because port numbers rarely change, especially for standard internet servers. Hard-wiring the IP address, however, is clearly unacceptable, because it would require recompiling the client source each time a different server machine was to be used. Typically, the client will read a host machine name from its command line arguments. (As we have seen, clients such as telnet, rsh and rcp all work this way.) Recall from Chapter 3 that the file /etc/hosts (or the NIS hosts map) provides a mapping from machine names to IP addresses, and the resolver routine gethostbyname() provides a way to query this mapping.

The gethostbyname() function returns a pointer to a hostent structure which is declared as follows:

```
struct      hostent {
    char    *h_name;        /* official name of host */
    char    **h_aliases;    /* alias list */
    int     h_addrtype;     /* host address type */
    int     h_length;       /* length of address */
    char    **h_addr_list;  /* list of addresses from name server */
};
```

This structure is flexible enough to handle hosts with multiple names and multiple addresses; h_addr_list can be an array of pointers to IP addresses. In a simple case, we require just the first (or only) of these addresses. For simplicity and backward compatibility, the following macro is provided:

```
#define     h_addr   h_addr_list[0]
```

Although we will not use it in our example, the resolver getservbyname() can be used in a similar way to obtain the port number of a given named service, by looking it up in /etc/services or in the NIS services map. The resolver returns a servent structure, the important member of which is the port number, s_port. Figure 4.17 shows the use of gethostbyname() and getservbyname() to fill in the fields in the server's socket address.

Here is the typical code, without error checking:

```
#define HANGMAN_TCP_PORT     1066;
struct hostent          *host_info;
struct sockaddr_in      server;

/* Take host name from command line */
host_info = gethostbyname(argv[1]);
```

```
memcpy(&server.sin_addr, host_info->h_addr,
                        host_info->h_length);
server.sin_port = htons(HANGMAN_TCP_PORT);

connect(sock, &server, sizeof server);
```

Why is the memcpy() call included? The motivation is to make the code independent of the form (and size) of a network address. The length of the address is returned in host_info->h_length; this value is used to control how much data memcpy() copies. If we were willing to assume that the address is the same size as a long (probably true for an IP address) we could replace the memcpy() call by an assignment as follows:

```
server.sin_addr = *(long *)host_info->h_addr;
```

Note the use of the htons() macro to ensure that the port number is in network byte order (i.e. big-endian). This is assumed by the socket routines. Omitting the htons() call will do no harm on a big-endian machine, but will create a nasty latent bug just waiting for the code to be ported to a little-endian machine.

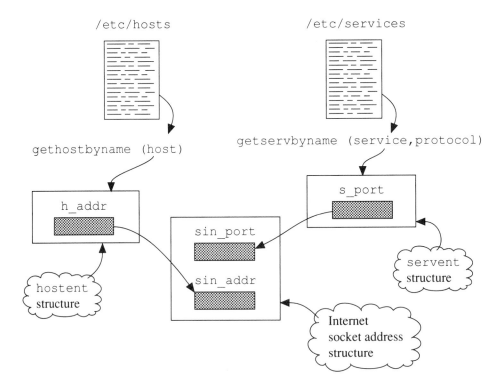

**Figure 4.17** Finding the required service.

Normally we would check the return value of the `connect()`. Zero implies success, −1 indicates various kinds of failure. Assuming that the operation succeeded, the descriptor `sock` is now connected, and can be used to do I/O to the server. Notice that whilst the server has two descriptors (the rendezvous descriptor and the connection descriptor), the client has only one.

Here is the complete source of a client for our hangman server. Having established the connection using the boiler-plate code just described, it merely ferries lines of text from the keyboard to the server, and from the server back to the screen.

```c
/* File hangclient.c  -   Client for hangman game. */

#include <stdio.h>
#include <sys/types.h>
#include <sys/socket.h>
#include <netinet/in.h>
#include <netdb.h>

#define LINESIZE            80
#define HANGMAN_TCP_PORT    1066

main(argc, argv)
int argc;
char *argv[];
{
    struct sockaddr_in  server; /* Server's address assembled here */
    struct hostent *host_info;
    int sock, count;
    char inline [LINESIZE];  /* Buffer to copy from user to server */
    char outline[LINESIZE];  /* Buffer to copy from server to user */
    char *server_name;

    /* Get server name from command line. If none, use 'localhost' */
    server_name = (argc>1) ? argv[1] : "localhost" ;

    /* Create the socket */
    sock = socket(AF_INET, SOCK_STREAM, 0);
    if (sock < 0) {
        perror("creating stream socket");
        exit(1);
    }

    host_info = gethostbyname(server_name);
    if (host_info == NULL) {
        fprintf(stderr, "%s: unknown host: %s\n", argv[0], server_name);
        exit(2);
    }

    /* Set up the server's socket address, then connect */
    server.sin_family = host_info->h_addrtype;
    memcpy((char *)&server.sin_addr, host_info->h_addr,
```

```
                                        host_info->h_length);
    server.sin_port   = htons(HANGMAN_TCP_PORT);

    if (connect(sock,(struct sockaddr *)&server,sizeof server) < 0) {
        perror("connecting to server");
        exit(3);
    }

    /* OK now we are connected to the server. Collect a line from the
       server, print it, collect a line from the user, send it to the
       server, and loop round until the server closes the connection.
    */

    printf("connected to server %s\n", server_name);
    while ((count = read(sock, inline, LINESIZE)) > 0) {
        write(1, inline, count);
        count = read(0, outline, LINESIZE);
        write(sock, outline, count);
    }
}
```

Note that in this case, the server is the first to communicate once the connection has been established. This is reflected in the ordering of the `read()` and `write()` calls in our client's main loop. This approach assumes that the interchanges between client and server are conveniently interleaved. Writing a client that will copy lines of text between the user and the server in an arbitrary order is a little harder, but we have seen the techniques needed to do it: we could create a second process, or we could use `select()`.

# 4.7  Connectionless clients and servers

In this section, we look at the sequence of operations used by *connectionless* clients and servers. We illustrate this with an example of a connectionless client which connects to the standard internet service, TFTP (trivial file transfer protocol).

## 4.7.1  Connectionless server design issues

The sequence of operations performed by connectionless servers and clients is shown in Figure 4.18. This figure shows a single server interacting with two clients. As shown, the server has a single socket on which it receives datagrams. Many clients may send datagrams to this socket, and in general the server will find itself retrieving datagrams from several clients in an arbitrary, interleaved order. If the server is *stateless* (that is, if it does not need to remember anything from one client interaction to the next), then this does not present a problem. The server simply reads the datagram, formulates a reply, sends it back to the client and forgets about it. Some of the trivial internet servers, such as `daytime` and `echo`, operate in this way.

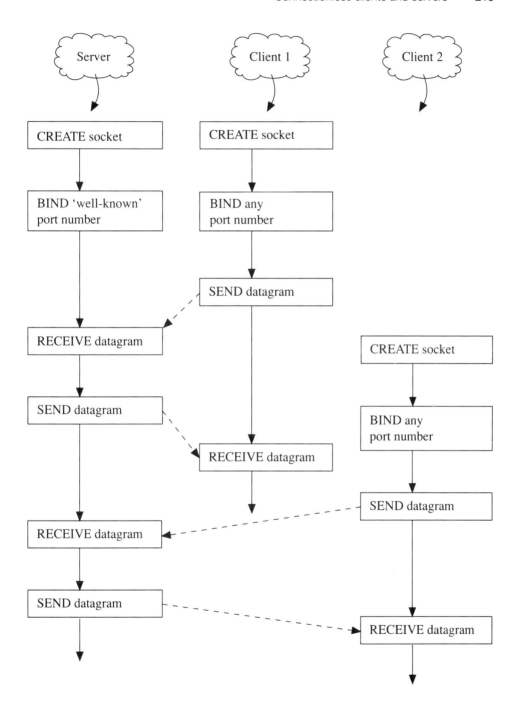

**Figure 4.18** Connectionless client and server operations.

Things get more complicated for servers which maintain state. One approach is to parcel the per client state information into a structure, and maintain some form of indexed data structure which uses as its search key a composite value formed from the client's socket address (i.e. its port number and IP address). Another approach is for the server to create a child process for each client it finds itself dealing with. Each child may create a new datagram socket, whose port number is duly notified to the client, and which is used by the client for the remainder of the interaction. (The TFTP server works this way.) Because each client is handled by a separate process, it is easy to keep track of the state information required by each client.

Another problem faced by connectionless clients and servers, at least those that use UDP as their transport protocol, is the 'unreliability' of UDP. One should not get too paranoid about this. When we describe UDP as unreliable, we do not mean that there is anything inherently 'flaky' about it. We simply mean that there is no mechanism built into the protocol to detect (and correct) problems such as dropped or misordered packet deliveries. Client–server pairs intended to operate between machines on a single LAN should not find this a problem. If the LAN is dropping packets, the appropriate response is not to implement a retransmission policy, but to notify the network manager of the problem, and encourage him or her to fix it. If the client and server are separated by intervening gateways, and particularly if they are spread across a wide area internet, the prospect of dropped or misordered packets is more real.

Essentially, the developer of a connectionless client–server pair has two choices:

1.  Assume that the underlying delivery system is 'reliable enough', and accept that the application will fail if the network fails.
2.  Demand that the application is more reliable than the network. In this case, a timeout/retransmit mechanism must be built in at the application level. We will look at one way to do this later in this section. (The alternative, of course, is to move to a connection-oriented service, and let TCP worry about the network failures.)

The asymmetry between client and server is much less marked in the connectionless case than in the connection-oriented case. In the latter case, as we saw earlier, the server calls `listen()` and `accept()` whereas the client calls `connect()`. None of these calls is used in the connectionless case. Here, both client and server simply create a socket, bind a port, and then send and receive datagrams. The client–server relationship is mainly a question of 'who goes first'. The client sends a datagram, the server responds. For some services, such as `daytime`, `chargen` and `time`, the client sends a zero-length datagram just to say that it is there, and the server obligingly doles out its fragment of wisdom. In the connectionless case, the client *must* transmit first, of course; otherwise the server is not aware that it is there.

## 4.7.2 Connectionless client and server operations

Connectionless clients and servers both begin by creating a datagram socket:

```
int sock;
sock = socket(AF_INET, SOCK_DGRAM, 0);
```

The earlier comments about address families apply equally here; again, we choose AF_INET addressing.

The server, of course, needs to bind its 'well-known' port number to this socket, so the client knows where to find it. The code looks exactly the same as in the connection-oriented case. The client does not need to make a call to bind(); if it attempts to transmit a datagram and there is no address bound, the system will automatically bind one.

The usual read() and write() calls cannot be used with unconnected sockets. Instead, a set of six new calls is provided: three for sending and three for receiving. For details, look up send(3) and recv(3).

The most straightforward of these calls are sendto() and recvfrom(), shown in Figure 4.19. In these calls, the first three arguments are as for write() and read(); namely, a descriptor, a pointer to the data buffer and a byte count. The flags argument can be used to specify special delivery options, but is usually zero. As expected, we have to specify the destination address on every call. This is done via the addr and addrlen arguments.

We will not review the other two pairs of calls in detail, but briefly, they are:

```
send(sock, data_addr, data_len, flags);
recv(sock, data_addr, data_len, flags);

sendmsg(sock, msg_info, flags);
recvmsg(sock, msg_info, flags);
```

The send() and recv() calls do not supply a peer address in their argument list, and may only be used on datagram sockets to which a connect() call has been applied to specify the peer address 'in advance', as it were. The name connect() is a misnomer when applied to datagram sockets as it does not make contact with the peer, it merely establishes a default address to be used when sending to that socket. In this context, 'peer' means 'the entity at the other end'.

The msg_info parameter in the sendmsg() and recvmsg() calls points to a structure which supports *gather-write* and *scatter-read* operations. Gather-write means that a collection of separate data buffers, at different places in memory, can be gathered together into a single datagram. Scatter-read means that a single datagram may be split up and delivered into several separate buffers. These can be useful, for example where the user's application protocol uses messages containing a header and a data portion. Sometimes (especially if the header is of variable length), it is not convenient to keep the two contiguous in memory.

## 4.7.3  A connectionless client example

We will illustrate the use of connectionless services by developing a client for the TFTP server. The client will be a 'remote' version of the cat program, called rcat, which might be invoked as follows:

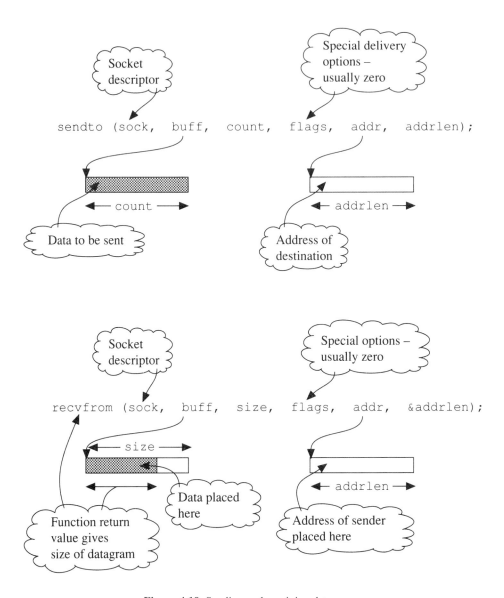

**Figure 4.19** Sending and receiving datagrams

```
rcat  trillian  /etc/passwd
```

This command will display the contents of the file /etc/passwd from the remote host trillian.

Although TFTP is certainly 'trivial' compared with other file transfer protocols such as ftp, rcp or FTAM (the OSI offering), the protocol is considerably more complicated than the simple ASCII text protocol of our earlier hangman service. The TFTP protocol is fully described in RFC 783. Here is a less formal description.

There are five packet types defined by the protocol, as shown in Figure 4.20. Each packet begins with an 'op-code' (a two-byte integer) whose value indicates the type of packet. A file transfer is initiated by the client which sends either a READ REQUEST or a WRITE REQUEST packet. This packet contains the filename (to be interpreted on the server), a terminating zero byte, and a second string indicating the *mode* of the transfer. A READ REQUEST, using *octet* mode, is appropriate for our `rcat` example.

The request is sent to the TFTP server at its 'well-known' port number (69). It does not matter what port number the client binds, but it must keep to the same one throughout. The server establishes a new socket (at a new port number) for its dialogue with this client. In the case of a READ REQUEST, the server responds by sending a sequence of DATA packets back to the client. Each DATA packet contains exactly 512 bytes of data (i.e. the total length of the datagram is 516 bytes), except for the last, which

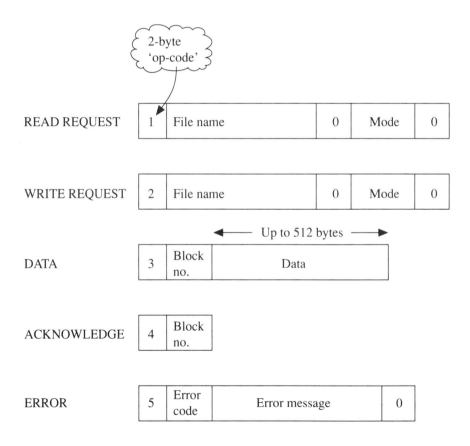

**Figure 4.20** TFTP packet formats.

contains from 0 to 511 bytes of data. This short packet signals the end of the data stream to the client. The block number in the DATA packet starts at 1 and increments for each block. The client must acknowledge each block by sending an ACKNOWLEDGE packet containing the number of the block to be acknowledged. The server will then proceed to send the next block. Note that the acknowledgements are sent to the UDP port that the server used to send the DATA packet, and not to port 69. The dialogue is illustrated in Figure 4.21.

If the server detects an error (for example, a request to copy a nonexistent or unreadable file), it will return an ERROR packet instead of a DATA packet. This error packet contains a numeric error code, and an error message text, which may be printed out by the client.

The op-codes and the block numbers are sent in network byte order (MS byte first). Of course, any machine-specific disagreements about the interpretation of the file data are someone else's problem. The data are opaque (i.e. not interpreted) as far as TFTP is concerned.

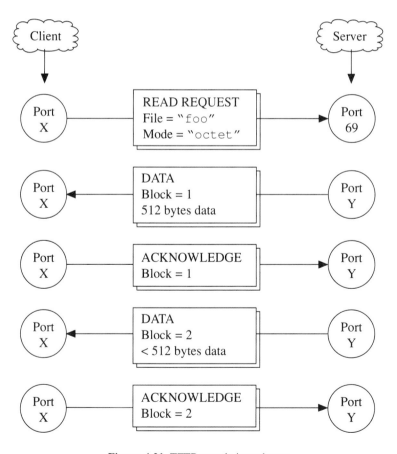

**Figure 4.21**  TFTP sample interchange.

You will notice that the client passes no information to the server about the identity of the user making the request. Consequently, the server has no meaningful user ID against which to check file access permissions. Most implementations of the TFTP server solve this problem by allowing read access only to files which have 'world' read permission, and allowing write access only to files which already exist and are publicly writable. Some versions execute a chroot() system call to a specified directory when they start up, to give even more security. In practice, these restrictions reduce the usefulness of our rcat client.

Given our earlier discussion on connectionless client and server operations, and the above description of the TFTP protocol, the client code shown below should come as no surprise. The only slightly messy part is the building of the READ REQUEST packet. Since the fields have variable length, we cannot use a structure, and must resort to explicit string copying and pointer manipulation.

```c
/* Remote cat client using TFTP server (UDP socket implementation).
   Usage: rcat hostname filename
*/

#include <sys/types.h>
#include <sys/fcntl.h>
#include <netinet/in.h>
#include <sys/socket.h>
#include <netdb.h>
#include <stdio.h>

#define TFTP_PORT       69      /* TFTP's well-known port number */
#define BSIZE           600     /* size of our data buffer */
#define MODE            "octet"

#define OP_RRQ          1       /* TFTP op-codes */
#define OP_DATA         3
#define OP_ACK          4
#define OP_ERROR        5

main(int argc, char *argv[])
{
    int    sock;                        /* Socket descriptor */
    struct sockaddr_in server;          /* Server's address  */
    struct sockaddr_in client;          /* Client's address  */
    struct hostent *host;               /* Server host info  */
    char   buffer[BSIZE], *p;
    int    count, server_len;
    if (argc != 3) {
        fprintf(stderr, "usage: %s hostname filename\n", argv[0]);
        exit(1);
    }
    /* Create a datagram socket */
    sock = socket(AF_INET, SOCK_DGRAM, 0);
```

```
/* Bind a local address. Any port number will do.
   This step isn't essential in the client. The system
   will pick an (arbitrary) port number if we don't.
*/
client.sin_family      = AF_INET;
client.sin_addr.s_addr = htonl(INADDR_ANY);
client.sin_port        = 0; /* 0 says choose any port */
if (bind(sock, &client, sizeof client) < 0) {
    fprintf(stderr, "rcat: bind failed\n"); exit(1);
}
/* Get the server's address */
host = gethostbyname(argv[1]);
if (host == NULL) {
    fprintf(stderr, "unknown host: %s\n", argv[1]);
    exit(2);
}
server.sin_family      = AF_INET;
memcpy(&server.sin_addr.s_addr, host->h_addr, host->h_length);
server.sin_port        = htons(TFTP_PORT);

/* Build a TFTP READ REQUEST packet. This is messy because the
   fields have variable length, so we can't use a structure.
*/
*(short *)buffer = htons(OP_RRQ);    /* The op-code   */
                                     /* in network byte order */
p = buffer + 2;
strcpy(p, argv[2]);                  /* The file name  */
p += strlen(argv[2])    + 1;         /* Keep the null */
strcpy(p, MODE);                     /* The mode       */
p += strlen(MODE) + 1;               /* Keep the null */

/* Send READ REQUEST to TFTP server. The length is computed from
   the pointer difference p-buffer
*/
count = sendto(sock, buffer, p-buffer, 0, &server, sizeof server);

/* Loop, collecting data packets from the server, until a short
   packet arrives. This indicates the end of the file.
*/
do {
    server_len = sizeof server;
    count = recvfrom(sock, buffer, BSIZE, 0, &server, &server_len);
    if (ntohs(*(short *)buffer) == OP_ERROR) {
        /* Ignore the error code; just print the error message */
        fprintf(stderr, "rcat: %s\n", buffer+4);
    }
    else {
        /* Got a good block. Write it to standard output. */
        write(1, buffer+4, count-4);
```

```
            /* Send an ACK packet. The block number we want to ack is
               already in the buffer so we just need to change the
               opcode and send the first 4 bytes of the buffer back.
               Note that the ACK is sent to the port number which the
               server just sent the data from, NOT to port 69. The
               required address is already in the server struct, after
               the recvfrom() call.
            */
            *(short *)buffer = htons(OP_ACK);
            sendto(sock, buffer, 4, 0, &server, sizeof server);
        }
    } while (count == 516);
}
```

## 4.7.4  TFTP packet traffic

We can use the `snoop` packet monitor to examine the network traffic generated by this program. Here is the interchange resulting from running the command

```
    rcat  desiato  /etc/passwd
```

on the host `magrathea`. It corresponds closely to the TFTP sample interchange shown in Figure 4.21. The `/etc/passwd` file on `desiato` is evidently 517 bytes long.

```
    magrathea -> desiato     TFTP Read "/etc/passwd" (octet)
    desiato -> magrathea     TFTP Data block 1 (512 bytes)
    magrathea -> desiato     TFTP Ack  block 1
    desiato -> magrathea     TFTP Data block 2 (15 bytes) (last block)
    magrathea -> desiato     TFTP Ack  block 2
```

## 4.7.5  Implementing a timeout and retry policy

Our TFTP client as shown makes no provision to recover from lost datagrams. If the network drops an incoming data packet, or an outgoing acknowledgement, the client will block forever. Note that in this case, misordered datagram deliveries are not an issue; the lock-step acknowledgement scheme guarantees that there is at most one datagram in transit.

As a simple example of implementing a timeout and retransmit policy, we will add code to recover from the loss of an outgoing acknowledgement packet. In practice, on a healthy LAN, it might be difficult to prove that such code was working. To simulate a LAN that drops packets, we will randomly 'lose' 25 per cent of the acknowledgement packets, by replacing the `sendto()` call in our `rcat` client with:

```
if (rand() % 4)
sendto( ... );
```

If the acknowledgement goes missing, the server will never send the next data packet, so the client will block forever on the next `recvfrom()` call. (This is not strictly true, because the TFTP server itself implements a timeout-and-retransmit policy, but we will ingore that for now!) There are a number of ways to force the read-datagram operation to time out.

One approach is to mark the socket as *nonblocking* – this can be done by adding the call:

```
fcntl(sock, F_SETFL, FNDELAY);
```

after the socket has been created. (This call can be applied to most open file descriptors, not just sockets. The symbolic constants `F_SETFL` and `FNDELAY` are defined in `<sys/fcntl.h>`.) If this is done, a call to `recvfrom()` when there is no datagram waiting to be read will return $-1$ immediately, with `errno` set to `EWOULDBLOCK`. A timeout can then be implemented by placing the `recvfrom()` call inside a loop, testing for an `EWOULDBLOCK` error return, and repeating up to some maximum retry count. There are two major disadvantages to this approach.

First, it is difficult to know how the maximum retry count relates to actual elapsed time. For example, what retry count should we use to get a two second timeout? Obviously this depends on the processor speed, and on how many other processes are in the scheduler queue. A second (and worse) problem is that spinning round in a polling loop like this is a waste of CPU time, and is best avoided in a multitasking operating system.

---

**An aside:** in fact, it will be our own process that suffers most if we do this. The UNIX scheduling algorithm reduces the priority of processes which are using a lot of CPU time. This helps to give fast interactive response to programs like shells and editors which spend much of their time waiting for input from the keyboard. Thus, the polling loop would push our process into a less-favourable scheduling priority.

---

Returning to our timeout-and-retransmit problem, clearly what we need is a way to block until either a datagram arrives, or a specified time has elapsed. The problem is rather similar to the `t_gets()` example from Chapter 2, and the solution is essentially the same – we arrange for a `SIGALRM` signal to be generated after the required timeout. This is done by calling:

```
alarm(t);
```

where `t` is the required timeout in seconds.

We also need to ask for the signal to be delivered to the process, by specifying a signal-handler function:

```
signal(SIGALRM, alarm_catcher);
```

Recall from our discussion in Chapter 2 that 'slow' system calls (i.e. those liable to block for a long time) will get interrupted if a signal is delivered, and will return with an 'apparent' error of EINTR. By checking the return value of recvfrom() and the errno value, we can distinguish a valid datagram from a timeout, and respond accordingly. The alarm_catcher function does not have to do anything in this case, except return. Thus, it may be written simply as:

```
void alarm_catcher() { }
```

If the recvfrom() call returns normally (i.e. a datagram is received without timing out), then we call

```
alarm(0);
```

which cancels the alarm signal. There is a small time window after returning from recvfrom() and before cancelling the alarm, during which a SIGALRM may still be delivered. Since the signal handler does nothing, this is benign. One further issue to resolve is: if the recvfrom() times out, which datagram should we retransmit? Clearly, the last one we sent. This could be an acknowledgement, or it may be the initial READ REQUEST packet. In the code shown below, the variables buffer, length and server are used to remember the source, length and destination of the most recently transmitted datagram.

The code of our new version of the client is shown below:

```
/* Remote cat client using TFTP server (UDP socket implementation).
   This version includes a simple timeout/retransmit mechanism
   Usage: rcat hostname filename
*/

#include <sys/types.h>
#include <sys/fcntl.h>
#include <netinet/in.h>
#include <sys/socket.h>
#include <netdb.h>
#include <signal.h>              /* Added for this version */
#include <errno.h>              /* Added for this version */
#include <stdio.h>

#define TFTP_PORT       69       /* TFTP's well-known port number */
#define BSIZE           600      /* size of our data buffer */
#define MODE            "octet"
#define TIMEOUT         2        /* Retransmit timeout in seconds */
```

```
#define OP_RRQ          1       /* TFTP op-codes */
#define OP_DATA         3
#define OP_ACK          4
#define OP_ERROR        5

void alarm_catcher() {}   /* This is the signal handler. It doesn't
                             do anything, except return
                          */

main(int argc, char *argv[])
{
    int    sock;                        /* Socket descriptor */
    struct sockaddr_in server;          /* Server's address  */
    struct sockaddr_in client;          /* Client's address  */
    struct hostent *host;               /* Server host info  */
    char   buffer[BSIZE], *p;
    int    count, server_len, length;

    if (argc != 3) {
        fprintf(stderr, "usage: %s hostname filename\n", argv[0]);
        exit(1);
    }

    /* Create a datagram socket */
    sock = socket(AF_INET, SOCK_DGRAM, 0);

    /* Bind a local address. */
    client.sin_family      = AF_INET;
    client.sin_addr.s_addr = htonl(INADDR_ANY);
    client.sin_port        = 0;  /* 0 says choose any port */

    if (bind(sock, &client, sizeof client) < 0) {
        fprintf(stderr, "rcat: bind failed\n"); exit(1);
    }

    /* Get the server's address */
    host = gethostbyname(argv[1]);
    if (host == NULL) {
        fprintf(stderr, "unknown host: %s\n", argv[1]);
        exit(2);
    }
    server.sin_family      = AF_INET;
    memcpy(&server.sin_addr.s_addr, host->h_addr, host->h_length);
    server.sin_port        = htons(TFTP_PORT);

    /* Build a TFTP READ REQUEST packet. This is messy because the
       fields have variable length, so we can't use a structure.
    */
    *(short *)buffer = htons(OP_RRQ);   /* The op-code   */
    p = buffer + 2;
    strcpy(p, argv[2]);                      /* The file name */
    p += strlen(argv[2])    + 1;        /* Keep the null */
```

```
    strcpy(p, MODE);                          /* The Mode     */
    p += strlen(MODE) + 1;

    /* Send READ REQUEST to TFTP server */
    length = p-buffer;
    count = sendto(sock, buffer, length, 0, &server, sizeof server);

    /* Loop, collecting DATA packets from the server, until a short
       packet arrives. This indicates the end of the file.
    */
    do {
        await_reply:
        server_len = sizeof server;
        /* Arrange for an ALARM signal to be delivered after TIMEOUT */
        signal(SIGALRM, alarm_catcher);
        alarm(TIMEOUT);
        count = recvfrom(sock, buffer, BSIZE, 0, &server, &server_len);
        alarm(0);               /* Cancel alarm signal */
        if (count == -1) {
            if (errno = EINTR) {
                /* Timed out - resend the last datagram */
                sendto(sock, buffer, length, 0, &server, sizeof server);
                goto await_reply;
            }
            else {      /* Must be a REAL error! */
                fprintf(stderr, "rcat: read error\n");
                exit(3);
            }
        }
        /* Reach here when got a valid datagram */
        if (ntohs(*(short *)buffer) == OP_ERROR) {
            fprintf(stderr, "rcat: %s\n", buffer+4);
        }
        else {
            write(1, buffer+4, count-4);
            /* Send an ACK packet. The block number we want to ack is
               already in the buffer so we just need to change the
               opcode. Note that the ACK is sent to the port number
               which the server just sent the data from, NOT to port
               69
            */
            *(short *)buffer = htons(OP_ACK);
            length = 4;
            if (rand() % 4) {
                sendto(sock, buffer, length, 0, &server, sizeof server);
            }
        }
    } while (count == 516);
}
```

In reality, clients and servers implementing a timeout-and-retransmit policy need to be smarter than this. When our client times out waiting for the next data block from the server, it does not know whether it was the previous outgoing acknowledge packet which got lost, or the new incoming data packet. Examples of the two scenarios are shown in Figure 4.22.

In the first case, the acknowledgement for block 2 is lost and retransmitted. The server sees nothing unusual. In the second case, the data for block 2 are lost. The client times out and retransmits the acknowledgement for block 1. The server will see two copies of this acknowledgement. It must be smart enough to realize this, and to respond by resending data block 2. When the client receives this block, it knows that the server has transmitted it at least once, and possibly twice. Transmitting a file block a second time does no harm – the operation is said to be *idempotent* – that is, it has no harmful effect if repeated. In this case, our concern is to ensure that the operation has happened at least once – if it has happened more than once, no harm is done.

Not all operations are idempotent. Consider a server responsible for maintaining your bank account. A request comes in to transfer £250 to the local tax office. The server performs the operation, and sends an acknowledgement, which gets lost. The client, tiring of waiting for a reply, times out and resends the request. Clearly, the server must *not* repeat the transfer of funds. It must be smart enough to realize 'I've already done that', and simply resend the acknowledgement. Typically, this is achieved by including some form of unique *transaction identifier* with each request. The server, maintaining a cache of recently processed transaction identifiers, along with the result of that transaction, is able to reject the duplicate request, return the cached result, and so preserve a guarantee of having performed the operation 'exactly once' even in the face of lost or duplicated packets.

# 4.8  A concurrent, distributed application

We will conclude this chapter with an example of a true distributed, concurrent application. The problem we are going to tackle can be stated very simply: we want to know how many prime numbers there are between 1 and 1 000 000. It is, of course, conceivable that you do not wish to know this. Nonetheless, the example has some merit; finding prime numbers is a relatively time-consuming business, and the idea is to get several servers working concurrently on different parts of the problem, to reduce the overall time to reach a solution. This is a clear-cut example of *data distribution*, discussed back in Section 1.3.1.

## 4.8.1  A nondistributed program to count prime numbers

To begin, here is an ordinary, nondistributed program to do the job:

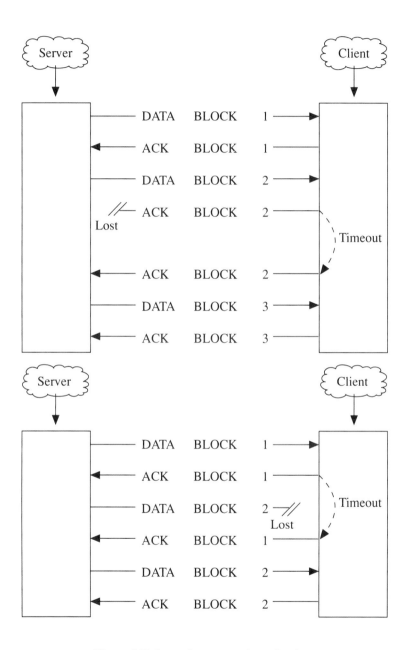

**Figure 4.22** Loss of request vs. loss of reply.

```
#define SMALLEST        1L
#define BIGGEST         1000000L

main(argc, argv)
int argc;
char *argv[];
{
    long count;
    count = count_primes(SMALLEST, BIGGEST);
    printf("Between %ld and %ld there are %ld primes\n",
        SMALLEST, BIGGEST, count);
}

long count_primes(min, max)
long min, max;
{
    long i, count = 0;
    for (i=min; i<=max; i++)
        if (isprime(i)) count++;
    return count;
}

int isprime(n)
long n;
{
    int i;
    for (i=2; i*i <= n; i++)
        if (n%i == 0)
            return 0;
    return 1;
}
```

This program takes 277 seconds to execute on a Sparcstation 2, and 935 seconds on a Sun 3/50. Clearly, with run-times this long, a concurrent distributed solution would be useful. (The answer, by the way, is 78 499.)

## 4.8.2  A server to count prime numbers

Before writing a distributed version of this program, there are two key design decisions to be taken. The first is: how do we divide the work between the client and the (multiple) servers? The second is: should the servers be connection-oriented or connectionless?

There are two possible places to draw the line between server and client. The first is to implement just the isprime() function on the server. That is to say, we send the server a number, and it sends back a boolean telling if the number is prime or not. This is clearly an appalling choice; the amount of work the server needs to do on each transaction is much too small. The communications overhead would far exceed the actual computation time, and we would end up with a distributed version which ran *slower* than the original single-processor version. The second choice is to implement `count_primes()` on the server. On each transaction we send the server two numbers specifying the lower and upper limits of the number range to be searched, and the server returns the count of primes within that range. Providing the range is fairly large, the computational load dominates and the communication overhead becomes negligible. The client, then, simply needs to divide up the total range into a number of subranges in some way, pass each subrange over to a server, collect the replies from the servers, and add them up. This is the basic model we will implement. The idea is to start up servers on multiple machines, so that they may operate concurrently.

The second decision, about whether to implement a connection-oriented or connectionless server, is much less clear-cut. It could be satisfactorily done either way. The fact that each transaction with the server is self-contained and makes no reference to previous transactions possibly argues for a connectionless service. Also, it is a little easier for the client to retrieve replies from multiple servers if they are all sent to the same UDP socket, rather than to separate TCP connections. On the other hand, use of UDP may force us to add in a timeout and retransmit mechanism to recover from lost packets if the subnetwork is not reliable. Choosing a suitable timeout value would be difficult because there is no easy way to estimate how long a particular request ought to take. It is easier to have the timeout and retransmission handled 'underneath' the application code. Consequently, we will choose to implement a connection-oriented server, using TCP.

As just discussed, the client-to-server protocol will consist simply of a pair of numbers specifying the subrange. In reply, the server just sends a single value back to the client, indicating the number of primes in that range.

With these design decisions out of the way, it is a simple matter to write the server. Indeed, as we have already seen the boiler-plate code for a TCP server, and we already have the `count_primes()` function, there is very little new to write.

There are a couple of things about which the client and server need to agree – which port number to use, and the format of the request packet. We will place these shared definitions in a header file, `primes.h`:

```
/* primes.h */

#define PRIME_PORT 1066

struct subrange {
    long        min;
    long        max;
};
```

Now here is the complete server:

```
/* Server for counting prime numbers */

#include <sys/types.h>
#include <sys/socket.h>
#include <netinet/in.h>
#include <stdio.h>
```

```c
#include "primes.h"

main()

{
    int sock, msgsock, client_len;
    struct sockaddr_in server, client;
    long count;
    struct limits limits;

    sock = socket(AF_INET, SOCK_STREAM, 0);
    if (sock < 0) {
        exit(1);
    }

    server.sin_family      = AF_INET;
    server.sin_addr.s_addr = htonl(INADDR_ANY);
    server.sin_port        = htons(PRIME_PORT);

    if (bind(sock, (struct sockaddr *) &server, sizeof (server)) < 0) {
        exit(2);
    }

    listen(sock, 5);
    while (1) {
        client_len = sizeof(client);
        msgsock = accept(sock, (struct sockaddr *) &client, &client_len);
        if (msgsock < 0) {
            exit(3);
        }

        /* Once a connection is made, we accept multiple requests from
           the client, until the client drops the connection.  At that
           point, we get an error back from the read()
        */

        while (1) {
            if(read(msgsock, &limits, sizeof limits) != sizeof limits)
                /* Assume 'end of file'; drop the connection */
                break;
            count = count_primes(limits.min, limits.max);
            write(msgsock, &count, sizeof count);
        }
        close(msgsock);
    }   /* Go wait for the next client */
}

/* The count_primes() and isprime() functions go here. They are the same
   as in the previous example.
*/
```

## 4.8.3  A simple prime number counting client

The client is a little harder. How does it know on which machines the server is available? How does it divide up the range? How does it keep track of which server is doing what? How does it collect the answers? How does it know when they are all in?

We will make a few simplifying assumptions to keep our client as easy as possible. Later, we will develop a more sophisticated version. To begin with, we assume that the servers have all been started up manually, for instance by logging in to each remote workstation in turn. Therefore, we know precisely where the servers are running, and can supply the appropriate machine names to the client on the command line. The range subdivision will be accomplished simply by dividing the 1–1 000 000 range into a number of equal sized subranges, depending on how many servers we were given. We will open a TCP connection to each server and send it a subrange. Then we will read back (in the same order) the responses from the servers, and total them.

---

**An aside:** our choice of a binary protocol implicitly assumes that the machines running the client and the server are using compatible binary data representations. We will examine this problem further – and present a solution to it – in Chapter 6.

---

Here is our initial, simple-minded client:

```
/* Client for counting prime numbers: Version 1
   C.R.Brown   24 June 1992
*/

#include <sys/types.h>
#include <sys/socket.h>
#include <netinet/in.h>
#include <stdio.h>
#include <netdb.h>
#include "primes.h"

#define MAX_HOSTS       10
#define SMALLEST        1
#define BIGGEST         1000000

main(int argc, char *argv[])
{
    int connection[MAX_HOSTS];
    char *host[MAX_HOSTS];
    int i, nhosts;
    long count, total;
    struct subrange limits;
    long start_time;

    nhosts = argc - 1;
```

```
    if (nhosts < 1) {
        fprintf(stderr, "%s: no hosts specified\n", argv[0]);
        exit(1);
    }

    if (nhosts > MAX_HOSTS) {
        nhosts = MAX_HOSTS;
        fprintf(stderr, "Too many hosts, using only the first %d\n", nhosts);
    }

    /* Try to obtain connections to each server */
    for (i=0; i<nhosts; i++) {
        host[i] = argv[i+1];
        switch (connection[i] = connect_to_server(host[i], PRIME_PORT)) {
            case -1: fprintf(stderr, "Problem creating socket - bye!\n");
                     exit(2);
            case -2: fprintf(stderr, "Unknown host: %s - bye!\n", host[i]);
                     exit(3);
            case -3: fprintf(stderr, "Cannot find server on host %s - bye!\n",
                             host[i]);
                     exit(4);
            default: printf("connected to host %s\n", host[i]);
        }
    }

    /* Send a subrange to each server */
    start_time = time(0);
    limits.max = SMALLEST - 1;
    for (i=0; i<nhosts; i++) {
        limits.min = limits.max + 1;
        limits.max = limits.min + (BIGGEST - SMALLEST + 1)/nhosts;
        if (i == nhosts-1) limits.max = BIGGEST;
        printf("sending range (%d,%d) to host %s\n",
                limits.min, limits.max, host[i]);
        write(connection[i], &limits, sizeof limits);
    }

    /* Read responses back from servers, in same order */
    total = 0;
    for (i=0; i<nhosts; i++) {
        read(connection[i], &count, sizeof count);
        printf("got reply = %ld from host %10s after %ld sec\n",
                count, host[i], time(0)-start_time);
        total += count;
    }
    printf("answer is %ld\n", total);
}

int connect_to_server(char *host, int port)
{
```

```
      int sock;
      struct sockaddr_in server;
      struct hostent *host_info;

      if ((sock = socket(AF_INET, SOCK_STREAM, 0)) < 0)   return -1;

      if ((host_info = gethostbyname(host)) == NULL)      return -2;

      server.sin_family      = AF_INET;
      server.sin_port        = htons(port);
      memcpy(&server.sin_addr, host_info->h_addr, host_info->h_length);

      if (connect(sock, &server, sizeof server) < 0)      return -3;

      return sock;
  }
```

Now suppose we have compiled and somehow started the server on the remote hosts `douglas`, `benjie` and `frankie`. We could then run our client, telling it to use these three hosts, as follows:

```
eddie% prime_client douglas frankie benjie
connected to host douglas
connected to host frankie
connected to host benjie
sending range (1,333334) to host douglas
sending range (333335,666668) to host frankie
sending range (666669,1000000) to host benjie
got reply = 28666 from host   douglas after 151 sec
got reply = 25405 from host   frankie after 163 sec
got reply = 24428 from host    benjie after 404 sec
answer is 78499
eddie%
```

Whilst our client clearly works, it has some major limitations. For one thing, it does not react well to the situation in which some of the servers cannot be contacted. It simply gives up completely, and exits. It would be better simply to ignore the servers we cannot find, and carry on with the rest. This requires a little additional logic, which we will incorporate in the next version.

## 4.8.4  Load-balancing issues

A much more interesting problem with the client becomes apparent if you examine the timings on the output shown above. Hosts `douglas` and `frankie` take approximately the same time to complete their work, but `benjie` takes nearly three times as long. Why is this? It is mainly because `benjie` is dealing with larger numbers and it takes longer, on average, to test a large number for prime-ness than to test a small one. The timings are also affected, of course, by the speed of the individual processors. Whatever the reasons, we are clearly not exploiting the machines as well as we might, because `douglas`'s and `frankie`'s servers are both spending about 60 per cent of their time idle. In the jargon of the parallel processing fraternity, we say that the load is *unbalanced*.

How can we fix this? One possible solution is to split the (1–1000000) range into unequal-sized pieces, such that each piece presents roughly the same computational load. To do this, we need some way of estimating the computational load of a given subrange. Unfortunately, prime numbers being what they are, there is no easy way to do this. (This is not always the case with this type of application. Sometimes, there is a cheap way to estimate the effort to process a given server request, which can be used to perform 'up front' load-balancing.)

Similar difficulties with a priori load-balancing arise in other, less trivial applications. For example, a distributed image processing application used spatial parallelism, dividing the image into horizontal strips, in order to speed up a stereo matching algorithm. The execution time of this algorithm was strongly dependent on the amount of edge detail in the image, so that dividing the image into equal-sized strips did not generally balance the load very well. The problem, as in our prime number example, is that there is no cheap way of estimating the amount of work involved in processing a given subset of the data.

Even if such a cost metric were available, it would not take into account the effect of different processor speeds, which are, usually, not known to the client. Furthermore, the timings will be affected by how heavily the host machines are loaded by other, unrelated tasks.

## 4.8.5  Implementing a processor farm

To fix this problem we will adopt a particular type of client–server paradigm known in parallel computing circles as a *processor farm*. The idea is as follows: a single client (called a master, in processor farm jargon) farms out the work to multiple servers (or slaves). It divides the work up into a large number of 'work packets'. It does not matter if the packets are not all 'equally difficult', but there should be several times as many work packets as there are servers. To begin, it sends a work packet to each server. Then, it waits until any server replies. The reply is recorded, and the next work packet is sent to that server. The process continues, with each server receiving a new work packet as soon as it has finished the last one, until all the packets have been sent out, and all the replies have been received. Notice that the processor farm, with its one client serviced by many servers, is almost the opposite of the usual client–server model, in which one server serves many clients.

The biggest advantage of the processor farm is that it keeps all the servers busy all the time, i.e. it balances the load. There is no need for an up-front estimate of how long each work packet will take. It does not matter if the servers run at different speeds. The biggest disadvantage is that processor farms are only appropriate if the task can be broken into a relatively large number of *independent* work packets. There should be several times as many work packets as there are slave processors. If the servicing of one work packet depends on results from previous work packets, the client logic gets *much* harder. Fortunately, in our example, each subrange work packet can be processed without reference to any other subrange, making the processor farm a good choice.

---

**An aside:** in the early days of transputers, the computation of the Mandelbrot set was a favourite amongst vendors as a demonstration of parallel computing. (The Mandelbrot set is a pattern based on fractal geometry which can be explored at arbitrary levels of detail.) There were three reasons for its popularity: it is very computationally intensive, it is very easy to implement as a processor farm, and you get a rather pretty picture at the end of it. Consequently at exhibitions one could walk through the hall seeing screen after screen of Mandelbrot. After a while the market sobered up, Mandelbrot-free zones were declared, and vendors finally started showing development and debugging tools which the users had by then discovered were essential if one was to have any hope of programming anything other than the Mandelbrot set. . . .

There are, however, some important image-rendering applications, such as ray tracing, which can also be parallelized using a processor farm.

---

No changes are needed to the server to implement the processor farm. On the client side, we now find that our decision to use a connection-oriented server makes life a little difficult for us. The central issue is that the client needs to retrieve responses from the servers in the order in which they occur, which will not in general be the same as the order in which the requests were sent out. If the service was connectionless, the client could collect the responses from all the servers by simply reading from a single datagram socket. In our connection-oriented client, we have a separate file descriptor to read for each server, and of course, we do not know in which order they will become ready.

Earlier in the chapter we saw the use of the `select()` system call to allow a process to block until any one of several specified file descriptors became ready for reading. There, we used it at the server end, to implement a concurrent server without using multiple processes. In our present example, we will use it in the client to concurrently feed data to multiple servers.

Here is our new 'processor farm' version of the client:

```
/* Client for counting prime numbers: Version 2
   Implements a processor farm, using sockets and select()
*/

#include <sys/types.h>
#include <sys/socket.h>
#include <netinet/in.h>
#include <stdio.h>
#include <netdb.h>
#include "primes.h"

#define FD_TABLE_SIZE   32
```

```
#define SMALLEST        1
#define BIGGEST         1000000
#define GRANULARITY     100   /* This controls the number of subranges
                                    (i.e.  work packets)  which the total
                                    range is divided into */

long next_min = SMALLEST;     /* Tracks the lower bound of the next
                                    work packet to be sent out */

char *host[FD_TABLE_SIZE];

void send_next_work_packet();
main(int argc, char *argv[])
{
    int i, fd;
    int prospects;          /* Prospective number of hosts */
    int outstanding;        /* Number of unanswered work packets */
    long count, total;
    long start_time;
    fd_set select_set;      /* Set of descriptors to select on */
    fd_set ready_set;

    start_time = time(0);
    prospects = argc - 1;
    if (prospects < 1) {
        fprintf(stderr, "%s: no hosts specified\n", argv[0]);
        exit(1);
    }

    /* Try to obtain connections to each server */
    outstanding = 0;
    argv++;          /* Bump pointer past the command name */
    FD_ZERO(&select_set);
    for (i=0; i<prospects; i++) {
        switch (fd = connect_to_server(argv[i], PRIME_PORT)) {
            case -1: fprintf(stderr, "Problem creating socket\n");
                     exit(2);
            case -2: fprintf(stderr, "Unknown host %s: ignored\n",
                                        argv[i]);
                     break;
            case -3: fprintf(stderr,"No server on host %s: ignored\n",
                                        argv[i]);
                     break;
            default: if (fd >= FD_TABLE_SIZE) {
                        fprintf(stderr,"too many hosts: %s ignored\n",
                                        argv[i]);
                       break;
                     }
                     printf("connected to host %s\n", argv[i]);

                     /* It is not  essential to  record the host name,
```

```
                        but it helps us print more meaningful messages
                */

                host[fd] = argv[i];

                /* We do not explicitly  record the value of the
                   descriptor for this connection, we simply add
                   it into the select set.  Later, when a select
                   returns,  we can find out which descriptor is
                   ready for reading.
                */

                FD_SET(fd, &select_set);
                send_next_work_packet(fd);
                outstanding++;
        }
}

/* At this point, since we have not retrieved any responses,
   the value of outstanding tells us how many hosts we found
*/
if (outstanding == 0) {
    fprintf(stderr, "No servers found!\n");
    exit(3);
}
total = 0;         /* Total count is accumulated in here */

/* Keep the servers busy until the job is done */
while (outstanding > 0) {

    /* We copy select_set  onto ready_set because  select() over-
       writes its argument, and we need to keep select_set intact
    */

    memcpy(&ready_set, &select_set, sizeof select_set);
    select(FD_TABLE_SIZE, &ready_set, NULL, NULL, NULL);

    /* Now we have to scan through the  file descriptor set which
       select()  returned to see which is ready  for reading.  We
       always scan the entire set, because it is possible (though
       unlikely)  for several  descriptors to become ready at the
       same time.
    */

    for (fd=3; fd < FD_TABLE_SIZE; fd++) {
        if (FD_ISSET(fd, &ready_set)) {
            read(fd, &count, sizeof count);
            printf("got reply = %ld from host %10s after %ld sec\n",
                    count, host[fd], time(0)-start_time);
            total += count;
            outstanding --;

            /* If there are more work packets to process, send
```

```
                           the next one out.  Otherwise,  just  mop up the
                           outstanding requests
                    */

                    if (next_min <= BIGGEST) {
                        send_next_work_packet(fd);
                        outstanding++;
                    }
                }
            }
        }
    }
    printf("answer is %ld\n", total);
}

int connect_to_server(char *host, int port)
{
    int sock;
    struct sockaddr_in server;
    struct hostent *host_info;

    if ((sock = socket(AF_INET, SOCK_STREAM, 0)) < 0)  return -1;

    if ((host_info = gethostbyname(host)) == NULL)     return -2;

    server.sin_family      = AF_INET;
    server.sin_port        = htons(port);
    memcpy(&server.sin_addr, host_info->h_addr, host_info->h_length);

    if (connect(sock, &server, sizeof server) < 0)     return -3;

    return sock;
}

void send_next_work_packet(int fd)
{
    struct subrange limits;

    limits.min = next_min;
    limits.max = limits.min + (BIGGEST - SMALLEST)/GRANULARITY;
    if (limits.max > BIGGEST) limits.max = BIGGEST;
    write(fd, &limits, sizeof limits);
    printf("sent range (%d,%d) to host %s\n",
            limits.min, limits.max, host[fd]);
    next_min = limits.max + 1;
}
```

Here is the dialogue when we run it:

```
douglas% prime_farm localhost eddie magrathea desiato benjie
connected to host localhost
sent range (1,10000) to host localhost
```

```
connected to host eddie
sent range (10001,20000) to host eddie
connected to host magrathea
sent range (20001,30000) to host magrathea
connected to host desiato
sent range (30001,40000) to host desiato
No server on host benjie: ignored
got reply = 1230 from host  localhost after 1 sec
sent range (40001,50000) to host localhost
got reply = 983 from host  magrathea after 2 sec
sent range (50001,60000) to host magrathea
got reply = 958 from host   desiato after 2 sec
sent range (60001,70000) to host desiato
got reply = 1033 from host     eddie after 3 sec
sent range (70001,80000) to host eddie
got reply = 924 from host  magrathea after 4 sec
sent range (80001,90000) to host magrathea
```

... and so on ...

```
got reply = 720 from host  magrathea after 138 sec
sent range (980001,990000) to host magrathea
got reply = 711 from host    desiato after 140 sec
sent range (990001,1000000) to host desiato
got reply = 710 from host  magrathea after 144 sec
got reply = 732 from host  localhost after 146 sec
got reply = 721 from host    desiato after 146 sec
got reply = 717 from host      eddie after 150 sec
answer is 78499
```

The operation of the processor farm is clearly visible from the above dialogue. Although not obvious from what is shown (most of it has been elided out), each host managed to process a different number of work packets, as follows:

| | |
|---|---|
| `localhost` | 22 packets handled |
| `eddie` | 16 packets handled |
| `magrathea` | 31 packets handled |
| `desiato` | 31 packets handled |

Since all the machines were more or less otherwise idle when this test was run, these numbers are indicative of the relative performance of the four machines used.

## 4.8.6 Starting up the remote servers

We have assumed in the above tests that servers had somehow been started on each machine. This could be done, of course, with an appropriate entry in a boot-time script (or by starting up the server via `inetd` – both these issues are discussed in Chapter 7). However, let us consider how we might take our client one final step further by having it explicitly startup servers as required on the remote machines.

To make the task a little easier we will make a small modification to the server, so that it automatically creates a child to do the real work. This is easily done by adding the lines

```
if (fork())  exit(0);
close(0);
close(1);
close(2);
```

at the beginning of the `main()` function in the server. The first line causes the parent to exit, leaving the child to get on with the work. The other lines explicitly close the server's `stdin`, `stdout` and `stderr` streams. This step is necessary to ensure that the `rsh` commands shown below do not wait until the child has exited. Of course, closing your `stdout` and `stderr` streams in this way restricts your options for error reporting – any calls to `perror()`, for example, are doomed to failure. We will examine the issue of error logging from background servers in Chapter 7.

This change immediately makes it easier to start up the required servers manually. Rather than logging in on each machine, we can now use a sequence of `rsh` commands on the local machine:

```
eddie% rsh douglas prime_server
eddie% rsh benjie prime_server
eddie% rsh magrathea prime_server
```

We can also bury these operations inside the client. One way is to use the `system()` function:

```
system("rsh douglas prime_server");
system("rsh benjie prime_server");
system("rsh magrathea prime_server");
```

This call causes the specified command to be executed 'as if it had been typed at a terminal'. This is wonderfully easy in terms of programming effort, but expensive in terms of execution. Each call to `system()` performs a `fork/exec` of a Bourne shell and supplies the argument string to that shell. A `fork()` and an `exec()`, particularly of a big program like a shell, consume significant resources.

A more efficient approach is to use functions such as `rcmd()` or `rexec()`, which we examined in Chapter 3, to contact the remote execution server directly.

# Chapter 5

# The transport level interface

## 5.1 Introduction

The transport level interface (TLI) is a library of functions that provide an application program interface to STREAMS-based transport services. (STREAMS is explained in Section 5.1.3, below.) As such, it is at the same conceptual level as sockets, and provides much the same functionality. Indeed, the names of the functions we will meet in this chapter will bear a more than passing resemblance to those of the last. TLI is more 'modern' than sockets, and more closely modelled on the OSI transport layer definition. It is, in a sense, the 'officially recommended' transport interface of UNIX. For example, it forms the basis of the XTI (X/Open Transport Interface) specification of the X/Open Group (X/Open, 1988). Despite all this, sockets remain as a popular and easy-to-use interface, and are unlikely to go away in the foreseeable future – too much existing code depends on them.

It is important to understand that TLI is not of itself a transport provider, it is merely an interface to one. Indeed, TLI is carefully designed to be independent of any specific transport protocol. This does not mean that all code written using TLI will automatically be independent of the transport provider – it is quite difficult, in practice, to write a client or a server using TLI which is not aware of which protocol it is using.

### 5.1.1 TLI's extra functionality

Before seeing the details it is worth summarizing some of the extra functionality of TLI compared with sockets. This includes the following:

1. The capability to send data along with a connection request.
2. The capability to send data along with a connection release.
3. The capability to retrieve a connection request from an endpoint without actually accepting the connection. A server may then examine the identity of the client requesting the connection, and either accept or forcefully reject the request. Using sockets, the most anti-social a server can be is to accept the connection, find who the client is, and then close the connection.

4.  The capability to query the transport provider, to find out, for example, how many bytes a transport endpoint address occupies, how much data can be sent in one lump (TLI calls them *transport service data units* – it could surely not bear to use a term as colloquial as 'lump'), whether *expedited* data can be sent, and so on.
5.  The capability to retrieve notification of special conditions or errors within the transport provider which the provider 'posts to' the transport endpoint. Special conditions include the arrival of expedited data, or a disconnection request.
6.  The capability to maintain record boundaries within a byte stream delivered by a connection-oriented transport, if the transport supports it.

To repeat our earlier point, it should be stressed that TLI does not 'provide' any of these capabilities, it merely supplies the interface to them.

## 5.1.2  Differences in style

Apart from the extra functionality, the most striking difference that the application programmer will notice between sockets and TLI is one of style. The manual pages are very formal – even more than usual. For example, the valid sequence of operations to obtain a network connection is described in terms of a set of endpoint *states*, a set of *events*, and a finite state machine. Another example of this ultra-hygienic approach is that each major TLI function has an associated structure type which neatly parcels up most of the data required by that call. The `t_bind()` function, for example, takes a pointer to a `struct t_bind` as argument, whereas the `t_connect()` function takes a pointer to a `struct t_call` and the `t_optmgmt()` function takes a pointer to a `struct t_optmgmt`. Whilst this makes the TLI function calls themselves very succinct (most of them have only two or three arguments), the business of squirrelling all the data away into the structures before the call, and/or grovelling around inside the structure to fish it all out again afterwards, can become rather tiresome.

There are other differences between TLI and sockets which are pure terminology. The most obvious is the term *transport endpoint*, which is essentially the same concept as a socket, and, like a socket, is referred to by a UNIX file descriptor. Another term drawn from OSI terminology is *transport service data unit* (TSDU), meaning a sequence of bytes sent as a single message.

## 5.1.3  TLI and STREAMS

TLI was introduced into System V Release 3 UNIX in 1985, along with a new and (then) mysterious mechanism called STREAMS, which had been developed by Dennis Ritchie. Historically (and, to some extent, technically) TLI and STREAMS are linked. STREAMS is a flexible framework for building I/O systems within the kernel. It defines a set of standard interfaces (based on message passing) between STREAMS *modules* (which exist inside the kernel), device drivers and user programs. It allows the construction of protocol stacks, multiplexors and demultiplexors within a standardized and documented framework between a user program and a device such as a terminal port or a network interface.

---

**An aside:** the name STREAMS is possibly not the best of choices. It has nothing directly to do with the general notion of a stream, as in 'standard output stream', or with the notion of a stream (as opposed to datagram) transport service. The name STACKS might have been better, or maybe MODULES, or perhaps some totally new word not as yet commandeered by the computing fraternity. As it is, we are obliged to write it in upper case to make clear what we mean. Dennis Ritchie showed similar reluctance to use up another word when he used the `static` keyword in C to mean two totally unrelated things in two different contexts. Generations of C programmers have been confused ever since.

---

A STREAM is constructed out of zero or more *modules* which are arranged in a stack between a *STREAMS driver* at the bottom end and a *STREAM head* at the top end. The stream head is the part on which the application programmer's system calls operate. Each module consists of a pair of *queues*, one for each direction of data flow. The general arrangement is shown in Figure 5.1. When a STREAMS device is opened, special data structures within the kernel's device tables control the assembly of an initial STREAMS configuration. For example, opening a device name such as `/dev/tcp` results in the creation of a stream supporting the TCP/IP stack. Thereafter, user programs can modify the configuration by pushing and popping modules on to the stack, using `ioctl()` calls applied to the stream head. However, it is *not* possible to prepare such modules in 'user space', and push them down into the kernel at run-time in this way. The modules must be compiled and linked into the kernel when the kernel is built. There is an excellent, more detailed introduction to STREAMS in Chapter 2 of Padovano (1993).

Prior to the introduction of STREAMS, the I/O subsystems in UNIX were monolithic and largely impenetrable (certainly without access to their source code). Adding new network protocols, or new character editing capabilities for terminal input, for example, required surgery deep within the kernel. Using STREAMS, such additions are much more straightforward.

Of what concern is all this to the user of TLI? The answer is, very little. The writing of STREAMS modules is a specialized business, much as the writing of device drivers is. For details, refer to the USL book *UNIX System V Release 4 Programmers' Guide: STREAMS*, or to SunSoft's *SunOS 5.1 STREAMS Programmers' Guide*. As Figure 5.1 shows, the TLI library functions are the application programmer's normal interface to the STREAMS mechanism, and the programmer will not normally be aware of the details of the STREAMS. (We will, however, meet one example of explicit pushing and popping of STREAMS modules later in the chapter.) For example, to construct a stream which supports the UDP/IP protocol stack, and obtain a transport endpoint, the TLI programmer simply makes a call of the form:

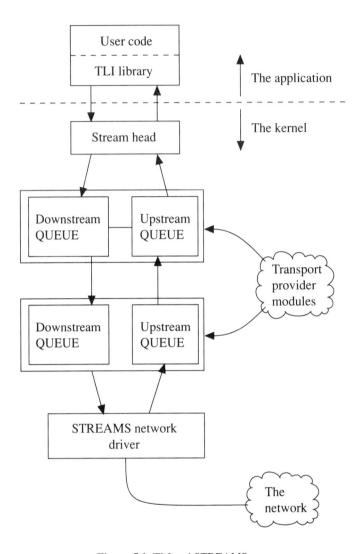

**Figure 5.1** TLI and STREAMS.

```
t = t_open("/dev/udp", O_RDWR, &info);
```

where /dev/udp is the name of the appropriate STREAMS driver. t_open() returns a file descriptor relating to the transport endpoint.

Sockets and STREAMS are occasionally promoted as being 'opposites', or 'alternatives'. This is not the case. There is no law which says that TLI *must* be implemented on top of STREAMS. Other implementations would be possible. For example, work is in hand on a TLI interface for Microsoft Windows. There is similarly no law that sockets must *not* be implemented on top of STREAMS. Indeed, in SunOS, sockets are implemented in precisely this way.

## 5.2 TLI data structures

The place to start learning about TLI is its data structures. As mentioned above, each data structure is designed to draw together all the data required by one particular operation.

### 5.2.1 The netbuf structure

The most widely used data structure in TLI is the netbuf structure shown in Figure 5.2. A netbuf is a general-purpose buffer structure which is used to pass data both in and out of TLI functions. It is declared as follows:

```
struct netbuf {
        unsigned int maxlen;
        unsigned int len;
        char *buf;
};
```

These structures are used to hold a variety of information such as transport endpoint addresses, protocol-specific options and user data.

When a netbuf is used to pass data into a function, the programmer allocates a buffer, places data into it and sets the buf member of the netbuf to point to it. The len member must also be set to say how many bytes of data are present. When a netbuf is used to pass data out of a function, the programmer allocates a buffer to receive the data, sets the buf member to point to it, and sets the maxlen member to the total length of the buffer. On return, the len member will be set to indicate the amount of data actually placed into the buffer. This allows the TLI functions to be 'safe' – if the function has

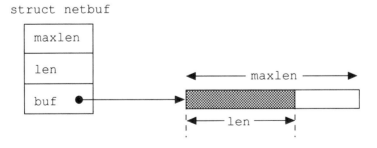

**Figure 5.2** The netbuf structure.

more data to pass back than `maxlen` says there is room for, the function returns an error rather than overwriting beyond the end of the user's buffer. The same `netbuf` is not usually used to send and receive data in the same call, so usually it is necessary to initialize either `len` or `maxlen` – not both.

## 5.2.2 The `t_bind` and `t_unitdata` structures

Here are two examples of data structures built using `netbuf`s. The first is a `t_bind` structure, used by the `t_bind()` function to bind a local address to a transport endpoint, and illustrated in Figure 5.3. The structure is defined as follows:

```
struct t_bind {
        struct netbuf   addr;
        unsigned        qlen;
};
```

The single `netbuf` called `addr` contained within the `t_bind` structure is used to hold the address of the transport endpoint to be bound. The form of this address depends on the underlying transport protocol, of course, and is not defined by TLI. In the case of TCP/IP, the address would simply be a `sockaddr_in` structure which we met in the previous chapter.

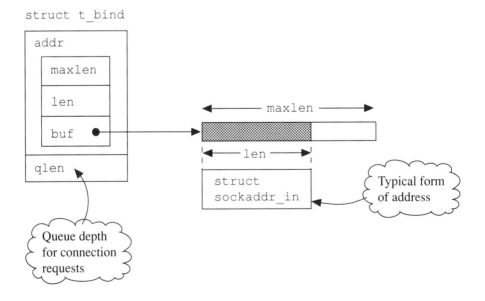

**Figure 5.3** The `t_bind` structure.

The `qlen` member of `t_bind` specifies the maximum number of connection requests which can be queued on this endpoint. This serves the same purpose as the parameter passed to the `listen()` call when using sockets.

The second example of a data structure using `netbufs` is a little more spectacular. The `t_unitdata` structure, shown in Figure 5.4, is used when sending and receiving datagrams over a connectionless transport. It is defined as follows:

```
struct t_unitdata {
        struct netbuf addr;
        struct netbuf opt;
        struct netbuf udata;
};
```

The `addr` component holds the address of the transport endpoint to which the datagram is to be delivered; again, this will typically be a `sockaddr_in` structure. The `opt` component holds 'protocol-specific options'. For example, when using the ISO connectionless transport protocol, the `opt` field contains a structure of type `isocl_options`, which contains parameters relating to 'quality of service'. Often, the `opt` field is unused, and the resulting 'empty' `netbuf` is usually marked as such by setting its `len` field to zero. Finally, the `udata` field contains the user data which are to be transmitted.

`struct t_unitdata`

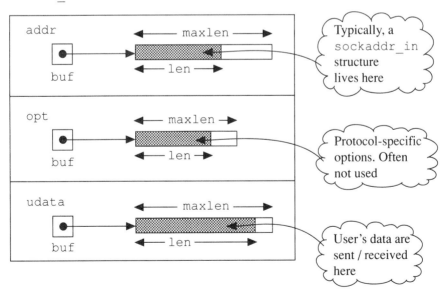

**Figure 5.4** The `t_unitdata` structure.

The following code fragment shows the use of a t_unitdata structure in sending a 100-byte datagram using UDP:

```
int    t;                    /* Descriptor for transport */
struct t_unitdata u;
struct sockaddr_in server; /* Address of recipient */
struct hostent *host;
char   buffer[100];          /* User data to be sent */

/* Open the transport */
t = t_open("/dev/udp", O_RDWR, 0);

/* Get the recipient's address (same as for sockets) */
host = gethostbyname("trillian");
server.sin_family      = AF_INET;
memcpy(&server.sin_addr.s_addr, host->h_addr,
                               host->h_length);
server.sin_port            = htons(SERVER_PORT);

/* Build the t_unitdata structure */
u.addr.len    = sizeof server;
u.addr.buf    = (char *)&server;
u.opt.len     = 0;         /* No options */
u.opt.buf     = (char *)0;
u.udata.len   = 100;
u.udata.buf   = buffer;

/* Assume there are some data in the buffer */
/* Send the datagram */
t_sndudata(t, &u);
```

## 5.2.3 Allocating TLI data structures

As the previous example shows, some of the TLI data structures are moderately complex, with several user buffers attached to them. To simplify the task of allocating these structures, the function t_alloc() is provided.

t_alloc() may be thought of as a specialized version of malloc(), which 'knows about' the TLI data structures. It is declared as follows:

```
char *t_alloc(int fd, int type, int fields)
```

The argument fd refers to the transport endpoint for which the structure is to be allocated. TLI uses this to determine the sizes of some of the data structures. The type argument specifies what sort of structure to allocate. Common values are:

```
T_BIND          /* Allocates a struct t_bind     */
T_CALL          /* Allocates a struct t_call     */
T_UNITDATA      /* Allocates a struct t_unitdata */
      .
```

The `fields` argument specifies which of the `netbuf` buffers associated with the structure should be allocated. The allowable values, which may be or-ed together, are:

```
T_ADDR          /* Allocate the address buffer   */
T_OPT           /* Allocate the options buffer   */
T_UDATA         /* Allocate the user data buffer */
T_ALL           /* Allocate all relevant buffers */
```

For each buffer specified, memory is allocated for the buffer, the `buf` field of the `netbuf` is set to point to it, and the `maxlen` field is set to its length.

As an example of its use, the following call will dynamically allocate a `t_unitdata` structure, along with buffers for the `addr` and `udata` components:

```
struct t_unitdata *u;

u = t_alloc(fd, T_UNITDATA, T_ADDR | T_UDATA);
```

How does `t_alloc()` know how large to make the buffers? It does not, but the transport provider does, and this information is accessible through the file descriptor passed as the first argument. It follows from this that `t_alloc()` may not be called until a transport endpoint has been created by calling `t_open()`, and a file descriptor obtained.

Storage occupied by these data structures may be released back to the system by calling `t_free()`. For example, the `unitdata` structure allocated by the above call to `t_alloc()` could be released by calling:

```
t_free(u, T_UNITDATA);
```

This call releases the `t_unitdata` structure and any associated buffers. Beware, however, that if any of the `netbuf` buffers were allocated explicitly, and not by a call to `t_alloc()`, they should be freed explicitly, and their `buf` pointers set to `NULL`, before calling `t_free()`. The following code fragment illustrates this:

```
#define MYBUFSIZE 1200
/* Get a t_unitdata and its address buffer */
u = t_alloc(fd, T_UNITDATA, T_ADDR);

/* Allocate the user data buffer ourselves  */
u.udata.buf    = malloc(MYBUFSIZE);
u.udata.maxlen = MYBUFSIZE;

/* Now use it ...

    ... assume we're done now  */

/* Free the user data buffer ourselves */
free(u.udata.buf);
u.udata.buf = NULL;

/* Free the rest */
t_free(u, T_UNITDATA);
```

# 5.3  TLI operations

## 5.3.1  Types of service

TLI can interface to three types of transport service:

1.   T_COTS – connection-oriented service (like a stream socket).
2.   T_COTS_ORD – connection-oriented service with orderly release (orderly release is a way of gracefully terminating a connection without loss of data).
3.   T_CLTS – connectionless service (like a datagram socket).

The normal sequence of operations is different for each type. We will look at the T_COTS and T_CLTS operations, but we will not consider the T_COTS_ORD service further here.

## 5.3.2  The TLI state machine

As mentioned earlier, the valid sequences of operations which can occur on a transport endpoint are described in terms of states, events and state transitions – in other words, a finite state machine. (The official programmers' guide says 'Users of TLI should understand all state transitions before writing software using the interface'. Since there are eight states, about twenty-five events and almost forty valid state transitions, the average programmer is in fact unlikely to understand all state transitions until after writing a *considerable amount* of software using the interface.)

The states are as follows:

1.   T_UNINIT – Uninitialized (initial and final state).
2.   T_UNBND – Initialized but not bound.
3.   T_IDLE – Bound, but no connection established.
4.   T_OUTCON – Outgoing connection pending (client waiting to connect).
5.   T_INCON – Incoming connection pending (server ready to accept).
6.   T_DATAXFER – Connected; data may be transferred.
7.   T_OUTREL – Waiting for orderly release indication.
8.   T_INREL – Waiting to send orderly release request.

Of these states, a connectionless service uses only the first three. A connection-oriented service (without orderly release) uses the first six, and a connection-oriented service with orderly release uses all eight.

The events fall into two groups:

1.   *Outgoing* events; that is, ones that are the result of an action (usually a call to a TLI function) at the local end.
2.   *Incoming* events; that is, ones that are received by a transport endpoint in response to an action at the remote end.

Figure 5.5 shows the state transitions and the events (TLI function calls) which occur during normal operation of a connectionless server and client. Figure 5.6 shows the same

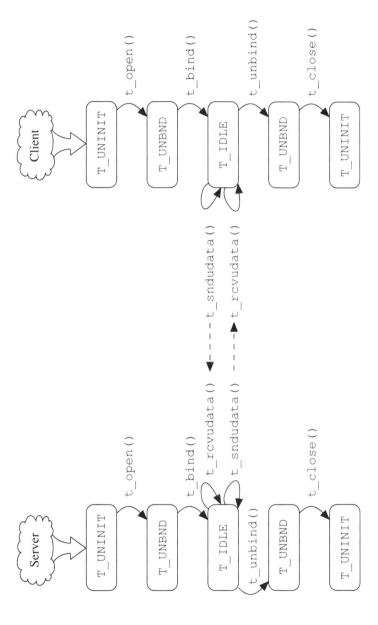

**Figure 5.5**  TLI state transitions for connectionless server and client.

thing for the connection-oriented case. There is clearly much in common with the equivalent sequence of operations using sockets (see Figures 4.18 and 4.12). The following sections discuss these operations in more detail, and point out some of the differences between TLI and sockets.

## 5.3.3 Connectionless service operations

Referring to Figure 5.5, we see that in terms of TLI operations, there is little to distinguish the server from the client in the connectionless case. Both endpoints spend most of their time in the T_IDLE state, in which they can both send and receive datagrams. The major difference is over 'who goes first' in the sending and receiving of datagrams.

Both server and client begin by selecting a transport provider, and creating a transport endpoint:

```
int  t;
struct t_info info;

t = t_open("/dev/udp", O_RDWR, &info);
```

The first argument must be the name of a STREAMS device which implements the protocol stack of the required transport provider. These names are implementation-specific. The third argument points to a t_info structure wherein will be returned various values relating to this transport provider, for example, the maximum size of a transport endpoint address and the maximum size of a TSDU. A program may choose to ignore this information (as we will in our examples) by passing a null pointer here.

Both server and client need explicitly to bind an address (port number) to their local endpoint, by calling t_bind(). TLI does not support the notion of implicitly binding an address for you if the endpoint is used for I/O without being explicitly bound first; at least, such a facility is not mentioned in the manual.

The server must build a t_bind structure prior to the t_bind() call. The addr component of this structure, which is shown in Figure 5.3, must contain the protocol-specific endpoint address to be bound. In the case of UDP or TCP, this will be a struct sockaddr_in. (It may seem strange to encounter a structure with 'sock' in the name when we are using TLI. Of course, a sockaddr_in structure is simply an 'internet endpoint address', whether sockets are being used or not.) Some of this code is familiar from the previous chapter:

```
struct sockaddr_in server;
struct t_bind      bindreq;

server.sin_family      = AF_INET;
server.sin_addr.s_addr = htonl(INADDR_ANY);
server.sin_port        = htons(MYPORT);
```

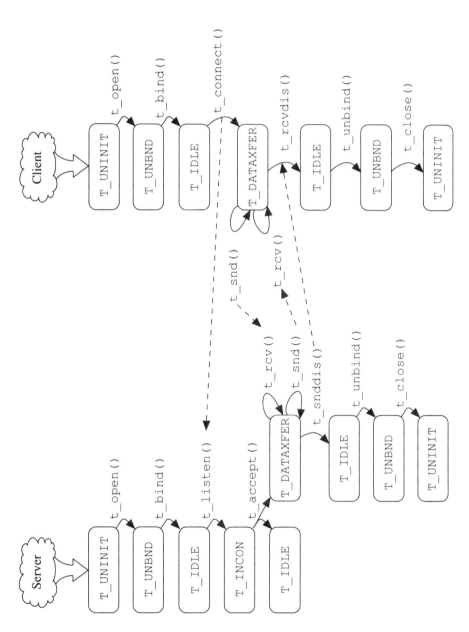

**Figure 5.6** Simplified TLI state transitions for connection-oriented server and client.

```
bindreq.addr.buf    = (char *)&server;
bindreq.addr.len    = sizeof server;
bindreq.addr.maxlen = sizeof server;

t_bind(t, &bindreq, &bindreq);
```

The first argument to t_bind() is the file descriptor for the transport endpoint. The second argument points to a t_bind structure containing the address to be bound. If the requested port cannot be bound, t_bind() will choose some other arbitrary port and bind that instead. Of course, this is convenient for the client but no good at all for the server. The third argument to t_bind() points to another structure in which is returned the actual address that was bound. We use the same structure for both in the example above. Thus, the prudent server should check that the correct port has been bound on return from t_bind() as follows:

```
if (ntohs(server.sin_port) != MYPORT) {
   /* complain ... */
}
```

An alternative style of coding is to allocate the t_bind structure and its associated buffer dynamically, using t_alloc(). Some language gymnastics are then needed to reference through this buffer to reach the components of the sockaddr_in structure within it. There is an example in the luserver program which follows.

The client has an easier time of the t_bind() call. Since it does not care what port gets bound, it can pass null pointers in place of both t_bind structures:

```
t_bind(t, NULL, NULL);
```

Once the client and server have bound addresses to their endpoints, they both enter the data transfer phase. Datagrams are sent and received using the following functions:

```
int t_sndudata(int t, struct t_unitdata *u)

int t_rcvudata(int t, struct t_unitdata *u, int *flags)
```

For both functions, the first argument is the descriptor for the transport endpoint, and the second points to a t_unitdata structure. It is around this structure (shown in Figure 5.4) that the action revolves. The sender of a datagram must set u->udata.buf to point to a buffer containing the data to be sent, and set u->udata.len to the length of the buffer. The u->addr.buf and u->addr.len fields must be set to the address to which the datagram is to be sent. Again, this will usually be a sockaddr_in structure. The *options* are often unused, so that u->opt.buf should be set to null, and u->opt.len to zero. These operations are illustrated in the luserver program, which follows.

The receiver of a datagram must allocate a buffer for it, set u->udata.buf to point to it, and u->udata.maxlen to its length. The receiver gets to know the address of the endpoint from which the datagram was sent, via the u->addr field, after the t_rcvudata() call has returned. We must allocate a buffer for this address, set u->addr.buf to point to it, and set u->addr.maxlen to its length. The t_rcvudata() function takes a third argument, flags. On return, this will be set to T_MORE if the datagram was too big to fit into the user's buffer, as determined from u->udata.maxlen. If this happens, the receiver should call t_rcvudata() again to retrieve the remainder of the datagram. If t_alloc() has been used to allocate the data buffer, it will ensure that the buffer is big enough to hold the largest datagram that the transport provider can deliver. In this case, T_MORE will never be set.

When data transfers are complete, the tidy-minded client should unbind the endpoint, and close it, as follows:

```
t_unbind(t);
t_close(t);
```

The t_unbind() call is not really necessary. If a bound endpoint is closed, it will be automatically unbound.

## 5.3.4  A simple connectionless server

Here is a simple connectionless server which illustrates many of the operations discussed in the previous section. It is essentially just an echo server, but it also performs lower-to-upper case translation.

```
/* File luserver.c - UDP echo server using TLI -
   Performs echoing with lower-to-upper case translation
   NB The error checking in this example is minimal.
*/

#include <stdio.h>
#include <sys/types.h>
#include <sys/fcntl.h>
#include <sys/socket.h>
#include <netinet/in.h>
#include <netdb.h>
#include <tiuser.h>

#define MYPORT  4444    /* The 'well-known' port number */

void process_datagram(struct t_unitdata *u);
main(int argc, char *argv[])
{
    int             t;          /* Transport endpoint handle */
    int             flags;
    struct t_bind   *bindreq;   /* Required endpoint address */
    struct t_bind   *bindret;   /* Actual endpoint address   */
    struct t_unitdata *u;       /* Datagram structure        */
```

```
    /* Create a connectionless endpoint */
    t = t_open("/dev/udp", O_RDWR, 0);

    /* Allocate two t_bind structures */
    bindreq = (struct t_bind *)t_alloc(t, T_BIND, T_ALL);
    bindret = (struct t_bind *)t_alloc(t, T_BIND, T_ALL);

    /* Allocate a t_unitdata structure */
    u = (struct t_unitdata *)t_alloc(t, T_UNITDATA, T_ALL);

    /* Bind our  'well-known' port.  The messy expressions with the
       casts are needed to make the 'generic' address buffer within
       the t_unitdata  structure look like a sockaddr_in structure.
    */
    ((struct sockaddr_in *)(bindreq->addr.buf))->sin_port
                                        = htons(MYPORT);
    ((struct sockaddr_in *)(bindreq->addr.buf))->sin_addr.s_addr
                                        = htonl(INADDR_ANY);
    bindreq->addr.len = sizeof (struct sockaddr_in);
    t_bind(t, bindreq, bindret);

    /* t_bind will not fail if the requested port is already
       bound, it will simply bind some other port. Because we
       are a server we MUST check that the correct port was bound
    */
    if (ntohs(((struct sockaddr_in *)(bindret->addr.buf))->sin_port)
       != MYPORT) {
       printf("bound the wrong port!\n");
       exit(1);
    }

    /* Main service loop */
    while(1) {
        /* Get a datagram from a client */
        t_rcvudata(t, u, &flags);

        /* Process the data and return the result.  Notice that the
           return address is conveniently in the addr buffer of the
           t_unitdata structure, following the t_rcvdata() call.
        */
        process_datagram(u);

        ((struct sockaddr_in *)u->addr.buf)->sin_family = AF_INET;
        t_sndudata(t, u);
    }
}
/* Think of this as symbolizing a real-world processing function.
   All it does is convert any lower case characters in the buffer
   to upper case.
*/
void process_datagram(struct t_unitdata *u)
```

```
{
    int i;

    for (i=0; i < u->udata.len; i++)
        u->udata.buf[i] = toupper(u->udata.buf[i]);
}
```

## 5.3.5  Connection-oriented service operations

The sequence of operations performed by connection-oriented clients and servers is shown in Figure 5.6. Just as for the connectionless case, both client and server begin by opening a transport endpoint and binding an address to it, with the obvious difference that now we must open a connection-oriented transport, typically /dev/tcp. Notice also that the t_bind structure includes a qlen field which specifies the maximum queue depth for pending connection requests. This field has meaning only for the server. It replaces the listen() call, which sockets use to establish the queue depth.

Once the server has bound an address and set a queue depth, it awaits incoming connection requests by calling t_listen(). Here we see a significant difference from the socket operations. Using sockets, the accept() call both waits for a connection request and accepts it, creating a new file descriptor for the connection. Using TLI, the actions of retrieving a connection request from the endpoint and accepting it are separate, using the calls t_listen() and t_accept() respectively.

t_listen() is declared as follows:

```
int t_listen(int t, struct t_call *call)
```

The first argument is the file descriptor for the transport endpoint on which the connection request was received. The second argument points to a user-supplied t_call structure in which is returned information about the client. This structure is declared as follows:

```
struct t_call {
    struct netbuf addr;     /* address          */
    struct netbuf opt;      /* options          */
    struct netbuf udata;    /* user data        */
    int sequence;           /* sequence number  */
};
```

The udata field here is used to retrieve any data that were passed along with the connection request – something that few protocols support. The field most likely to be of interest is the addr field which contains the endpoint address of the client who sent the connection request. The server may examine this address to decide whether to accept the connection. If it chooses to reject the client, it may call t_snddis() to send a rejection to the client. If it chooses to accept the client's request, it calls t_accept(). This scheme differs from the socket scheme, in which a server cannot identify the client until after accepting the connection request. The most unsociable a socket-based server can be is to accept the connection and close it down again immediately.

The t_accept() function, too, is significantly different from its sockets counterpart. Firstly, t_accept() should only be called *after* a connection request has been retrieved. It is not used to wait for a connection request; t_listen() does that. Secondly, it is the programmer's responsibility to create a new endpoint, and bind an address to it, before accepting the connection on it. This concept is strange to die-hard socket programmers who are accustomed to having accept() do all the work for them. In practice, it is usual to write a user-level function which mimics the accept() call. Here is a minimalist version. It takes two arguments: the first is the descriptor of the endpoint on which the connection request was received. In Chapter 4, we called this the *rendezvous* descriptor. The second argument points to the t_call structure which t_listen() returned to us. The accept_call() function returns a descriptor for the newly accepted connection. In Chapter 4, we called this the *connection* descriptor. The rendezvous descriptor reverts back to the T_IDLE state, and the connection descriptor enters the T_DATAXFER state, as shown in Figure 5.6.

```
int accept_call(int fd, struct t_call *call)
{
    int         conn_fd;

    /* Get a new endpoint to accept the connection on */
    if ((conn_fd = t_open("/dev/tcp", O_RDWR, 0)) < 0)
        return -1;

    /* Bind any local address */
    if (t_bind(conn_fd, 0, 0) < 0) {
        t_close(conn_fd);
        return -2;
    }

    /* Accept the connection request on the new descriptor */
    if (t_accept(fd, conn_fd, call) < 0) {
        t_close(conn_fd);
        return -3;
    }

    /* All's well, return the new descriptor to the caller */
    return conn_fd;
}
```

On the client side, the connection is made by calling t_connect(). This function is declared as follows:

```
int t_connect(int t, struct t_call *sndcall,
                     struct t_call *rcvcall);
```

This function is almost directly equivalent to the socket `connect()` call. The `sndcall` argument points to a `t_call` structure which contains (at minimum) the address of the server. Optionally, it may also carry protocol-specific options, and a buffer of user data to be passed along with the connection request. The `rcvcall` argument points to an 'empty' `t_call` structure which will be filled in on return with the address of the remote endpoint on which the connection has been established, plus protocol-specific options and a buffer of user data which was returned when the connection was accepted. Again, both of these are usually unused. If the client is not interested in any of this information, it may pass a null pointer as the third argument.

Once a connection has been accepted, the server and client may begin to transfer data. Unlike the socket scheme, we cannot use ordinary `read()` and `write()` system calls on the connection descriptor returned by `accept_call()`. Instead, the functions `t_rcv()` and `t_snd()` are used. These are declared as follows:

```
int t_rcv(int conn_fd, char buf, unsigned nbytes, int *flags)
int t_snd(int conn_fd, char buf, unsigned nbytes, int  flags)
```

These functions closely resemble `read()` and `write()` except for the additional `flags` argument. This argument has two purposes:

1. Setting the `T_EXPEDITED` bit requests that the data be sent as expedited data.
2. It provides a way to send a single TSDU split across several `t_snd()` calls. This is done by setting the `T_MORE` flag bit in all but the last call. This only works if the transport provider preserves message boundaries in the first place, which of course TCP does not.

In fact, it *is* possible to use normal `read()` and `write()` calls with a TLI connection, but it is first necessary to push onto the STREAM's head a special module designed to support the read/write interface. This is one of the few cases when a programmer may wish to manipulate the STREAMS module stack explicitly. Having done this, the descriptor can be used like a normal UNIX file descriptor – and we can use calls such as `read()`, `write()` and `dup()` on it. There are two situations where this can be useful:

1. When we want to do an `exec()` to pass the connection to some other program which knows nothing about TLI or networks and which simply uses `read()` and `write()` for its I/O.
2. When it is convenient to use higher level `stdio` library functions such as `printf()` to perform I/O on the network connection. In this case, care must be taken to defeat the buffering within the `stdio` library, either by calling `setbuf()` to turn buffering off for the stream altogether, or by calling `fflush()` at appropriate points.

The following code fragment illustrates the latter usage:

```
#include <stdio.h>
#include <stropts.h>
/* Get a TLI endpoint descriptor */
```

```
conn_fd = accept_call(t, &call_info);

/* Convert it  to a  regular  UNIX  file descriptor.
   'tirdwr'  is the name of the 'transport interface
   read/write' module which is built into the kernel
*/
ioctl(conn_fd, I_PUSH, "tirdwr");

/* Duplicate it onto our standard output */
close(1);
dup(conn_fd);

/* Turn off buffering */
setbuf(stdout, NULL);

printf("This will be sent to the connection");
```

## 5.3.6  A simple connection-oriented client

The following program illustrates a simple connection-oriented client using TLI. It connects to the chargen service on port 19. This service (described in RFC 864) just repeatedly sends lines of text containing a test character pattern. Any data sent *to* the service are discarded. The error handling in this example is more thorough and is discussed in the section below.

```
/* TLI-based version of chargen client using TCP */

#include <stdio.h>
#include <tiuser.h>
#include <fcntl.h>
#include <sys/socket.h>
#include <netdb.h>
#include <netinet/in.h>
#include <stropts.h>

/* Macro to make the casts look shorter */
#define SAD struct sockaddr_in *

#define CHARGEN_PORT        19

extern int  t_errno;

main(int argc, char *argv[])
{
    struct t_call    *call;
    char             outbuf[BUFSIZ];
    int              count;
    int              fd;
    int              flags;

    /* Open a transport endpoint */
```

```
if ((fd=t_open("/dev/tcp", O_RDWR, 0)) < 0) {
    t_error("t_open failed");
    exit(1);
}

/* Bind an arbitrary address */
if (t_bind(fd, 0, 0) < 0) {
    t_error("t_bind failed");
    exit(2);
}

/* Build the call structure to connect to the server */
call = (struct t_call *)t_alloc(fd, T_CALL, T_ADDR);
if (call == 0) {
    t_error("t_alloc failed");
    exit(3);
}

/* Place the server's address into the call structure.
   This is the only messy part. The (SAD) cast allows
   us to view the generic addr.buf as a sockaddr_in
   structure. For simplicity, the machine name
   'localhost' is hard-wired into the code.
*/
call->addr.len = sizeof (struct sockaddr_in);
((SAD)call->addr.buf)->sin_family = AF_INET;
((SAD)call->addr.buf)->sin_port   = htons(CHARGEN_PORT);
((SAD)call->addr.buf)->sin_addr.s_addr =
    *(u_long *)gethostbyname("localhost")->h_addr;

/* No options or user data to be passed with the connect */
call->opt.len   = 0;
call->udata.len = 0;

/* Connect to the server */
if (t_connect(fd, call, 0) < 0) {
    t_error("t_connect");
    printf("t_errno = %d\n", t_errno);
}

/* The chargen service will send data to us indefinitely.
   We'll just receive one buffer-full, to prove the point
*/
count = t_rcv(fd, outbuf, BUFSIZ, &flags);
write(1, outbuf, count);
}
```

When executed, this client delivers the following line of output:

```
!"#$%&'()*+,-./0123456789:;<=>?@ABCDEFGHIJKLMNOPQRSTUVWXYZ[\]^_'abcdefg
```

which corresponds to one message sent by the `chargen` server.

### 5.3.7 TLI error reporting

Like system calls, TLI library functions flag errors by returning −1. Unlike system calls, they do not use the global variable `errno` for the error code, or the `perror()` function for printing error messages. Instead, they have their own global variable, `t_errno`, and their own error message printing routine, `t_error()`. The error codes returned in `t_errno` are defined in the header file `<tiuser.h>`. For example, an attempt to call `t_connect()` on a connectionless endpoint returns an error with `t_errno` set to `TNOTSUPPORT`, and the corresponding error text generated by `t_error()` is `"Primitive not supported by provider"`.

Two error codes deserve special mention. The first is `TSYSERR`, which indicates an error not within the TLI library itself, but during a system call. In this case, the traditional `errno` can be consulted for more detail, and `t_error()` prints out the text which `perror()` would have printed, prefixed by the text `"System error:"` ; for example:

```
System error: Out of stream resources
```

The second special error code is `TLOOK`, which indicates that an asynchronous event (not necessarily an error as such) has been received at the transport endpoint. When this happens, the programmer is expected to call `t_look()` on the transport endpoint to retrieve an integer code indicating the type of event that has been received. These codes are also defined in `<tiuser.h>`, and are as follows:

```
T_LISTEN         connection indication received
T_CONNECT        connect confirmation received
T_DATA           normal data received
T_EXDATA         expedited data received
T_DISCONNECT     disconnect received
T_ERROR          fatal error occurred
T_UDERR          datagram error indication
T_ORDREL         orderly release indication
```

## 5.4  TLI example – a service registry

### 5.4.1  Overview of the registry

This example of TLI-based client and server programs constitutes one of the more ambitious projects in the book – we will build a system that maintains a network-wide registry of services, and allows clients to find and connect to those services knowing only a simple service name. We noted in Chapter 3 that UNIX lacks such a service. The idea is to write a service *broker* program, which accepts *registration requests* from servers around the network. The broker maintains a table of mappings from the service names onto the transport endpoint addresses (machine IP addresses and port numbers, for example) of the corresponding server. A potential client contacts the broker, supplies the name of the service he or she requires (for example, 'hangman'), and receives the transport endpoint address.

As well as showing use of TLI, this example provides an illustration of the typical development process of a client–server protocol.

The client–server relationships are more complex here, and in an attempt to reduce the confusion we will refer to the programs that make use of the service registry as *application servers* and *application clients*. Of course the application servers are clients of the broker at the point when they register.

To add to the confusion, we will use both connectionless and connection-oriented protocols. In our implementation, the broker itself uses a connectionless protocol, but the services that it registers are connection-oriented.

The registration service itself has three main components, shown in Figure 5.7:

1.  The service broker, which maintains a service map, linking text service names with transport endpoint addresses. The broker is the only program in this system which operates at a 'well-known' endpoint address.
2.  A small library of support functions, `brokerlib`, used by the application servers and application clients to contact the broker.
3.  An administrative utility, `svclist`, which simply reads out the entire service map from the broker and displays it.

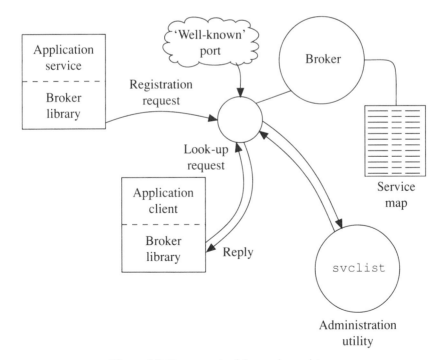

**Figure 5.7** Components of the service registry.

Before getting into details of the implementation, let us examine our 'end product' from the point of view of the application clients and servers who will use it. Services register themselves with a call of the form:

```
fd = register_service("hangman");
```

and receive a descriptor on which to accept client connections.

To use the service, a client simply makes a call of the form:

```
fd = connect_to_service("hangman");
```

and receives a file descriptor already connected to the server. These two functions make up the broker library. As you can see, from the point of view of the application clients and servers, the registry is very easy to use.

---

**An aside:** Brad Cox, in his book *Object Oriented Programming: An evolutionary approach* (1986), makes a distinction between the *bulk* of a software package and its *surface area*. Bulk is a measure of the amount of code in the package, and surface area is a measure of the number of things that must be understood about the package, and correctly handled, in order to use it successfully. There is sometimes a tendency to think that because a package has a large surface area, it must be very powerful. A programmer leafs through the manual for the new graphics library he has just bought, marvelling at the huge number of functions it provides. In reality, most of the functions are there so that the programmer can take care of a lot of low level detail that really ought to be hidden inside the package. An analogy might be made with a modern SLR camera. Very complex internally, the camera automatically handles focusing, exposure control and film winding, leaving the user simply to 'point and click'. In Cox's terminology, the camera has a large bulk but a small surface area.

Our point here is that despite the internal complexity of the service registration package, it has a simple, easy-to-use interface, i.e. a small surface area.

---

These two functions handle most of the work of obtaining a connection between the application server and client. Note the following in particular:

1.  The application client does not need to know which machine the application server is running on. All it needs to know is the service's name.
2.  Neither the application servers nor the clients are aware of the underlying transport protocol in use. The only code which knows what a transport endpoint looks like is in the broker library.

In order to keep our example tolerably short, we make a number of simplifying assumptions:

1.  Only one instance of each service is registered on the network. (If two services are registered with the same name, the broker just scans linearly through its service map,

and would always find the first one.) A more sophisticated broker might recognize the existence of multiple servers, and balance the load between them.

2. The broker service is not replicated, i.e. there are no *slave brokers* analogous to the slave NIS servers to help spread the load or to provide continuity of service if the master fails.

3. The machine on which the broker is running is known to all hosts, via an alias name `brokerhost` in the `/etc/hosts` file or the NIS `hosts` map. A better way to handle this might be to have the functions in the broker library *broadcast* requests in order to find the broker.

## 5.4.2  Designing the protocol

It may be instructive to work through the design decisions that were taken in the development of this example. These steps are typical of the design process for many client–server applications. Development began with the design of the broker protocol, and the format of the service map held by the broker. It was decided to make the broker service itself 'transport-independent', in the sense that the broker does not know the internal structure of the application servers' transport endpoint addresses which it holds in the service map. Thus, a map entry is a relatively opaque object defined as follows:

```
struct map_entry {
    char svc_name[SVC_NAME_LEN];   /* Name of service  */
    char svc_tsap[SVC_TSAP_LEN];   /* Endpoint address */
};
```

Here, `svc_name` is a text string identifying the service, and `svc_tsap` is the protocol-specific 'transport service access point' – for example, a `sockaddr_in` structure.

The next step was to identify the requests that the broker must handle. The first two are obvious:

1. The `OP_REGISTER` request, used by the application servers to add entries to the service map.

2. The `OP_FIND` request, used by the application clients to locate a server.

In the interests of simplicity, there is no de-register request to remove an entry from the map. Two further commands were added to support the `svclist` utility which lists the map entries:

3. The `OP_FIRST` request, which returns the first entry in the map.

4. The `OP_NEXT` request, which returns the next entry in the map.

To list the entire map, `svclist` sends a single `OP_FIRST` request followed by multiple `OP_NEXT` requests. As an alternative, it would be possible to implement a single command to retrieve the whole map in one go. Although potentially more efficient, this idea was rejected because it would fail if the map was too big to fit into a single datagram.

The next step was to flesh out the details of these commands by defining the structure of the requests and the replies. Each request is sent as a datagram which begins with an integer *op-code* identifying the request. The op-code is one of the values OP_REGISTER, OP_FIND, OP_FIRST or OP_NEXT. After reading the datagram, the broker does a switch on this op-code to select the appropriate action. Following the op-code, the OP_REGISTER and OP_FIND requests contain additional message-specific data. All requests are acknowledged. In every case, the acknowledgement begins with an integer *status* code indicating if the request was successful. The following status values were defined:

- STAT_OK          Request successful
- STAT_NOSVC       Non-existent service requested
- STAT_NOMORE      Reached end of service map
- STAT_BADOP       Undefined op-code received

The OP_REGISTER command returns no data other than the status value. For the other three commands, the status value is followed by an entry from the service map. The broker protocol is summarized in Table 5.1.

The message formats are defined in a header file, broker.h, which serves to define the interface to the broker. Here it is:

```
/* broker.h - Header File for Network Service Broker */

/* This is the broker service's 'well-known' port number.
   The 'proper' way to do this is to add an entry into
   /etc/services and look up the port using getservbyname()
*/
#define BROKER_PORT 5432

/* Operation codes for broker commands */
#define OP_REGISTER 1
#define OP_FIND     2
#define OP_FIRST    3
#define OP_NEXT     4

/* Status values within broker acknowledgements */
#define STAT_OK     1
#define STAT_NOSVC  2          /* Non-existent service */
#define STAT_NOMORE 3          /* Reached end of service map */
#define STAT_BADOP  4          /* Undefined op-code received */
```

**Table 5.1**   The broker protocol

| Operation | Message to broker | Reply from broker |
|-----------|-------------------|-------------------|
| Register | OP_REGISTER + map entry | STAT_OK |
| Find service | OP_FIND + service name | STAT_OK + map entry or STAT_NOSVC |
| Get first service | OP_FIRST | STAT_OK + map entry or STAT_NOMORE |
| Get next service | OP_NEXT | STAT_OK + map entry or STAT_NOMORE |

```
/* Implementation Limits - sizes are in bytes */
#define SVC_NAME_LEN       32       /* Size of a service name */
#define SVC_TSAP_LEN       32       /* Size of transport endpoint addr */

/* A Service Entry as maintained by the broker */

typedef struct map_entry {
    char name[SVC_NAME_LEN];    /* Name of service */
    char tsap[SVC_TSAP_LEN];    /* Endpoint address of service */
} Map_entry;

/* Broker Message Formats */

/* OP_REGISTER message format */

typedef struct registration_request {
    int   opcode;                   /* == OP_REGISTER */
    char name[SVC_NAME_LEN];
    char tsap[SVC_TSAP_LEN];
} Registration_request;

/* OP_FIND message format */

typedef struct service_request {
    int   opcode;                   /* == OP_FIND */
    char name[SVC_NAME_LEN];
} Service_request;

/* Reply format for OP_FIND, OP_FIRST and OP_NEXT */

typedef struct service_reply {
    int   status;     /* OK, not found, etc. */
    struct map_entry svc;
} Service_reply;
```

## 5.4.3  The service broker

We are now in a position to write the broker, which is fairly typical of the code for a connectionless service. The logical structure is straightforward enough: first, create a connectionless endpoint to receive commands, and bind our well-known port. Then, enter our service loop. Each time round the loop we retrieve a request datagram, do a `switch` on the op-code, then build and return a reply. The only murky parts are the casts used to impose an appropriate structure on the buffer which receives request datagrams. Here is the code:

```
/* broker.c  -  Network-wide service registration broker */

#include <stdio.h>
#include <sys/types.h>
#include <sys/fcntl.h>
```

```
#include <sys/socket.h>
#include <tiuser.h>
#include <netinet/in.h>
#include "broker.h"

#define NON_FATAL       1               /* Error severity codes */
#define FATAL           2
#define MAP_SIZE        100             /* Size of service map */

Map_entry               map[MAP_SIZE];  /* The service map */
int                     count = 0;      /* No. of entries in map */
int                     eh;             /* Endpoint handle */
struct t_unitdata       *u;             /* Datagram structure */

/* This error logging is naive  because in reality the broker's
   stdout may be closed. Logging to a file or via syslogd would
   be preferable.
*/

void log_error(char *message, int severity)
{
    printf("broker: %s\n", message);
    if (severity == FATAL) exit(1);
    else return;
}

void acknowledge(int status)
{
    u->udata.buf = (char *)&status;
    u->udata.len = sizeof status;
    t_sndudata(eh, u);
    return;
}

main(int argc, char *argv[])
{
    int                 flags;
    int                 pos;
    int                 found;
    int                 n;
    char                buffer[BUFSIZ];  /* For receiving datagrams */
    struct t_bind       bindreq, bindret;
    struct sockaddr_in  broker_addr;
    struct sockaddr_in  actual_addr;
    Register_request    *reg_req;
    Service_request     *svc_req;
    Service_reply       reply;

    /* Create a connectionless endpoint to talk to our clients */
    eh = t_open("/dev/udp", O_RDWR, (struct t_info *) 0);
    if (eh < 0)
```

```
        log_error("t_open failed", FATAL);

/* Bind our local address so the clients know where we are */
broker_addr.sin_family      = AF_INET;
broker_addr.sin_addr.s_addr = htonl(INADDR_ANY);
broker_addr.sin_port        = htons(BROKER_PORT);

/* Set up the data structure for the t_bind call.
   Note we set up the len field for the 'outgoing' structure
   and the maxlen field of the 'incoming' structure
*/
bindreq.addr.len    = sizeof broker_addr;
bindreq.addr.buf    = (char *)&broker_addr;
bindret.addr.buf    = (char *)&actual_addr;
bindret.addr.maxlen = sizeof actual_addr;

if (t_bind(eh, &bindreq, &bindret) < 0)
    log_error("t_bind failed", FATAL);

/* t_bind may bind a port different from the one requested. This
   is NOT considered a failure.  Therefore, we should check that
   the right port was bound.
*/
if (actual_addr.sin_port != htons(BROKER_PORT))
    log_error("t_bind bound the wrong port", FATAL);

/* Allocate a t_unitdata structure to receive datagrams.
   We will provide our own udata buffer,  and we are not
   interested in options, so the only part of the struct
   we want t_alloc to allocate is the address.
*/
u = (struct t_unitdata *)t_alloc(eh, T_UNITDATA, T_ADDR);

/* Enter our main service loop */
while(1) {
    /* Retrieve a request and do whatever the op-code says */
    u->udata.buf    = buffer;
    u->udata.maxlen = sizeof buffer;
    u->opt.maxlen   = 0;  /* Not interested in options */
    if (t_rcvudata(eh, u, &flags) < 0) {
        log_error("t_rcvudata failed", FATAL);
    }

    /* Note that the address of the sender of the request is
       now in u->addr.  This is convenient for returning the
       reply.  The op-code is the first  thing in the buffer.
    */
    switch (*(int *)(buffer)) {
    case OP_REGISTER:
      /* Copy a new service name and address into the map.
         We really ought to check if the map is full! The
```

```
                following line establishes a pointer which gives
                an 'appropriate' view of the data in the buffer.
            */
            reg_req = (Register_request *)(u->udata.buf);
            /* Copy the map entry into the map */
            memcpy(map[count].name, reg_req->name, SVC_NAME_LEN);
            memcpy(map[count].tsap, reg_req->tsap, SVC_TSAP_LEN);
            count++;
            acknowledge(STAT_OK);
            break;

        case OP_FIND:
          /* Find a service in the map, and return its address */
            svc_req = (Service_request *)(u->udata.buf);
            for (n=0,found=0; n<count && !found; n++) {
                if (strcmp(map[n].name, svc_req->name) == 0) {
                    /* Found service, assemble a reply */
                    reply.svc    = map[n];
                    reply.status = STAT_OK;
                    u->udata.buf = (char *)&reply;
                    u->udata.len = sizeof reply;
                    t_sndudata(eh, u);
                    found = 1;
                }
            }
            if (! found) acknowledge(STAT_NOSVC);
            break;

        case OP_FIRST:
            pos = -1;              /* Initialize position in map */
                                  /* Fall through ... */
        case OP_NEXT:
            pos++;
            if (pos >= count) acknowledge(STAT_NOMORE);
            else {
                /* Assemble a reply */
                reply.svc    = map[pos];
                reply.status = STAT_OK;
                u->udata.buf = (char *)&reply;
                u->udata.len = sizeof reply;
                t_sndudata(eh, u);
            }
            break;
        default:
            /* We don't recognize the opcode */
            acknowledge(STAT_BADOP);
            break;
        }
    }
}
```

## 5.4.4 The `svclist` utility

Next, we examine the code for `svclist`. This shows the boiler-plate code for a connectionless client using TLI. Whereas the broker was ignorant of the structure of the endpoint addresses it held in its map, `svclist` must know the structure in order to print out a meaningful representation. It is assumed that the address is a 'socket address', beginning with a tag value such as `AF_INET` to indicate the address family in use. In the implementation shown, only `AF_INET` is supported, but other protocols could easily be added. Here is the code:

```c
/* svclist.c - Service Registration Admin Tool */

#include <stdio.h>
#include <sys/types.h>
#include <sys/fcntl.h>
#include <sys/socket.h>
#include <tiuser.h>
#include <netinet/in.h>
#include <netdb.h>
#include "broker.h"

extern int t_errno;             /* TLI error codes returned here */
void print_IP_host(struct in_addr *ip_addr);

main(int argc, char *argv[])
{
    int             eh;             /* Endpoint handle      */
    int             flags;
    struct t_unitdata   *u;             /* Datagram structure   */
    struct sockaddr_in  broker;         /* Address of broker    */
    struct sockaddr_in  *svc_addr;      /* Service's address    */
    int             request;        /* Packet to broker     */
    Service_reply       reply;          /* Packet from broker   */
    struct hostent      *host;          /* Host info for broker */

    /* Create a connectionless endpoint to talk to the broker.
       We should bind an address, but we don't care which.
    */
    eh = t_open("/dev/udp", O_RDWR, (struct t_info *) 0);
    if (eh < 0) {
        t_error("t_open failed");
        exit(1);
    }

    t_bind(eh, NULL, NULL);

    /* Get the broker's address. We assume there is an entry
       'brokerhost' in the /etc/hosts file to identify this
       machine
    */
```

```
if ((host = gethostbyname("brokerhost")) == NULL) {
    fprintf(stderr, "Do not know brokerhost\n");
    exit(2);
}

broker.sin_family      = AF_INET;
memcpy(&broker.sin_addr.s_addr, host->h_addr, host->h_length);
broker.sin_port        = htons(BROKER_PORT);

/* Allocate a t_unitdata structure for datagrams */
u = (struct t_unitdata *)t_alloc(eh, T_UNITDATA, T_ADDR);

/* Now loop, requesting service entries from the broker until
   the broker says there are no more.  The op-code OP_FIRST is
   used for the first request, OP_NEXT for all subsequent.
*/

request = OP_FIRST;

while (1) {
    /* Build the unitdata structure to send the op-code */
    u->udata.buf     = (char *)&request;
    u->udata.len     = sizeof request;
    u->addr.buf      = (char *)&broker;
    u->addr.len      = sizeof broker;
    /* The maxlen fields are ignored since we are outputting */
    if (t_sndudata(eh, u) < 0) {
        t_error("svclist: error sending datagram");
        exit(1);
    }

    /* Set up the unitdata structure to read the broker's reply */
    u->udata.buf     = (char *)&reply;
    u->udata.maxlen  = sizeof reply;
    u->addr.buf      = (char *)&broker;
    u->addr.maxlen   = sizeof broker;
    /* The len fields are ignored since we are inputting */
    if (t_rcvudata(eh, u, &flags) < 0) {
        t_error("svclist: error receiving datagram");
        exit(1);
    }
    if (reply.status != STAT_OK) break;   /* End of map? */

    /* OK, now decode the reply and print it. We assume here
       that the 'tsap' address is in fact a sockaddr
    */

    printf("Service name: %-12s", reply.svc.name);
    svc_addr = (struct sockaddr_in *)reply.svc.tsap;

    /* This could be extended to handle other address families.
       For simplicity, we have implemented AF_INET only.
```

```
        */
        switch (svc_addr->sin_family) {
            case AF_INET:
                printf("host = ");
                print_IP_host(&(svc_addr->sin_addr));
                printf(", port = %5d\n", ntohs(svc_addr->sin_port));
                break;
            default:
                printf(" unknown protocol\n");
                break;
        }

    request = OP_NEXT;
    }

    if (request == OP_FIRST)
        printf("No services registered\n");
}
/* This function prints the host name for a given IP address
   If the host does not appear in the host's map, the IP addr
   is printed in dotted decimal notation.
*/
void print_IP_host(struct in_addr *ip_addr)
{
    struct hostent *h;

    h = gethostbyaddr(ip_addr, sizeof (struct in_addr), AF_INET);
    if (h == 0) {
        /* Host not known, print raw IP address */
        printf("%d.%d.%d.%d", (ip_addr->s_addr >> 24) & 0xff,
                              (ip_addr->s_addr >> 16) & 0xff,
                              (ip_addr->s_addr >> 8 ) & 0xff,
                              (ip_addr->s_addr >> 0 ) & 0xff);
    }
    else {
        /* Host known, print the host text name */
        printf("%-12s", h->h_name);
    }
}
```

## 5.4.5  The support library

Next we show the functions in the support library `brokerlib.c`. These are the functions the application clients and servers use to hide the details of talking to the broker. They are the trickiest parts of the system, but still fairly straightforward.

The first function is `connect_to_service()`, which the application clients use to obtain a connection to a named service. This function shows the client-side code for both a connectionless service (the broker) and a connection-oriented service (the application server requested by the application client). The steps are as follows:

1. Create and bind a connectionless endpoint.
2. Use it to send an OP_FIND request to the broker.
3. Read the broker's reply, containing the application server's address.
4. Create and bind a connection-oriented endpoint.
5. Connect this endpoint to the application server's endpoint whose address was returned by the broker.
6. Return the descriptor for the connected endpoint to the caller.

The second function is register_service(), which the application servers use to register themselves with the broker. This function shows client-side code for a connectionless service (the broker again), and some of the server-side code for a connection-oriented service. The steps are as follows:

1. Create a connection-oriented endpoint for the application service to use.
2. Bind a local address to it. We do not care which, but we need to know, so it can be registered.
3. Create and bind a connectionless endpoint.
4. Use the connectionless endpoint to send an OP_REGISTER message to the broker, containing the service name (passed by the caller) and the address we bound at step 2.
5. Return the connection-oriented endpoint descriptor to the caller. It is then up to the caller (i.e. the application server) to perform t_listen() and t_accept() on this endpoint to obtain client connections.

The third function in the broker library is accept_call(), which we saw in Section 5.3.5. Here is the code of the broker library:

```
/* brokerlib.c  --  Library Support for Broker Service */

#include <stdio.h>
#include <sys/types.h>
#include <sys/fcntl.h>
#include <sys/socket.h>
#include <netinet/in.h>
#include <netdb.h>
#include <tiuser.h>
#include "broker.h"

extern int t_errno;

/* This is the function the application clients use to obtain
   a connection to a  named  service.  The function returns a
   transport endpoint already connected to the server.
*/
int connect_to_service(char *svc_name)
```

```
{
    int                 seh;    /* Stream endpoint handle   */
    int                 deh;    /* Datagram endpoint handle */
    int                 flags;
    Service_request     request;
    Service_reply       reply;
    struct hostent      *host;
    struct sockaddr_in  broker;
    struct t_unitdata   u;
    struct t_call       call;

    /* Create a connectionless endpoint to talk to the broker */

    if ((deh = t_open("/dev/udp", O_RDWR, 0)) < 0)
        return -1;

    if (t_bind(deh, 0, 0) < 0)
        return -1;

    /* Build a 'find service' request */

    request.opcode = OP_FIND;
    strcpy(request.name, svc_name);

    /* Get the broker's address */
    if ((host = gethostbyname("brokerhost")) == NULL)
        return -2;

    broker.sin_family      = AF_INET;
    memcpy(&broker.sin_addr.s_addr, host->h_addr, host->h_length);
    broker.sin_port        = htons(BROKER_PORT);

    /* Build a t_unitdata structure for datagrams */
    u.udata.buf    = (char *)&request;
    u.udata.len    = sizeof request;
    u.addr.buf     = (char *)&broker;
    u.addr.len     = sizeof broker;
    u.opt.len      = 0;

    /* Send the request to the broker */
    t_sndudata(deh, &u);

    /* Get the broker's reply */
    u.udata.buf    = (char *)&reply;
    u.udata.len    = 0;
    u.udata.maxlen = sizeof reply;
    u.addr.maxlen  = 0;
    u.opt.maxlen   = 0;
    t_rcvudata(deh, &u, &flags);

    /* Finished with the connectionless endpoint now */
        t_close(deh);

    /* If broker reported error, return error to caller */
```

```
    if (reply.status != STAT_OK)
        return -3;

    /* Create a connection-oriented endpoint for the application
       service to use, and bind an (arbitrary) local address to
       it.
    */
    if ((seh = t_open("/dev/tcp", O_RDWR, 0)) < 0)
        return -4;

    if (t_bind(seh, 0, 0) < 0) {
        close(seh);
        return -5;
    }

    /* Connect this  endpoint to the  server's endpoint whose
       address  was returned by the  broker.  First, build a
       t_call  struct.  The first line here is  the heart of
       the whole system.  We pass the endpoint  address that
       the broker sent us directly into the t_call structure
       without examining it.
    */
    call.addr.buf    = (char *)(reply.svc.tsap);
    call.addr.len    = sizeof (struct sockaddr_in);
    call.opt.len     = 0;
    call.udata.len   = 0;
    if (t_connect(seh, &call, 0) < 0) {
        close(seh);
        return -7;
    }

    /* All's well, return the endpoint handle to the caller */
    return seh;

}

/* This is the function the application servers use to register
   themselves with the broker. The function returns a transport
   endpoint on which the server may accept connections
*/
int register_service(char *svc_name)
{
    Register_request    request;
    int                 reply;
    int                 seh;
    int                 deh;
    int                 flags;
    struct hostent      *host;
    struct t_bind       bindreq;
    struct t_bind       bindrep;
```

```
struct sockaddr_in   svc_addr;
struct sockaddr_in   broker;
struct t_unitdata    u;
char                 this_host[32];

/* Create a connection-oriented endpoint for the application
   service to use.
*/

if ((seh = t_open("/dev/tcp", O_RDWR, 0)) < 0)
        return -1;

/* Bind a local address. We don't mind which port we use, but
   we must find out and register it with the broker.
*/

bindreq.addr.buf    = (char *)0;
bindreq.addr.len    = 0;
bindreq.qlen        = 5;          /* Max queue length */
bindrep.addr.buf    = (char *)&svc_addr;
bindrep.addr.maxlen = sizeof svc_addr;

if (t_bind(seh, &bindreq, &bindrep) < 0)
    return -2;
/* bindrep tells us what port we have got, but we still need to
   look up our own IP address
*/
gethostname(this_host, sizeof this_host);
if ((host = gethostbyname(this_host)) == 0) {
    return -3;
}
memcpy(&svc_addr.sin_addr.s_addr, host->h_addr, host->h_length);

/* Create a connectionless endpoint to talk to the broker */

if ((deh = t_open("/dev/udp", O_RDWR, 0)) < 0)
    return -3;

if (t_bind(deh, 0, 0) < 0)
    return -3;

/* Build a registration request */

request.opcode = OP_REGISTER;
strcpy(request.name, svc_name);
memcpy(request.tsap, &svc_addr, sizeof svc_addr);

/* Get the broker's address */
if ((host = gethostbyname("brokerhost")) == NULL)
    return -4;

broker.sin_family     = AF_INET;
memcpy(&broker.sin_addr.s_addr, host->h_addr, host->h_length);
broker.sin_port       = htons(BROKER_PORT);
```

```
    /* Build a t_unitdata structure for datagrams */
    u.udata.buf    = (char *)&request;
    u.udata.len    = sizeof request;
    u.addr.buf     = (char *)&broker;
    u.addr.len     = sizeof broker;
    u.opt.len      = 0;

    /* Send the request to the broker */
    t_sndudata(deh, &u);

    /* Get the broker's reply (= status only) */
    u.udata.buf    = (char *)&reply;
    u.udata.maxlen = sizeof reply;
    u.addr.maxlen  = 0;
    u.opt.maxlen   = 0;
    t_rcvudata(deh, &u, &flags);

    /* If broker reported error, return error to caller */
    if (reply != STAT_OK)
        return -5;

    /* All's well, return the application server's endpoint */
    return seh;
}

/* This is the function the application servers call to accept a
   connection once a connection request has been received. A new
   endpoint handle for the connection is returned.
*/
accept_call(int fd, struct t_call *call)
{
    int             conn_fd;

    /* Get a new endpoint to accept the connection on */
    if ((conn_fd = t_open("/dev/tcp", O_RDWR, 0)) < 0)
        return -1;

    /* Bind any local address */
    if (t_bind(conn_fd, 0, 0) < 0) {
        close(conn_fd);
        return -2;
    }

    /* Accept the connection request on the new descriptor */
    if (t_accept(fd, conn_fd, call) < 0) {
        close(conn_fd);
        return -3;
    }

    /* All's well, return the new descriptor to the caller */
    return conn_fd;
}
```

## 5.4.6  An example application server

To round off the example, and to allow us to test everything we have written so far, we will show a simple application client and a pair of application servers. The servers offer a trivial 'arithmetic service' – reading a pair of numbers from the client, performing an arithmetic operation on them, and returning a single integer to the client. The two servers we will implement perform addition and multiplication. This is a simple example of the *algorithmic distribution* discussed in Chapter 1.

As usual, we need a header file describing the message formats used by the servers. This time, it is rather trivial:

```
/* arith.h  - data types for arithmetic services */

typedef struct int_pair {
    int     num1;
    int     num2;
} Int_pair;

/* Each of the arithmetic servers reads an Int_pair
   from the client and returns a single int
*/
```

Here is the code for the addition service. We will not show the code for the multiplication service – it is almost identical.

```
/* This is the 'adder' service.  */

#include <stdio.h>
#include <tiuser.h>
#include "arith.h"

main(int argc, char *argv[])
{
    int                 rendezvous;
    int                 connection;
    struct t_call       *call;
    int                 flags;
    Int_pair            request;
    int                 reply;

    /* Register with the broker. We get back a descriptor for an
       endpoint on which we can receive connection requests.
    */
    rendezvous = register_service("adder");

    /* Allocate a t_call structure */
    call = (struct t_call *)t_alloc(rendezvous, T_CALL, T_ADDR);

    while(1) {          /* Main service loop */
        /* Wait for a connection request */
```

```
        t_listen(rendezvous, call);
        connection = accept_call(rendezvous, call);
        if (connection < 0) {
            t_error("adder: problem accepting call");
        }

        /* This is the application-specific part. Get a message
            (an integer pair) from the client.
        */
        while (t_rcv(connection, &request, sizeof request,
                &flags) > 0) {

            /* Formulate a reply and send it back */
            reply = request.num1 + request.num2;
            t_snd(connection, &reply, sizeof reply, 0);
        }
        t_close(connection);
    }
}
```

## 5.4.7  An example application client

The final piece of code is the application client. The most exciting part of this is the calls
to connect_to_service(). Note that, whilst this function hides all the details of setting
up the connection to the application server, it is left up to the client to conduct the
dialogue, using t_snd() and t_rcv().

```
/* Example client of arithmetic servers */

#include <stdio.h>
#include "arith.h"

main(int argc, char *argv[])
{
    int         fd_add;
    int         fd_mult;
    int         n;
    int         flags;
    /* Structures for dialogue with servers */
    Int_pair    add_request;
    Int_pair    mult_request;
    int         add_reply;
    int         mult_reply;

    /* Establish connections to the servers */
    fd_add  = connect_to_service("adder");
    fd_mult = connect_to_service("multiplier");

    /* Now we will print our 5 times table */
```

```
n = 1;
while (n <= 10) {

    /* Multiply n by 5 using the multiplication server */

    mult_request.num1 = n;
    mult_request.num2 = 5;
    t_snd(fd_mult, &mult_request, sizeof mult_request, 0);
    t_rcv(fd_mult, &mult_reply,   sizeof mult_reply, &flags);
    printf("5 times %d is %d\n", n, mult_reply);

    /* Add one to n using the addition server */

    add_request.num1 = n;
    add_request.num2 = 1;
    t_snd(fd_add, &add_request, sizeof add_request, 0);
    t_rcv(fd_add, &add_reply,   sizeof add_reply, &flags);
    n = add_reply;
}
}
```

## 5.4.8  A demonstration run

A certain amount of setup is required to run this example. First, a machine must be chosen as brokerhost. An alias for this machine must be entered into the host's map, or into the /etc/hosts files. The broker should then be started on this machine. Root permissions are not required to run the broker.

Next, the application servers should be started. Let us suppose that the addition server is started on trillian, and the multiplication server is started on zaphod:

```
trillian%  adder &
zaphod% multiplier &
```

Now we may run svclist to check that these servers have registered:

```
eddie% svclist
Service name: adder       host = trillian    , port =  1088
Service name: multiplier  host = zaphod       , port =  1244
eddie%
```

Finally, we may start the client. The results are fairly uninspiring, as befits a transparent network service!

```
eddie% client
5 times 1 is 5
5 times 2 is 10
5 times 3 is 15
5 times 4 is 20
```

```
5 times 5 is 25
5 times 6 is 30
5 times 7 is 35
5 times 8 is 40
5 times 9 is 45
5 times 10 is 50
eddie%
```

## 5.5  TLI or sockets?

Since TLI and sockets offer much the same facilities, and are often both supported by the UNIX system, programmers are sometimes uncertain which to choose. It is not possible to give a definitive answer here, but the following points may at least help ensure that the uncertainty is fairly balanced!

1.  Sockets existed long before TLI, and there is a lot of socket code out in the world. If your work involves the maintenance of older network applications, you will need to understand sockets.
2.  Purely from a coding standpoint, sockets 'feel' better integrated into UNIX; for example, in their use of regular UNIX file descriptors, and in their use of `errno` rather than a specific error-reporting mechanism.
3.  The TLI coding style imposed by the use of all the `netbuf` structures can become awkward and verbose. It is true that there is more flexibility, but much of it is often not wanted. However, style is a matter of personal taste.
4.  TLI is the 'officially supported' way forward. The SVR4 manual says that: 'TLI is the preferred programming interface for accessing transport services and it is recommended that programmers writing new applications for System V Release 4 use TLI'. Also, the X/Open XPG3 standard for networking interfaces is essentially the TLI interface. Software products seeking to carry the X/Open trademark to advertise compliance with X/Open definitions would necessarily have to use TLI.

An issue we have not addressed here is the writing of true 'transport-independent' code. SVR4 UNIX includes 'network selection' mechanisms which allow run-time selection of an appropriate transport provider and of the correct set of name-to-address mapping functions. These mechanisms mesh in well with the TLI interface. (See Chapter 3 of Padovano, 1993.) If you need to write code which must run over multiple protocol stacks, or which you anticipate will need to move to other transport protocols in the future, then TLI offers some significant advantages.

Much more important than the question of whether to use sockets or TLI is the question of whether we should be talking directly to the transport provider *at all*. Remote procedure calls, discussed in the next chapter, provide a much higher level and more elegant mechanism for network communication. Other object-oriented paradigms, such as the *ToolTalk* messaging facility in Solaris, are perhaps how the distributed applications of the future will be integrated.

# Chapter 6

# Distributed programming using remote procedure calls

## 6.1 Introduction

### 6.1.1 A new view of client–server communication

In the last two chapters we have looked in some detail at the business of communicating between clients and servers by dealing explicitly with the transport provider. We have used the socket and TLI libraries to interface directly to the transport layer. In this type of distributed programming we are very aware, as programmers, of the communication which is taking place between the various parts of the program because this communication appears as explicit I/O operations in the code, using calls such as `read()` and `write()`, or `t_snd()` and `t_rcv()`. Indeed, the structure of a client or server written in this way tends to be centred around the exchanges with the remote peer; see Figure 6.1. There are other 'overheads' involved in writing client–server applications at this level, for example, the code needed by the client to find the address of, and connect to, the server. Another complication, briefly mentioned in Chapter 4, arises when data are sent between machines with differing architectures, and consequently with different binary data representations.

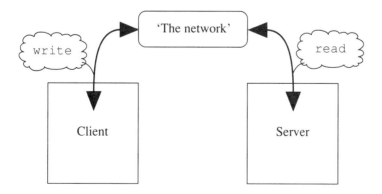

**Figure 6.1** Client–server communication using explicit I/O.

In this chapter, we explore an alternative method for writing distributed applications which handles most of these issues automatically and in which the interactions between the local and remote parts take place in a much less visible way. We will be working at a 'higher level of abstraction', away from the transport layer. First, consider for a moment the program below:

```c
/* Print a list of primes between 1 and 1000 */
main()
{
    int i, how_many, primes[1000];
    how_many = find_primes(1, 1000, primes);
    for (i=0; i<how_many; i++)
        printf("%d is prime\n", primes[i]);
}

/* Find all primes between min and max, return them in array */
int find_primes(int min, int max, int *array)
{
    int i, count=0;
    for (i=min; i<=max; i++)
        if (isprime(i))
            array[count++] = i;
    return count;
}

/* Return TRUE if n is prime */
int isprime(int n)
{
    int i;
    for (i=2; i*i <= n; i++) {
        if ((n % i) == 0)
            return 0;
    }
    return 1;
}
```

We will be returning to this program later in the chapter, but for the moment the details of this code are not important. Notice, however, the layered structure of the program: `main()` calls `find_primes()`, and `find_primes()` calls `isprime()`. Most programs show this layered structure; high level functions decide what is to be done, and low level functions do the dirty work. This caller–callee relationship is similar to the client–server relationship used in distributed programming. We do not usually speak of a client–server relationship in this context, but it is there nonetheless. Like servers, low level functions sit passively waiting to be called. Like clients, high level functions actively decide to make the call. See Figure 6.2.

Remote procedure calls, the subject of this chapter, give the best of both worlds by retaining a traditional layered structure to a program, whilst allowing different pieces of it

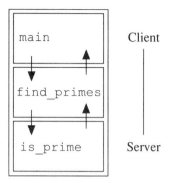

**Figure 6.2** Client–server relationships in nondistributed programs.

to reside on different machines. As the name implies, a remote procedure call (RPC) is a call to a procedure (or function, or subroutine; call it what you will) which exists, and will execute, on a remote machine. The mechanism is illustrated in Figure 6.3. The client code (high level function) makes a call to a client *stub* procedure, passing arguments as required. To the program that called it, the stub looks as if it were the 'real' procedure. In fact, it simply parcels up the arguments, along with additional data specifying which procedure is to be called, and builds a message, which is sent via the network transport provider to the remote machine. There, a server *wrapper* program picks apart the message, selects which procedure is to be called, retrieves the parameters from the message, and passes them to the procedure. When the procedure is done, any return data are again parcelled into a message by the server wrapper, and returned to the client stub. The stub retrieves the data and returns them to the original client caller, just as if the stub had done the work locally. (The server wrapper is also often referred to as the server stub; wrapper seems a more appropriate description.)

RPC hides the interprocess communication from us behind an ordinary function call. In other words, it allows a program to communicate with its remote parts using exactly the same mechanism (a procedure call) as it uses to communicate with its local parts. The ideal RPC mechanism, perhaps, would allow programmers to call procedures without even *knowing* if they were local or remote, in the same way that NFS lets them access files without knowing which machines those files are on. In practice, RPC is not quite that transparent. There may be some constraints on how parameters may be passed to the remote procedure, and how the results may be returned.

## 6.1.2 RPC implementations

The RPC concept described in the previous section is clearly an elegant and rather general idea, and several significant RPC implementations have been produced. Generally, an RPC implementation provides the following components:

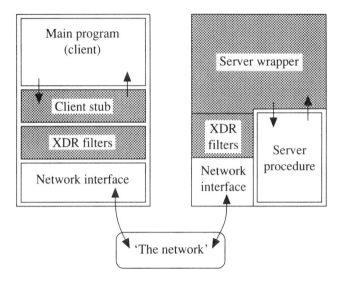

**Figure 6.3** Client–server communication using RPC.

1.  Some form of language, or notation, for specifying the remote procedures present in the server, and the format of the arguments and return values of those procedures.
2.  A tool that automatically generates the client stub and server wrapper code (the parts shown shaded in Figure 6.3), based on the programmer's specification of the argument and return types of the remote procedures.
3.  A set of rules defining the format of data as they pass across the network between client and server, together with support for converting between the machine's internal representation and the external representation. This component is labelled 'XDR filters' in Figure 6.3.
4.  Some form of service registry to make it easier for the clients to find the server they need without knowledge of specific transport endpoint addresses such as port numbers. Such services are known variously as port mappers, brokers or binding services.
5.  A library of functions to handle the details of obtaining a connection to the client, serializing and de-serializing the arguments, and so on.

All RPC mechanisms, of course, rely on some underlying transport protocol to send call messages and reply messages across the network. Some use a connection-oriented transport, some use connectionless transport, and some can use either.

The RPC mechanism described in this chapter is sometimes called 'Sun RPC' because Sun invented it, and is sometimes called 'ONC RPC' because it forms part of the 'open network computing' facilities which are generally taken to include RPC, and the major services built on top of it, such as NFS and NIS. It is not the only RPC mechanism in use, and (arguably) it is not the best. It is, however, the most widespread at the present time.

A much earlier RPC implementation is the Courier RPC mechanism developed by Xerox, which forms the basis of XNS (Xerox network systems). This runs on top of SPP (sequenced packet protocol) which is part of the XNS protocol suite. This is a connection-oriented, reliable protocol, similar to TCP. An implementation of Courier was provided in 4.3 BSD; however, Courier cannot be considered a mainstream distributed programming environment amongst the UNIX community at large.

Another RPC mechanism originated with Apollo's NCS (network computing system) and is generally known as NCS RPC. This RPC is significant because it was adopted as the basis of the Distributed Computing Environment (DCE) from the Open Software Foundation. It is probably the major alternative to Sun RPC at the present time.

## 6.1.3 The ONC RPC system

The ONC RPC system, which is the main focus of this chapter, consists of the following major components:

1. A standard external data representation (XDR) used for all message traffic between client and server. XDR not only defines the way the bits and bytes have to look, it also provides a language for describing the data types passed to and from the remote procedure.
2. A library of XDR *filters*. These are the routines which convert between the data representation used within the local machine and the XDR representation. Each filter operates in either direction. There are predefined filters for all of C's basic data types, plus additional routines which aid the development of filters for user-defined data types – arrays, structures, and more complex graph structures involving pointer chains.
3. An extension to the XDR language, a sort of RPC description language, allows the programmer to describe the client–server interface in a formal, precise way. This is referred to as a *protocol specification*.
4. A tool called rpcgen which reads the RPC description language and generates the C source code for the client stub and server wrapper. rpcgen will also generate any additional XDR filters required for user-defined data types.
5. A library of RPC support functions.
6. A service registry called the port mapper, which keeps track of all RPC services registered on a machine, and their transport endpoint addresses. In later implementations the port mapper is called rpcbind.

## 6.1.4 Identifying an RPC service

A remote procedure is identified by three numbers:

{ program number, version number, procedure number }

Each of these is simply a numeric integer value, although the programmer rarely has to embed the actual numbers into the code.

The two numbers

{ program number, version number }

identify a specific server *program*, and the procedure number identifies a procedure within that program.

Each host runs a portmapper (itself an RPC-based service) which maintains a register of all RPC servers running on that host. The portmapper is similar to the simple service broker program we wrote in Chapter 5, with one important difference: our service broker maintained a network-wide registry, but the portmapper only maintains a registry for servers on the local machine.

The steps involved in locating an RPC service are shown in Figure 6.4. When a server starts up, it creates a transport endpoint to accept connections on, and binds an arbitrary port number to it. It then registers with the portmapper, sending a message which effectively says something like: 'Hello, I'm serving program number 100007, version 1, using UDP protocol, and I'm listening on port 1061.' The portmapper adds this mapping to its list. This is step (1) in Figure 6.4.

When a client wishes to make a remote procedure call, it contacts the portmapper on the machine where the remote service is running, passing it the program number, version number and protocol of the desired service (step (2) in Figure 6.4). The portmapper returns the port number at which the service is listening (step (3) in the figure). The client may then call the server procedure by sending an RPC call message to the port it just got from the portmapper (step 4 in the figure). The call message contains the serialized arguments to the procedure and also the procedure number, which the server uses to dispatch the request to the correct procedure.

Notice the two stages in locating the remote procedure:

1. The portmapper locates the correct port for the service, based on the program number and version number.
2. The server wrapper selects the correct service procedure, based on the procedure number passed in the call message.

The command

```
rpcinfo  -p
```

may be used to query the portmapper to provide its entire list of mappings. rpcinfo is the administrative component of RPC, analogous to our svclist utility in Chapter 5. A typical output (from Solaris 2.1) appears below:

```
deepthought% rpcinfo -p
   program vers proto   port  service
    100000    4   tcp    111  portmapper
    100000    3   tcp    111  portmapper
```

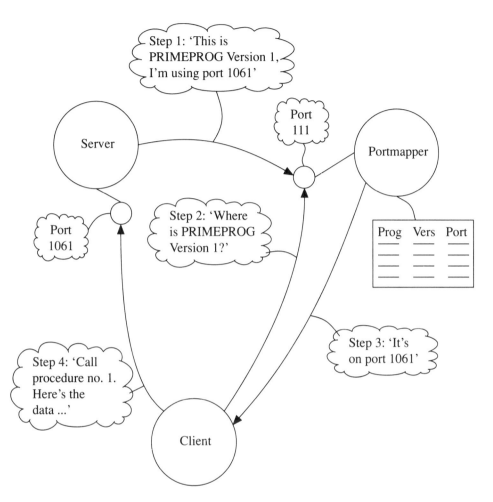

**Figure 6.4** Registering and locating an RPC server.

```
100000    2    tcp    111    portmapper
100000    4    udp    111    portmapper
100000    3    udp    111    portmapper
100000    2    udp    111    portmapper
100007    3    udp   1029    ypbind
100007    3    tcp   1027    ypbind
100024    1    udp   1035    status
100021    1    udp   1036    nlockmgr
100024    1    tcp   1028    status
100021    1    tcp   1029    nlockmgr
100087   10    udp   1038
100021    3    udp   1036    nlockmgr
100021    3    tcp   1029    nlockmgr
```

. . . edited for brevity

```
100083   1   tcp   4046
100003   2   udp   2049   nfs
100005   1   udp   1056   mountd
100005   2   udp   1056   mountd
100026   1   udp   1057   bootparam
100005   1   tcp   4048   mountd
100026   1   tcp   4047   bootparam
100005   2   tcp   4048   mountd
```

There are some interesting points to note about this output. First, most of the port numbers are arbitrary, and indeed may well be different next time if the machine is rebooted. The program and version numbers are *not* arbitrary – it is these numbers which the client and server must agree about. Secondly, note that some servers register for more than one protocol; ypbind, for example, is listening on TCP port 1027 and UDP port 1029. Thirdly, some services are registered under more than one version. mountd, for example, has registered versions 1 and 2. The idea behind having multiple version numbers is to allow evolution of the server protocols without losing backward compatibility. Here mountd version 2 provides the newest version of the service; version 1 continues to support older clients. The two can coexist without conflict or confusion about which version is required. Indeed, since both versions are registered at the same UDP port (1056), it is evident that a single mountd program has registered both versions of the protocol.

The names appearing in the column headed service are simply symbolic names for the program numbers. rpcbind looks these up in the file /etc/rpc (or in the rpc map, if NIS is running). This file will probably have many more entries than there are servers present on the machine. Here is an extract:

```
rpcbind         100000   portmap sunrpc rpcbind
nisd            100300   rpc.nisd
rstatd          100001   rstat rup perfmeter
rusersd         100002   rusers
nfs             100003   nfsprog
ypserv          100004   ypprog
mountd          100005   mount showmount
ypbind          100007
walld           100008   rwall shutdown
yppasswdd       100009   yppasswd
etherstatd      100010   etherstat
rquotad         100011   rquotaprog quota rquota
sprayd          100012   spray
3270_mapper     100013
rje_mapper      100014
selection_svc   100015   selnsvc
database_svc    100016
rexd            100017   rex
```

The first column gives the 'official' name for the service, the second column shows the program number, and the remaining columns show alternative names for the service.

These are the 'standard' program numbers for these services, in much the same way that 'well-known' port numbers are standard for socket based servers. These program numbers are allocated in the following groups:

-       0 – 1fffffff     Administered by Sun Microsystems
- 20000000 – 3fffffff     User-defined
- 40000000 – 5fffffff     Transient
- 60000000 – ffffffff     Reserved for future use

# 6.2 External data representation

In this section we examine the external data representation (XDR) used by Sun RPC in transporting procedure arguments and return values between the RPC server and client. A machine-independent data format such as XDR finds use in other contexts, too. In fact, whenever binary data generated by one computer need to be processed by another dissimilar computer, XDR or some such format must be used. We will first look at some of the problems caused by dissimilar machine architectures, and then we will see how XDR solves these problems.

## 6.2.1 Data representation differences

Whenever we wish to transfer binary data between computers we come up against an unfortunate fact of life: different computer architectures use different representations for binary data.

One of the most common differences in representation concerns byte ordering. Typically, a computer has a 32-bit wide data path between processor and memory. Thus, the 'natural' unit of data for the processor to address is a 32-bit word. Most computers, however, support the notion of a byte-addressable memory. In effect, they use the bottom two bits of a 'byte address' to select one 8-bit byte within the 32-bit memory location identified by a 'word address', as shown in Figure 6.5.

Unfortunately, computer architects do not agree on the order of these bytes within the word. The example of Figure 6.5 shows the so-called *big-endian* byte ordering. This means that within a word, the most significant byte is stored 'first', that is, at the lowest byte address. Architectures such as the 68000 family and SPARC are big-endian. Architectures such as the VAX, the transputer and the Intel 486 family are little-endian.

The endian-ness of the architecture determines the order in which bytes are transmitted across a byte-oriented data path such as a network or a magnetic tape. Consider the following two programs:

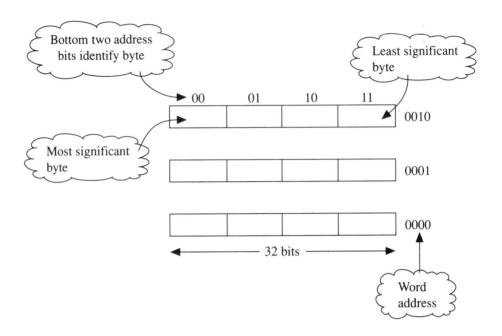

**Figure 6.5** Big-endian byte ordering.

```
/* PROGRAM A */
main()
{
    int i = 0x12345678;

    write(1, &i, sizeof i);
}


/* PROGRAM B */
main()
{
    int i;
    read(0, &i, sizeof i);
    printf("%x\n", i);
}
```

Suppose that Program A is run on a little-endian 486-based machine, and its output is passed (using rsh) to Program B running on a big-endian SPARC-based machine.

The little-endian machine sends the least significant byte first, i.e. the bytes are sent in the order 78, 56, 34, 12. The big-endian machine places the first byte it receives at the most significant end of the word. The output appears as follows:

```
78563412
```

Examination of this result (bearing in mind that the numbers are in hexadecimal, i.e. two digits to a byte) shows the effects of the byte reversal clearly.

The byte reversal is also easily seen if we examine the output of `proga` directly, using `od`. On a little-endian machine it appears as follows, with the least significant byte appearing first in the data stream:

```
nunc% proga | od -b
0000000 170 126 064 022
0000004
```

whereas on a big-endian machine it appears as follows, with the most significant byte appearing first in the data stream:

```
douglas% proga | od -b
0000000  022 064 126 170
0000004
```

Note that `od` is showing the bytes in octal (just to confuse the issue!).

Similar experiments can be done with doubles or other data types, and, similarly, we get the wrong answers.

After byte ordering, the most common causes of differences in data representation are the 'alignment rules' of the processor architecture. A typical alignment rule might be '32-bit integers must be at an address which is a multiple of 4' (i.e. must be aligned with the processor's 32-bit word). Such rules may require a compiler to generate 'holes' in data structures, to ensure that all items in the structure meet their alignment requirement. Consider the following structure:

```
struct demo {
    char c;
    int i;
    long x;
}
```

Figure 6.6 shows three possible binary representations for this structure, for different machine word lengths and alignment rules. Combined with the big-endian vs. little-endian differences discussed above, we can see at least six possible representations for this structure.

```
struct demo {
  char c;
  int  i;
  long x;
}
```

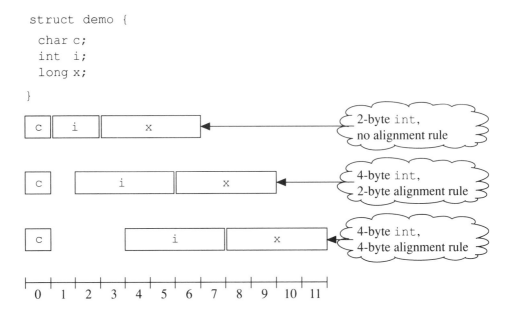

Figure 6.6 Structure alignment examples.

---

**An aside:** what is surprising is not that these data representation differences exist, but how relatively minor they actually are. Everyone uses two's complement binary numbers to represent signed integers. One might imagine that a computer might have evolved which did arithmetic in base 9, using a pair of three-state signals ('trits'?) to represent each digit, but none has. Silly though that example may be, it is not all that far removed from the situation twenty years ago, when each manufacturer had its own representation for floating point numbers. Moving floating point data between, say, a Data General NOVA and a DEC PDP-15 would have been a major job – not that many people would have ever considered such a thing. Nowadays, everyone uses the IEEE 754 standard for binary floating point arithmetic, and these problems have gone away. If intelligent beings exist elsewhere in the universe, it would be interesting to compare not only their body chemistry, but also how their computers represent data (and whether their operating system is POSIX conformant . . . ).

---

In addition to variations in data representation resulting from architectural differences, there are language-specific differences too. For example, in Pascal a string is stored with a string length in the initial byte; in C a string is delimited by a null terminator byte.

Finally, we must consider the issues of passing pointers from machine to machine. Of course, any architecture-specific differences in pointer representation are rather academic – there is a more fundamental problem. An address on one computer has no validity on another, even if it has an identical architecture. I cannot pass the address of some variable across the network to a remote host, and expect that address to mean something. The remote machine has a separate address space. Nonetheless, there are situations in which we wish to pass to a remote procedure some form of graph structure held together with pointers – a linked list or a binary tree, for example. The problem here is: how can we send such a structure down a serial byte stream, and have the machine at the other end reconstruct it? (The self-assembly furniture sold at budget furniture shops provides an analogy: it is packed flat for transit, but can be reconstituted into its proper three-dimensional form, using the instructions provided, once you get it home.)

## 6.2.2  XDR formats

XDR solves the problems of different data representations by defining a standard representation for data whilst 'in transit' between machines. These XDR formats are described in RFC 1014, which is also reproduced in Sun's *SunOS 4.1: Network Programming Guide*, and in AT&T's *UNIX SVR4 Programmers' Guide: Networking Interfaces*. There is nothing very unusual about the formats themselves; three examples are shown in Figure 6.7.

We can make a few general observations about the XDR formats:

1.  XDR is basically a 'big-endian' representation, as the integer example in Figure 6.7 shows.
2.  XDR does not support the notion of protocol *negotiation*; in particular, two little-endian machines communicating using XDR cannot mutually agree to use little-endian byte ordering, they must stick to the XDR rules and convert everything to/from big-endian ordering, inefficient though this may be. XDR is said to use a *single canonical form*.
3.  All XDR items are a multiple of four bytes long. If necessary, items are padded with trailing zero bytes to ensure this rule is obeyed. The choice of the XDR unit size is a trade-off. Four is large enough to meet the alignment requirements of most machines, and small enough to avoid being grotesquely inefficient for data types such as booleans.
4.  XDR uses *implicit typing*. If machine A were to send, say, an integer, a double and a string to machine B, it would transmit exactly those bytes illustrated in Figure 6.7. To make sense of this byte stream (i.e. to convert it to the correct local representation) machine B must know *a priori* that it is expecting an integer, a double and a string. This information is *not* passed as part of the message.

    In contrast, the basic encoding rules (BER) of ASN.1 use *explicit typing*. Every data type transmitted is encoded using three fields: a *tag*, explicitly specifying the type of data, a *length*, specifying the number of bytes taken up by the value, and finally the encoded value itself.

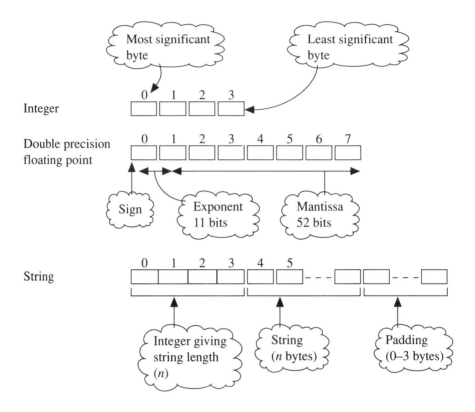

**Figure 6.7** Examples of XDR formats.

5.  XDR assumes the data are to be encoded onto a *byte* stream. It assumes that the bytes will be delivered in the order they were sent, but it says nothing, for example, about the order in which bits should be transmitted within the bytes. That is left up to the lower layers of the protocol stack.

The full list of primitive data types for which XDR formats are defined is given in Table 6.1.

## 6.2.3 XDR filters

The RPC library includes a collection of functions for encoding data to, and decoding data from, XDR format. These functions are called XDR *filters*. There is a separate filter for each basic data type in Table 6.1; for example, the filter xdr_double() handles doubles, and xdr_int() handles integers. Each filter handles both encoding and decoding. These filters take two parameters: the first is a handle on the XDR stream

**Table 6.1**

| Data type | Definition |
|---|---|
| Integer | 4 bytes – equivalent to an `int` in C. |
| Unsigned integer | 4 bytes. |
| Enumeration | Encoded as signed integers, but can only take on a specified set of values. |
| Boolean | Encoded as signed integers, but can only take on the values 0 (false) and 1 (true). |
| Hyper integer | 8 bytes – no equivalent in C. |
| Unsigned hyper integer | 8 bytes. |
| Float | 4 bytes; uses the IEEE representation for single-precision floating point data. |
| Double | 8 bytes; uses the IEEE representation for double-precision floating point data. |
| Fixed length array | A fixed length array is used when the sender and receiver know that the array will always be (say) 80 elements long. The array is encoded simply by encoding its individual elements in order. |
| Variable length array | A variable length array is used when the sender and receiver do not know *a priori* how long the array will be. Consequently when the array is encoded, it is preceded by an integer (in XDR format, of course) specifying the number of elements in the array. |
| String | A string is, in effect, a variable length array of bytes. It is encoded as an integer specifying the length of the string followed by the bytes of the string. If necessary, bytes containing zero are added to the end to make the total byte count a multiple of four. Notice that this is not the same as the usual C representation for a string, and there is no guarantee of a zero terminator byte in the XDR representation. |
| Fixed length opaque | It is possible to pass data via XDR without any special interpretation. Such data are termed *opaque*. For example, when NFS sends a block of file data to a client, those data are not interpreted by NFS itself. Of course, any machine-dependent issues in interpreting those data are then someone else's problem. Fixed length opaque data are simply sent as an uninterpreted sequence of bytes. If necessary, bytes containing zero are appended to make the total byte count a multiple of four. The sender and receiver must agree *a priori* on the length of the data. |
| Variable length opaque | Similar to fixed length opaque, but used when the sender and receiver do not know *a priori* how long the data will be. Consequently when the data are encoded they are preceded by an integer specifying the number of bytes of data present. |
| Structure | XDR specifies that a structure is encoded simply by encoding each of its members in turn. XDR filters can be written automatically to do this, working from a declaration of the structure. |
| Discriminated union | A discriminated union allows the sending of any one of a set of pre-arranged types. Each possible type is called an *arm* of the union. A user-defined tag, called the *discriminant*, tells XDR which arm of the union is present. The discriminant is encoded (as an integer) in the XDR data stream prior to the data within the arm. In effect, the discriminated union allows the user to send explicitly tagged data, using data types and tags of the user's own choosing. |

(analogous to a file handle obtained from a call to `fopen()`), and the second is a pointer to the data item to be encoded, or a pointer to where the decoded data item is to be placed. The direction of the XDR stream (either encode or decode) is stored as part of the XDR stream handle, so that the filter knows which way to operate when it is called. In addition to the XDR filters for the primitive data types, there are more complex filters which handle the encoding and decoding of fixed length and variable length arrays.

XDR streams can be associated either with a memory buffer, or with an existing 'standard I/O' stream of type `FILE *`.

We can gain some insight into how the filters operate by comparing the following two program fragments:

```
FILE *fd;                        /* File handle */
int    i = 0x12345678;
double d = 123.456;

fd = fopen("demo", "w");       /* Open a file */
fprintf(fd, "%d %f", i, d);    /* Serialize some data to it */
```

```
/* The program xdr_to_file.c */

#include <stdio.h>
#include <rpc/rpc.h>

main()
{
    FILE *fd;                        /* File handle */
    XDR  xd;                     /* XDR stream handle */
    int    i = 0x12345678;
    double d = 123.456;

    fd = fopen("demo", "w");         /* Open a file */
    /* The next call creates an XDR stream associated
       with an existing stdio stream.  The XDR handle
       is returned in xd
    */
    xdrstdio_create(&xd, fd, XDR_ENCODE);
                              /* Associate XDR stream */
    xdr_int(&xd, &i);  /* Serialize some data to it */
    xdr_double(&xd, &d);
}
```

Both examples serialize binary data (the values of variables `i` and `d`), and write them to the file `demo`. The XDR filters such as `xdr_int()` are included in the RPC library and are rather like `fprintf()` in that they take some sort of 'stream handle' as argument, and output a serial data representation to that stream. There are significant differences, however:

1.  XDR filters work both ways, depending on the direction encoded in the XDR stream handle, whereas we use two separate functions, `fprintf()` and `fscanf()`, for output and input.

2.  There is a separate XDR filter for each data type, whereas `fprintf()` handles all data types, according to the format codes it receives. By convention, the XDR filter which encodes the type T is named `xdr_T()`.

3.  `fprintf()` generates an ASCII representation of the data, whereas XDR filters generate a binary representation. Converting data to an ASCII representation is another way of deriving a machine-independent representation, but in most cases it is less efficient, in terms of both the time taken to perform the encoding or decoding, and the number of bytes in the resulting data stream.

We can use XDR filters in this way to rewrite the sample programs we used in Section 6.2.1, so that instead of communicating via `write()` and `read()`, the data are passed through an XDR filter. Here is the XDR version of Program A:

```
/* The Program xdr_writer.c */

#include <stdio.h>
#include <sys/types.h>
#include <rpc/rpc.h>

main(int argc, char *argv[])
{
    int     i = 0x12345678;
    XDR     handle;

    xdrstdio_create(&handle, stdout, XDR_ENCODE);
    xdr_int(&handle, &i);
}
```

and here is the XDR version of Program B:

```
/* The Program xdr_reader.c */

#include <stdio.h>
#include <sys/types.h>
#include <rpc/rpc.h>

main(int argc, char *argv[])
{
    int     i;
    XDR     handle;

    xdrstdio_create(&handle, stdin, XDR_DECODE);
    xdr_int(&handle, &i);

    printf("%x\n", i);
}
```

In both programs the call to `xdrstdio_create()` associates an XDR stream with an existing `stdio` stream. The third parameter in this call (either `XDR_ENCODE` or `XDR_DECODE`) is stored within the XDR stream handle. These versions do interoperate correctly (and give the right answer!) between little-endian and big-endian machines.

Whilst XDR filters might occasionally be used in this way (for example, to write a magnetic tape which was destined to be read on an incompatible machine), the commonest use of XDR is in the transmission of arguments and return values during a remote procedure call. Figure 6.8 shows the role of XDR filters in the context of a client calling a service procedure, passing an argument of type `struct foo` and receiving a result of type `struct bar`.

The numbered steps shown in this figure are as follows:

1. The client program wishing to make the RPC call assembles the data to be passed to the remote procedure. If just a single item is to be passed (say an `int`), then the client simply stores a value into an `int` variable. If several items of data must be passed, the client must bundle them up into an appropriate structure.
2. The client calls the client stub function, passing the address of the data it wishes to transmit. The stub in turn passes this address to the appropriate XDR filter.
3. The client XDR filter, operating in the `ENCODE` direction as defined by the direction specified within the XDR stream handle, serializes the data, which are then transmitted across the network to the server.
4. The server XDR filter, operating in the `DECODE` direction, de-serializes the data, rebuilding the original data structure using the correct representation for the server machine and passing it to the server wrapper.
5. The server wrapper passes the address of the data to the service procedure.
6. When the service procedure is done, it places its results in an outgoing variable (again, a structure must be used if several data items are to be returned).
7. The server procedure returns the address of the data to its server wrapper, which in turn passes it to the appropriate XDR filter.
8. The server XDR filter, operating in the `ENCODE` direction, serializes the data which are then transmitted across the network to the client.
9. The client XDR filter, operating in the `DECODE` direction, de-serializes the data, and rebuilds the original data structure.
10. The client stub passes the address of this returned data structure back to the client program as its return value.

This sequence of operations highlights some key restrictions that apply when passing arguments to, and retrieving results from, a remote procedure:

1. Only a single data item can be passed in. If several values are to be passed, they must be parcelled up into a structure.
2. Likewise, only a single data item can be returned. If several values are to be returned, they must be parcelled up into a structure.
3. Both the client and the server procedure always deal in terms of pointers to the data items they receive and return, never directly with the items themselves.

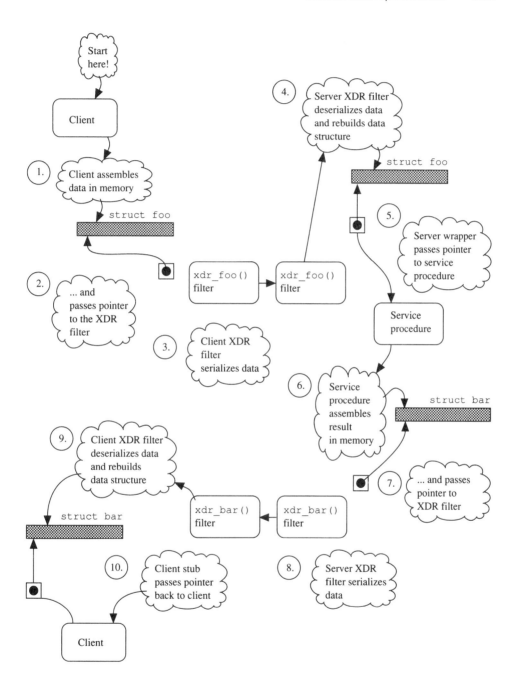

**Figure 6.8** XDR filters.

## 6.2.4 The XDR data description language

When we write a distributed application using RPC we begin by writing an XDR *protocol specification* which defines the data types passed to and from the remote procedures. This specification is placed into a .x file and is written using a special XDR data description language. The .x file is then submitted as input to the rpcgen utility, which will generate (among other things) a C header file containing declarations for the C data types corresponding to the XDR data types, and a file containing the C source code for XDR filters corresponding to any user-defined data types appearing in the .x file.

The idea of having a notation to describe data is not new to us – whenever we declare a variable in a C program, we describe the type of data held in that variable. For example:

```
double x;

struct person {
    char name[50];
    int  age;
} me;
```

We see here various keywords (double, char, int) which specify primitive data types, as well as various notations (the structure and array declarations) which specify more complex derived data types.

XDR provides a similar notation for describing data – indeed, much of the syntax of the XDR language is taken directly from C. This notation is used primarily in describing the format of the data to be sent and returned in an RPC call. As such, it provides a formal, precise way of specifying the protocol used between server and client in an RPC-based distributed application. Rather than present the formal grammar of XDR, we show some examples in Table 6.2, and explain them. You will undoubtedly draw on your knowledge of C as you read these, but keep in mind that XDR's basic types and type constructors are *not* always the same as those in the C language.

## 6.2.5 An XDR example

Here is an example which illustrates the use of XDR data types, shows how they correspond to C data types, and provides a further example of an encoded XDR output stream.

We start with the XDR protocol specification, in a file named play.x. This file uses the XDR notations described in Table 6.2.

```
/* Protocol specification file play.x */
const MYSIZE = 4;

union myunion  switch (int mytag) {
    case 0:
```

**Table 6.2**

| Type | Definition |
| --- | --- |
| `void;` | An explicit way of saying 'no data'. Used when RPC procedures take no parameters, or when an arm of a discriminated union is empty (see example below). |
| `int    page_number;` | Same as an `int` in C, except guaranteed 4 bytes long. |
| `int    week[7];` | A fixed length array of integers (just as in C). It is encoded simply by encoding the elements in turn. Sender and receiver must know at compile-time how big the array is. |
| `double density<50>;` | A variable length array of doubles up to 50 elements long. Remember, when a variable length array is encoded, the actual length is encoded into the data stream prior to the data. There is no directly equivalent type in C, so it is represented as a structure in which the first element holds the length, and the second element points to the data. |
| `int    scores<>;` | A variable length array of integers with no upper limit on the number of elements. |
| `enum {`<br>`    MONDAY = 0;`<br>`    TUESDAY = 1;`<br>`    WEDNESDAY = 2;`<br>`} weekday ;` | An integer data type which supports only a restricted set of values, with the specified names. |
| `const BLOCKSIZE = 512;` | Defines a symbolic name for a numeric constant; similar to a `#define` in C. |
| `opaque filedata[BLOCKSIZE];` | Defines a fixed size block of opaque data exactly `BLOCKSIZE` bytes in length. |
| `opaque mydata<1000>;` | Defines a variable size block of opaque data up to 1000 bytes in length. |
| `string myname<50>` | Defines a string of maximum length 50. |
| `typedef opaque fhandle[32];` | Defines a new type name '`fhandle`' to mean a fixed length array of 32 bytes of opaque data. Equivalent to a `typedef` in C. |
| `union switch mystatus {`<br>`    case 0:`<br>`        void;`<br>`    case 1:`<br>`        int    x;`<br>`    case 2:`<br>`        int    y;`<br>`        double z[50];`<br>`}` | Defines a discriminated union. '`mystatus`' is the tag value which specifies which 'arm' of the union is present. Each arm is described by a 'case' construct. In this example, if `mystatus` is 0, no further data appear in the union. If `mystatus` is 1, a single `int` follows. If `mystatus` is 2, an `int` and an array of 50 doubles follow. |

```
        void;
    case 1:
        int    x;
    case 2:
        double z[50];
} ;
struct play {
    int            i;
    opaque         odata[MYSIZE];
    int            vai<60>;
    string         myname<50>;
    myunion        foo;
} ;
```

This file defines a structure containing an integer, a four-byte array of opaque data, a variable lenth array of integers, a string and a discriminated union. The discriminated union, in turn, contains three arms: arm 0 is empty, arm 1 contains a single integer and arm 2 contains an array of 50 doubles.

Next, we run rpcgen:

```
rpcgen  play.x
```

which will result in the creation of two new files, play.h and play_xdr.c. The play.h file contains a set of C declarations equivalent to the XDR declarations in the .x file. Here it is:

```
/*
 * Please do not edit this file.
 * It was generated using rpcgen.
 */

#include <rpc/types.h>

#define MYSIZE 4

struct myunion {
        int mytag;
        union {
                int x;
                double z[50];
        } myunion_u;
};
typedef struct myunion myunion;
bool_t xdr_myunion();

struct play {
        int i;
        char odata[MYSIZE];
```

```
        struct {
                u_int vai_len;
                int *vai_val;
        } vai;
        char *myname;
        myunion foo;
};
typedef struct play play;
bool_t xdr_play();
```

Let us dissect this in detail. The discriminated union `myunion` in the `.x` file has become a `struct` in the `.h` file. The first member of the struct, `mytag`, is the discriminant of the union. Embedded within the `struct` is a C union whose members correspond to the arms of the discriminated union. To transmit such a union using XDR, we must set the discriminant value to say which arm is present, place data into the appropriate arm and call the XDR filter. Notice also that a `typedef` has been generated for this structure.

The line

```
bool_t xdr_myunion();
```

is a function declaration for the XDR filter for a `myunion` struct. This follows the naming convention for all XDR filters, i.e. the filter for data type `T` is called `xdr_T()`. The return type, as for all XDR filters, is of type `bool_t`, that is, a boolean.

The declaration of the `play` structure has changed considerably between the `.x` and the `.h` files. First, the array of opaque data has become an array of `char`. Secondly, the variable length array `vai` in the `.x` file has turned into a structure. The first member of this structure, `vai_len`, holds a count of the number of elements of data in the array, and the second member, `vai_val`, points to the beginning of the array itself. The string `myname` in the `.x` file has turned into a `char *`. Note that a `typedef` has been generated for this structure also.

Finally, we have a declaration for the XDR filter for a `play` structure.

The second file generated by `rpcgen` is named `play_xdr.c`. It contains the source code for the XDR filters for the `myunion` and `play` structures.

To see these data structures and filters in operation, here is a small test harness, `play.c`:

```
/* play.c  --  demonstrates XDR data types */

#include <stdio.h>
#include <rpc/rpc.h>
/* Include the header file generated by rpcgen */
#include "play.h"

main()
{
    int    i;
    /* Note that rpcgen generates a typedef for the play
```

```
        structure so we just declare it as type "play"
*/
play    p;
XDR     handle;

xdrstdio_create(&handle, stdout, XDR_ENCODE);

/* Now put some data into our play structure.
   Values are given in octal to make it easier to
   tie them in with the output from od -b.
*/
p.i = 033;
for (i=0; i<4; i++)
    p.odata[i] = 0100 + i;
/* Allocate and initialize the variable length array */
p.vai.vai_len = 2;
p.vai.vai_val = (int *)malloc(2 * sizeof (int));
p.vai.vai_val[0] = 044;
p.vai.vai_val[1] = 055;
p.myname = "chris";
/* Select arm 1 of the union and put some data into it */
p.foo.mytag = 1;
p.foo.myunion_u.x = 077;
/* Now XDR the structure to stdout, to see what we get */
xdr_play(&handle, &p);
}
```

This file, along with the file `play_xdr.c` generated by `rpcgen`, may be compiled and linked to produce an executable program. Running this program, and examining the output using `od`, yields the following. Bytes are shown in octal, in groups of four, with added comments:

```
000 000 000 033    # The integer i in big-endian order
100 101 102 103    # 4 bytes of opaque data, not re-ordered
000 000 000 002    # Length of variable length array
000 000 000 044    # First element of variable length array
000 000 000 055    # Second element of variable length array
000 000 000 005    # Length of text string
143 150 162 151    # The characters 'c', 'h', 'r', 'i'
163 000 000 000    # 's' plus 3 bytes of padding
000 000 000 001    # The discriminant of the union
000 000 000 077    # Data in arm 1 of the union
```

## 6.2.6 XDR and linked data structures

As mentioned earlier, the transmission of linked data structures from machine to machine presents a particular problem because pointers generated in the address space of one machine are not valid in the address space of another. XDR provides a special filter called xdr_pointer() which *is* capable of following pointer chains and encoding the result into a serial byte stream – at least for certain types of linked structure. Within a .*x* file, pointers are declared using a notation deceptively similar to the one used in C. For example, this file, point.x, defines a rectangle structure as containing pointers to two point structures:

```
struct point {
    int x;
    int y;
};

struct rectangle {
    point *topleft;
    point *botright;
};
```

When a pointer is encountered in a structure which is being XDR'ed, the xdr_pointer filter first encodes the integer value 1 into the data stream, then calls the appropriate filter to XDR whatever the pointed-to item is. The '1' in the encoded stream basically says 'I am following a non-null pointer; the next thing in the data stream is the encoding of what it pointed to.' It is interesting to examine the sequence of XDR calls as a rectangle structure is encoded:

1. xdr_rectangle calls xdr_pointer to encode the topleft item.
2. xdr_pointer writes a 1 to the stream and calls xdr_point to encode the pointed-to item.
3. xdr_point calls xdr_int twice to encode the *x* and *y* items in the structure to which topleft points.
4. Back in the top level call to xdr_rectangle, the whole process repeats to encode the botright pointer.

We can demonstrate this using the following program which builds a rectangle structure and XDRs it to stdout:

```
#include <stdio.h>
#include <sys/types.h>
#include <rpc/rpc.h>
#include "point.h"

/* Values in octal for easy tie-up with od output */
point p1 = { 022, 033 };
point p2 = { 044, 055 };

rectangle r = { &p1, &p2 };

main(argc, argv)
int argc;
```

```
char *argv[];
{
    XDR handle;
    xdrstdio_create(&handle, stdout, XDR_ENCODE);

    xdr_rectangle(&handle, &r);
}
```

If this program is run and the output piped into od -b we see the following sequence of values (these are bytes, in octal):

```
000 000 000 001    # This says a pointer is being followed
000 000 000 022    # This is the encoding of point p1
000 000 000 033
000 000 000 001    # This says a pointer is being followed
000 000 000 044    # This is the encoding of point p2
000 000 000 055
```

If xdr_pointer() encounters a null pointer, it will encode a '0' into the stream. This says 'I have been asked to encode a null pointer. There is no pointed-to item, so nothing further will be encoded into the stream.' This handling of null pointers means that XDR can correctly serialize some recursive types of data structure, such as linked lists and binary trees. Consider the following file, list.x, which defines a node in a linked list of integers:

```
struct intlist {
    struct intlist *next;
    int             data;
};
```

This structure is self-referential. When it is XDR'ed (by calling its XDR filter, xdr_intlist()) the filter first calls xdr_pointer() to encode the first 'next' pointer. Finding this pointer to be non-null, xdr_pointer() encodes a '1' to the stream and because the pointed-to item happens to be another intlist, it calls xdr_intlist() recursively to encode this item. Thus we have mutual recursion – xdr_intlist() calls xdr_pointer(), and xdr_pointer() calls xdr_intlist(). Each pair of calls walks one node down the list. This continues until xdr_pointer() finds the null pointer, at which point it encodes a '0' to the stream and returns. The innermost instance of xdr_intlist() now calls xdr_int() to encode its 'data' item, and so on. Confused?

Perhaps an example would help. Here is a program, list.c, which builds a simple linked list then XDRs it to stdout:

```
/* The program list.c */

#include <stdio.h>
#include <sys/types.h>
```

```
#include <rpc/rpc.h>
#include "list.h"

/* Values in octal for easy tie-up with od output */
intlist n1 = { NULL, 022 },
         n2 = { &n1,  033 },
         n3 = { &n2,  044 },
         n4 = { &n3,  055 };

main(argc, argv)
int argc;
char *argv[];
{
    XDR handle;

    xdrstdio_create(&handle, stdout, XDR_ENCODE);

    xdr_intlist(&handle, &n4);
}
```

The initialization clauses in this program construct a simple four-element list, as shown in Figure 6.9(a), with n4 at the head of the list, and n1 at the tail. Running this program, and examining the output using od, yields the following. As before, bytes are shown in octal, in groups of four, with added comments:

```
000 000 000 001    # These 1's are generated as xdr_pointer()
000 000 000 001    # ... walks down the list to the tail
000 000 000 001
000 000 000 000    # This marks the end of the list
000 000 000 022    # Now we get the list data, in reverse
000 000 000 033    # order, as the recursive calls to
000 000 000 044    # xdr_pointer() unstack.
000 000 000 055
```

Using these techniques, acyclic (i.e. loop-free) linked data structures such as linked lists and binary trees can be serialized and de-serialized. The technique does *not* work, however, on cyclic data structures, such as the circular list shown in Figure 6.9(b), or the doubly-linked list shown in Figure 6.9(c). For these structures, the XDR filters get stuck in an infinite loop, chasing the pointer chains round and round.

## 6.3  Building clients and servers using rpcgen

### 6.3.1  rpcgen: the big picture

Having examined the role of XDR in remote procedure calls, we now look at the mechanics of building RPC clients and servers, and present a complete example.

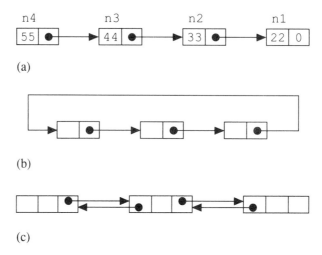

**Figure 6.9** Acyclic and cyclic linked structures: (a) singly-linked list; (b) circular linked list; (c) doubly-linked list.

The `rpcgen` utility handles most of the donkey work of building a distributed RPC application. As input, `rpcgen` reads a protocol specification file, prepared by the user, which contains two things:

1. Declarations of any user-defined data types passed into, or returned from, the remote procedures. The declarations are written using the XDR language described earlier in the chapter.
2. A list of the procedures which make up the server, including their names, and the types of their input parameters and return values.

Conventionally, the protocol specification file has the extension `.x`, for example, `demo.x`. This file is submitted as input to `rpcgen`, using the command:

```
rpcgen   demo.x
```

As shown in Figure 6.10, this generates four output files:

1. `demo_clnt.c`: source code of the client stub.
2. `demo_svc.c`: source code of the server wrapper.
3. `demo_xdr.c`: source code of the XDR filters for any user-defined data types.
4. `demo.h`: a header file containing structure declarations and `typedefs` corresponding to the XDR data types defined in `demo.x`.

These files correspond to the 'boiler-plate' components of the application, the components shown shaded in Figure 6.3.

In addition to the `.x` file, the user must provide:

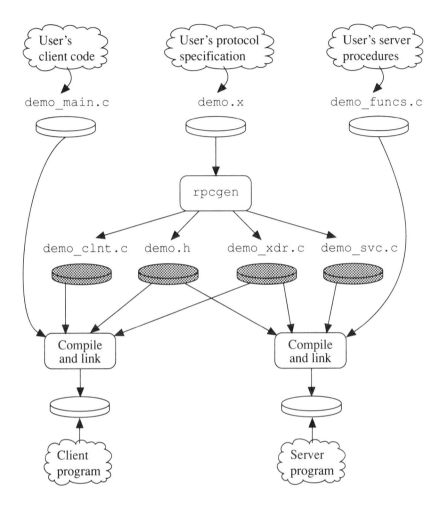

**Figure 6.10** Input and output files for rpcgen.

1.  The source code of the service procedures themselves. In Figure 6.10, this is shown as demo_funcs.c. This is not a complete program, just a collection of service procedures. The server wrapper provides (among other things) the main() function of the server.

2.  The source code of the client. In Figure 6.10, this is shown as demo_main.c.

**An aside:** it is a great shame that rpcgen does not write these parts as well, working from, say, a sketch on the back of an old envelope.

To build the server, the following files are compiled and linked:

```
demo_svc.c
demo_xdr.c
demo_funcs.c
```

To build the client, the following files are compiled and linked:

```
demo_main.c
demo_xdr.c
demo_clnt.c
```

## 6.3.2 Defining an RPC protocol

We will illustrate this process with a simple example – a distributed version of our prime number printing program from earlier in the chapter. We will use rpcgen to do much of the hard work for us.

If we are building a new server from scratch, the first question is: exactly what service will it provide? If we are taking an existing non-distributed application and splitting it up so that parts run remotely, the first decision is where to 'draw the line' between the local and remote components. Let us return to the prime-number program of Figure 6.2. The code for this program is reproduced below.

```c
/* Print a list of primes between 1 and 1000 */
main()
{
    int i, how_many, primes[1000];
    how_many = find_primes(1, 1000, primes);
    for (i=0; i<how_many; i++)
        printf("%d is prime\n", primes[i]);
}

/* Find all primes between min and max, return them in array */
int find_primes(int min, int max, int *array)
{
    int i, count=0;
    for (i=min; i<=max; i++)
        if (isprime(i))
            array[count++] = i;
    return count;
}

/* Return TRUE if n is prime */
int isprime(int n)
{
    int i;
    for (i=2; i*i <= n; i++) {
        if ((n % i) == 0)
```

```
            return 0;
    }
    return 1;
}
```

For this example, we might choose to place the `find_primes()` and `isprime()` functions remotely, and keep the `main()` function local.

---

**An aside:** in reality there would probably be no reason to distribute a program as simple as this *at all*. It would be simpler, and probably quicker, to do all the work on the local machine. This program does not require any remote resources which are not available locally, except – possibly – we might wish to reach out to find a faster CPU to do the number-crunching. This is a toy example, intended merely to examine the mechanisms of RPC programming.

---

Whether we are distributing an existing application or building a brand new one, we must begin by defining the application protocol – that is, the form of the messages by which the client and server will communicate. The XDR data description language gives us a formal way to describe this protocol.

Suppose we have chosen to distribute our prime number program, as suggested above, by placing the `find_primes()` function (and its support function `isprime()`) remotely. Thus, we must define the protocol between `main()` and `find_primes()`.

As it stands, there are two things wrong with the interface to `find_primes()` which prevent it being used as a remote procedure:

1. There are *two* input parameters. An RPC procedure can have only one. We will need to bundle the `min` and `max` parameters up into a structure.
2. The result (a list of prime numbers) is currently returned into an array provided by the caller, through the pointer passed in as the third argument. This technique just will not work for an RPC call. We need to return the list as the return value of the function. Since we do not know in advance how long the list will be, a variable length integer array is an appropriate choice of XDR data type for this return value.

---

**An aside:** please remember that these rules about RPC argument passing only apply to the ONC implementation of RPC and not to the RPC concept as a whole. Other implementations, such as DCE (Distributed Computing Environment), have different rules.

---

## 6.3.3 The protocol specification file

With these two issues in mind, we can now write XDR declarations for the 'request' and 'reply' data types of our single service procedure, `find_primes()`. These will form the first part of our `.x` file:

```
/* Max size of array of primes we can return */
const  MAXPRIMES = 1000;

/* The input parameters: a min-max range */
struct prime_request {
    int  min;
    int  max;
};

/* The output parameters: a variable length array */
struct prime_result {
    int  array<MAXPRIMES>;
};
```

This information allows `rpcgen` to generate XDR filters for our data types. It will also generate 'C equivalent' data definitions in the .h file.

Also in our protocol specification file we must give our server a program number and a version number, and specify the service procedures which make up the server, along with their input and output data types. Extensions to the XDR language are provided by `rpcgen` to allow us to do this. Insofar as it relies on the use of nested curly brackets, the notation will seem fairly natural to C programmers. Here are the required statements for our prime number service. This example is rather degenerate, in that it defines only a single server, with a single version, and a single service procedure:

```
program PRIMEPROG {
    version PRIMEVERS {
        prime_result FIND_PRIMES(prime_request) = 1;
    } = 1;        /* The version number */
} = 0x2000009a;   /* The program number */
```

This definition might be read as follows:

1. We are defining a server whose program number is 0x2000009a. This value is fairly arbitrary, except that it lies within the 'user-defined' range of service numbers.
2. This is version 1 of the program.
3. The server has a single procedure, called FIND_PRIMES, which is procedure no. 1. This procedure takes a parameter of type `prime_request` and returns a result of type `prime_result`.

The curly bracket notation seems unnecessarily complicated in this example, but it is designed to give the flexibility to define multiple versions and multiple service procedures. For example, suppose our prime number server had evolved by acquiring an additional service procedure called COUNT_PRIMES. We might call this new version of the server version 2, and describe both versions in a single protocol specification file as follows:

```
program PRIMEPROG {
    version PRIMEVERS1 {
```

```
            prime_result FIND_PRIMES(prime_request)  = 1;
      } = 1;
      version PRIMEVERS2 {
            prime_result FIND_PRIMES(prime_request)  = 1;
            int          COUNT_PRIMES(prime_request) = 2;
      } = 2;
} = 0x2000009a;
```

Putting the two parts together, the complete protocol specification file for our distributed prime number example appears as follows. Note the use of C-style comments, which are ignored by rpcgen.

```
/* This is the protocol specification file primes.x */

/* Max size of array of primes we can return */
const  MAXPRIMES = 1000;

/* The input parameters: a min-max range */
struct prime_request {
    int  min;
    int  max;
};

/* The output parameters: a variable length array */
struct prime_result {
    int  array<MAXPRIMES>;
};

/* The program definition. There is only one program,
   with only one version and only one procedure
*/
program PRIMEPROG {
    version PRIMEVERS {
        prime_result FIND_PRIMES(prime_request) = 1;
    } = 1;         /* The version number */
} = 0x2000009a;   /* The program number */
```

Submitting this file as input to rpcgen, we create the following four files:

```
primes.h
primes_clnt.c
primes_svc.c
primes_xdr.c
```

The only one of these four we really need to look inside is the header file primes.h, which tells us what the C equivalents of the XDR data types look like. Here it is:

```
/*
 * Please do not edit this file.
```

```
* It was generated using rpcgen.
*/

#include <rpc/types.h>

#define MAXPRIMES 1000

struct prime_request {
        int min;
        int max;
};
typedef struct prime_request prime_request;
bool_t xdr_prime_request();

struct prime_result {
        struct {
                u_int array_len;
                int *array_val;
        } array;
};
typedef struct prime_result prime_result;
bool_t xdr_prime_result();

#define PRIMEPROG ((u_long)0x2000009a)
#define PRIMEVERS ((u_long)1)
#define FIND_PRIMES ((u_long)1)
extern prime_result *find_primes_1();
```

Let us dissect this file:

1. The `const` statement in the `.x` file has generated a `#define` in the header file.
2. The declaration of the `prime_request` structure has been copied through unchanged into the header file. However, a `typedef` for `prime_request` has been generated, allowing us to define variables of type `prime_request` instead of type `struct prime_request`. Notice that a declaration of the XDR filter for our new data type has also been generated.
3. The declaration of the `prime_result` structure has changed somewhat between the `.x` file and the header file. We see that a variable length array is actually represented within our C program by a structure with two components; the first, `array_len`, holds the number of elements in the array, and the second, `array_val`, points to the initial element. The name 'array' in this example is the name we chose in our `.x` file; it is not some naming convention hard-wired into `rpcgen`. As for the `prime_request` declaration, we also get a `typedef` for our new data type, and a declaration of its XDR filter.
4. The program definition part of the `.x` file has generated symbolic constants for `PRIMEPROG`, `PRIMEVERS` and `FIND_PRIMES` in the header file. We will use the first two of these symbolic constants in our client program, to identify the server.
5. The last line of the header file is a declaration of the remote procedure as it will appear in our C program. It shows two important features. First, the name of the

remote procedure is derived by converting the name in the `.x` file into lower case, and appending an underscore followed by the version number. Thus, the function we actually call in our client code, and the function we must define in our server code, is `find_primes_1()`. The second thing to notice is that the return value of this function is a pointer to a `prime_result`, although in the `.x` file we defined it to return a `prime_result`. Also (although not apparent from the header file) the function takes a pointer to a `prime_request` as argument and not a `prime_request` as we wrote in the `.x` file. This is true of all ONC RPC procedures – they accept and return *pointers to* the data types as specified in the `.x` file.

## 6.3.4 The server procedure

Next, we need to modify the `find_primes()` function to operate as an RPC service procedure. Changes are needed to both the argument-passing and the result-returning parts of the function. Here is the modified version:

```c
/* The file primes_funcs.c */
/* Prime number printing: RPC Server, Version 1 */

#include <rpc/rpc.h>
#include "primes.h"          /* Header file from rpcgen */

prime_result *find_primes_1(prime_request *request)
{
    /* Reserve storage for the results. This MUST be static,
       else it will  have blown  away  off the  stack by the
       time the xdr_prime_result filter gets to serialize it
    */
    static prime_result result;
    static int   prime_array[MAXPRIMES];
    int i, count=0;

    /* Loop over the range limits in the request "packet" */
    for (i=request->min; i<=request->max; i++)
       if (isprime(i))
           prime_array[count++] = i;

    /* Assemble the reply packet. Note that the variable
       length  array we are returning  is really a struct
       with the element count, and a pointer to the first
       element.
    */
    result.array.array_len = count;
    result.array.array_val = prime_array;
    return &result;
}

/* This is a 'private' support function and is not directly
```

```
    called via RPC. Returns TRUE if n is prime
*/
int isprime(int n)
{
    int i;
    for (i=2; i*i <= n; i++) {
        if ((n % i) == 0)
            return 0;
    }
    return 1;
}
```

Comparing this with the original (nondistributed) version, we note the following changes:

1.  The function find_primes() is now called find_primes_1(). The '1' is the protocol version number.
2.  Both the arguments and the return value of the function have had to be 'repackaged' to fit the RPC rules.
3.  Static storage is reserved for the function's return value, including the array of primes itself. These items are passed (by reference) back to the XDR filter when the function returns, for transmission back to the caller. It is *essential* that these data are not on the stack frame of find_primes_1() because the function will have returned (and its stack frame reclaimed) before XDR gets to see the data. This consideration is not specifically to do with RPC or XDR. Functions which return pointers to data within their own stack frame are broken in any context!
4.  The 'guts' of the function, the part that actually finds prime numbers, is unchanged. A major benefit of distributing an application using RPC is that it requires minimal alteration to the application-specific parts of the code. Because this example is rather trivial, it barely manages to make the point, but it is an important benefit of RPC nonetheless.
5.  Once the array of primes has been filled in, we must enter the count and the start address of the array into the result structure. Finally, we return the address of this structure.

## 6.3.5 The client code

Now we must write some client code to test our RPC server. Our client program is derived from the main() function of our original nondistributed example. Although most of the detail of obtaining a connection to the RPC server is hidden by the RPC library, the client must make a call to the function clnt_create() to obtain a *client handle*, which it subsequently passes as a parameter whenever it wishes to make an RPC call to the server.

The clnt_create() function is illustrated in Figure 6.11. Notice that the client must be aware of which remote host the RPC will be made to. Our client – like most – simply

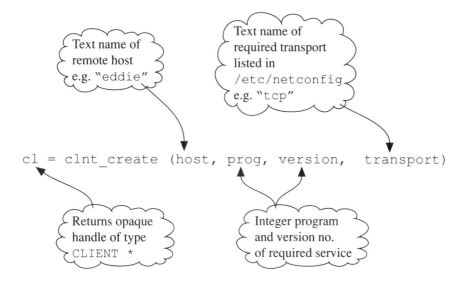

**Figure 6.11** The `clnt_create()` function.

takes the host name off the command line. The `clnt_create()` call takes care of contacting the portmapper on the specified host, and querying it for the specified RPC program and version number. The portmapper returns the appropriate transport endpoint address for the service.

The client may see errors occurring at three different stages of the RPC call:

1. The call to `client_create()` may fail, most likely because the specified host is not known on the local machine, or because the specified {program, version} pair is not registered on the remote host. If `client_create()` fails, it returns a null pointer, and the convenience routine `clnt_pcreateerror()` may be called to print a more detailed error message.
2. The RPC call may fail to reach the remote procedure. This is less likely, assuming that the client stub is the one which `rpcgen` produced. In this case, the RPC call will return a null pointer, and the convenience routine `clnt_perror()` may be called to print a more detailed error message.
3. Some form of application-specific error may be detected within the service procedure itself. For example, our `find_primes()` server procedure may notice that the `min` and `max` parameters passed to it are wrongly ordered, i.e. `max` is smaller than `min`. Reporting of such errors is entirely up to the application protocol. Typically, a status value is included as part of the returned structure, which can be examined by the caller. Using an XDR discriminated union with the return status as the discriminant provides a good way of saying 'here's all the good stuff you get back if it succeeded, and here's the measly error status you get back if it failed'.

Our client code handles the first two error types, but not the third. The program takes three command line arguments; the first is the name of the host on which the server is running; the second and third specify the lower and upper limits of the number range to be searched. Here is the code:

```
/* The file primes_main.c                          */
/* Prime number printing: RPC Client, Version 1 */

#include <rpc/rpc.h>
#include "primes.h"              /* Header file from rpcgen */

main(int argc, char *argv[])
{
    int i;
    CLIENT *cl;                  /* Client handle            */
    prime_result *result;        /* Pointer to result 'packet' */
    prime_request request;       /* Request 'packet'           */

    if (argc != 4) {
        printf("usage: %s host min max\n", argv[0]);
        exit(1);
    }

    /* Connect to the client on the host specified as argv[1] */
    cl = clnt_create(argv[1], PRIMEPROG, PRIMEVERS, "tcp");
    if (cl == NULL) {
        clnt_pcreateerror(argv[1]);
        exit(2);
    }

    /* Build a request 'packet', taking the min and max values
       from the command line
    */
    request.min = atoi(argv[2]);
    request.max = atoi(argv[3]);

    /* Call the remote procedure */
    result = find_primes_1(&request, cl);
    if (result == NULL) {
        clnt_perror(cl, argv[1]);
        exit(3);
    }

    /* Print the results */
    for (i=0; i< result->array.array_len; i++)
        printf("%d is prime\n", result->array.array_val[i]);
    printf("count of primes found = %d\n", result->array.array_len);

    /* Free the memory allocated for the results */
    xdr_free(xdr_prime_result, result);
}
```

The following points are worth noting:

1. request is declared to be of type prime_request rather than of type struct prime_request. The typedef for prime_request was generated by rpcgen and appears in the header file primes.h.
2. Note carefully the remote procedure call itself. It takes as argument the address of a prime_request structure, and it returns as its function value the address of a prime_reply structure. It also takes, as its second argument, the client handle obtained from the call to clnt_create().
3. The memory which holds the result data structure is allocated for you by the xdr_prime_result() filter, operating in the DECODE direction. This memory should be explicitly freed by calling xdr_free(), as shown.

## 6.3.6  Putting all the pieces together

To summarize, we have created three files:

```
primes.x          The protocol specification
primes_funcs.c    The service procedure
primes_main.c     The client program
```

The rpcgen utility has generated four more files:

```
primes.h          Header file for inclusion in user code
primes_xdr.c      XDR filters for user-defined data types
primes_clnt.c     The client stub
primes_svc.c      The server wrapper
```

To compile and link the server and client programs requires commands of the form:

```
cc primes_funcs.c primes_svc.c primes_xdr.c -lnsl -o primes_server

cc primes_main.c primes_clnt.c primes_xdr.c -lnsl -o primes_client
```

Here, we have used the flag -lnsl to load the library holding the RPC functions. The name of this library varies from system to system. On some systems, it may be part of the standard C library, so that no special flags are needed.

## 6.3.7  Testing RPC servers

Our RPC server may now be started and tested. It is convenient (but not essential) to place an entry for our new service in /etc/rpc (or in the RPC map, if NIS is running). We just add the line:

```
primes            536871066
```

which simply serves to give a name to our program number for use by the RPC administrative utility, rpcinfo. Where does this funny number 536871066 come from? It is the decimal equivalent of the hex number 0x2000009a which we selected as the program number in our protocol specification file. (It is unfortunate that /etc/rpc needs program numbers in decimal, when the ranges of allowed values are specified in hexadecimal.)

Now we can start the server, on (say) the host trillian:

```
trillian% primes_server
trillian%
```

Why do we not launch the server in the background, and why does it apparently exit immediately? The answer is that the server wrappers generated by rpcgen include code to create a child process. The parent simply exits, leaving the child to get on with the work.

Back on our local machine eddie, we can check that the server has registered by querying the portmapper on trillian:

```
eddie%  rpcinfo -p trillian
   program vers proto    port
    100000   3   udp    111   rpcbind
    100000   2   udp    111   rpcbind
    100000   3   tcp    111   rpcbind
    100000   2   tcp    111   rpcbind
    100008   1   tcp   1027   walld
    100008   1   udp   1027   walld
    ...
    100021   2   tcp   1031   nlockmgr
    100021   2   udp   1034   nlockmgr
 536871066   1   tcp   1045   primes
 536871066   1   udp   1039   primes
```

Most of the list has been elided out, for brevity. The interesting lines are the last two which correspond to our newly registered primes_server. We see that the server wrapper has registered our service for both TCP and UDP transports.

As an aid to testing RPC servers, rpcgen includes within the server wrapper a 'ping' procedure, which is always procedure 0. (Recall from the example that our FIND_PRIMES procedure is procedure 1.) The ping procedure takes no argument and returns an 'empty' result. It is there simply to provide a way to test that the server is alive and is receiving RPC requests from the network. The -t and -u flags on rpcinfo can be used to request a call to the ping procedure for a given host, program and version, using TCP and UDP transports respectively. For example:

```
eddie% rpcinfo -t trillian primes 1
program 536871066 version 1 ready and waiting
```

```
eddie% rpcinfo -u trillian primes 1
program 536871066 version 1 ready and waiting

eddie% rpcinfo -t trillian primes 2
rpcinfo: RPC: Program/version mismatch;
            low version = 1, high version = 1
program 536871066 version 2 is not available

eddie% rpcinfo -t trillian 12345 1
rpcinfo: RPC: Program unavailable
program 12345 version 1 is not available

eddie%
```

The first two examples succeed, showing that our server is indeed listening on `trillian` using both TCP and UDP transports. The third example fails because there is no version 2 of our prime server. The fourth example fails because there is no server registered as program 12345.

Finally, we can run our client, connecting to the server on `trillian`, and specifying a number range from 1 to 20:

```
eddie% primes_client trillian 1 20
1 is prime
2 is prime
3 is prime
5 is prime
7 is prime
11 is prime
13 is prime
17 is prime
19 is prime
count of primes found = 9
eddie%
```

# 6.4  RPC authorization

## 6.4.1  Credentials and verifiers

The 'prime number' server of the previous section had no knowledge of the identity of its clients – either the machine on which the client was running, or the ID of the user. As a result, it had no way to implement any form of access control; for example, to restrict the service to specific machines or users. It is a sad reflection on standards of human behaviour that any modern distributed computing system is expected to provide some measure of security to prevent unauthorized access to certain services or resources.

Methods for authorization of client requests by a server are usually based on the notion of a *credential* and a *verifier*, both of which are passed from the client to the server. The credential is a statement of the client's identity – the name of the client host machine, and the user ID perhaps. The verifier is a piece of data which only the 'real client' would know. A good (and well-worn) analogy may be drawn with an identity card, used to restrict access within a company's premises. The name and employee number on the card are your credentials – a statement of your identity. The photograph on the card is your verifier – it prevents anyone else from stealing your card and using the credentials it carries to impersonate you.

In some situations it is equally important for the client to be able to verify the identity of the server. For example, if a client intends to hand over some confidential piece of information to a database server for storage, it needs to be sure that the server is the real server, and not some stand-in which is going to e-mail the data to the neighbourhood hacker.

In previous chapters we examined a number of TCP/IP-based servers which spoke directly to the transport layer, using sockets or TLI. For some of these, such as the `rexecd` server, a credential (a user name) and a verifier (a password) is passed as part of the application-level protocol. In other cases, such as the `rlogind` server, the notion of *reserved ports* provides the verifier which enables the server to be confident that it is talking to a valid client.

The reserved port concept is not appropriate for RPC-based clients and servers because they choose essentially random (and nonreserved) port numbers, or because they are running over some protocol other than TCP/IP which does not support the notion of reserved ports. In this section we will examine the alternative authentication mechanisms used with RPC.

## 6.4.2 RPC authentication 'flavours'

The RPC protocol itself does not define an authentication mechanism – that is, it does not specify the type or format of the credentials or verifier that should be sent as part of an RPC request. It does, however, provide a 'slot' within the RPC request packet in which authentication data can be placed.

In reality, three forms of authentication are supported by most implementations of RPC. By 'supported', we mean that there are header files defining the format which the authentication data should take, and there are routines within the RPC library to form the authorization data on the client side, and to retrieve it on the server side. These three forms of authentication are referred to as *flavours*, and are as follows:

1. `AUTH_NONE`: Neither a credential nor a verifier is passed.
2. `AUTH_UNIX`: Credentials consist of the client machine name, the user's numeric ID and group ID, and a list of groups to which the user belongs. There is no verifier.
3. `AUTH_DES`: The credentials consist essentially of a 'netname' of the form `unix.221@eddie` where 221 is my user ID and `eddie` is my machine name. The verifier consists of a timestamp encrypted using the data encryption standard (DES) algorithm.

There is little more to be said about AUTH_NONE authentication. The server simply does not know who the client is, and is unable to implement any access control policy. This is the flavour of authentication you get by default, as in the case of our prime number server in the previous section.

The AUTH_UNIX flavour allows the server to discover the identity of the client (in terms of his machine name and his UNIX user and group IDs, and so on), enabling it to implement some form of access control policy, or at least to check accessibility of files against the correct user ID. An example of this is provided in the next section. However, as there is no verifier, it is straightforward for a user-written RPC client to fake these credentials. Consequently, the authentication provided by AUTH_UNIX is not adequate to defend a server against a hostile programmer.

The AUTH_DES flavour provides what is generally known as 'secure RPC' which in turn forms the basis of 'secure NFS'. The security stems from the use of the DES algorithm to encrypt measures of the current time passed between client and server. A server checks the validity of a client by decrypting the timestamp and comparing it with its own local time. The client can likewise check the validity of the server by decrypting the timestamps which are passed back to it. The benefit of using a timestamp for this purpose is that it reduces the chances of a program listening in to the network traffic, capturing a verifier and later replaying it in the hope of impersonating the original sender of the verifier. For this arrangement to work, the clocks on the two systems must be synchronized. The *conversation key* used to encrypt the timestamps is chosen at random by the client and passed to the server on the first transaction using another form of encryption known as Diffie–Hellman public key cryptography. The conversation key may also, if the client and server wish, be used to encrypt and decrypt the application data which pass between them.

Because US federal law prohibits the export of implementations of the DES algorithm, UNIX vendors do not (usually) ship secure RPC outside the US. We will not consider it further here.

## 6.4.3 Sending and receiving credentials

Let us examine some code fragments which show the use of AUTH_UNIX authentication in an RPC call. In order to pass the AUTH_UNIX credentials, the client must attach an *authorization* structure to the handle obtained from the call to clnt_create(). The RPC library function authunix_create_default() may be used to create this structure. The code typically looks like this:

```
cl = clnt_create( ... )
cl->cl_auth = authunix_create_default();
```

and that's about all there is to it on the client side.

In the server, the service procedure can retrieve the credentials via the second argument which is passed to it. This argument (which we ignored in our earlier example) is of type (struct svc_req *). The svc_req structure is declared as follows:

```
struct svc_req {
    u_long          rq_prog;      /* service program number */
    u_long          rq_vers;      /* service protocol version */
    u_long          rq_proc;      /* the desired procedure */
    struct opaque_auth rq_cred;   /* raw creds from the wire */
    caddr_t         rq_clntcred;  /* read-only cooked cred */
    SVCXPRT         *rq_xprt;     /* associated transport */
};
```

The fields of interest in here are `rq_cred` which holds a structure containing (among other things) the flavour type, and `rq_clntcred` which points to a (flavour-specific) structure holding the actual authentication data.

The server first needs to check what flavour of authentication is present. The flavour is represented by one of the constants AUTH_NONE, AUTH_UNIX and AUTH_DES, which are defined in the header file `<rpc/auth.h>`.

Having satisfied itself that AUTH_UNIX authentication is present, the server can delve a little deeper into the `svc_req` structure to find the client's machine name, user ID and so on. Before the service procedure is called, this information is extracted from the RPC message and placed into an `authunix_parms` structure which is declared in `<rpc/auth_sys.h>` as follows:

```
struct authunix_parms {
        u_long  aup_time;
        char    *aup_machname; /* Client host name     */
        uid_t   aup_uid;       /* Client user ID       */
        gid_t   aup_gid;       /* Client group ID      */
        u_int   aup_len;       /* Length of group list */
        gid_t   *aup_gids;     /* List of groups       */
};
```

In later versions of RPC, the `authunix_parms` structure is renamed to `authsys_parms`, and the AUTH_UNIX flavour is renamed to AUTH_SYS.

The following code fragment illustrates how the server can retrieve the authorization flavour and the AUTH_UNIX credentials:

```
int *my_service_proc_1(my_request *r, struct svc_req *rqstp)
{
    struct authunix_parms *ucred;

    fprintf(stderr,"flavour = %d\n", rqstp->rq_cred.oa_flavor);

    if (rqstp->rq_cred.oa_flavor == AUTH_UNIX) {
        ucred = (struct authunix_parms *)(rqstp->rq_clntcred);
        fprintf(stderr, "host = %s\n", ucred->aup_machname);
        fprintf(stderr, "uid  = %d\n", ucred->aup_uid);
        fprintf(stderr, "gid=%d\n",    ucred->aup_gid);
    }
```

```
      /* Now the service procedure proper ... */

}
```

Note that what we have seen so far simply gets the client's credentials across to the server. It does not, of itself, enforce any form of access restrictions. That is left up to the application. Our example in the next section shows a simple access control policy based on a list of trusted users held in a file.

# 6.5  An extended RPC example

## 6.5.1  Enhancements to the prime number server

To illustrate some additional RPC features, let us take our prime number service a stage further. We will add the following:

1. UNIX-flavour authentication, and an access control policy on the server side based on a list of trusted users held in a file.
2. A second service procedure, count_primes().
3. Some user-level error checking and reporting by the server. The error checking consists simply of a test that the min and max parameters passed to the service procedures satisfy the relation min < max.
4. The use of discriminated unions to pass back different data in the cases of successful and unsuccessful calls to the service procedures.

We will retain the same program number for this service, but it will become version 2.

## 6.5.2  The new protocol specification file

The place to begin our new version is the same place we began the original version – the protocol specification file. We will make the following changes:

1. We define new data types find_result and count_result for the return values of find_primes() and count_primes() respectively. Both of these data types are discriminated unions; the *discriminant* of the union is a status value indicating the success or failure of the call. The possible status values are defined as an enumeration and are as follows:

```
      STAT_OK          Call was successful, data returned
      STAT_BAD_RANGE   Min, max values not valid, no data returned
      STAT_BAD_AUTH    Authorization failed, no data returned
```

From the client's viewpoint, what these discriminated unions say is 'You'll get a status value back to tell you whether the call succeeded or failed. If it succeeded, you'll get back more data – the result of the service procedure. If it failed, you get nothing else back.' The XDR keyword `void` is used to indicate the 'empty' arms of the union.

A discriminated union is a little like a `switch` statement in C (and has stolen much the same syntax); however, a discriminated union selects one of several pieces of *data*, whereas a `switch` selects one of several pieces of *code*.

2.   We add the definition of our new procedure, `count_primes()`, which becomes procedure 2.
3.   We change the protocol version number to 2, with the symbolic name `PRIME_AUTH_VERS`.

The input parameter type `prime_request` remains unchanged, and is used as input by both service procedures. The program number, `PRIMEPROG`, is also unchanged.

Here is our revised protocol specification:

```
/* This is the protocol specification file primes2.x */
/* Protocol specification for V2 of primes service  */

/* Max size of array of primes we can return */
const  MAXPRIMES = 1000;

/* Return status values */
enum prime_status {
    STAT_OK       = 1,
    STAT_BAD_RANGE = 2,
    STAT_BAD_AUTH  = 3
};

/* The input parameters: a min-max range          */
/* Used by both find_primes() and count_primes() */
struct prime_request {
    int  min;
    int  max;
};

/* Output parameters for find_primes:          */
union find_result switch(prime_status status) {
    case STAT_OK:
        int array<MAXPRIMES>;
    case STAT_BAD_RANGE:
        void;
    case STAT_BAD_AUTH:
        void;
};

/* Output parameters for count_primes:          */
union count_result switch (prime_status status) {
    case STAT_OK:
        int count;
```

```
    case STAT_BAD_RANGE:
        void;
    case STAT_BAD_AUTH:
        void;
};

/* The program definition.                        */

program PRIMEPROG {
    version PRIME_AUTH_VERS {
        find_result   FIND_PRIMES (prime_request) = 1;
        count_result COUNT_PRIMES(prime_request) = 2;
    } = 2;          /* The version number */
} = 0x2000009a;    /* The program number */
```

As before, it is instructive to examine the header file generated by rpcgen which defines the C data types corresponding to the XDR types. What is new here is the C version of the discriminated unions. This becomes a C *structure*, with two members: (1) the discriminant, and (2) a C union describing the arms of the discriminated union. In this example, these unions are rather degenerate, having only one member. This is because there is only one non-empty arm in the XDR discriminated unions. Note that rpcgen invents a name for this union by taking the name of the data type being defined and appending '_u', giving find_result_u, for example. It is helpful when writing the client and server code to keep the header file in view as a guide to accessing the components of the input parameters and return values of the service procedures. Here is the new version of the header file, primes2.h:

```
/*
 * Please do not edit this file.
 * It was generated using rpcgen.
 */

#include <rpc/types.h>

#define MAXPRIMES 1000

enum prime_status {
        STAT_OK = 1,
        STAT_BAD_RANGE = 2,
        STAT_BAD_AUTH = 3,
};
typedef enum prime_status prime_status;
bool_t xdr_prime_status();

struct prime_request {
        int min;
        int max;
};
typedef struct prime_request prime_request;
bool_t xdr_prime_request();
```

```
struct find_result {
        prime_status status;
        union {
                struct {
                        u_int array_len;
                        int *array_val;
                } array;
        } find_result_u;
};
typedef struct find_result find_result;
bool_t xdr_find_result();

struct count_result {
        prime_status status;
        union {
                int count;
        } count_result_u;
};
typedef struct count_result count_result;
bool_t xdr_count_result();

#define PRIMEPROG ((u_long)0x2000009a)
#define PRIME_AUTH_VERS ((u_long)2)
#define FIND_PRIMES ((u_long)1)
extern find_result *find_primes_2();
#define COUNT_PRIMES ((u_long)2)
extern count_result *count_primes_2();
```

## 6.5.3  The revised service procedures

Next we will revise the service procedures. The major changes are as follows:

1. The addition of a new service procedure `count_primes()`. This is similar to `find_primes()` except that instead of returning a list of primes, it just returns a count of the number found.

   Note that the service procedures now have names ending '_2' because this is version 2 of the protocol. This naming convention is used to allow service procedures for several versions of the protocol to coexist in the same program.

2. The addition of a support function, `validate_user()`. This is called by both our service procedures and is passed a service request handle. It returns 1 if the user is deemed 'OK', and 0 if not.

   This function extracts the client's user ID from the service request handle, having first checked that `AUTH_UNIX` credentials have indeed been passed. The code here is what we saw in Section 6.4.3. It then calls `getpwuid()` to map this user ID back onto a login name. Note that this mapping is performed on the server machine; thus, the login name we look up in the authorization file is the one in the server's password file corresponding to the numeric user ID the client sent us. The situation is reminiscent of the user identity mapping with NFS which we explored in Section 3.4.6. This is perhaps not surprising, as NFS uses RPC with AUTH_UNIX credentials! Next we open our chosen authorization file, /etc/primeusers, which is expected to contain a list of authorized users, one per line. We scan this file looking for a match. If we find one, the user is deemed to be validated.

We see here a clear separation between what RPC does (carry the credentials from client to server) and what the user code does (implement an access control policy). Clearly, more complex validation schemes could be used, involving other components of the client's credentials such as the group ID or machine name.

3. The service procedures make checks on both the user's authorization (by calling validate_user()), and the validity of the (min,max) range they receive. Each procedure must be sure to set an appropriate return status in the return value, and to fill in whichever arm of the discriminated union is implied by that status.

Here is the revised server code:

```
/* The file primes2_funcs.c                      */
/* Prime number printing: RPC Server, Version 2 */

#include <stdio.h>
#include <pwd.h>
#include <rpc/rpc.h>
#include "primes2.h"          /* Header file from rpcgen */

find_result *find_primes_2(prime_request *request,
                           struct svc_req *rqstp)
{
    /* Reserve storage for the results. This MUST be static,
       else it will  have blown  away  off the  stack by the
       time the XDR filter gets to serialize it.
    */
    static find_result result;
    static int   prime_array[MAXPRIMES];
    int i, count=0;

    /* Validate the user */
    if (validate_user(rqstp) == 0)
        result.status = STAT_BAD_AUTH;

    /* Validate the input parameters */
    else if (request->min >= request->max)
        result.status = STAT_BAD_RANGE;
    else {
        /* Loop over the range limits in the request */
        for (i=request->min; i<=request->max; i++)
            if (isprime(i))
                prime_array[count++] = i;
```

```
        /* Assemble the reply packet. Note that the variable
           length  array we are returning  is really a struct
           with the element count, and a pointer to the first
           element.
        */
        result.status                    = STAT_OK;
        result.find_result_u.array.array_len = count;
        result.find_result_u.array.array_val = prime_array;
    }
    return &result;
}

count_result *count_primes_2(prime_request *request,
                             struct svc_req *rqstp)
{
    /* Reserve storage for the results. This MUST be static,
       else it will  have blown  away  off the  stack by the
       time the XDR filter gets to serialize it.
    */
    static count_result result;
    int i, count=0;

    /* Validate the user */
    if (validate_user(rqstp) == 0)
        result.status = STAT_BAD_AUTH;

    /* Validate the input parameters */
    else if (request->min >= request->max)
        result.status = STAT_BAD_RANGE;
    else {
        /* Loop over the range limits in the request */
        for (i=request->min; i<=request->max; i++)
            if (isprime(i))
                count++;

        /* Assemble the reply */
        result.status              = STAT_OK;
        result.count_result_u.count = count;
    }
    return &result;
}
/* This is a 'private' support function and is not directly
   called via RPC. Returns TRUE if n is prime
*/
int isprime(int n)
{
    int i;
    for (i=2; i*i <= n; i++) {
        if ((n % i) == 0)
            return 0;
```

```
    }
    return 1;
}

/* This function is  called to validate the client  using the
   credentials in the service request. Returns TRUE if client
   is OK, FALSE if not
*/
int validate_user(struct svc_req *rqstp)
{
    struct authunix_parms *ucred;
    struct passwd          *pwent;
    char                   *client_name;
    FILE                   *fd;
    char                    name_in_file[50];

    /* Print out the credentials, for debugging */
    fprintf(stderr,"Authorization flavour = %d\n",
            rqstp->rq_cred.oa_flavor);
    if (rqstp->rq_cred.oa_flavor != AUTH_UNIX)
        return 0; /* Client has not supplied credentials */
    ucred = (struct authunix_parms *)(rqstp->rq_clntcred);
    fprintf(stderr, "host = %s\n", ucred->aup_machname);
    fprintf(stderr, "uid = %d\n",  ucred->aup_uid);
    fprintf(stderr, "gid = %d\n",  ucred->aup_gid);

    /* Map the uid onto a login name on the SERVER machine */
    pwent = getpwuid(ucred->aup_uid);
    if (pwent == NULL)
        return 0; /* User has no account on this machine */

    client_name = pwent->pw_name;
    fprintf(stderr, "client name is %s\n", client_name);

    /* It would be much more efficient to read the file only
       on the first call,  and cache the  list of names in a
       local array
    */
    if ((fd = fopen("/etc/primeusers", "r")) == NULL)
        return 0; /* No authorization file */

    while (fscanf(fd, "%s", name_in_file) != EOF) {
        fprintf(stderr, "comparing %s with %s\n",
                client_name, name_in_file);
        if (strcmp(client_name, name_in_file) == 0) {
            fclose(fd);
            return 1; /* User is authenticated */
        }
    }
    fclose(fd);
    return 0; /* User not in list */
}
```

## 6.5.4  The revised client code

Finally here is the revised client code. The changes here are less extensive. The most important addition, conceptually, is the addition of the line

```
cl->cl_auth = authunix_create_default();
```

to ensure that the appropriate credentials are passed with the RPC call.

Our new client tests only the count_primes() routine; a test of find_primes() could easily be added. We must check the return status (the discriminant of the union) to determine whether our call succeeded, so that we can print an appropriate error message, or print out the data that were returned.

Here is the revised client code:

```c
/* The file primes2_main.c                    */
/* Prime number printing: RPC Client, Version 2 */

#include <rpc/rpc.h>
#include "primes2.h"            /* Header file from rpcgen */
main(int argc, char *argv[])
{
    int i;
    CLIENT *cl;                 /* Client handle            */
    count_result *result;       /* Pointer to result 'packet' */
    prime_request request;      /* Request 'packet'         */

    if (argc != 4) {
        printf("usage: %s host min max\n", argv[0]);
        exit(1);
    }

    /* Connect to the client on the host specified as argv[1] */
    cl = clnt_create(argv[1], PRIMEPROG, PRIME_AUTH_VERS, "tcp");
    if (cl == NULL) {
        clnt_pcreateerror(argv[1]);
        exit(2);
    }

    /* Create UNIX credentials */
    cl->cl_auth = authunix_create_default();

    /* Build a request 'packet' */
    request.min = atoi(argv[2]);
    request.max = atoi(argv[3]);

    /* Call the remote procedure */
    result = count_primes_2(&request, cl);
    if (result == NULL) {
        clnt_perror(cl, argv[1]);
        exit(3);
    }
```

```
        /* Check the return status */
        switch(result->status) {
            case STAT_OK:
                printf("No. of primes found = %d\n",
                        result->count_result_u.count);
                break;
            case STAT_BAD_RANGE:
                printf("Server rejected us: bad range\n");
                break;
            case STAT_BAD_AUTH:
                printf("Server rejected us: bad authorization\n");
                break;
        }

        /* Free the memory allocated for the results */
        xdr_free(xdr_count_result, result);
}
```

Note that the service procedure failures (bad authorization and bad range) are both handled at the user level; as far as the RPC service is concerned, the call has succeeded. It might be preferable, in the case of an authorization failure, to have the RPC call itself fail (so that the client receives a null pointer back from the call). This is also possible, but requires the use of lower level routines in the RPC library.

## 6.5.5  A packet trace

It may be helpful to look at the packet traffic on the network when this program is run. This example was gathered using Sun's packet monitor snoop which we previously met in Chapter 4. Running the primes2_client program generated thirteen network packets as shown below. A, B and C are the names of the three machines concerned (abbreviated to keep the lines short). The prime client is running on A, the prime server is running on B, and C is the NIS server for B.

```
 1    A -> B    PORTMAP C GETPORT prog=536871066 (?) vers=2 proto=TCP
 2    B -> A    PORTMAP R GETPORT port=3422
 3    A -> B    TCP D=3422 S=1046 Syn Seq=419712000 Len=0
 4    B -> A    TCP D=1046 S=3422 Syn Ack=419712001 Seq=620096000 Len=0
 5    A -> B    TCP D=3422 S=1046     Ack=620096001 Seq=419712001 Len=0
 6    A -> B    RPC C XID=735372650 PROG=536871066 (?) VERS=2 PROC=2
 7    B -> C    NIS C MATCH 21 in passwd.byuid
 8    C -> B    NIS R MATCH OK
 9    B -> A    RPC R (#6) XID=735372650 Success
10    A -> B    TCP D=3422 S=1046 Fin Ack=620096033 Seq=419712089 Len=0
11    B -> A    TCP D=1046 S=3422     Ack=419712090 Seq=620096033 Len=0
12    B -> A    TCP D=1046 S=3422 Fin Ack=419712090 Seq=620096033 Len=0
13    A -> B    TCP D=3422 S=1046     Ack=620096034 Seq=419712090 Len=0
```

Taken in turn, these packets are as follows:

1.   A call to the portmapper on machine B from the primes client, as a result of the `clnt_create()` call. The portmapper is being queried for program number 536871066, version 2. The (?) is shown because this program number does not appear in machine B's `/etc/rpc` file, so `snoop` is unable to display a proper name for the program.

2.   A reply from the portmapper saying that the service is registered on port 3422.

3–5. These three TCP packets handle the setting up of the TCP connection from port 1046 on machine A (an arbitrary port bound by the client) to port 3422 on machine B (the port at which the server is registered).

6.   This is the actual RPC call request transmitted using the TCP connection which has just been set up. The call is to procedure 2 (`count_primes`) of program 536871066, version 2. We will examine this packet in more detail below.

7.   Machine B now makes an RPC call to its NIS server (machine C) asking it to look up user ID 21 in the `passwd.byuid` map. This results from the call to `getpwuid()` made by the user validation routine in the primes server. 21 is the ID of the user running the primes client. If machine B was not running NIS, this enquiry would have been resolved by a local lookup in `/etc/passwd` and no NIS call would have been seen.

8.   The NIS server on machine C replies.

9.   The call to `count_primes()` returns.

10–13. These four packets close down the TCP connection between machine A, port 1046, and machine B, port 3422.

The 'verbose' output from `snoop` is too extensive to reproduce fully here, but we will delve a little further into packets 1 and 6. Here are the verbose reports for the TCP and RPC layers of these two packets. (The IP and ethernet header information is also reported, but has been omitted here.)

```
----------- Packet 1 ------------
UDP:  ----- UDP Header -----
UDP:
UDP:  Source port = 1148
UDP:  Destination port = 111 (Sun RPC)
UDP:  Length = 64
UDP:  Checksum = 0000 (no checksum)
UDP:
RPC:  ----- SUN RPC Header -----
RPC:
RPC:  Transaction id = 735426414
RPC:  Type = 0 (Call)
RPC:  RPC version = 2
RPC:  Program = 100000 (PMAP), version = 2, procedure = 3
RPC:  Credentials: Flavor = 0 (None), len = 0 bytes
RPC:  Verifier    : Flavor = 0 (None), len = 0 bytes
RPC:
PMAP:  ----- Portmapper -----
```

```
PMAP:
PMAP:  Proc = 3 (Get port number)
PMAP:  Program = 536871066 (?)
PMAP:  Version = 2
PMAP:  Protocol = 6 (TCP)
PMAP:
----------- Packet 6 ------------
TCP:  ----- TCP Header -----
TCP:
TCP:  Source port = 1046
TCP:  Destination port = 3422 (Sun RPC)
TCP:  Sequence number = 419712001
TCP:  Acknowledgement number = 620096001
TCP:  Data offset = 20 bytes
TCP:  Flags = 0x18
TCP:       ..0. .... = No urgent pointer
TCP:       ...1 .... = Acknowledgement
TCP:       .... 1... = Push
TCP:       .... .0.. = No reset
TCP:       .... ..0. = No Syn
TCP:       .... ...0 = No Fin
TCP:  Window = 4096
TCP:  Checksum = 0x753d
TCP:  No options
TCP:
RPC:  ----- SUN RPC Header -----
RPC:
RPC:  Record Mark: last fragment, length = 84
RPC:  Transaction id = 735372650
RPC:  Type = 0 (Call)
RPC:  RPC version = 2
RPC:  Program = 536871066 (?), version = 2, procedure = 2
RPC:  Credentials: Flavor = 1 (Unix), len = 36 bytes
RPC:     Time = 20-Apr-93 15:48:12
RPC:     Hostname = desiato
RPC:     Uid = 21, Gid = 90
RPC:     Groups = 90 21
RPC:  Verifier   : Flavor = 0 (None), len = 0 bytes
RPC:
```

Packet 1 is seen to be an RPC request carried by a UDP datagram. It is directed to port 111 on machine B – the portmapper's 'well-known' port number. We see that the portmapper is program 100000, version 2, and we are calling procedure 3, `get_port_number`. No credentials or verifier are passed.

Packet 6 is seen to be an RPC request carried by a TCP segment. Within the RPC header can be seen the authorization data inserted by the client's call to `authunix_create_default()` – a timestamp, the client machine name, the user's ID and group ID, and list of groups.

# 6.6 The RPC library

Our RPC examples in this chapter have all used `rpcgen` to generate the client stubs and server wrappers. The only calls to the RPC library made directly by our code were the `clnt_create()` call in the clients, and the error-printing routines `clnt_perror()` and `clnt_pcreateerror()`. Everything else was hidden by the stubs and wrappers.

Whilst using `rpcgen` is the easiest way to develop RPC applications, and is quite satisfactory for most purposes, it is not obligatory to use it. Indeed, some extra flexibility may be gained by using the RPC library directly to write one's own stubs and wrappers, perhaps using those generated by `rpcgen` as a starting point. The following are some of the things that can be done in this way but cannot be done using `rpcgen`:

1. Writing servers which register more than one version of an RPC service.
2. The implementation of novel authentication schemes.
3. RPC clients which broadcast to find a server.
4. Asynchronous RPC calls – that is, calls which do not wait on the client side until the server has finished. There are two cases to consider: (1) cases where the server returns no result – these are fairly easy to implement; and (2) cases where the server returns a result later, but the client is able to get on with something else in the meantime. This uses a mechanism known as *callback RPC* in which the server and the client briefly exchange roles. The notion of simultaneous execution of server and client does not fit well with the RPC concept, where the normal course of events (call the server, wait for a reply) explicitly precludes parallelism.

Futher details of using the RPC library may be found in the manual pages for `rpc(3N)` and in Bloomer (1992) and Corbin (1992).

# 6.7 Summary of RPC benefits

Experience teaching client–server programming to C programmers suggests that many programmers find the details of RPC difficult to master and may initially feel that it is actually harder to write distributed applications in this way than using sockets. This difficulty stems partly from the seemingly large amount of detail that must be mastered, and partly from the complexity of the C data types which RPC programmers inevitably encounter. Our humble `find_primes()` service procedure, for example, returned a pointer to a structure containing a union containing a structure containing a pointer to an array of integers.

However, you are strongly encouraged to overcome these initial difficulties, because once mastered, RPC offers substantial benefits for the writer of distributed applications. In summary, these benefits are as follows:

1. The user code in both client and server is independent of the underlying transport protocol. In particular, it makes no assumptions about the form of a transport endpoint address. There are no `sockaddr_in` structures!

2.  The XDR language aids the production of tightly defined and highly structured protocols. The protocol specification file plays a central role not only in generating the code (via `rpcgen`) for the stubs and wrappers, but also in providing a concise human-readable statement of the application-level protocol.

3.  RPC preserves traditional nondistributed program structure much more than sockets or TLI. The program does not have to be redesigned around the I/O operations between client and server; it continues to use the same mechanism (a function call) to access the remote parts of the program as it uses to access the local parts. The benefits are especially noticeable when there are multiple service procedures. It is not necessary to invent 'op-codes' to select the appropriate server action, or to wrap a large `switch` around the server to dispatch a request to the correct code, as we did with our TLI-based service registry in Chapter 5. These details are handled automatically by the client stub and server wrapper code.

4.  The external data representation, and the XDR filters which convert to and from the host-specific data representation, automatically handle differences in binary representation of data between computers of different architecture. Whilst this may seem like a non-issue to programmers who may be lucky enough to work on UNIX networks which are completely homogeneous, it would be a short-sighted developer indeed who stated categorically that his or her applications would *never* have to interoperate with a machine of different architecture. If byte-order and other differences have to be handled within the application code, the inconvenience is enormous.

5.  By providing a way to transport credentials and verifiers, RPC offers support for authentication of clients, and in the case of secure RPC, authentication of the servers as well.

# 6.8  Solaris ToolTalk

## 6.8.1  Introducing ToolTalk

We end this chapter by introducing a rather different way of building distributed applications, which abstracts the user even further from the transport layer than does RPC.

The *ToolTalk* message delivery service from SunSoft is a novel method of interprocess communication which allows applications to communicate without direct knowledge of one another. Instead of making connection with, and sending data to, a specific peer process, ToolTalk applications dispatch messages of specific *types* to the ToolTalk service. Potential message recipients register the message types they wish to receive by filling in a 'message pattern' and registering the pattern with the ToolTalk service. The service compares the type of a message it has been asked to deliver with the patterns registered by the potential recipients; if a match is found, the message is delivered to the application.

For example, as part of a system for writing computer-aided learning materials, the main authoring program needs to get some text edited. It dispatches a message to the ToolTalk service saying (in effect) 'I want to get the text in file `foo` edited. Please send this message to any ToolTalk application registered within the current X window session which is capable of handling `EDIT_TEXT` messages. I expect a reply'.

The above example is a *request*; that is, a message that needs to be acted upon and replied to. Messages may also be *notices*, that is, they advertise some event, but do not require a response.

ToolTalk is intended to facilitate a kind of 'plug and play' approach to integrated applications. Alternative implementations of tools can be substituted so long as their message protocols are compatible. By using a message protocol as the defining interface for an application, ToolTalk takes a sort of coarse grained, object-oriented view of distributed programming.

In some small way, ToolTalk message delivery is a little like the System V message queue facility described in Section 2.7. Using message queues, an application delivers a message to a specified queue, without necessarily knowing which application will retrieve that message. The message queue ID might be used to represent the 'scope' of delivery of the message, and the message type (which is a simple integer in the case of message queues) is analogous to the more complex message typing in ToolTalk. The 'downstream' applications might 'register an interest' in specific message types by retrieving only those specific types from the queue. However, the ToolTalk service is more sophisticated than message queues in several ways:

1.  Since ToolTalk uses RPCs to communicate between applications and the delivery service, ToolTalk communications operate 'network-wide'. Message queues work only within a single machine.
2.  ToolTalk will automatically start applications which are able to handle specific message types if no suitable application is currently running.
3.  The ToolTalk message patterns are much more complex than the simple integer message types used by message queues.

## 6.8.2  A ToolTalk example

ToolTalk is primarily designed to integrate applications which run under a windowing system such as `openwin`. There are library functions to set up callbacks out of a window application's main loop when a ToolTalk message is received.

To avoid getting drawn into the complexities of X Windows applications, we examine here a simple character-based ToolTalk demonstration, which interacts with the user via its standard input and standard output. Instead of retrieving messages within a callback routine registered with the window's main loop, our example includes an explicit service loop and uses the `select()` system call (described in Section 4.5) to multiplex between ToolTalk messages and user input appearing on `stdin`.

The program both sends and observes (i.e. reads, but does not reply to) messages of type `ttdemo_val`. The content of the message consists of a single integer value. A message is sent whenever the user enters a number on the keyboard. When a ToolTalk message is received, the program simply prints the integer value from the message to stdout.

Even in this minimal example, we will not review the purpose of every call. The ToolTalk package suffers from a large 'surface area' (to use our analogy from Chapter 5), consisting of approximately 160 different functions. Full details are given in SunSoft (1992b).

Here is the code:

```
/* ttdemo  --  Non-X-Windows based demonstration of ToolTalk */
#include <stdio.h>
#include <desktop/tt_c.h>

void        receive_tt_message();
void        send_tt_message(int);

void main()
{
        int val, ttfd;
        Tt_pattern pat;
        fd_set set;

        /* Initialize ToolTalk, and obtain a file descriptor
           that will  become active whenever  ToolTalk has a
           message for this process.
         */

        tt_open();
        ttfd = tt_fd();

        /* Create and register a pattern so ToolTalk knows we
           are interested in 'ttdemo_val' messages within the
           session we join.
         */

        pat = tt_pattern_create();
        tt_pattern_category_set(pat, TT_OBSERVE);
        tt_pattern_scope_add(pat, TT_SESSION);
        tt_pattern_op_add(pat, "ttdemo_val");
        tt_pattern_register(pat);

        /* Join the default session. The session name is taken
           from the _SUN_TT_SESSION environment variable which
           is set up when the session is started
        */

        tt_session_join(tt_default_session());

        /* The head of our main service loop */
        while (1) {

            /* Prepare a descriptor set for select() containing
```

```
                  just our stdin and the ToolTalk file descriptor.
              */

              FD_ZERO(&set);
              FD_SET(0,    &set);
              FD_SET(ttfd, &set);

              /* Wait until either stdin or ToolTalk has something
              */
              select(ttfd+1, &set, NULL, NULL, NULL);

              /* If receive keyboard input, read integer value and
                 broadcast it as a ToolTalk message
              */
              if (FD_ISSET(0, &set)) {
                  if (scanf("%d", &val) == EOF)
                      break;
                  send_tt_message(val);
              }

              /* If we received a message from ToolTalk, print
                 out the new integer value
              */
              if (FD_ISSET(ttfd, &set)) {
                  receive_tt_message();
              }
          }

          /* Allow ToolTalk to clean up.  */
          tt_close();
          exit(0);
}

/* Receive the ToolTalk message. If it's a ttdemo_val message,
   print it out
*/
void receive_tt_message()
{
    Tt_message msg_in;
    int mark, val_in;
    char *op;
    Tt_status err;

    msg_in = tt_message_receive();

    /* It's possible for the file descriptor to become active
       even though ToolTalk doesn't really have a message for
       us.  The returned message handle is NULL in this case.
    */
    if (msg_in == NULL) return;

    /* Get a storage mark so we can easily free the data
```

```
        ToolTalk returns to us.
    */
    mark = tt_mark();

    op = tt_message_op(msg_in);
    err = tt_ptr_error(op);
    if (err > TT_WRN_LAST) {
        printf( "tt_message_op(): %s\n",
                tt_status_message(err));
    } else if (op != 0) {
        if (strcmp("ttdemo_val", tt_message_op(msg_in))==0) {
            tt_message_arg_ival(msg_in, 0, &val_in);
            printf("Got ToolTalk message, val=%d\n", val_in);
        }
    }

    tt_message_destroy(msg_in);
    tt_release(mark);
    return;
}

void send_tt_message(int val_out)
{
    Tt_message msg_out;

    /* Create and send a ToolTalk notice message which contains
       the op-code 'ttdemo_val' and a single integer argument
    */
    msg_out = tt_pnotice_create(TT_SESSION, "ttdemo_val");
    tt_message_arg_add(msg_out, TT_IN, "integer", NULL);
    tt_message_arg_ival_set(msg_out, 0, val_out);
    tt_message_send(msg_out);

    /* Since this message is a notice, we don't expect a reply, so
       there's no need to keep a handle for the message.
    */

    tt_message_destroy(msg_out);
}
```

Usually, a tool joins a ToolTalk session that is associated with a specific X display. However, since this example is character-based, to run this program within the Solaris environment, the user must first start a ToolTalk session:

```
/usr/openwin/bin/ttsession  -c
```

The -c flag indicates that this session is not associated with an X windows display. A new shell is started, and the environment variable _SUN_TT_SESSION is set to the name that was chosen for the session. Within the session, instances of ttdemo may now be executed. If any instance receives input from the keyboard, it sends a `ttdemo_val` message to its session. All instances of `ttdemo` within the session will retrieve this message and report the new value. Notice that the programmer is concerned with session names and message types, not (for example) with host names and port numbers.

ToolTalk is perhaps too high level a service to replace RPC as a general-purpose distributed programming mechanism. Also, its complexity presents a significant learning hurdle. Nonetheless, it is an interesting new paradigm and one which we can expect to see more of in the future.

# Chapter 7

# Server administration

This chapter brings together a collection of topics under the general heading of 'server administration'. We will look at how servers can be reconfigured on-the-fly, and how they can best log their actions or errors. We examine the concept of a 'programmable' (extensible) server. First, however, we look at an easy way to start servers up.

## 7.1 The internet superserver, `inetd`

### 7.1.1 What does `inetd` do?

Following the introduction of TCP/IP support into UNIX, and the development of the real work-horse servers such as `telnetd` and `ftpd`, the number of services grew steadily, and after a while the number of daemon processes in the system began to get rather large. Of course, these daemons are not consuming processing time unless a client actually connects to them, because they are blocked awaiting the connection. However, they are using memory (or at the very least, swap space), and they are consuming slots in the kernel's scheduler tables.

To alleviate this problem, 4.3 BSD UNIX introduced the idea of a 'super-server', called `inetd` (or internet daemon). The `inetd` server waits for connection requests on behalf of many 'ordinary' servers. When a connection request is received, `inetd` forks a new process and duplicates the network connection onto the standard input and standard output of that process. The new process then executes the appropriate server program.

As well as reducing the number of idle processes in the machine, `inetd` further simplifies matters by taking care of the details of establishing a network connection, allowing the server itself to be completely 'network naïve', and simply communicate with the client using its standard input and standard output. This not only makes the server easier to write, it also makes it smaller, because it does not need to include any socket or TLI library code. In addition, `inetd` takes care of a number of rather trivial services by itself. These include the echo service, the time-of-day services, the `chargen` service and the discard service (the network equivalent of `/dev/null` ). It is even possible to start up RPC-based servers via `inetd`.

This explains why you will not necessarily see the `telnet,` `ftp,` `rshd` or other daemons running if you examine the process table using `ps`. You will see them only if

347

they are currently active, that is, in conversation with a client. In the dialogue below, we have `telnet`ted to the machine `zaphod` (which guarantees at least one active `telnet` daemon there!) and executed a `ps` command:

```
zaphod% ps -alx
         F UID   PID  PPID CP PRI NI  SZ  RSS WCHAN    STAT TT   TIME COMMAND
  20088000   0     1     0  0   5  0  56    0 child    IW   ?    0:00 /sbin/init -
     80003   0     2     0  0 -24  0   0    0 child    D    ?    0:07 pagedaemon
     88000   0    44     1  0   1  0  80    0 select   IW   ?    0:00 portmap
     88000   3    47     1  0   1  0  40    0 select   IW   ?    0:00 ypbind
     88000   0    49     1  0   1  0  56    0 select   IW   ?    0:00 keyserv
     88001   0    59     1  0   1  0  24    0 nfs_dnlc I    ?    0:08 (biod)
     88001   0    60     1  0   1  0  24    0 nfs_dnlc I    ·?   0:09 (biod)
     88001   0    61     1  0   1  0  24    0 nfs_dnlc I    ?    0:07 (biod)
     88001   0    62     1  0   1  0  24    0 nfs_dnlc I    ?    0:08 (biod)
     88000   0    73     1  0   1  0  64    0 select   IW   ?    0:01 syslogd
     88000   0    86     1  1   1  0  56    0 select   IW   ?    0:00 rpc.statd
     88000   0    87     1  0   1  0  96    0 select   IW   ?    0:00 rpc.lockd
     88000   0   109     1  0   1  0  56    0 select   IW   ?    0:05 inetd
  20088001   0   651   109  2   1  0  48  304 select   S    ?    0:01 in.telnetd
  20488201  21   652   651  1  15  0  72  160 kernelma S    p0   0:00 -csh (csh)
  20000001  21   672   652 17  29  0 168  432          R    p0   0:00 ps -alx
zaphod%
```

The example above is not complete; the lines for many of the processes which do not interest us have been edited out. The key point to note is that `inetd` (running with PID = 109) is seen to be the parent of our `telnet` server process, with PID = 651. Of course there may be other instances of `telnetd` running on the machine besides ours, or even some `telnet` clients.

Further examination of this list will reveal a number of daemons which have *not* been started via `inetd`, but directly by `init` at boot-time. These include the portmapper, `ypbind` and several copies of `biod`. (These daemons will all be seen to have PID = 1 as their parent.) The reason for not starting these daemons via `inetd` is primarily one of performance. Each time `inetd` launches a daemon, it requires a `fork()` and an `exec()` — both expensive operations in UNIX. To incur such an overhead in daemons which are likely to be contacted very frequently (perhaps many times a second) would impose an unacceptable performance penalty.

## 7.1.2 `inetd` configuration files

To find out which servers to listen on behalf of, and at which ports, `inetd` reads two files: `/etc/inetd.conf` and `/etc/services`. The `/etc/inetd.conf` file specifies which services to listen for, and the `/etc/services` file specifies at which ports to listen.

We have already examined `/etc/services` and found it to provide a simple mapping between a service name, and a port number and protocol. Here is a short extract:

```
echo              7/tcp
echo              7/udp
discard           9/tcp        sink null
discard           9/udp        sink null
ftp-data          20/tcp
ftp               21/tcp
telnet            23/tcp
smtp              25/tcp       mail
time              37/tcp       timserver
time              37/udp       timserver
...
exec              512/tcp
login             513/tcp
shell             514/tcp      cmd
```

The `/etc/inetd.conf` file is new to us. Here is an extract:

```
ftp      stream  tcp   nowait  root    /usr/etc/in.ftpd      in.ftpd -ld
telnet   stream  tcp   nowait  root    /usr/etc/in.telnetd   in.telnetd
shell    stream  tcp   nowait  root    /usr/etc/in.rshd      in.rshd
login    stream  tcp   nowait  root    /usr/etc/in.rlogind   in.rlogind
exec     stream  tcp   nowait  root    /usr/etc/in.rexecd    in.rexecd
comsat   dgram   udp   wait    root    /usr/etc/in.comsat    in.comsat
talk     dgram   udp   wait    root    /usr/etc/in.talkd     in.talkd
#finger  stream  tcp   nowait  nobody  /usr/etc/in.fingerd   in.fingerd
#systat  stream  tcp   nowait  root    /usr/bin/ps           ps -auwwx
time     stream  tcp   nowait  root    internal
time     dgram   udp   wait    root    internal
echo     stream  tcp   nowait  root    internal
echo     dgram   udp   wait    root    internal
```

Each line describes a service on whose behalf `inetd` is to listen. The fields are as follows:

1. The name of the service (as it appears in `/etc/services`).
2. The type of socket which `inetd` should create for this service.
3. The protocol to be used.
4. A flag which should have the value `nowait` for all except single-threaded connectionless servers. This flag controls whether the server waits a while for new service requests after it is done with the current client (`wait`), or exits immediately (`nowait`).
5. The user ID with which the server will run. This determines whose privileges you are carrying when you use the service.
6. The pathname of the server executable (or `internal` if `inetd` deals with the request directly).
7. The command line arguments to be passed to the server.

Why are two separate configuration files used, rather than merging the data into one file? Like many things in UNIX, the answer is largely historical and a desire to maintain backward compatibility. `/etc/services` is used for other, more general, purposes; and anyway, it was there first!

### 7.1.3 Starting a connection-oriented server via `inetd`

To illustrate the ease with which a network-naïve program can be installed as a server using `inetd`, we will take a standard UNIX utility, `who`, and turn it into a server. This does not require us to write any new C code at all. To begin, we need to add entries into `/etc/services` and `/etc/inetd.conf`.

The entry in `/etc/services` appears as follows:

```
wserve      2100/tcp
```

where 2100 is the 'well-known' port number we have selected for this service. The entry in `/etc/inetd.conf` is as follows:

```
wserve  stream  tcp    nowait  root    /usr/bin/who    who
```

Unfortunately, `inetd` will not magically notice that we have made these changes; we need to send it a SIGHUP signal to tell it to re-read the files. We will see how to use this technique in our own servers later in this chapter. We can use `ps` to find the process ID of `inetd` prior to sending the signal:

```
eddie# ps -ae | grep inetd
  231 ?         0:02 inetd
eddie# kill -HUP 231
```

We must be logged in as `root` to do the above step. Now we can check that `inetd` is listening on behalf of this new service using `netstat`:

```
eddie# netstat -a | head
Active Internet connections (including servers)
Proto Recv-Q Send-Q  Local Address    Foreign Address    (state)
tcp        0      0  *.wserve         *.*                LISTEN
tcp        0      0  *.xserver0       *.*                LISTEN
tcp        0      0  *.chargen        *.*                LISTEN
tcp        0      0  *.daytime        *.*                LISTEN
tcp        0      0  *.discard        *.*                LISTEN
tcp        0      0  *.echo           *.*                LISTEN
tcp        0      0  *.time           *.*                LISTEN
tcp        0      0  *.nntp           *.*                LISTEN
eddie#
```

We see that there is now a socket in the LISTEN state at the expected `wserve` port, which is encouraging.

Finally, we can log in to some other machine (`trillian` in the example below), and attempt to `telnet` to our new service back on `eddie`. Note that since `trillian` does not have `wserve` in its `/etc/services` map, we must specify the port which `telnet` is to connect to by number, not by service name:

```
trillian% telnet eddie 2100
Trying 200.1.1.61 ...
Connected to localhost.
Escape character is '^]'.
michael   console Feb 22 09:54
michael   ttyp0   Feb 22 09:56
michael   ttyp1   Feb 22 09:56
michael   ttyp2   Feb 22 10:17
michael   ttyp3   Feb 22 10:17
henry     ttyp5   Feb 22 15:22    (picard)
Connection closed by foreign host.
trillian%
```

Our new network service seems to work!

---

**An aside:** many sites would consider servers such as our `wserve` to be a security risk. The problem is that they allow users on other machines to obtain a list of valid account names – always a useful first step for a potential intruder. If you examine the `/etc/inetd.conf` example shown earlier, you will notice that the entries for `finger` and `systat` have been commented out, for much the same reason.

---

## 7.1.4 Writing filters to use as network servers

Using `inetd`, can we take *any* UNIX filter program (i.e. one which communicates solely via its standard input and standard output) and turn it into a network server in this way? In theory, yes, but in practice there can be problems as a result of the buffering carried out either within the filter itself, or within the standard I/O library. Attempting to use `grep` as a server in this way, for example, does not yield any response until `grep` has accumulated a whole buffer full of output – typically 1024 bytes.

The problem – and its solution – is readily demonstrated with this trivial example of an echo server, intended for start-up via `inetd`:

```
/* echo server using stdio library */
#include <stdio.h>

main()
{
    char line[100];

    while (fgets(line, 100, stdin) != NULL)
```

```
        fputs(line, stdout);
    }
```

As it stands, this echo server returns nothing until it has a full buffer of output data. The fix is to defeat the buffering of the stdout stream, either by calling fflush() whenever we want to ensure that the client gets to see the reply, or by calling setbuf() to disable buffering on stdout altogether. Here is the fflush() fix:

```
/* echo server using stdio library and fflush() */
#include <stdio.h>

main()
{
    char line[100];

    while (fgets(line, 100, stdin) != NULL) {
        fputs(line, stdout);
        fflush(stdout);
    }
}
```

and here is the setbuf() fix:

```
/* echo server using stdio library and setbuf() */
#include <stdio.h>

main()
{
    char line[100];

    setbuf(stdout, NULL);
    while (fgets(line, 100, stdin) != NULL)
        fputs(line, stdout);
}
```

Of course the alternative is to avoid using the stdio library altogether, at least for output. The following implementation is fine:

```
/* echo server using low level read() and write() */
main()
{
    char line[100];
    int count;

    while ((count = read(0, line, 100)) > 0)
        write(1, line, count);
}
```

If formatted output is wanted, it is safest to use sprintf() into a buffer, followed by write(). This example prepends line numbers to the text which is echoed:

```
/* echo server using sprintf() and write() */
#include <stdio.h>

main()
{
    char line1[100], line2[120];
    int count=0;

    while (fgets(line1, 100, stdin) != NULL) {
        sprintf(line2, "reply %d: %s", ++count, line1);
        write(1, line2, strlen(line2));
    }
}
```

A filter such as sort cannot really be made to work at all in this way. The sorted output, by definition, cannot be produced until all the input has been read. However, sort will not see EOF on its input until the network connection has been closed, by which time there is no way to return the reply.

## 7.1.5  Starting an RPC server via inetd

It is also possible to start RPC servers via inetd. A different syntax is required for the entries in inetd.conf. The exact details vary from implementation to implementation, but a typical entry is:

```
rexd/1    stream  rpc/tcp wait root /usr/sbin/rpc.rexd rpc.rexd
```

Here, the notation rexd/1 indicates that this is version 1 of the rexd server. Some versions of rpcgen require a special flag, usually -I, to request that they should generate server wrappers which can be started either stand-alone or via inetd. More recent versions of rpcgen generate such wrappers by default.

## 7.1.6  Other network listener services

In SVR4 UNIX, inetd is one of a small family (three) of programs known as *port monitors*. The other two are listen and ttymon. The term *port* is used here in a very general way, to mean any kind of access point into the system. The servers' transport endpoints at 'well-known' network addresses constitute ports in this context; so do serial interfaces to which log-in terminals may be connected.

The listen port monitor fulfils a similar role to inetd, that is, it waits for connection requests, and starts up specified servers on demand. However, listen was designed specifically to work with STREAMS and TLI, and is able (for example) to push specified STREAMS modules before invoking the server. It is possible to run multiple instances to handle multiple transport protocols. The inetd port monitor, as we have seen, is administered by editing `/etc/inetd.conf` and signalling the server. In contrast, `listen` is administered via a command-line utility, `nlsadmin`.

The other SVR4 port monitor, `ttymon`, monitors serial ports, setting up the terminal modes, baud rates and so on for the port, and starting up the services associated with those ports. It replaces the `getty` program found in earlier versions of UNIX. `ttymon` has its own administrative utility, `ttyadm`.

The port monitors themselves are controlled by a kind of 'port monitor monitor' called `sac`, the service access controller, which is responsible for starting up port monitors under control of the configuration file `/etc/saf/_sactab`. Periodically, `sac` polls the port monitors under its jurisdiction to see if they are alive. Of course, `sac` has its own administration utility, `sacadm`. Jointly, these utilities make up the so-called *service access facility* shown in Figure 7.1.

---

**An aside:** in principle, these new arrangements give greater flexibility – users can write their own port monitors if they wish, and install them using `sacadm`. The administrative utilities eliminate the need to know the format of the underlying configuration files, replacing it with the need to know several dozen option flags. In fact, the administrative tools are themselves often hidden behind menu-driven configuration aids such as `sysadm`. In practice, these arrangements seem to be part of System V's unwritten mission to provide one extra layer of configurability than anyone can actually think of a use for.

---

# 7.2 Logging server actions and errors

Service daemons normally operate without an associated terminal. Usually, their `stdout` and `stderr` streams are not available. If the daemon was started by `inetd` as discussed in the previous section, these streams will refer to the network connection and are used for the dialogue with the client. In any event, the server almost certainly cannot use `printf()` to generate diagnostic output, either to report errors, or simply to log its actions. In this section, we explore some alternative approaches.

## 7.2.1 Logging to a terminal

Daemons that really *must* get a message on to the screen can usually do so by opening `/dev/console` and writing to it. This is an unsatisfactory approach – if the console terminal is in use, the user's work may be disrupted by the message. If the terminal is not in use, the message may go unheeded. If the console is running a window manager, the message may get written to the 'login screen' from which the window manager was launched, and will only be revealed when the window manager is terminated.

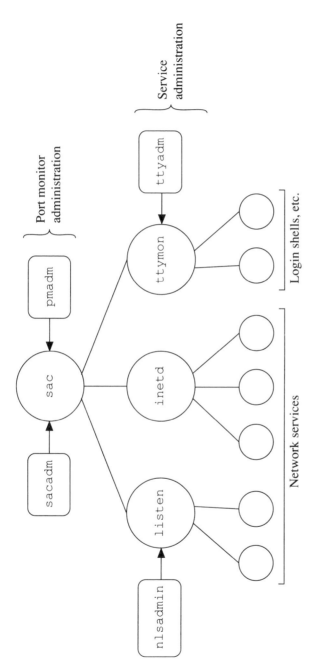

**Figure 7.1** The SVR4 service access facility.

## 7.2.2 Logging to a file

Daemons may, of course, open a file and log messages to that. Usually, the file is opened for appending, so that previously logged output is not overwritten. Such files grow without limit, and will need periodic attention from the system administrator to trim them to a reasonable size. Sometimes, simple scripts are written, and fired up by entries in `crontab` each day, to parcel up the log into daily files. For example, the current log might be renamed to `old_log`, and a new (empty) log started. Fancier schemes are sometimes used to keep, say, the last week's worth of log under files with names such as `log_Tue_23_Feb`.

An example of a program which logs to files is the service access controller (we met this briefly in the previous section) which keeps today's and yesterday's logs in the files `/var/saf/tcp/log` and `/var/saf/tcp/o.log` respectively. Another example is the `uucp` program suite, which maintains a whole collection of log files under the directory `/usr/spool/uucp/.Log`.

## 7.2.3 Logging via `syslogd`

The best way for a daemon to log errors and actions is via the `syslogd` daemon, which was specifically designed for the purpose. The main advantage of `syslogd` is that it offers great flexibility in determining where the messages should go, without building specific knowledge of this into the daemon itself.

Messages logged by `syslogd` have a *priority*, which is made up of two components, a *facility* and a *level*. The facility indicates where (approximately) in the system the message is coming from, and the level indicates how important the message is. Figure 7.2 shows the `syslogd` message priorities. For example, the priority `lpr.debug` (note the separating dot) indicates debug-level messages coming from the printer spooling system.

The programmer's main interface to `syslogd` is the function `syslog()`, which is illustrated in Figure 7.3. Here is an example:

```
syslog(LOG_USER | LOG_INFO,
       "%s: cannot open config file: %m", argv[0] );
```

The second argument to `syslog()` is a `printf`-style format string, with one additional format code, `%m`, which will be replaced by the current error message (as would be printed out by `perror()`).

The function `openlog()` may be called to initialize the log, to set a default *facility* for the messages, and to ask for specific information to be prepended to each message. For example, the call

```
openlog("mydaemon", LOG_PID, LOG_USER);
```

causes each logged message to be preceded by the text 'mydaemon', and the process ID of the daemon logging the message. It also sets the default facility to `LOG_USER`. In some

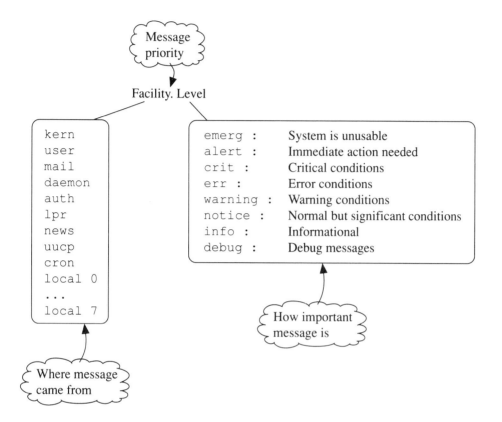

**Figure 7.2** `syslogd` message priorities.

implementations a call to `openlog()` appears to be mandatory for the logging to work at all. In other versions, it is optional.

The following trivial program illustrates the use of `openlog()` and `syslog()`:

```
#include <stdio.h>
#include <syslog.h>

main(int argc, char *argv[])
{
    int count;

    openlog("mydaemon", LOG_PID, LOG_USER);
    for (count=0; count<5; count++) {
        syslog(LOG_NOTICE, "log message %d", count);
    }
}
```

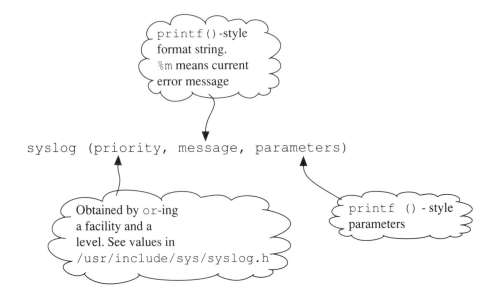

**Figure 7.3** Using `syslog()`.

The messages logged by the above program are of the form:

```
Apr  9 22:27:35 mydaemon[344]: log message 0
```

The `syslogd` daemon is controlled by the file `/etc/syslog.conf` which determines where each type of message is to be sent. Each entry in this file consists of a *selector* and an *action*. The selector specifies a list of message priorities (remember, a priority consists of a facility and a level), and the action specifies what to do with the message. There are three possible types of action:

1. The message can be appended to a specified file.
2. The message can be sent to a specified list of users.
3. The message can be forwarded to the `syslogd` on another machine.

Here is an example:

```
lpr.debug                       /usr/adm/lpd-errs
kern.debug;daemon.notice        /usr/adm/messages
*.alert; kern.err               root
auth.notice                     @trillian
```

Taken in turn, these four lines specify that:

1. Messages with the priority `lpr.debug` should be appended to the file `/usr/adm/lpd-errs`.

2. Messages with the priority `kern.debug` or `daemon.notice` should be appended to the file `/usr/adm/messages`.
3. Messages from any facility at the `alert` level (note the use of `*` as a wildcard) or with priority `kern.err` should be sent to the user `root`, if he or she is logged in.
4. Messages with the priority `auth.notice` should be forwarded to the `syslogd` on the machine `trillian`. What happens to them there will depend upon the `/etc/syslog.conf` file on `trillian`.

If the file `syslog.conf` is changed, a `SIGHUP` signal should be sent to the `syslogd` daemon to force it to re-read the file. To make this easier, `syslogd` writes its process ID to the file `/etc/syslog.pid` when it starts up. Thus, `syslogd` may be signalled using the shell command:

```
kill -HUP  `cat /etc/syslog.pid`
```

without the need to run `ps` to find the process ID.

The `logger` command provides a command-level interface to the `syslogd` facility, allowing messages to be logged manually (for testing, or to record some administrative operation) or from within shell scripts. For example, the command:

```
logger  -p  user.notice  Deleted Yr 4 Student Accounts
```

logs a message at the `user.notice` priority.

Some implementations of `syslogd` maintain a one-line message buffer which they use to eliminate repeated identical messages. This can be useful, for example, in preventing the kernel appending a million lines to the system log telling you that the disk is full!

# 7.3  Configurable servers

## 7.3.1  Server configuration files

Daemons often have an associated configuration file which establishes some set of operating parameters. We have met two examples of such daemons earlier in the chapter: `inetd`, with its configuration file `inetd.conf`, and `syslogd`, with the file `/etc/syslog.conf`. Another example, though not within the scope of this book, is `gated`. This daemon is responsible for exchanging internet routing information, and has an associated configuration file `/etc/gated.conf`.

---

**An aside:** `gated` should be pronounced 'gate-dee' and not 'gate-ed'. Similarly, `vi` should be pronounced 'vee-eye' and not 'vie'. Either of these blunders would carry penalty points amongst the UNIX *cognoscenti*.

---

## 7.3.2 Reconfiguration on receipt of a signal

Usually, the daemon reads its `config` file when it starts up. If we wish to change the configuration, we edit the file. Of course, editing a `config` file does not by itself reconfigure the daemon. The daemon must be told to re-read the file. A very heavy-handed way to do this is to reboot the system. A better way is to find the daemon in a `ps` listing, kill it off and start a new one. Of course, this will not please any clients which happened to be talking to it at the time. Even better is to write the daemon so that it re-reads the `config` file upon receipt of an agreed signal. We saw an example of this technique in operation earlier in the chapter when we added an entry to the `inetd.conf` file and then signalled `inetd`.

The program schema to do this is one we showed in Chapter 2; it typically appears as follows:

```
void read_config_file()
{
    int fd;

    fd = open("my_config_file", O_RDONLY);
    /* Do the hard part
        ... i.e. read configuration parameters
    */
    close(fd);
    signal(SIGHUP, read_config_file);
}

main()
{
    /* Set up initial configuration */
    read_config_file();

    /* Enter service loop */
    while (1) {
        ...
    }

}
```

# 7.4  Starting daemons at boot-time

## 7.4.1 Boot-time scripts

In Section 7.1 we discussed the business of installing a daemon via `inetd`, and mentioned some of the pitfalls. Suppose, however, that our daemon is to run 'stand-alone', rather than being started via `inetd`. In this case, we need to make entries in the appropriate boot-time scripts so that the daemon is automatically run each time the system starts up.

When UNIX boots, a single user-level process, with process ID = 1, is created by the kernel. This process runs a program called `init`. All other processes in the machine are created as a result of `fork()` system calls, and are directly or indirectly descendants of `init`. It is `init` which executes the boot-time scripts responsible for starting the system services.

The BSD version of `init` executes the scripts `/etc/rc.boot`, `/etc/rc` and `/etc/rc.local`. The `rc.local` script is the place to put start-up code for locally developed or machine-specific services. This is a Bourne shell script and may simply be edited to add the required commands. A typical fragment follows:

```
if [ -f /usr/lib/sendmail -a -f /etc/sendmail.cf ]; then
        (cd /var/spool/mqueue; rm -f nf* lf*)
        /usr/lib/sendmail -bd -q1h; echo -n ' sendmail'
fi
```

These lines are responsible for starting up the mail delivery daemon, `sendmail`. The `if` test is typical; it tests for the presence both of the executable file itself (`/usr/lib/sendmail`) and of an associated configuration file (`/etc/sendmail.cf`). This allows the daemon to be 'disabled' by removing or renaming the configuration file. It is straightforward to add entries to `rc.local` for user-written daemons.

In SVR4, things are more complicated. Here `init` supports the notion of multiple *run levels*. The allowable run levels are 0 through 6, and 's' (single-user). A default run level is established when the system boots, but the run level can subsequently be changed (by the super-user) without rebooting the system. Roughly speaking, larger run levels correspond to greater degrees of activity within the system, although a number of special cases disrupt this pattern, as follows:

```
0    System is shut down, power may be removed.
1    System administrator mode. All file systems are accessible,
     but no regular users may log in.
2    Multi-user mode. All terminal processes and daemons to support
     multi-user operation are started.
3    Remote file-sharing mode. In addition to the level 2 services,
     distributed file system daemons are started.
4    An alternative multi-user state, usually unused.
5    Shuts UNIX down and transfers control to the bootstrap ROM.
6    Shuts UNIX down and auto-reboots.
```

The actions taken by `init` when a particular run level is entered are controlled by a hierarchy of configuration files and shell scripts. At the top level of this hierarchy is the file `/etc/inittab`. This is not a shell script, but uses a special notation understood by `init`. A typical fragment from this file follows:

```
is:3:initdefault:
r0:0:wait:/sbin/rc0 off 1> /dev/sysmsg 2>&1 </dev/console
```

```
r1:1:wait:/sbin/rc1  1> /dev/sysmsg 2>&1 </dev/console
r2:23:wait:/sbin/rc2 1> /dev/sysmsg 2>&1 </dev/console
r3:3:wait:/sbin/rc3  1> /dev/sysmsg 2>&1 </dev/console
```

The fields within each line are separated by colons and are as follows:

1. A label, which serves very little purpose.
2. A list of run levels at which this entry is to be processed. For example, if init enters run level 1, it will process the entry labelled r1 in the example.
3. An *action*, which tells init how to manage the process. The commonest action types are wait, which means to run the specified command once on entering the run level and wait for its termination, and respawn which means to run the specified command, without waiting for its termination, and then restart the command if it should subsequently terminate. An action type of initdefault is a special entry used to tell init its default run state when the system boots.
4. The (Bourne shell) command to be executed. These appear complex in the example above because of the notations used to redirect the I/O streams, but basically this inittab runs the scripts /sbin/rc0, /sbin/rc1, /sbin/rc2 and /sbin/rc3 on entering run levels 0, 1, 2 and 3 respectively. These scripts form the second level in the boot file hierarchy.

It is possible to put daemon start-up commands directly into files such as /sbin/rc2, or even into inittab itself, but examination of these files reveals a third level in the boot file hierarchy. For example, here is the important part of /sbin/rc2:

```
echo 'Changing to state 2.'
if [ -d /etc/rc2.d ]
then
    for f in /etc/rc2.d/K*
    {
        if [ -s ${f} ]
        then
            /sbin/sh ${f} stop
        fi
    }
fi

if [ -d /etc/rc2.d ]
then
    for f in /etc/rc2.d/S*
    {
        if [ -s ${f} ]
        then
            /sbin/sh ${f} start
        fi
    }
fi
```

For those not fluent in shell programming, what this script does is to run all the scripts in the directory `/etc/rc2.d` whose names begin with K (for kill), with the argument `stop`. Then it runs all the scripts whose names begin with S (for start) with the argument `start`. Examination of the directory `/etc/rc2.d` shows a set of files such as:

```
K20nfs          S02PRESERVE     S69inet       S80merge
K30fumounts     S05RMTMPFILES   S70uucp       S80sendmail
K40rumounts     S06syslogd      S75cron       S85merge
K50rfs          S11uname        S75rpc        S86sysetup
S01MOUNTFSYS    S25mse          S80lp         S94osm
```

Each file name starts with a K or an S, then a two digit number. The numbers are used to control the order in which the scripts are executed – the 'master' script `/sbin/rc2` executes the scripts in sorted order. These scripts form the third level in the boot file hierarchy. A typical script is `S06syslogd` which launches the `syslogd` daemon described in Section 7.2. Here it is:

```
if [ ! -d /usr/sbin ]
then                             # /usr not mounted ??
    exit
fi
case "$1" in
'start')
    if [ -x /usr/sbin/syslogd ]
    then
        /usr/sbin/syslogd &
    else
        echo $0: /usr/sbin/syslogd not found >/dev/console
        exit 1
    fi
    ;;
'stop')
    kill `cat /etc/syslog.pid`
    ;;
esac
```

Rather mysteriously, this script tests for the two arguments `start` and `stop`, and uses them to start and shut down the `syslogd` daemon respectively. A rummage through the file system (using `find`) reveals that the same script is referenced under the name `K06syslogd` in the directories `/etc/rc0.d` and `/etc/rc1.d`, where it is used to shut down the `syslogd` daemon.

The hierarchy of boot-time files in SVR4 is summarized in Figure 7.4. For a user-written daemon, the best place for a start-up script is probably the `/etc/rc2.d` directory. Using the existing scripts as examples, it is fairly easy to add your own.

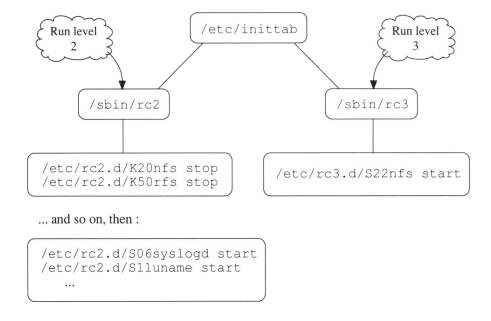

**Figure 7.4**  Part of the SVR4 boot file hierarchy.

## 7.4.2  Robustness of daemons

Daemons started at boot-time (as discussed in the previous section) are very long-lived processes. They are expected to continue to operate correctly from the time the machine is booted to the time it is shut down, perhaps weeks later. Consequently, such programs need to be especially robust. Robustness is a difficult topic, but the following are key issues:

1.  Extra care must be taken to test for, and recover from, all conceivable errors. If a parameter passed by a client is out of range, for example, it should be rejected before it has time to do any real harm. Error recovery is essential, and can often dominate the code. Clearly, it is *not* acceptable for a daemon to simply exit if it encounters a problem, except as a last resort.

2.  During its lifetime, the daemon may service a huge number of client requests. It is essential that any per client resources used by the daemon are released when that client is done. For example, any unwanted file descriptors must be closed so that they may be re-used. Every process has a limit (sixty-four is a typical value) on the number of descriptors available. If this limit is reached, calls such as `open()` and `socket()` which create new descriptors will fail. Similarly, any per client shared memory segments, semaphores or message queues should be destroyed. There is a

system-wide limit, which is usually quite small, on the number of such objects which can exist at any one time.

3. A less obvious problem (and one it is more difficult to eradicate with certainty) relates to the freeing of dynamically allocated memory which is no longer required. If a daemon allocates complex linked data structures for each client, every nook and cranny of these structures must be freed when the client is done. The cumulative effect of failing to free memory is known as a *memory leak*, and can be very hard to track down. The program may run apparently correctly for days, gradually eating away at the virtual memory space of the machine, until at some stage, an operation such as `fork()` or `malloc()` fails. There may be no obvious symptoms to point to the offending daemon. There are one or two third-party software tools available to help identify memory leaks, but the real answer is to draw lots of pictures of the data structures, wrap a cold towel around your head and think hard!

4. All signals should either be explicitly handled, or be ignored.

Points (2) and (3) above do not apply with such force to daemons started via `inetd` or some other port monitor, because a fresh copy of the daemon is started for every request.

# 7.5 Extensible servers

## 7.5.1 The extensible server concept

The servers that we have encountered in this book have each offered a fixed repertoire of services. In the case of the RPC-based servers, this repertoire corresponds to the defined set of RPC procedures within the server. In the case of the 'service registry' server of Chapter 5, we implemented four commands, identified by an 'op-code' and separated by a `switch` in the server. In both cases, the set of available commands is hard-wired into the server source code and can be extended only by editing and recompiling the server.

*Extensible* servers offer an alternative approach. The basic idea is that the client may download a sequence of operations to the server, give that sequence some sort of identifier, then subsequently request that the sequence be carried out, simply by sending the identifier, and perhaps some additional parameters. In effect, the server becomes an interpreter for a command language which can be extended on-the-fly by incrementally defining new procedures in the language.

## 7.5.2 Extensible languages

There are a number of general-purpose programming languages that work this way. FORTH, a language developed by astronomer Charles Moore, is one example (Brodie, 1981). PostScript, the language developed by Adobe Systems to support laser printers, is another. Both these languages use a stack-oriented approach to expression evaluation, using 'reverse polish' notation. For example, the sequence

```
2  3  +
```

means 'push 2 on to the stack, push 3 on to the stack, replace the top two numbers on the stack by their sum'.

Both languages are also dictionary-driven (this is what makes them extensible – the language includes primitives to define new dictionary entries). In FORTH, the primitives ':' and ';' are used to begin and end the definition of a new *word*. For example, the following sequence defines a new word FAC, which computes factorials:

```
: FAC DUP 1 - SWAP BEGIN OVER * SWAP 1 - SWAP
  OVER 0= UNTIL SWAP DROP ;
```

Because FORTH expression evaluation refers explicitly to an evaluation stack, named variables are rarely used within procedures. The FAC procedure shown above uses no variables. However, the important point is that such definitions may be entered into the FORTH interpreter on the fly – there is no distinction between *compile-time* and *run-time*, as is normally found with languages such as C. Following the entry of such a definition, a factorial may be computed as follows:

```
5 FAC
```

The ability to teach a server new 'high level' operations on top of the 'low level' ones it already knows has two advantages:

1.  The client has much greater control over how much work is off-loaded to the server, and how much remains in the client.
2.  The volume of network traffic between client and server may be greatly reduced. This reduction comes about because long command sequences only need to be sent once. In particular, the client can download a loop to the server, then invoke the loop with a single message. With a non-extensible server, the looping goes on at the client end, with a message passed to the server each time through the loop.

FORTH is not a widely used language within the UNIX community. However, the PostScript language has given rise to what is perhaps the best-known extensible UNIX server, the *Network Extensible Window System*, or *NeWS*.

## 7.5.3 NeWS and PostScript

The PostScript language on which NeWS is based is designed to drive such things as laser printers, bitmapped displays or other devices able to make marks on some kind of drawing surface. The language includes many drawing operators such as moveto, lineto, curveto, show and fill, as well as operators that establish a drawing context, such as `translate, rotate, scale` and `setfont`. However, PostScript also has a full range of features which are more general in purpose, including variables, arrays, arithmetic, loops, branches and so on, making it suitable for a wide range of programming tasks (Adobe Systems Inc., 1990).

The NeWS server was introduced by Sun Microsystems and heavily promoted as *the* network window system, in much the same way that NFS had been promoted as *the* network file system. Whilst support for NFS was widespread, NeWS never caught on in the same way. Over time, it lost the market-place battle against the X Window System, despite being – arguably – a more elegant protocol. Nonetheless, Sun continue to support it, alongside X.

The following NeWS example illustrates the concept of off-loading work to the server, and the resultant reduction in network traffic. A client wishing to draw multiple instances of a graphical object (in this case, a ten by ten square grid) adds a suitable procedure to the NeWS server's dictionary by sending the following commands:

```
/Grid {
    0.1  1  {
        dup  0  moveto  0  1  rlineto
        0  exch  moveto  1  0  rlineto
    } for
    stroke
} def
```

Thereafter, specific instances of the grid may be drawn at specified positions, rotations and scalings by sending commands to establish the desired context, then invoking the new procedure. For example:

```
1  0  translate  Grid
45  rotate  1.414  dup  scale  Grid
```

For comparison, the (roughly) equivalent code to draw a grid using the X window protocol might appear as follows:

```
for (v = 0; v < 100; v += 10) {
    XDrawLine(display, d, gc, 0, v, 100, v);
    XDrawLine(display, d, gc, v, 0, v, 100);
}
```

The key difference is that the X protocol is data-driven. The `for` loop is executed in the client, not in the server, and each call to `XDrawLine()` results in message traffic to the server.

## 7.5.4  An extensible file server protocol

Interestingly, an extensible file server protocol was developed by Sun in 1990. This, too, used a tokenized language based on PostScript (Arnold, 1991). The idea was that the client could download a procedure to the server to perform some (high level) operation on the file system, ranging from a simple file rename to a recursive removal of an entire directory hierarchy. This extensible file server protocol was named NeFS (Network Extensible File System), but was never released.

# 7.6  A final aside

Having refrained, for the most part, from writing this book in the first person, I should like to finish with a few personal comments about the philosophy and evolution of UNIX.

My first contact with UNIX, in (I guess) about 1979, was with a version known as Edition 6. It ran on a PDP-11 minicomputer. The entire distribution, including the source code, which lived in directories with nice friendly names like ken (Ken Thompson) and dmr (Dennis Ritchie), fitted on to two 2.5 Mbyte disk cartridges. A kernel could be configured to fit into 48 kbytes – the maximum the memory architecture of the PDP-11 would allow. The documentation consisted of two manuals, each about one inch thick. To quote John Lions, '. . . the whole documentation is not unreasonably transportable in a student's briefcase'. Kernighan and Pike comment on this with the telling remark: 'This has been fixed in recent versions' (Kernighan and Pike, 1984). In fact nowadays you can fill a briefcase simply by collecting together all the pieces of paper that say 'Read This First'.

In the early days, there was no vendor support for UNIX. That is not to say that no help was available – on the contrary, there were plenty of well-informed people, most of whom were only too pleased to share their knowledge with you. E-mail proved extremely effective at unifying a user community which was tightly focused technically despite being widely dispersed geographically. User group conferences provided a slightly more formal forum. Most of the axes to be ground were intellectual, not commercial. No one was really trying to 'sell' UNIX, except in the way that you might try to persuade a friend to go to see a good play. No one pretended that UNIX was perfect; the manual pages had a standard section called BUGS.

This pioneering spirit has largely disappeared. Nowadays, most users get their help through impersonal (and expensive) 'hotline support' services, in much the same way, I suppose, that people pay psycho-analysts to get a shoulder to cry on. (It has been said that people who pay to visit psycho-analysts need their heads examining.) It is gratifying to note, however, that the spirit of communal self-help lives on in the e-mail and newsgroup services of the internet. The documentation has become more sanitized (and a great deal thicker!), with the BUGS section retitled CAVEATS or NOTES. Even some of the vendor-sponsored textbooks have a stilted quality born, presumably, of a fear of sullying the corporate image by actually pointing out the shortcomings of the product or letting slip that a member of the workforce has a sense of humour. The kernel on the machine I am running occupies 1.77 Mbytes – some thirty-six times the size of my original PDP-11 version. Perhaps this does not matter – my machine has forty-six times as much memory as the PDP, and cost maybe one-tenth as much. In my more cynical moments, however, I wonder why it does not have thirty-six times the productivity.

Those early versions of UNIX were guided by a principle which was never made explicit but which in retrospect we might call the *principle of no surprises*. By this, I mean that one could form a fairly simple mental model of the underlying mechanisms; the processes, streams, system calls, files and so forth, which was sufficient to understand the whole system, and which let you predict the effect of any command or change in system configuration which you were contemplating. I can still remember the pleasure of seeing the elegance of these underlying features. Unfortunately, this 'principle of no surprises' has been violated time and again in recent versions of UNIX, and in a myriad of ways, ranging from symbolic links to the discovery that you have to pay extra for the C compiler.

As each new release has come along, I have managed – just – to assimilate the new features, or at least, those that seemed useful to me. But I sometimes wonder if the newcomer to UNIX, opening the 'Read This First' document from the latest version (and wondering which of the other twenty-seven manuals to read next), can ever be expected to see the elegance that attracted me to the system in the first place.

Many of the changes we have seen in UNIX represent genuine increases in functionality: virtual memory, networking, window managers and so on. Few of the features discussed in this book, for example, were present in that early PDP-11 version of UNIX. Other changes reflect the move which UNIX has made from the land of the *cognoscenti* – people who know what they are doing – to the land of the 'naïve' user. In my view, this represents the biggest challenge that UNIX has faced so far. I wish it well.

# Appendix: Summary of UNIX IPC mechanisms

This appendix provides a summary of the UNIX IPC mechanisms. Each mechanism is described under the following headings:

| | |
|---|---|
| • **Name:** | The general name of the mechanism. |
| • **Description:** | A short description of its operation. |
| • **Rendezvous:** | What must two processes agree on to communicate via this mechanism? |
| • **Access control:** | Who can do what and to whom. |
| • **Strengths:** | Things this mechanism is good at; when to use it. |
| • **Weaknesses:** | Things this mechanism is bad at; when not to use it. |
| • **Reference:** | Where to find more detail in this book. |

| | |
|---|---|
| **Name:** | Pipe. |
| **Description:** | Simple stream connection between two processes. Bidirectional in SVR4, unidirectional in earlier versions. |
| **Rendezvous:** | Processes must share a common ancestor which created the pipe. |
| **Access control:** | None. |
| **Strengths:** | Automatic loose synchronization between sender and receiver. Ideal for 'single producer, single consumer' scenario. |
| **Weaknesses:** | Must be pre-arranged by common ancestor. Cannot traverse the network; both processes must be on the same machine. |
| **Reference:** | Section 2.4. |

| | |
|---|---|
| **Name:** | Named pipe. |
| **Description:** | Simple stream connection between two processes. |
| **Rendezvous:** | An entry in the UNIX filesystem, e.g. `/tmp/mypipe`. |
| **Access control:** | Normal UNIX file access controls based on the file system entry for the pipe. |
| **Strengths:** | Very simple to use. Automatic loose synchronization between sender and receiver. No need to be pre-arranged. |
| **Weaknesses:** | Cannot traverse the network; both processes must be on the same |

machine. (Not true if RFS running, the named pipe can then be exported and opened remotely.)

**Reference:** Section 2.4.5.

---

**Name:** File.
**Description:** Linear byte sequence stored on disk.
**Rendezvous:** An entry in the UNIX filesystem, e.g. `/usr/julian/mydata`.
**Access control:** Separate read, write and execute permission for owner, group and 'other' user categories.
**Strengths:** Handles very large volumes of data (100s of Mbytes). Random access. Includes locking mechanism for arbitrary byte ranges. Huge number of existing utilities to manipulate files. Nonvolatile (i.e. survives power-down or reboot). Network file system allows files to be used as network-wide IPC.
**Weaknesses:** No automatic synchronization between producers and consumers. Potentially inefficient as data must be copied to/from disk.
**Reference:** Section 3.4, 3.5.

---

**Name:** Shared memory.
**Description:** Allows a region of memory to be allocated and mapped into the address space of two or more processes.
**Rendezvous:** Shared memory regions are identified by an integer key value.
**Access control:** Similar to file access control. Segments have ownerships, and read/write permissions for user, group and other.
**Strengths:** Very efficient as data do not need to be copied. Provides random access to shared data. Provides many-to-many communication.
**Weaknesses:** No implied sychronization. May need semaphores to protect critical updates, and signals or some other synchronization to coordinate producer/consumer activity. Does not work across the network (all processes must be on same machine).
**Reference:** Section 2.5.

---

**Name:** Semaphore.
**Description:** Multi-valued semaphores, provide a sleep/wakeup mechanism to synchronize access to shared resources and/or protect critical code sections against simultaneous execution by more than one process.
**Rendezvous:** An array of semaphores is identified by an integer key value. An element of the array is further identified by its index within the array.
**Access control:** Similar to file access control. Semaphores have ownerships, and read/write permissions for user, group and other.
**Strengths:** Solves the classical computer science problems of locking access to shared resources. Supports the automatic release of locks held by a process when it terminates.
**Weaknesses:** Unnecessarily complicated for most applications. Does not work

|  |  |
|---|---|
| | across the network (all processes must be on same machine). |
| **Reference:** | Section 2.6. |

| | |
|---|---|
| **Name:** | Message queue. |
| **Description:** | Provides a serial queue of discrete messages which can be attached and accessed by many processes. |
| **Rendezvous:** | A message queue is identified by an integer key value. Messages on the queue may be further identified by an integer message type. |
| **Access control:** | Similar to file access control. Message queues have ownerships, and read/write permissions for user, group and other. |
| **Strengths:** | Suitable for both one-to-many and many-to-one producer/consumer scenarios. Message type values allow implementation of priority messages and message demultiplexing schemes. |
| **Weaknesses:** | Typically, there is a rather small system-wide limit on the amount of data which can be held in mesage queues. Does not work across the network (all processes must be on same machine). |
| **Reference:** | Section 2.7. |

| | |
|---|---|
| **Name:** | Signal. |
| **Description:** | Provides a way for one process to 'get the attention' of another process asynchronously. |
| **Rendezvous:** | Sender must know the process ID of the recipient. Each signal has a type (a small integer value); the types have strong conventional meanings. |
| **Access control:** | Signals can only be sent to processes with the same user ID as the sending process. |
| **Strengths:** | Asynchronous, i.e. recipient does not need to be blocked waiting for the signal in order to receive it. |
| **Weaknesses:** | No data (other than the signal type) may be transferred along with the signal. Unsolicited and unexpected signals usually cause the recipient process to terminate. Details of BSD and SVR4 implementations have diverged. Does not work across the network (all processes must be on same machine). |
| **Reference:** | Section 2.8. |

| | |
|---|---|
| **Name:** | Socket. |
| **Description:** | General-purpose interface to both connectionless and connection-oriented network transport services. |
| **Rendezvous:** | Depends on the underlying transport protocol. For TCP and UDP, clients contact servers at a known 16-bit port number on a machine with a specified IP address. |
| **Access control:** | Port numbers below 1024 are 'reserved', i.e. can only be used by processes with root privilege. |
| **Strengths:** | Enables communication between processes across a network. Widely |

|                  |                                                                                                                           |
|------------------|---------------------------------------------------------------------------------------------------------------------------|
|                  | supported/copied by non-UNIX systems.                                                                                      |
| **Weaknesses:**  | Access control is primitive and weak. Minimal support for communication between machines of different architectures.       |
| **Reference:**   | Chapter 4.                                                                                                                 |

|                     |                                                                                                                                                                                             |
|---------------------|---------------------------------------------------------------------------------------------------------------------------------------------------------------------------------------------|
| **Name:**           | Transport level interface (TLI).                                                                                                                                                             |
| **Description:**    | General-purpose interface to both connectionless and connection-oriented network transport services.                                                                                        |
| **Rendezvous:**     | Depends on the underlying transport protocol. For TCP and UDP, clients contact servers at a known 16-bit port number on a machine with a specified IP address.                               |
| **Access control:** | Port numbers below 1024 are 'reserved', i.e. can only be used by processes with root privilege.                                                                                              |
| **Strengths:**      | Enables communication between processes across a network. Integration with 'network selection' service in SVR4 UNIX eases writing of applications which are independent of the transport protocol. |
| **Weaknesses:**     | Access control is primitive and weak. No support for communication between machines of different architectures. Not widely used outside UNIX.                                                |
| **Reference:**      | Chapter 5.                                                                                                                                                                                  |

|                     |                                                                                                                                                                                                       |
|---------------------|-------------------------------------------------------------------------------------------------------------------------------------------------------------------------------------------------------|
| **Name:**           | Remote procedure call (RPC).                                                                                                                                                                           |
| **Description:**    | Mechanism that allows parts of an application to be placed remotely and accessed by a normal procedure call.                                                                                           |
| **Rendezvous:**     | Client must know host IP address, program number and version number of required service. In addition, individual service procedures are identified by a procedure number.                              |
| **Access control:** | None within the RPC mechanism itself, but support for UNIX-style and (much stronger) DES encrypted authentication of both server and client.                                                           |
| **Strengths:**      | High degree of transparency of network transport. High degree of independence from transport protocol. Automatic conversion of data types allows interoperation between machines of different architectures. |
| **Weaknesses:**     | Amount of data which can be passed or returned in a single RPC call is limited (typically < 8 kbytes). Data conversion is needlessly expensive between little-endian machines. Significant constraints on passing parameters and returning rules. |
| **Reference:**      | Chapter 6.                                                                                                                                                                                            |

# Bibliography

Adobe Systems Inc. (1990), *Postscript Language Reference Manual* (2nd edn), Reading, MA: Addison-Wesley.

Aho, A.V., Kernighan, B.W. and Weinberger, P. (1988), *The AWK Programming Language*, Reading, MA: Addison-Wesley.

Arnold, G. (1991), *Change and Non-change in NFS*, Sun User '91 Conference Proceeding, Sun UK User Group, Owles Hall, Buntingford, Hertfordshire, SG9 9PL, UK.

AT&T (1990), *UNIX SVR4 Programmers' Guide: Networking Interfaces*, Englewood Cliffs, NJ: Prentice Hall.

Bloomer, J. (1992), *Power Programming with RPC*, Sebastopol, CA: O'Reilly and Associates, Inc.

Brodie, L. (1981), *Starting FORTH*, Englewood Cliffs, NJ: Prentice Hall.

Comer, D.E. and Stevens, D.L. (1993), *Internetworking with TCP/IP*, Volume 3: *Client–Server Programming and Applications*, Englewood Cliffs, NJ: Prentice Hall.

Corbin, J.R. (1992), *The Art of Distributed Applications*, New York: Springer-Verlag.

Cox, B.J. (1986), *Object Oriented Programming: An evolutionary approach*, Reading, MA: Addison-Wesley.

Custer, H. (1993), *Inside Windows NT*, Redmond, Washington: Microsoft Press.

Eykholt, J.R., Kleiman, S.R., Barton, S., Falkner, R., Shivalingiah, A., Smith, M., Stein, D., Voll, J., Weeks, M. and Williams, D. (1992), *Beyond Multiprocessing – Multithreading the SunOS Kernel*, USENIX Conference Proceedings, San Antonio, TX.

Fox, G., Johnson, M., Lyzenga, G., Otto, S., Salmon, J. and Walker, D. (1988), *Solving Problems on Concurrent Processors*, Englewood Cliffs, NJ: Prentice Hall.

Hofstadter, D.R. (1979), *Godel, Escher, Bach: An Eternal Golden Braid*, New York, Basic Books.

Jones, G. and Goldsmith, M. (1989), *Programming in Occam 2*, Englewood Cliffs, NJ: Prentice Hall.

Kernighan, B.W. and Pike, R. (1984), *The UNIX Programming Environment*, Englewood Cliffs, NJ: Prentice Hall.

Krol, E. (1993), *The Whole Internet Users Guide and Catalog*, Sebastopol, CA: O'Reilly and Associates, Inc.

Leffler, S.J., McKusik, M.K., Karels, M.J. and Quarterman, J.S. (1988), *The Design and Implementation of the 4.3 BSD UNIX Operating System*, Reading, MA: Addison-Wesley.

Lynch, D.C. and Rose, M.T. (1993), *Internet System Handbook*, Reading, MA: Addison-Wesley.

McManis, C. (1991), *Naming Systems: A replacement for NIS*, Sun UK User Group Conference Proceedings, Birmingham, UK, September 1991 (available through SunSoft offices).

Malamud, C. (1992), *Analysing SUN Networks*, New York, NY: Van Nostrand Reinhold.

Nemeth, E., Snyder, G. and Seebas, S. (1989), *UNIX System Administration Handbook*, Englewood Cliffs, NJ: Prentice Hall.

Open Software Foundation (1991), *Guide to OSF/1: A technical synopsis*, Sebastopol, CA: O'Reilly and Associates, Inc.

Padovano, M. (1993), *Networking Applications on UNIX System V Release 4*, Englewood Cliffs, NJ: Prentice Hall.

Perihelion Software (1989), *The Helios Operating System*, Hemel Hempstead, UK: Prentice Hall.

POSIX P1003.4a (1990), *Threads Extension for Portable Operating Systems* (Draft Vsn 6), Piscataway, NJ: IEEE.

Powell, M.L., Kleiman, S.R., Barton, S., Shah, D., Stein, D. and Weeks, M. (1991), *SunOS Multi-thread Architecture*, Winter '91 USENIX Conference Proceedings, Dallas, TX.

Rieken, B. and Weiman, L. (1992), *Adventures in UNIX Network Programming*, New York: John Wiley and Sons.

Rochkind, M.J. (1985), *Advanced UNIX Programming*, Englewood Cliffs, NJ: Prentice Hall.

Schuilenburg, A., Malagardis, N. and Ginzinger, P. (1992), *Trends in Parallel Operating Systems*, EEC Esprit Directorate, report from Esprit Project 5665.

Stern, H. (1991), *Managing NFS and NIS*, Sebastopol, CA: O'Reilly and Associates, Inc.

Stevens, W.R. (1990), *UNIX Network Programming*, Englewood Cliffs, NJ: Prentice Hall.

Sun (1990), *SunOS 4.1: Network Programming Guide*, Mountain View, CA: Sun Microsystems.

SunSoft (1992a), *SunOS 5.1 STREAMS Programmers' Guide*, Mountain View, CA: Sun Microsystems.

SunSoft (1992b), *ToolTalk 1.0.2 Programmer's Guide*, Mountain View, CA: Sun Microsystems.

Tanenbaum, A.S. (1988), *Computer Networks* (2nd edn), Englewood Cliffs, NJ: Prentice Hall.

Tanenbaum, A.S. (1992), *Modern Operating Systems*, Englewood Cliffs, NJ: Prentice Hall.

Trew, A. and Wilson, G. (Eds) (1991), *Past, Present, Parallel: A survey of available parallel computing systems*, New York: Springer-Verlag.

USL (1992), *UNIX System V Release 4 Programmers' Guide: STREAMS*, Englewood Cliffs, NJ: Prentice Hall.

X/Open Company Ltd (1988), *X/Open Portability Guide (Issue 3): Networking Services*, Englewood Cliffs, NJ: Prentice Hall.

# RFC (Request for Comments) Documents

In total there are currently over 1400 RFC documents, though a good number of these are obsolete. Listed below are the RFCs mentioned in the text plus a few others of general interest. These may be obtained from a variety of archive servers, including `nic.ddn.mil`, using anonymous FTP.

783  Sollins, K.R. TFTP protocol (revision 2). 1981 June.

791  Postel, J.B. Internet Protocol. 1981 September.

793  Postel, J.B. Transmission control protocol.

821  Postel, J.B. Simple Mail transfer protocol. 1982 August.

854  Postel, J.B.; Reynolds, J.K. Telnet protocol specification.

855  Postel, J.B.; Reynolds, J.K. Telnet option specifications.

864  Postel, J.B. Character generator protocol.

959  Postel, J.B.; Reynolds, J.K. File transfer protocol.

1014  Sun Microsystems, Inc. XDR: external data representation standard.

1057  Sun Microsystems, Inc. RPC: remote procedure call protocol.

1094  Sun Microsystems, Inc. NFS: network file system protocol specification.

1325  Malkin, G.; Marine, A. FYI on questions and answers – answers to commonly asked 'new internet user' questions.

1350  Sollins, K. The TFTP protocol (revision 2).

1360  Postel, J. (ed.) IAB official protocol standards. 1992 September.

1392  Malkin, G.; Parker, T.; LaQuey (eds) Internet users' glossary.

# Index